# A HODDER CHRISTIAN OMNIBUS

## Jennifer Rees Larcombe

### WHERE HAVE YOU GONE GOD?
### BEYOND HEALING
### TURNING POINT

# WHERE HAVE YOU GONE GOD?

# BEYOND HEALING

# TURNING POINT

Jennifer Rees Larcombe

**Hodder & Stoughton**
LONDON SYDNEY AUCKLAND

This omnibus edition first published in Great Britain 1998

*Where Have You Gone God?* first published in Great Britain
in this edition 1989
Copyright © 1989 Jennifer Rees Larcombe

*Beyond Healing* first published in Great Britain
in this edition 1994
Copyright © 1986 Jennifer Rees Larcombe

*Turning Point* first published in Great Britain in this edition 1994
Copyright © 1994 Jennifer Rees Larcombe

The right of Jennifer Rees Larcombe to be identified as the
Author of these Works has been asserted by her in accordance
with the Copyright, Designs and Patents Act 1988.

10 9 8 7 6 5 4 3 2 1

British Library Cataloguing in Publication Data
A record for this book is available from the British Library

ISBN 0 340 71398 4

Printed and bound in Great Britain by
Clays Ltd, St Ives plc

Hodder and Stoughton Ltd
A Division of Hodder Headline PLC
338 Euston Road
London NW1 3BH

# Where Have You Gone, God?

Jennifer Rees Larcombe

Hodder & Stoughton
LONDON SYDNEY AUCKLAND

All scripture quotations are from the
Good News Bible, unless otherwise stated.
The following abbreviations are used:

Amplified Bible – AMP
Authorised Version – AV
Living Bible – LB
New International Version – NIV

First published in Great Britain 1989

10 9 8 7 6 5 4 3

British Library Cataloguing in Publication Data
A record for this book is available from the British Library

ISBN 0 340 64169 X

Printed and bound in Great Britain


Hodder and Stoughton
A Division of Hodder Headline PLC
338 Euston Road
London NW1 3BH

'Jesus was led by the Spirit into the desert. (Luke 4:1) The best of God's saints have their deserts. The dearest of His children have to walk through a weary wilderness. There is no believer who can always sing for joy. But the Spirit Who led Him was with Him and He is always with us.'
Charles Haddon Spurgeon

# CONTENTS

# PREFACE TO THE SECOND EDITION:

# PLEASE DON'T THROW THIS BOOK AWAY

'Where have you gone, God?' I remember muttering that in a blend of fury and despair as I lay in a London hospital in 1984. I had been there for weeks; I was in a lot of pain and too far from home for friends and family to visit regularly. Yet the worst part of the experience was the total absence of God – just when I needed Him most. I felt bereaved and utterly forsaken.

At the time I thought I was the only Christian who had these awful patches of spiritual darkness and doubt, but I have since come to realise that many of us go through them at some stage and in varying degrees during our lives with God. Of course, few of us will ever admit it, because by doing so we lay ourselves open to a barrage of irritating advice and the endless, well-meaning clichés that set our teeth on edge. Worse still, our friends may even write us off as unspiritual, sin-ridden failures.

During one of my 'bad patches', someone gave me a book because she thought 'it would do me good'. I threw it straight in the dustbin! The very last thing we want, when we are feeling dried up inside, dazed by suffering and downright angry with God, is a book by smug 'experts' who have never had to struggle with their faith and always feel triumphant. But please don't throw *this* book away until you have at least 'nibbled' at it. You will see that all of us who have contributed to it have also gone through 'dark nights of the soul'. Far from losing our faith, we have come out on the far side, knowing and loving God in a deeper and more durable way. Only those who have lived through this experience can possibly understand others who are still trapped inside it. I have written this book in the hope that it will be the personal contact and encouragement that so many of us need. It is simply a patchwork of all the things I have gleaned from people who know from bitter experience what they are talking about.

When I was asked to write a preface for this new edition I found it quite a painful experience. Reading through the book again took me back to when I first wrote it, sitting in my wheelchair. Since then I have been healed and restored to full health and energy, but the memories of those eight years of illness are still very easily brought back to mind. Would I want to change anything in the book now that I am well again? I still agree with what I wrote, but I think I would want to underline more heavily the chapter about being angry with God. When I first wrote the book I did not realise how many spiritual deserts are caused by anger and resentment and how dangerous it is to hold on to these negative feelings. I have written about this much more fully in a subsequent book, *Turning Point*.

Recently someone said to me, 'After being healed by God in such a remarkable way, you must always feel so close to Him now and so full of faith.' If only she was right! These dry patches do not only occur during times of loss, pain and suffering: they can hit us only too easily when everything is easy and comfortable. In fact we can lose God just as easily under the featherweight piles of happy, ordinary things as we can under tons of the black coals of grief.

Well-meaning friends always seem to think our 'deserts' are our own fault and often they may be right, yet I believe that sometimes God does withdraw the feeling of His closeness when He wants to help our faith grow larger. Faith, like a mushroom, appears to grow best in the dark! Something my mother once said frequently comes to my rescue and I have passed it on to many other desert travellers: 'Jesus promised us that His presence would always be with us, but He never promised that we would always feel it.'

Fortunately these deserts need not last for ever, and often they can be the prelude to something new and exciting. I hope and pray that this book will help you to find the courage to keep going until you discover your own particular 'treasure of darkness' (Isa. 43:5).

Jennifer Rees Larcombe
1995

> *How much longer will you forget me, Lord? For ever? How much longer will you hide yourself from me? How long will sorrow fill my heart day and night? I rely on your constant love: I will be glad because you will rescue me.* Psalm 13

# 1
# WHAT IS A SPIRITUAL DESERT?

---

'Don't hide yourself from me . . . You have been
my help; don't leave me, . . . , O God, my Saviour.'
*Psalm 27:9*

---

Dear Jen,
Help! Something's gone wrong and I'm not quite sure
what! I'm not ill or depressed, I just feel God has
withdrawn Himself from me. I go to church and house
group, but I'm a fly on the wall, not *part* of what's going
on. Prayer is like talking on the phone to someone
who's hung up. I'm just as busy as ever with church
activities, but leading the youth group is such a grind
these days now my enthusiasm's all gone.

It wouldn't be so bad if I could blame all this on to
something, but the circumstances of our lives are as
happy as ever. Outwardly I'm functioning normally,
but inside I know I've lost my joy. So I dread church
now because everyone there looks so maddeningly
happy, all the clapping and singing make me feel I'm
being rubbed with sandpaper. If I told them how I feel
they would start probing me for secret sins. I know I

---

O God, you are my God, and I long for you. My
whole being desires You; like a dry, worn-out and
waterless land, my soul is thirsty for You. Psalm
63:1

must have done something wrong, and I keep saying 'sorry', so why does God go on looking the other way? I want Him back desperately, but the more hassled I become, the farther He seems to recede.

I see from your book *Beyond Healing* that you had a similar experience so I thought you might understand. I just don't know anyone else who would. So on Sundays I put on my 'gleaming Christian face' and hope they won't realise I'm just a well disguised heap of rubbish.

Yours sincerely, Jill R

I put the letter down on the table beside me and sat gazing into space. I have known Jill for years and greatly admired the way she was always 'on fire' for God.

'Why should this happen to someone like her, Lord?' I whispered. 'Why does it happen to any of us?' I added ruefully. Once I, too, had thought no one else would understand, because no other Christian ever had the experience of losing God for no apparent reason.

Suddenly, in my memory I saw myself sitting at the dining table at a friend's house. My six, and her five children were making the baked beans on toast seem like the Lord Mayor's banquet. I had come a long way to see this friend because I was desperate and, like Jill, I had no wish to hang out my dirty washing in my local churchyard!

Before tea, while the children played in the garden I had tried to explain how I felt.

'When I was filled with God's Spirit, I thought my life would stay permanently full of joy, peace and power. I

---

*Lord, why are you standing aloof and far away. Why do you hide when I need you the most?*
Psalm 10:1, LB

didn't think I would ever be ill, or have money problems, and close contact with God would be a constant part of life.'

Earlier that same year I had been told by the consultant neurologist that the disease I had developed had permanently damaged my body, and was not only incurable, but it would probably keep recurring and sentence me to life in a wheelchair. I had smiled kindly at him, as I commented under my breath.

'That's what you think. It's *never* God's will for Christians to be ill.' When our minister had prayed for me in hospital I had expected to be healed instantly, but was quite happy to concede that God's healing might be gradual. What mattered to me far more during those long months in hospital was the new and intimate relationship with God that I was discovering.

On a flood tide of hope I had come home from hospital and plunged into the worst experience of my life. The more I believed I was getting better and tried to act as if I was, the more ill I became. Worse than that, I suddenly felt God had abandoned me. All the faith and joy that had sustained me over the previous months trickled away and was lost in the sand of a spiritual desert.

'Whatever did I do to bring this on myself?' I asked my friend. 'One thing after another keeps going wrong in our lives, so somehow I must have stepped outside God's protection. It just doesn't seem as if God's there any more.'

'Its a matter of faith dear,' she said gently. 'I *know* that,' I snapped crossly, 'but what are you supposed to do when your faith's all gone?'

---

*Jesus answered him, 'You do not understand now what I am doing, but you will understand later.'* John 13:7

Before she could answer, the children clattered in with roaring appetites and dirty knees, and soon we were all squashed round the table.

'Never mind, Jen,' soothed my friend, as she cleared away my plate of untouched food, 'just think how you will be able to use this experience to help other people one day.'

That remark was *the end*! The dam that I had so carefully constructed to contain my emotions burst violently.

'*How stupid!*' I thought, How could such a complete failure *ever* be used by God again? He had chucked me on the scrap heap like a rusty old car. I wanted so desperately to stay near Him, but I could not have felt further away if I had been Judas Iscariot. No! this humiliating experience could never be of use in any way. It was totally negative and destructive.

I could never have said all that, with eleven baked-bean-smeared faces gazing at me in astonishment. But the intensity of my feelings must have been obvious for I can still remember my friend pouring an apparently endless stream of tea all over her best table-cloth!

You are probably not supposed to write Christian books until you have all the answers tied up in neat bundles, but I could not wait for that. I began to write *Beyond Healing* as a kind of therapy and certainly, when it was finished, I saw my illness in a totally different light. But the thing that blessed me most was the mass of letters that followed its publication. From all over the world people wrote to say something like this;

What a relief, at long last to discover someone else who feels the same way as I do.

*Where is the blessedness I knew when first I saw the Lord? / Where is the soul refreshing view of Jesus and His word?* William Cowper

Jill was obviously only feeling a bit dry and spiritually 'switched off', while many other letters were from people who were going through much deeper and more painful experiences. Some were physically ill or depressed, while others grappled with unanswerable questions, such as 'Why did God allow my child to die?'

Soon the family began to dread breakfast-time when I opened the post and invariably dissolved into tears. Many of these people have become my friends – on paper – and I realise that one of the privileges God has given me is the time to communicate with them.

As I sat thinking how to answer Jill's letter that day, more than a year ago, I began to wonder just how many Christians there are like the two of us who hide their difficulties behind a smiling mask, while inwardly feeling like a modern leper without a bell.

Looking back over my life I could remember several bad patches, and I had thought I was the only 'un-spiritual' Christian to experience that kind of thing. Was I wrong? Do other people also feel they ought to convey the impression that since their conversion or baptism in the Holy Spirit their lives have been one song of praise?

So I began to ask all my friends if they had ever felt separated from God, and after some initial reluctance I received a whole range of answers.

'Yes, I've had several patches when my Christian life felt rather dull and drab.'

'Twice I've had to go to my Bishop and tell him I suddenly could not believe a word I was preaching. He told me many clergymen go through patches like that.'

---

*Thou wouldst not be seeking God, if thou hadst not already found Him.* Pascal

'I seem prone to recurring bouts of depression during which I always feel God no longer loves me personally.'

## Deserts are much more common than I thought

Soon I began to discover that these private feelings are shared by an astonishing number of other Christians.

'I'd like to write a book about these deserts,' I said as yet another letter fell in the marmalade, 'not just for people in them but also for their families and friends.'

Of course, I knew I could never do such a thing on my own. I am not a theologian; my only qualification is that I have been through several deserts and I know how much they hurt. So I plucked up enough courage to write to literally hundreds of Christians all over the world: clergymen, charismatic leaders, missionaries, doctors and scores of ordinary people like me. I asked them the following questions:

* Have you ever had a 'difficult patch' as a Christian?
* Do you know why?
* Did you gain anything from it?
* How did you escape?'
* Could you put me in touch with anyone else you know of who has been through the dark night of the soul?

I thought no one would bother to answer, but the letters came back like a freak wave, and many sent me several other names to follow up. 'It is such a relief to be able to tell someone how I really feel at long last,' was a recurring refrain.

---

*Such is the nature of our trials that while they last we cannot see the end.* Martin Luther

'Why,' asked one person, 'are we all so frightened to admit that our faith, joy and spiritual enthusiasm can sometimes flicker like a candle flame? Have we all been suppressing our feelings because "problems" are unfashionable these days?'

Some people hate writing letters so they talked to me on cassette, by phone or arrived in person on the door step. Soon I was in contact with over a thousand other Christians who were willing to allow me to draw on their experiences. My collection of letters and notes filled eight bulging files and provided me with a much clearer picture of what a spiritual desert is.

## What a spiritual desert is
* A period of time during which a Christian's relationship with God becomes stale or strained.
* Difficult or tragic circumstances that make us feel God is angry with us or powerless to help.
* It can last from a few hours to several years. If we do not want to get out of it, it will last a lifetime.
* Deserts are felt very differently. For some sensitive people they are intense and devastating, while the easy going, placid types may find them a mere irritation.
* Sometimes the cause is obvious and easily put right, but the maddening part of many desert experiences is that at the time there is no apparent cause.

---

*And don't tell me suffering ennobles people. I might punch you on the nose.* Wendy Green. From *Facing Bereavement* (Ann Warren, ed.)

## The letters kept arriving

You might think that looking into over a thousand 'deserts' was a very depressing way to spend a year! Actually it was deeply exciting. My own faith in the sheer love of God has been strengthened enormously by hearing of the things people learnt about God *not* when they were being successful, prosperous and on a spiritual 'high', but when they had reached the end of their own faith, courage and even their desire to live. Letters like this:

Dear Jen,

Yes, I went into one of your deserts after my husband died, and it was pure hell. After the funeral I floated along on a cotton-wool cloud of other people's prayers. God was so close I used to think I would touch Him in the night if I reached out my hand in the darkness. But then suddenly, just when I needed Him most, He vanished.

One night in the bath I reached the depths of despair. As I lay there I suddenly thought, am I going to take God at face value or not? He said, 'I will never leave you; I will never abandon you.' (Hebrews 13:5) Either it was true, or He was a liar. Does He keep His promises or doesn't He? I asked myself, and amid the steam and soap I decided that definitely He does.

Just knowing that in my head, and setting my mind on it, regardless of feelings, has made all the difference and gradually my joy in Him has returned. Now I actually feel I am closer to God than I was before, something between us is stronger. Perhaps I've simply discovered that He really is always there, regardless of how I may *feel* at the time. That discovery was my

---

*What we learn in the dark we possess for ever.*
Edith Schaeffer

'treasure of darkness'. There's a verse in Isaiah (45:3) which says, 'I will give you the treasures from dark secret places; then you will know that I am the Lord, and that the God of Israel has called you by name.' Under the desert sands lie deep caverns and mines where we chisel out these gemstones, facts about God that we only discover at the darkest moments of our lives. They make us far richer when we come out of our deserts than we were before.

Much love, Mary.

## No trite sayings

That letter might be irritating you if you happen to be going through a period of suffering. Perhaps you feel like my friend Dawn when she said:

> 'If one more person tells me, "We know that in all things God works for good with those who love Him", (Romans 8:28) I think I'll punch them! I don't want to be "done good to", I just want my son well again.'

These 'treasures of darkness' don't feel valuable at the time, more like lumps of hard rock. It is not until we are safely 'home' that we discover how 'rich' we have become. All the others who joined me in writing this book know what it is like to wait tensely for the next tactless remark made by someone who knows nothing about

> *I hate the darkness and fears that beset me, and I love high spirits, health, success and fun with friends, yet I have learned more in the darkness of unhappiness and pain than by hours of well being. Sufferings pass but what is learnt through suffering is treasure for ever more.* Leslie Weatherhead

suffering. The treasures of darkness we want to share are not sugary jingles or trite sayings. They are the priceless facts we discovered about God during the darkest times in our lives. Things that could only have been mined down there in the darkness.

# 2

# THE BEGINNING OF THE END

---

Some wandered in the trackless desert and could not find their way . . . They were . . . thirsty and had given up all hope. Then, in their trouble they called to the Lord and He saved them from their distress. He led them by a straight road to a city where they could live. *Psalm 107:4–7*

---

It would be marvellous if from the experience of a thousand deserts I could offer you an instant formula for escape, an air ticket to 'green pastures'. But there is no easy way out. Those on the outside may say there is, but they are wrong!

Many people have discovered various escape routes, but they are only paths, not launching pads. You have to *walk* along a path, step by step, before it eventually takes you where you want to go. The first four steps of the journey are crucial. They are – realising where you are; wanting to escape; asking 'why?'; and seeking help.

---

*The Lord said, 'I was ready to answer My people's prayers, but they did not pray, I was ready for them to find Me, but they did not even try.'*
Isaiah 65:1

## 1: REALISING WHERE YOU ARE

Most people drift into their deserts so gradually they do not realise what is happening.

'There was no dramatic turning away from God, He just faded slowly over the horizon,' was the way one person described it.

'I was sitting on the underground one morning,' said Malcolm, 'when a young man with a fish badge on his lapel sat down beside me. I felt irritated when he began talking about his faith. But after he got out, it suddenly struck me that I had once been as enthusiastic as he was. So excited about God, I even wanted to share Him with strangers in the rush hour. I had become so used to the boring routine of Christianity I'd been grinding along without thinking about it.

'For several days after that I would not admit to myself (or to God) that my Christian life was not what it had once been, or yet how I wished it could be. That weekend, I went for a long walk in the park and at last I realised I had been trying to kid the Lord for ages. That young man on the train had shown me how much I was actually missing the Lord. So I stopped by the duck pond and cried out to Him for help – silently of course! "Please get me out of this boring lethargy." It seemed to take months before anything really changed, but I would say the turning point in any desert is being honest with yourself and with God.'

> *In my alarm I said, 'I am cut off from Your sight!'*
> *Yet You heard my cry for mercy when I called to*
> *You for help.* Psalm 31:22, NIV

Recognising where we are and asking for God's help are often the most difficult things to do in a desert, but they are also the most important.

'That's ridiculous,' you may be thinking, 'my main trouble is I can't believe He'll hear me.'

That does not matter, it is not our faith or lack of it that causes God to hear our voice. He is so eager to help He says,

'Before they call I will answer, while they are still speaking I will hear.' (Is. 65:24, NIV.) He'll hear you all right.

'But I'm far too ashamed to speak to God,' someone else might say. Sometimes we know we have walked into our wilderness deliberately and when we realise where we are, we feel we have forfeited our right to God's love. He seems millions of miles away and the steep, rocky path back to Him is too hard to attempt.

Someone once said that if you walk a thousand steps away from God, you only have to turn, and take one step back towards Him again, because He has followed you all the way. God does not wait until we have cleared up our lives, organised our relationships and changed our attitudes, He meets us just where we are, right at the very lowest point of our desert, and it is only God Himself who can help us climb back out of them again.

*Though you have made me see troubles, many and bitter, you will restore my life again; from the depths of the earth you will again bring me up.*
Psalm 71:20, NIV

## 2: DO YOU REALLY WANT TO GET OUT?

'Stupid question!' you may be thinking, but if we are honest, we have to admit that sometimes we are quite comfortable staying where we are.

David once said, 'I wish I had wings, like a dove, I would fly away and find rest . . . and live in the wilderness.' (Psalm 55:6–7) Deserts can actually become a refuge that we are reluctant to leave, an identity or even a way of life.

I am ashamed to say I quite enjoyed throwing 'pity parties' all round the district, rehearsing my many grievances to anyone who would listen. I wanted them to be as sorry for me as I was for myself! Sometimes we can almost feel proud of our deepest hurts and nurture them carefully because our problems are all we have left, and cuddling them close to our hearts can seem like a comfort. In the end that only makes us bitter, but we do not always recognise that at the time.

'If all my problems were solved,' said Karen to her house group leaders, after they had spent months counselling her, 'You wouldn't be interested in me any more.' Her desert had become her means of importance. We can actually *like* being the person they all pray for and ask round for meals. Remove the problems and our personality goes as well.

### The desert can provide a good excuse
When we want to duck out of irksome responsibilities, we can use the desert as an excuse.

> *You will seek Me and find Me when you seek Me with all your heart.* Jeremiah 29:13

'Oh well, if I've lost my faith I don't need to bother getting up for Church on Sunday, I'll have a nice sleep on, instead.'

'It would be hypocritical of me to lead that youth group now, so I'll resign. (Those boys were making my life a misery anyway.)'

## There can also be a security in boredom
If we had to climb out of our rut we might feel exposed.

'Yes my Church does bore me to snoring point,' said Janice, 'my friend wants me to go to hers, but I'm not sure about this new kind of worship. What would people think if I started going there?'

It can take a lot of courage to walk out of a desert.

## Has something else become more important to us than God?
It might be something wrong, but it could equally be very good in itself.

'We bought a boat, it was a great way to relax but soon we were off sailing most weekends, and we lost contact with our Church.'

'Once we had our baby we found it was difficult to get along to services and anyway we liked being a family together at home.'

'I put all my energy into running the Sunday School, and in the end that became more important to me than my relationship with God Himself.'

'We moved to an old house and doing it up ourselves took all our spare time.'

God wants us to live rich lives, full of relationships and activities. He simply asks that we share them all with Him and always put Him first in our lives.

## The desert crisis

Robbie was the least likely candidate for a desert experience that I ever knew. Her love for the Lord had the same quality as that of the apostle John. Being single and nearly thirty-three did not seem to matter to her. The Lord filled her life, and the church music group was the pivot of her existence.

Then one day Keith joined the staff of the school where she worked. There always seemed so much to talk about during break, they both taught the same subject and shared so many interests. Soon it seemed logical to do their marking together and the staffroom was always so peaceful after school.

The evening that Keith told her how unhappily married he was, Robbie went into her desert. Oh, she did not recognise it for what it was, Satan saw to that. After all, she was doing nothing wrong, just talking to a lonely, misunderstood man, but church suddenly became boring.

Everything came to a head during a geography field trip. A week in the Brecon Beacons was like the daydreams she had enjoyed as a teenager. Their love was so enormous that they hardly noticed the two other teachers or their twenty sniggering pupils.

'I can't go back to Wendy after this,' whispered Keith, as they watched the sun set over Pen-y-fan on the last

---

*Keep away from anything that might take God's place in your hearts*. 1 John 5:21, LB

night. 'I'm going to leave her. I'll have to find somewhere else to live, I was wondering . . . if . . . could I move into your flat?'

A few days later Robbie was playing her guitar in church. The decision was still unmade and God did not seem to be around to help her make it! There was something very poignant about the music that day; perhaps it would be the last time she would be part of it. Church was *not* one of the interests she shared with Keith and what would people think about them living together? What would the Lord think?

That evening the sermon was about the Israelites coming out of the desert after their forty years of wandering and how they crossed the river Jordan into their Promised Land. During the closing prayer, Robbie saw a vivid picture in her mind. God had often communicated with her like that, but this was clearer than anything else had ever been. She was standing on the desert bank of the Jordan, covered with dust and her clothes encrusted with sand. On the far side she could see Caanan, the fruit trees on the sloping hills and the wild flowers in the meadows. There stood Jesus Himself, His arms open wide, His face twisted with longing as He called her over the water to join Him. Everything inside her wanted to leap forward, wade across the river and fling herself into His arms for ever. Instead she looked back over her right shoulder, back towards the dry, empty desert. There stood Keith, silently beckoning her. The decision was agonising. Like Lot's wife she stood on the bank, frozen between two worlds.

Did she want to be out of her desert enough to say

> *Oh God, I don't love You, I don't even want to love You, but I want to want to love You!* St Teresa

goodbye to Keith and the companionship, security, even the children he could give her?

## When the desert is at its most dangerous

There is, I believe, a crisis point in every desert when we have to make a decision either to cry out to God for help or to shrug our shoulders and think, What's the point of carrying on with Christianity when I don't get anything out of it any more? Perhaps I should take a break for a while, mustn't get too intense. This is the stage when the desert is *most dangerous*. Many people have thought, 'I can always go back to Christianity when I feel like it.' But Satan makes sure they never *do* feel like it, and one day they realise they have wasted years wandering aimlessly round an unproductive wasteland.

God is not like a half-knitted jumper you can put down and pick up again when you feel like it. He is a person, who said, 'My spirit will not always strive with man.' If we push Him to the back of a drawer He won't just lie there until we 'feel like' Him again. Perhaps this is one of the reasons why He allows us to feel far from Him – to see if we love Him enough to *mind* when we lose Him.

For months Robbie remained poised on the river-bank. Sometimes she would manage to 'give Keith up' and turn back towards Jesus, but then Keith would look at her across the staff room, or arrive on her doorstep late at night, and the old longing for him would return. She was stuck in this agonising situation when she came to speak to me.

---

*If you hear God's voice today, do not be stubborn as your ancestors were when they rebelled against God . . . in the desert.* Hebrews 3:7–8

'Change your job,' I urged her, 'sell your house, move away. Jesus said it was better for you to cut off a foot or a hand rather than allow yourself to be drawn away from Him.'

At that time Robbie was unwilling to take such drastic action, and as the weeks went by she actually wanted Keith more than she wanted her relationship with Jesus.

When we deliberately separate ourselves from God by a sin that we are enjoying, He minds terribly. But because He did not create us as robots, but gave us the privilege of free will, there is nothing He can do to help us out of our deserts if we do not want to leave them.

## 3: ASKING THE QUESTION 'WHY?'

'Why should this happen to me?' we bellow, when we feel God is far away. Jesus Himself cried from the cross, 'My God, *why* have you forsaken me?'

Satan likes to make us think deserts are always our own fault, and other Christians frequently do the job for him! However, just because there is often no instant answer to the question 'why?' does not mean we should not ask it. It is a fact that we do cause some deserts ourselves and sometimes there is a specific reason for our misery that we could easily put right if only we asked God to show it to us. My friend Amy assumed she knew the answer so she did not bother to put the question.

> *O Lord, Who art as the shadow of a great rock in a weary land, Who beholdest Thy weak creatures, weary of labour, weary of pleasure, weary of hope deferred, weary of self; in Thine abundant compassion, and unutterable tenderness, bring us, I pray Thee, unto Thy rest.* Christina G. Rossetti

'Ron took early retirement, and we moved down to the west country, bought an old house and took in three old ladies to help pay the bills. It sounded like a good idea back in Orpington, but it's been sheer murder. I'm on the go twenty-four hours a day. Ron has his golf, while I'm left holding the baby – or should I say three very bad tempered babies! I missed my old church terribly but had no time to join a new one. My spiritual side was gradually eroded by endless little jobs, until one day I realised I simply wasn't communicating with God any more. I thought it was overwork that was separating me from God, but as there was nothing I could do about that, I continued in my desert and became bitter and frustrated. I would have saved myself such a lot of hassle if only I had asked God 'why?'

One day when I was loading my ever-hungry washing machine I came to the end of myself and shouted,

'Lord, why don't you help me?' Nothing happened, but then a few days later Ron and I had a terrible row. We never row, we're not the type, but he was putting his golf clubs into the back of the car yet again and something inside me erupted,

'It was *your* idea to come down here, I never wanted to leave my friends. This is your pipe-dream, and yet off you go to golf yet again! Do you think I'm just your slave?'

I'd often thought all that, but never actually put my resentment into words, but as Ron drove away I

---

*Answer me now Lord! I have lost all hope. Don't hide yourself from me . . . Remind me each morning of your constant love, for I put my trust in you.*
Psalm 143:7–8

realised that even before we left Orpington I had been seething with suppressed anger.

I made a cup of tea and thought, 'That's the real reason for your problem with the Lord. It's anger and self-pity, not exhaustion at all.' Once I had confessed this to the Lord I felt close to Him again. Soon I found a lovely little church, and I cope with the ladies while Ron plays his golf. He stays in while I go to church. He was perfectly reasonable about it when I put it to him.

It would be marvellous if we could all escape from our deserts as easily as Amy!

Of course we all know sin separates us from God, so when He feels far away we need to pray, 'Lord have I done something to upset you?' God is more anxious than we are to remove anything that divides us from Him, so if we ask Him to identify the obstacle, He most certainly will.

There is no sin, however big, that can go on separating us from God, once we are willing to renounce it and go to Jesus for forgiveness. He took the blame and the punishment on the Cross. Deserts occur when we will not confess those sins.

All those months when Robbie was sleeping with Keith, she was telling herself, 'God understands, He knows we need each other.' She was trying to make herself believe *what she wanted to believe*.

You can change the hands of your clock to convince yourself that you are not late for work, but you cannot change the time. Neither can we bend God's rules to suit

*Why am I so sad? Why am I so troubled? I will put my hope in God and once again I will praise Him.*
Psalm 42:5

our own desires and expect to remain close to Him. He loves us to the uttermost, but He is a Holy God and it is impossible for Him to come near sin.

Robbie complained because she felt so far from the Lord, but He was simply showing His disapproval.

There is a story of a child who stole a large toffee and was caught sucking it by her mother. 'Jesus will be very sad you stole that,' she said sternly. The child burst into tears of contrition and her mother, fearing she had been too hard, said, 'Never mind dear, just say you're sorry, He'll forgive you.'

'I will,' replied the child, 'but not until I finish the toffee.' It is while we still want to go on sucking the toffee that we stay in our desert.

## Deserts are never never a punishment for sin

When we finally want to regain our relationship with God, more than we want the 'obstacle' that is separating Him from us, we can be free instantly by asking God's forgiveness and turning away from that sin.

Satan hates that, so sometimes, *after* God has revealed the barrier of sin, and we have dealt with it, Satan still surrounds us with a vague cloud of guilt and worthlessness.

Mark allowed himself to be sucked into a dishonest business deal. For months afterwards he felt miles from God, but at last he went to his minister, confessed the whole sordid story and asked God to forgive him. Was

> *If we say that we have no sin, we deceive ourselves and there is no truth in us. But if we confess our sins to God He will keep His promise . . . He will forgive us our sins and purify us from all our wrongdoing.* 1 John 1:8–9

that the end of his desert? No, if anything it grew worse. Every time he went to church or tried to pray Satan would say,

'God may have forgiven you, but He won't ever want you near to Him again, not after all those filthy things you did. This feeling of isolation is your punishment.'

*Satan was lying of course.* Jesus died to take the punishment for Mark's sin, and after Mark had been forgiven, in God's eyes he was as innocent as if he had never sinned.

In desperation he went back to his minister. 'I just don't *feel* forgiven,' he explained.

'Suppose I handed you a cheque for a million pounds, just because I happen to be fond of you,' said the minister. 'You'd be a rich man wouldn't you?'

'Yes,' replied Mark.

'But the fact probably wouldn't sink in just at first – you wouldn't *feel* rich because you hadn't earned the money. So would that make the cheque worthless?'

'No,' smiled Mark, 'I'd take it straight to the bank.' The minister continued, 'God has forgiven you, that is a fact that your feelings can never alter. Jesus suffered instead of you, but I think you almost want to be punished because you cannot forgive yourself. You need to pick up this "cheque" that's lying here. Receive God's forgiveness and start enjoying it.'

That afternoon Mark walked out of his desert for good.

---

*But because of our sins, He was wounded, beaten because of the evil we did . . . All of us were like sheep that were lost, each of us going his own way, but the Lord made the punishment fall on Him, the punishment all of us deserved.*
Isaiah 53:5–6

Many deserts, however, are caused by enslaving habits and repeated defeat in the face of temptation. You will find more about these on page 97.

## Sometimes the question 'why?' can become dangerous

Sometimes we may never know the reason why we had to go through a desert. When the missionary doctor Helen Roseveare was kidnapped and raped, God said to her later, 'Will you trust Me if I never tell you why?'

I believe, now, that repeatedly asking the question 'why?' actually hindered my escape. The main trouble with 'why?' is that it faces us in the wrong direction. You walk through a desert from one side to the other and you come out a richer person at the far end. If you keep looking backwards over your shoulder trying to see what caused you to be there, you cannot see the path that leads to freedom.

I did not realise we need only ask God once, on one specific occasion, then leave it to Him to send us the answer *if and when* it would help us to know. Every Christian acquaintance I turned to for help seemed to give me a different answer, until I was totally confused and that question 'why?' nearly drove me mad.

## We must leave Him to answer in His time

If only I had stopped asking 'why?' and asked 'how?' instead. When you are lost in a geographical desert it

---

*He does not punish us as we deserve or repay us according to our sins and wrongs . . . As far as the east is from the west so far does He remove our sins from us.* Psalm 103:10–12

does not matter in the slightest if you got there because your plane crashed, your jeep broke down or you fell off a camel. What does matter is *'how'* am I going to get out of this? And *'what'* treasure can I discover on the way?

'I will wait for the Lord, who is hiding his face . . . I will put my trust in Him.' (Isaiah 8:17)

## 4: SIGNALLING FOR HELP

When a person is stranded alone in the Sahara, survival depends on letting someone else know where they are. Any signal will do – smoke rings, a mirror perhaps, or even a radio.

Shouting for help is just as vital in a spiritual Sahara, but not nearly so easy! When we have always been the one to whom people come for advice, it takes a lot of courage to admit we are floundering ourselves. Many sensitive people, when they are suffering, like to crawl off alone into a hole, and even when we do manage to tell our friends how we feel they may not understand.

'The worst thing about spiritual deserts,' said one man who came to see me, 'is the hostility they arouse in other people.'

It has been tragic to hear about the ways other desert travellers have been hurt by their fellow Christians. It is not our enemies who injure us most, but our friends.

Job said, 'In trouble like this I need loyal friends – whether I've forsaken God or not. But you, my friends, you deceive me like streams that go dry when no rain

---

*We don't know why we feel depressed, that's what's so depressing.* David Watson

comes.' (Job 6:14–17) Job desperately needed love and understanding in his illness and bereavement, and for a week his friends gave him just that, and then they turned on him. Our friends will also allow *us* a short excursion into our desert, and for a time we will be sustained by their love, attention and home-made sponge cakes.

Then, when their patience begins to wear thin we shall soon hear the familiar, trite remarks which feel like the sting of desert scorpions.

* Pull yourself together.
* You brought all this on yourself, you know.
* We all knew you were doing too much.
* You shouldn't be so negative.
* It's your own fault you aren't healed.
* You ought to read some books on 'triumphant living'.

Just a few days after Barbara's twenty-year-old son was killed on his motor bike, a 'friend' said to her,

'You must have allowed Satan in by some unconfessed sin.' The grief of losing her son was enough to bear without the guilt of perhaps having caused his death. That cruel remark plunged Barbara into three years of terrible depression.

'"Smile and the whole world smiles with you". That's true all right in churches. If you're full of joy you're full of friends, but if you're down people can't run away fast enough!' (Lesley)

---

*Deserts isolate us, but perhaps we need these times of being outcasts in order to teach us to form our own opinion, rather than mindlessly following the crowd.* Gloria Moody

'I feel as if they've all ganged up on me, talking about me, discussing what I ought to do, judging me.' (Wendy)

'People come and listen to your problems but it's only to bolster up their own spiritual ego – "doing counselling". Afterwards they go off and ask people to pray, but it's only a pious form of gossiping.' (Jenny)

'I'm constantly having to endure long counselling sessions when amateur psychiatrists go tramping round my subconscious in hobnail boots.' (Stephen)

## What is Satan up to in all this?

He is trying hard to isolate us from other Christians, because he knows we are more vulnerable when we are alone.

'I can always be with God in the woods and fields,' said my friend Gerry, when she felt people at church were criticising her. But God does not live in trees, He lives in people. That winter it snowed so heavily even the main roads were blocked. I was worried about Gerry whose cottage lay at the end of a lane, a couple of miles from the village where we were living. All she had were her chickens for company. So I put on my boots and floundered through the snowdrifts to see if she was all right.

'I'm fine,' she said, sticking her head out of the chicken house, 'and so are my hens.'

'Surely you don't leave them out there all night in these low temperatures,' I protested.

> *Is it nothing to you, all ye that pass by? Behold and see if there be any sorrow like unto my sorrow.* Lamentations 1:12, AV

'They're all right,' she laughed, 'they all huddle up together to keep warm. Of course if you left one on its own it would be ready for the deep-freeze by morning!'

'Christians must be a bit like chickens,' I said later as I warmed my hands round a mug of china tea. 'We survive if we stay close to each other and share our heat; isolate ourselves, and we've had it!' Gerry understood what I meant, but she is still in the deep-freeze.

Christians can seem poor company when we are feeling 'out at elbows' with God, but strangely, we still need them. While it is both unwise and unnecessary to 'bare our souls' in public, somewhere in our circle of friends there will be one or two people who are wise and sensitive enough to understand us.

The one thing we need above everything else is prayer, especially when we are finding it hard to pray ourselves. It is imperative that we find some mature Christian who will pray for us. Someone really close to God to whom we can talk honestly, knowing they will neither pepper us with shallow advice nor gossip about our problems later. God will come to comfort us wearing their body, and speak to us using their voice.

**Have you asked someone to pray for you?**
Only eternity will show how much our generation owes to Billy Graham, but once he too had his desert experience.

'I prayed and prayed but the Heavens seemed to be

---

*I kept quiet, not saying a word . . . but my suffering only grew worse and I was overcome with anxiety. The more I thought the more troubled I became. Psalm 39:2–3*

brass. I felt as though God had disappeared and that I was all alone with my trial and burden. It was a dark night for my soul, so I wrote to my mother . . . and will never forget her reply. "Son, there are many times when God withdraws to test your faith, He wants you to trust Him in the darkness. Now son, reach up by faith in the fog and you will find that His hand will be there." In tears I knelt by my bed and experienced an overwhelming sense of God's presence.'

It was possibly not so much his mother's good advice, as her earnest prayers that rescued Billy from his desert.

## Danger! Desert hazard

Don't let anyone make you feel guilty if during patches of severe stress or depression going to church is quite impossible (see Page 185). So long as you have that one Christian friend to pray for you and meet with you regularly, God can give you all you need until the worst pain is over.

## Don't signal in the wrong direction

Some people, of course, do not withdraw into solitude when they are suffering. They go to the opposite extreme. Satan has to change his tactics with these extroverts because they automatically reach out towards people when they need help. So he tempts them to trust people too much.

---

*I kept on believing even when I said, 'I am completely crushed', even when I was afraid and said, 'no one can be trusted'. Psalm 116:10–11*

When our lives are full of problems, so often instead of praying, we dash round asking all our friends for advice. When everyone at Church has heard our story, we travel round the country in search of 'super stars' with a gift of healing.

## Trusting people instead of God

When it is people we are trusting instead of God, the results are:

* confusion – they all tell us something different
* we are crushed by their condemnation
* our problems seem bigger every time we rehearse them
* we feel the church has let us down, so we leave
* and Satan has got his way.

Job said, 'Have pity upon me, have pity upon me O ye my friends; for the hand of God hath touched me.' (Job 19:21) If it is only the sympathy of *people* we want, we shall be disappointed as soon as he was.

The Lord says, 'I will condemn the person who turns away from Me and puts his trust in man . . . He is like a bush in the desert, which grows in the dry wilderness, on salty ground where nothing else grows . . . But I will bless the person who puts his trust in Me. He is like a tree growing near a stream and sending out roots to the water.'    (Jeremiah 17:5–8)

---

*God never fades from the vision of a person until he ceases to pray.* Oral Roberts

However well trained, famous or gifted people may be, they *themselves* will never get us out of our desert. God can only use people to help us when we first turn to Him in an act of the will.

## Treasure of darkness

When Marion came to see me, the muscles of her neck and face were so taut she could not have smiled if she tried. Orphaned as a child, rejected by the man she loved, she had just lost her home and was finding her job in a Christian organisation an impossible strain.

'I don't want any advice,' she said hastily, 'I've been positively suffocated by tons of it. Now I've reached a point where people don't exist any more. I feel I'm standing naked and alone before God possessing nothing. I have been hurt so much in a way I feel I'm dead. Everything in life is lost now except my relationship with God. It's funny really,' she added with a stiff attempt at a smile, 'but actually all I've ever wanted in life was God, and now He is literally all I *have*.'

Marion had been basing her faith and Christianity on the people around her and they let her down badly. Yet, perhaps she had just made the most important discovery of her life – her Treasure of Darkness.

---

*Let thy discontents be thy secret, if the world knew them t'will despise thee and increase them.*
Benjamin Franklin

It seems ironic that Satan had tried so hard to crush her by the condemnation of others and yet, he had only managed to remove all her earthly props, pushing her right into the arms of God!

*What else have I in heaven but You? Since I have You, what else could I want on earth? . . . God is my strength; He is all I ever need.* Psalm 73:25–26

# 3

# IN THE DESERT YOU ARE A VIP

---

Jesus said: 'I have told you all this so that you will
have peace . . . Here on earth you will have many
trials and sorrows, but take courage! I have overcome the world.' *John 16:33*

---

Just suppose your desert story began as Job's did, with
God sitting in Heaven smiling down on you with pride.
(See Job 1:8)

'*There's* someone who really loves Me,' murmurs God
happily and all the angels smile agreement. 'Just look at
him worshipping Me there in church, and trying to
please Me in every detail of his life.'

Satan is also watching you with his crafty eyes just as
he once watched Job. The way that you love God and His
obvious pleasure in you irritates Satan into action. (See
Job 1:9–11)

'He only loves you for what he gets out of You,' he
begins. 'Look at him – healthy – attractive personality –
happily married – comfortably off, he only has to pray
and You do anything he wants. Is it any wonder he's
constantly full of joy and peace! You lavish Your power
on his ministry, and give him success in every project.
He's no fool, he knows he's on to a good thing! But . . .
just suppose You let me take everything away from him
would he *still* love You *then*?'

## God hesitates. Why?

* Because He loves you so much He hates to think of you suffering in any way.
* Because of the risk. Satan might be right, a desert could cause you to reject Him for ever.

But God is prepared to take that risk . . .

* Because He knows this desert could bless you out of all recognition. He wants to add all kinds of new dimensions to your personality, and give you a deeper sympathy and understanding for other people, but He knows you can only gain these in a desert.
* Because He knows about the weak place that constantly defeats you, (impatience, selfishness, pride and so on.) He understands how much you long to be rid of these things but again He realises they can be eradicated only through adversity.
* Because He has mountains of riches stacked up for you in Heaven, and he wants you to look forward to them instead of being so preoccupied with the few grubby possessions you value down here.
* Because He wants you to love Him in the same way that He loves you. Not with selfish conditional cupboard love, but for Himself alone.

So, because God loves you enough to want only your best and highest good, and *not* to score points off his

> *Dear friends, don't be bewildered or surprised when you go through the fiery trials ahead, for this is no strange unusual thing that is going to happen to you.* 1 Peter 4:12

enemy, or play spiteful games with you, He gives His consent and your desert begins.

## Satan is powerless

Some people get so frightened of Satan they imagine him hiding behind every desert cactus. He is *completely powerless* to harm you in any way unless God first gives His permission, and God would never allow anything that was not ultimately for your total benefit. He knows you through and through and he will never allow Satan to send more than you can take. (See 1 Corinthians 10:13)

'If God is for us, who can be against us?' (Romans 8:31)

## Satan sits in hell working out his strategy

These are his objectives:

* To make you doubt God's love, and His ability and desire to help you, even His very existence.
* To make you think that your life is no longer in God's control because you or your parents sinned and stepped out of His protection.
* To make you feel sorry for yourself, resent God and complain about Him, turn to other people or things for comfort and finally to reject Him altogether.

## How will he achieve all this?

It is not only the dramatic events of life that Satan tries to

---

*It may now be necessary for you to be sad for a while because of the many kinds of trials you suffer. Their purpose is to prove your faith is genuine.* 1 Peter 1:6–7

use to separate us from God, he is just as active in the boring patches when nothing seems to be happening at all. He can use prosperity, success and ease. He knows when everything in our lives is going perfectly, including our Christian work, we don't need God at all. He tried to crush Job by adversity and failed but he managed to corrupt Solomon by wealth and fame.

## The first battle

Satan didn't do too well with Job – at first. When he was ruined financially and lost his ten children in a mass tragedy, he said,

'The Lord gave, the Lord has taken away, may His name be praised!' Satan must have been livid. Perhaps you too won the first battle. You turned *towards* God when your life collapsed round your ears. But Satan tried again – he always does. Soon Job was desperately ill, rejected by his community and even his own wife. Still he managed to say;

'When God sends us something good we welcome it, how can we complain when he sends us trouble?' Job 2:10

The second battle went to Job too, but Satan waited, knowing he held the trump card. The devastating effect of 'long-suffering'.

When our Church is watching us anxiously, cheering us on and admiring how well we are coping with our illness or bereavement, we manage wonderfully. However, as the months go by, everyone drifts back to their own lives again and no one notices us any more.

---

*The fruit of the Spirit is . . . long-suffering.* Galatians 5:22. *Anyone can suffer 'short', it takes a lot more guts to 'suffer long'.* Tom Rees

Then our suffering can seem endless, cruel and devoid of reason.

Satan can wait, time means nothing to him. When it is eighteen months since the funeral and people feel we should 'be over it by now'. Or when you *still* have not found a job after two years. When the doctors have done all they can, and say 'you've just got to live with it'. That is when Satan's time really comes. Job did not manage at all well then. He said; 'I was living in peace but God took me by the throat and battered me and crushed me . . . He wounds me again and again he attacks like a soldier gone mad with hate.' (Job 16:12–14)

Satan must have grinned when he heard all that. Job never knew Satan was behind all his misery, he blamed God and his friends blamed him! No one thought of Satan. We and our friends still act the same and Satan loves it.

## You are the VIP

You may feel totally alone in your desert, but you are watched by a countless number of beings. How you react *now* is important, not only to you, but also to them! You may feel your life is wasted and useless, but actually you are a vital part of the battle between light and darkness, good and evil.

## We decide who wins

We are not just pawns in a huge game of chess played by God against Satan. Chessmen have no power, they go

---

*Every battle of faith counts in God's sight, even if there is little or no victory to be seen at the time.*
Sister Basilea Schlink

where they are placed. Although God and Satan are watching us more closely than any chess champions, *we* decide who wins.

When we wake in the morning and face another endless pain-filled day, the pointlessness of it all makes us wish we had died in the night. Actually, each day is a challenge. We are not just a forgotten grain of desert sand, God and Heaven care intensely how we are going to manage the day. If we walk through it clinging to God regardless of whether we can feel His presence or receive His blessings, His face will shine with joy and Satan will scowl in defeat. We will not see it, but it will happen. If we whine, grumble or shake an angry fist at God and turn for comfort or help to some other 'god', his face will twist with pain and Satan will smirk in triumph.

Poor old Job said a lot of things he regretted later (see Job 42:3). But while Satan may have won several battles he did not win the war and by the end of his experience Job knew God in a new and deeper way, and said to Him, 'In the past I knew only what others had told me, but now I have seen You with my own eyes.' (Job 42:5)

The ultimate prize for this war in the desert is your relationship with God. That is what Satan is attacking. Just how important is that relationship to you? Is it worth fighting for over a lengthy period? Or is it so trivial you will chuck it away when the going seems tough? We may not always win every one of those daily skirmishes but a failure should never discourage us; it is the whole war we want to win. We must never forget:

> *It isn't the days of high tension that try us most, and so give us most, it's the days that seem all grey and dull, they test the quality of the gold.* Amy Carmichael, *Candles in the Dark*

* Abraham lied
* Jacob cheated
* Moses murdered
* Elijah ran away
* David committed adultery
* Peter denied Jesus

They all lost a few battles too. Jesus says to them and to all desert travellers who keep on going to the end, 'To those who win the victory I will give the right to sit beside Me on My throne, just as I have been victorious and now sit by My Father on His throne.' (Revelation 3:21)

Our prize is eternal, but not instant, and I know from bitter experience that deserts hurt! Let us never forget that God is not only up there, looking down on us, but also beside us, fighting with us on our side.

'When through fiery trials thy pathway shall lie,
His grace all-sufficient shall be thy supply,
The flame shall not hurt thee, His only design
Thy dross to consume and thy gold to refine.

'The soul that on Jesus has leaned for repose
He will not, He cannot desert to its foes;
That soul, though all hell should endeavour to shake,
He never will leave, He will never forsake.'

Richard Keen, *How firm a foundation*. From *Hymns of Faith*

# 4

# BEDROCK FACTS FOR DESERT SURVIVAL

---

The people . . . said, 'The Lord has abandoned us!
He has forgotten us.' So the Lord answers, 'Can a
woman forget her own baby, and not love the child
she bore? Even if a mother should forget her child,
I will never forget you . . . I have written your name
on the palms of My hands.' *Isaiah 49:14–16*

---

The worst part of travelling through a desert is the
endlessly shifting sand. When you want to camp for the
night there is nothing firm into which to drive the tent
pegs. Our survival depends on discovering firm, hard
ground on which to base our existence – the bedrock
facts.

## 1: GOD NEVER LEAVES US,
## HOWEVER WE MAY FEEL

My friend Jane looked distraught when she came to see
me in her desert.

'When something goes wrong,' she said, 'my immedi-
ate instinct is always to go to church to be there, in God's
presence. But when I went last week it was torture
observing other people finding the joy and comfort that
has been denied to me for so long. At the end I tried to
express to someone how I felt, and she simply said "If
God seems far away, guess who's moved!" But I haven't

moved. I'm running towards God as fast as I can. He's the one who's slammed the door in *my* face, why can't anyone understand that?'

The one thing a desert does to all of us is to make us feel God is far away, but that is never, never true.

## Does the sun go away?

A few years ago we decided to try the Lake District for our holiday, because everyone kept telling us how beautiful it was there. Two wet, miserable weeks later we drove home again, sneezing all the way. Mountains? Were there any? All we had seen were gloomy clouds hanging low over our heads. Lakes? The lashing rain obscured them. Views? We had seen nothing but misted car windows.

'The sun must've gone to Africa, ' my smallest son remarked crossly as we sped down the motorway.

'Don't be silly,' his knowledgeable elder sister replied. 'The sun is always up there shining.'

'If it *had* been I wouldn't have felt so cold,' snapped Richard.

'You just have to *know* it's there even when you can't feel it,' said Naomi with finality. She was right and the same principle applies to God.

> I believe in the sun, even when it is not shining
> I believe in love even when I cannot feel it
> I believe in God even when He is silent.

---

*Wherever God's children are — as they are still upon their Father's ground — so they are still under their Father's eye and care. They may lose themselves in a wilderness, but God has not lost them.*
Matthew Henry

---

Those words were scrawled on the walls of a dungeon in Cologne by a Jewish prisoner during the war. Where was God when he wrote that? There in the prison with him. Where was the sun when we shivered in the car park at the bottom of Helvellyn? Shining brilliantly behind the obscuring clouds. Where was God when I stumbled blindly along in my desert? Right there beside me.

## How do we know God is with us?

God said He would never leave us over and over again throughout the Bible. 1 Samuel 12:22 says, 'The LORD has made a solemn promise and He will not abandon you.' God never breaks promises, He *is* close to us whether we feel it or not.

'The best things in life are appreciated most after they have been lost,' says Roy Smith. Perhaps it is possible to take God for granted, just because He is always there. We do not think about oxygen, we just breathe it automatically. Stand on the moon without an oxygen mask and we would think of nothing else. Perhaps deserts make us more aware of God than ever before.

Of course there are many reasons why we feel God has left us and we will look at them later in the book, but I wonder if the main purpose of a desert is not to give us the chance to discover whether our feelings are actually more important to us than God Himself.

These days we lay great emphasis on finding inner healing, releasing ourselves in worship, gaining power for our ministry and acquiring spiritual gifts to make our

---

*Jesus said: 'I will be with you always'.* (Matt. 28:20) *He promised us that we would always have His presence, but He never promised that we would always feel His presence.* Jean Rees

devotional life more fulfilling. As R. T. Kendall says, 'We are living in a "what's in it for me?" generation.' Perhaps we have lost that simple, ardent desire for God Himself, without all the trappings. The desert often robs us of the enjoyable side of our Christianity, even the 'fizz and bubble' of feeling close to God. Could the desert actually force us to ask if it is God we really want, or just the 'perks'?

If we can go on loving, obeying and putting Him first even when we are no longer getting anything out of it for ourselves we are actually beginning to love Him in the way that He loves us – totally unselfishly. 'For our life is a matter of faith, not of sight (feelings).' 2 Corinthians 5:7.

## 2: GOD MINDS ABOUT OUR DESERT

'I had this mental picture of God standing with His arms folded while I was sucked down in quicksands,' wrote Emma. 'If He cared about all I was going through, He would have done something to stop it.'

I remember feeling that God is so big and important, He could not possibly be interested in my affairs.

'It's all very well for you, Lord, sitting up there in comfort,' I remember muttering one day, 'Leaving me alone in all this pain.' The next morning I was reading my Bible (very unenthusiastically) when this verse 'hit me in the eye'. 'In all their distress, He too was distressed.' (Is. 63:9 NIV) Suddenly I realised that because He loved me so much, naturally He would mind terribly if I was

---

*God Himself has said, 'I will never, never let go your hand; I will never, never forsake you.'* Hebrews 13:5. Weymouth

suffering, just as I would care if someone I loved was in pain.

## God suffers much more in our deserts than we do

Just before I began to think about this book, the encephalitis flared up again and I was rapidly admitted to the hospital's intensive care unit.

I can remember little about it. I had such a headache I wanted to die, as I lay there gasping into my oxygen mask with tubes and needles protruding from every part of my body.

I do, however, remember feeling extremely sorry for myself, until I opened my eyes and saw my husband Tony sitting by my bed. The look on his face cured my self-pity.

'This is bad for me, but it's a thousand times worse for him,' I thought.

Why was it worse for Tony? Because he loves me and it is always much worse to watch someone you love suffering than it is to suffer yourself.

## Why did Jesus cry?

When her beloved brother Lazarus became ill, Mary didn't worry, she knew Jesus. He even healed beggars so certainly He would use His power to save one of his best friends. She and Martha sent a message to Jesus and received this encouraging reply.

'The final result of this illness will not be the death of Lazarus.' (John 11:4)

Mary felt quite happy after that – until Lazarus died.

---

*Thou canst not shrink from pain more than He dislikes thy bearing it.* Cardinal J. H. Newman

Then she began to feel uneasy. Why had Jesus not bothered to come?

'He's probably on His way,' she comforted herself, 'after all He's raised the dead before now.'

It was not until after the funeral that Mary finally plunged into her desert. Jesus had let her down, even He could not raise a decomposing corpse. For four days she sat in a state of despair – then Jesus arrived. Martha dashed out to meet Him, but Mary stayed in her house. Was she too angry with Jesus to face Him?

'If He'd been here Lazarus would not have died,' she kept thinking, 'He doesn't really care after all.'

Many of us went into our deserts because we were totally bewildered by suffering. God did not answer our anguished prayers. The promises He appeared to give us became a hollow mockery. In our hurt and disillusionment we turned away from the comfort Jesus would have given us. If only we had got up, like Martha, and hurried out to meet Him.

Yet Jesus understood how Mary was feeling and He cared so much He sent Martha in to fetch her.

When Mary saw Jesus she told Him exactly what she thought of Him and then burst into tears. What did Jesus do? He wept. He did not cry for his friend Lazarus, He knew He was going to raise him from the dead at any moment. He wept for Mary in her agony of soul. He minded for her. He cries like that for us too, because He loves us just as much as he loved Mary.

> *He (God) found them wandering through the desert, a desolate, wind-swept wilderness. He protected them and cared for them, as He would protect Himself.* Deuteronomy 32:10

## How does God feel about the mildly drab patches?

God does not only grieve over us in our dramatic deserts, He misses our company during our 'dull times'. The story about Mary and Martha in Luke 10:38–41 proves that more than anything else He wants our company. So when we give up the habit of prayer and close our Bibles with a sigh of boredom because we feel cut off from God, it is actually God who is feeling cut off from *us*!

## 3: IT DOES NOT MATTER IF YOU HAVE LOST YOUR FAITH

One evening just before Christmas, Ann went over to her baby's carrycot to see if he was ready for his six o'clock feed and suddenly the world stopped. Andrew was dead.

'I remember reaching out towards God even before I screamed for my husband,' she told me. 'The doctor, police and friends came and went all that evening, but they were far less real to me than God, it was as if He was carrying me. At last, when I went up to lie down on my bed He allowed me to see right into Heaven and there was Andrew very much alive and completely happy.

---

*He has an especial tenderness of love towards thee for that thou art in the dark and hast no light, and His heart is glad when thou dost arise and say, 'I will go to my father'. For He sees thee through all the gloom through which thou canst not see Him.* George Macdonald

'That vision made life possible through the next few months – they were difficult, but I was coping. Then one day I was sitting by the fire, and suddenly a veil seemed to slip from my eyes. There was no such person as God, everything I'd believed all my life was a hoax invented by people to keep us happy. But I knew I was no longer deceived.

'It was rather a relief at first, no more struggling to understand God and His mysterious ways. Then as I sat there I began to feel icy cold. If there was no God then there was no Heaven, if there was no Heaven, my baby was dead and I would never see him again. If life finished at the grave then this precarious, unfair world was simply pointless. In a panic I realised my security had gone, without God who was there to turn to? I searched my mind desperately but it was as if my brain had clicked into a new programme of thought and I saw things from a totally different point of view. However hard I tried, I just could not believe anything the Bible said.

'As the days went by my Christian friends seemed like deluded fools. How could I go to them for help? But I had to talk to someone, so at last I made an appointment with our vicar and shaking like a leaf I sat down in his study. I thought he would be profoundly shocked when I told him my faith had gone – after all, I was the church youth leader. Instead he said gently. "I know how this feels, I've been through similar experi-

> *Even when we are too weak to have any faith left, He remains faithful to us and will help us, for He cannot disown us who are part of Himself and He will always carry out His promises to us.* 2 Timothy 2:13, LB

ences, a great many Christians have. This is a very
normal and common reaction to shock. Bereavement
affects us like a physical wound, and you have to give
wounds time to heal."

'He was right too. My faith did not return immediately but I was content after that go on acting as a
Christian outwardly while I waited for my faith to
return.'

This loss of faith is a ghastly part of many deserts.
Sometimes, it happens suddenly, 'like someone switch-
ing the light off in your brain and leaving you in total
darkness'. Others feel something like Pauline:

I kept having flashes of doubt. I suppressed them, but
they kept on happening until I felt all tensed up and
edgy.

After Ann's interview with her vicar she was 'content
to wait'. She was in fact exercising the faith she thought
she had lost. Faith is simply a willingness to wait. We do
not bother to wait for a bus unless we know one is due.
Faith means standing at the bus stop: you don't need
faith when the bus arrives.

## That God exists does not depend on our belief
One Easter Sunday my brother Justyn suddenly realised
he did not believe a word he was preaching. His complete
loss of faith persisted for well over a year.

> *It is not my grasp of God that matters most, but His
> grasp of me. The thing that matters most is not
> even my consciousness that He holds me fast, but
> just the blessed fact of it.* Francis James.

'I was *paid* to have faith and impart it to others,' he told me, 'so I felt I had to work hard to get it back. I sweated and struggled and spent sleepless nights pacing the floor or reading through mountains of theological books on faith!

'Then someone told me to relax and rest in the fact that God believed in me even if I did not believe in Him. My belief or lack of belief made no difference whatsoever to the fact that God exists and He loves me. Now when I meet other Christians who are hammered by doubts I tell them this;

* God chose you before you were born. (Jeremiah 1:5)
* While you were still a sinner Christ died for you. (Romans 5:8)
* He called you before you chose Him. (John 15:16)
* He loves you with an everlasting love. (Jeremiah 31:3)
* Nothing you do will ever make Him love you any less.
* Nothing you do will ever make Him love you any more.

## Whether you believe does not alter the fact

'Of course,' continued Justyn, 'for a Christian to doubt God is a sin and when I realised that, I had to repent. Even now, years later, those doubts sometimes return fleetingly, but I'm ready for them now, and I repent at once and turn to the Lord for help before they have the chance to take hold of me again.

---

*If from sheer physical weakness or from any other cause, you find faith faltering or failing, turn away from yourself and cling to this. God isn't faltering or even altering, 'He abideth faithful'.* Canon Guy H. King

'What always helps me most is to remember Peter. When he stepped out of the boat he had so much faith he could even walk on the water. Yet, when he lost his faith he was actually much safer, because at that moment the Lord reached out and grabbed him. His safety did not depend on his faith, but on Jesus and so does mine.

'People have too much faith in faith. It is God Himself we need to trust.'

## Do you want to have faith?

Once a man brought his handicapped child to Jesus for healing (Mark 9:14–29). Jesus said,

'Everything is possible for him who believes.' The poor man was devastated. He wanted to believe yet he felt he was letting his son down because his faith was not great enough to meet this challenge. When my baby son Duncan was ill I felt like that man. 'If he dies,' I thought, 'it will be my fault because I can't work up enough faith to save him.' When I explained my feelings to our vicar he said gently, 'It is not your faith that counts, but God's faithfulness.'

As that worried father stood before Jesus the tears ran down his face as he exclaimed,

'I do have faith, but not enough. Help me to have more!' For Jesus it was enough that the man *wanted* faith. He healed the boy at once and He did just the same thing for my son Duncan.

> *But what if some of them were not faithful? Does this mean that God will not be faithful? Certainly not!* Romans 3:3–4

**How do we cope when our faith has deserted us?**
How do we operate while we wait for faith to return?
Matthew Chapter 28 verses 17–18 gives us the answer.
'They worshipped Him, even though some doubted.
Jesus drew near . . .' We need to keep ourselves in the
company of people who are not doubting, even when our
faith has gone. It is while we keep on worshipping with
them that Jesus 'draws near' to us again.

## 4: GOD IS BIG ENOUGH TO COPE WITH OUR ANGER

---

The Lord is good, when trouble comes He is the
place to go! *Nahum 1:7*

---

It surprises me sometimes, that the files containing all my
'desert letters' do not actually burst into flames. So many
of them smoulder with rage. Deserts are full of very
angry people:

> *I prayed for faith, and thought that someday faith
> would come down and strike me like lightning
> from Heaven. But faith did not seem to come. One
> day I read in Romans 10:17, 'Faith comes by
> hearing and hearing by the word of God.' I had,
> up to that time closed my Bible and prayed for
> faith, I now opened my Bible and began to study
> and faith has been growing ever since. D. L.
> Moody*

'I just couldn't stand the new vicar, he's such a silly little man.'

'I'm sick of other Christians offering me gift-wrapped answers when my world has fallen apart.'

## The Bible tells us clearly

Many of us have every reason to be angry but, the Bible tells us clearly to:

* 'Get rid of all these things: anger, passion and hateful feelings.' (Colossians 3:8)
* and to do so before the end of the day. (Ephesians 4:26)

That is easier said than done! First we have to recognise who is the real object of our anger. Perhaps it is not the bald-headed vicar, but God Himself. Subconsciously we are furious with Him for allowing the misery He could so easily have prevented. Yet we dare not admit our feelings, even to ourselves. So we transfer our rage on to other people or turn it inwards and lash ourselves with remorse.

To suppress anger is positively dangerous. We must express it, but dare we actually do that to God Almighty?

Many of the greatest men in the Bible were very angry with God, and they dared to tell Him so.

'If you are going to treat me like this, take
pity on me and kill me, so that I won't have
to endure your cruelty any longer.'
That was Moses. (Numbers 11:15)

*The bad experiences of our lives can either make us bitter or better.* David Watson

'It's too much,' he prayed 'Lord, take away my life,
I might as well be dead!'
That was Elijah. (1 Kings 19:4)

'Listen to my bitter complaint. Don't
condemn me God . . . Is it right for You
to be so cruel?' (Job 10:1–3)

'Are you going to do nothing and make us suffer
more than we can endure?'
That was Isaiah. (Isaiah 64:12)

'Don't you care that we are about to die?'
That was the disciples. (Mark 4:38)

Have you ever felt like that? Did you tell God how you
felt, or did you withdraw from Him and redirect your
anger towards others?

I have always found the most special part of parent-
hood is being able to comfort my children when they are
hurt. I used to keep a jar of sweets in the first-aid box
along with the plasters and antiseptic. But Richard, my
youngest son, never wanted my love when things went
wrong, because he always seemed to blame *me*!

I would see him from the kitchen window falling down
with a terrible bang, but by the time I had hurried out into
the garden, he was nowhere to be found. Sometimes he
would hide for ages, frightened to express the anger he
felt. I was always so relieved when at last his adrenalin
level was high enough, forcing him to 'break cover' and
hurl himself on me, punching, kicking and bellowing out

---

*Spiritual distress is the heaviest cross and
greatest burden that a just, holy, wise and good
God sends His believers.* Christian Sciver

his rage. He was so tiny and helpless and I loved him so much I didn't care at all, and I knew he had to dissipate his anger before he would let me comfort him. When the tornado had spent itself, he would give me a rather sheepish hug by way of saying sorry, and our comfortable relationship was restored.

I was reminded of Richard when Shirley told me about her desert.

I waited until the house was empty one evening, and then I shut the windows tightly. I was furious with God, and I wanted to tell Him so – loudly. I banged the kitchen table until my knuckles hurt. 'You've let me down!' I stormed, *'You just aren't fair!'*

I went on and on like that, until suddenly I was frightened. Scared of my own anger. Would God strike me dead? I felt as if I had been behaving like a tiny child, deprived of sweets, beating his fists against his father's chest. I collapsed on the kitchen chair, feeling desolate and empty. It was then that I felt literally enclosed by His arms, bathed by His reassurance. It was as if he said, 'I'm big enough to take your anger. I love you and I understand.'

I sat there sobbing with relief as I asked Him to forgive me for doubting His love, and that really was the turning point in my desert.

As human beings we have to express our anger. God is the only person big enough not to be damaged by that, and He also loves us enough to absorb it. However, even God Himself can be hurt by:

*For we beat upon His chest from within the circles of His arms.* Susan Jenkins

## Chronic, persistent anger

One of my children had a school friend who struck me as a very strange little boy. He must have been about nine I suppose. He was quiet and 'good' at school, but his father told me he was impossible at home. His mother, to whom he was devoted, had died some years earlier, but it was not grief that made Gavin so difficult – it was anger. His father had married again within the year and Gavin would not forgive him for putting another woman in his mother's place. He expressed his anger constantly, and made his father's life a misery. The marriage broke up in the end, no one could stand the strain, and the last I heard of Gavin he was in a home for maladjusted children. Gavin's father had only wanted to provide him with the love and care of a substitute mother. He was doing the best thing possible for his son, but Gavin destroyed his father's plans by chronic anger.

An outburst of anger is obviously scriptural and it certainly lowers the blood pressure, but a long-term attitude of anger and resentment is quite another thing.

## We can hurt God intensely

When difficulties arose in John's building and decorating business he naturally took them to God, but when God appeared to do nothing to help, John became angry. One day he was struggling to paper a client's lounge. The pattern would not match and the paper refused to stick to the walls. For John this was the last straw.

---

*How often they rebelled against Him in the desert, how many times they made Him sad! Again and again they put God to the test and brought pain to the Holy God of Israel.* Psalm 78:40–41

'You just can't love me Lord,' he burst out, 'if you did You'd help!'

That night, still furious, he went to his house group. He had to – he was the leader! Someone had a prophecy which simply said,

'I *do* love you, are not My hands and feet proof enough?' Bowed in the quiet room, John 'saw' the Lord clearly before him, showing His wounded hands and side as once he had showed Thomas.

'Jesus said nothing,' John told me, 'but the look of hurt and pain on His face was too much for me, I realised with terrible clarity that my attitude was causing Him real suffering.'

There is nothing which hurts more than to love someone to the uttermost, and then to have that person reject your love completely. God could not possibly love each one of us more than He does, so when we continue in an attitude of sustained resentment, anger and rejection He hurts no less than we would, if the person we loved most did the same to us.


## The most vital fact

The most vital bedrock fact of all is that God only wants to bless us, whatever we are going through, just as Gavin's father wanted to do the best for his son. Our attitude can hinder God's plans or cause them to materialise – it is up to us. God loves us so deeply that when we deliberately throw away our chance of His blessing, He *minds* for us.

So, whether we express our anger and bewilderment in a childhood 'temper tantrum' or smoulder away for

---

*Let us return to the Lord! He has hurt us, but He will be sure to heal us; He has wounded us but He will bandage our wounds.* Hosea 6:1

many months, we need to follow the example of Job
before our communion with God can be restored. He was
perhaps more rude to God than any other person in the
Bible, but at the very end of his book he says;

'So I am ashamed of all I have said and repent in dust
and ashes . . .' Then the Lord made him prosperous
again and gave him twice as much as he had had before.
(Job 42)

# 5

# THE DESERT CRISIS

In the shadow of Thy wings will I make my refuge
until these calamities be overpast. *Psalm 57:1, AV*

Most people who have been through a desert look back
on one particular incident which they remember as their
desert crisis. They use different words to describe it, such
as: 'Reaching the end of myself,' 'rock bottom', or 'my
turning point', but they are all talking about the same
thing. One person put it like this.

When my husband was seriously ill I went on like
the perfect vicar's wife – said all the right things, and
kept my smile pinned on firmly. But inside I was in a
turmoil. I remember thinking, 'I'm hanging over a
black hole. If I let go I'll hit the bottom and dis-
integrate'. So I just went on holding on to the edge by
my finger nails, praying constantly that God would
spare Peter's life.

One day another clergy wife sensed I was not really
as 'all right' as I pretended to be. When I explained the
'black hole' feeling to her, she said, 'why don't you let
yourself fall, dear, because when you do, you'll land
right into the arms of Jesus. He's got this whole situation in His control.' I collapsed into a chair and burst
into floods of tears. I realised I had not been trusting
Him to care for me if Peter were to die. I had been
resisting His love while I tried to cope by myself. I felt I
was falling down and down and I tensed myself to feel
the sharp rocks on the bottom, but 'underneath were

the everlasting arms' and I have never felt so comforted in my life. (The eternal God is your refuge and dwelling place, and underneath are the everlasting arms. Deuteronomy 33:27)

## The 'black hole': the crucial point

It is not the difficult circumstances of our lives that cause our spiritual deserts, but our reaction to them. The human instinct is usually to fight, to try and escape from an unpleasant situation as quickly as possible. Of course we should declare war on our problems – it is never right to lie down in a defeated, self-pitying heap. If you did that in the Sahara you would certainly die within hours! We should try to escape our desert by:

* Prayer perhaps with fasting.
* Seeking God's healing or deliverance.
* Confessing our sins and changing our attitudes.

Yet when we have done every single thing we can do, sometimes the situation does not change at all. It is then that we reach our crisis, the 'black hole'.

At the lowest point of every difficult situation stands Jesus with his arms open wide, longing to comfort us. He is saying, 'Will you give this to Me and trust Me to sort it out?'

> *If we know how much He loves us, we should always be ready to receive equally and with indifference from His hand the sweet and the bitter, all would please that came from Him.*
> Brother Lawrence

If we turn to Him at that point, our spiritual desert will probably be over, even if our human suffering may have to continue. But when we argue with God our desert is prolonged and our misery increases.

God only intended the Jews to take a few weeks to cross the Sinai Desert after He rescued them from Egyptian slavery. Yet He could not give them the Promised land until they had learnt to trust Him completely. It was their grumbling, complaining and rebellion that kept them in the desert for forty long years.

To accept a desert in all its bleakness, confusion, or grief can be the hardest thing God ever asks of us. When Jesus was in the Garden of Gethsemane He fought against the thought of the cross which lay ahead of Him and prayed until He sweated blood.

'Let this cup pass from Me.' He wanted that suffering removed, but He knew that His Father would never allow anything unless it would bring ultimate and long term good. So He bowed his head and accepted it. 'Nevertheless not My will, but Thine be done.' He could accept even the horror of the cross because He knew that all things work together for good to those that love God.

## 'All things' means deserts, too

It was because I did not realise that 'all things', means, good *and* bad things that it hurt me so much to be in my desert.

> *God, grant me the serenity*
> *To accept the things I cannot change.*
> *The courage to change the things I can –*
> *And the wisdom to know the difference.*
> B. Niebuhr

'This illness can't be God's will,' I thought. 'So what caused it?' For months I used every gram of my energy trying different ways to find healing until in the end I became so exhausted my physical condition grew worse.

'Satan's won!' I cried, when my friend Grace found me in tears one day.

'That's just what I thought,' she replied. 'When my husband left me with four kids, I just would not accept the situation for months, so I wrestled in prayer and beat on the doors of Heaven. "Lord, You've got to bring him back, I can't cope without him." I used to shout until I was quite worn out. But still my husband didn't come back.

'One day I found a tiny phrase from a poem written by the missionary, Amy Carmichael: "In acceptance lieth peace". Who was I to say what God should do? That was up to Him. I've gone on praying for a reconciliation ever since, but from that moment I nestled into God, and began to live again.'

'But Grace,' I argued, 'Acceptance is a cop out. We must fight bad situations or they drown us.' Grace smiled her crooked smile at me as she replied.

'When the waves are coming at us they will drown us if we just weakly let ourselves sink under them – that's resignation. But acceptance is a strong action: it means flinging ourselves on to the crest of the wave and allowing it to take us into the shore.'

After that conversation with Grace I still went on trying to manipulate God for months – all the way to my Black

---

*Woe to the man who fights with His Creator. Does the pot argue with its maker? Does the clay dispute with him who forms it, saying, 'Stop, you're doing it wrong!'* Isaiah 45:9

Hole! But eventually I too found that 'in acceptance lieth peace'. I also discovered that,

## Door out of the desert

Acceptance is the door which leads out of the desert. Acceptance is an act of the will, a decision we make without the help of wonderful 'bubbly' sensations – we simply decide to take whatever God gives us, asking for His help *in it* and not by having it removed. When we accept a difficult situation God does not necessarily change it, though He might. What He *does* change is the way we feel about it.

## Acceptance is not a 'one off' decision

Ruth and Goff's 'black hole' happened as they sat in the hospital intensive care unit beside their sixteen-year old daughter. That day at school, Barbara had suffered a massive brain haemorrhage.

'How we prayed,' they told me. 'We had no doubt in our minds that God would heal her, so we sat there praying away in tongues for hours, regardless of the nurses and doctors. Suddenly, at the same moment we both knew the Lord wanted us to trust Barbara to Him. He was the one who knew what was really best for her. As we held hands across her bed we gave our daughter to God, to do what He wanted, and we stopped demanding that He should do what we wanted. Complete peace seemed to settle round all three of us and a little while later the Lord took Barbara home to complete safety.'

*God wants us to accept everything and anything with a smile, not with gritted teeth.* Mother Teresa

'Did that feeling of peace remain with you?' I asked.

'We have always known that Barbara is in the safest place in the universe,' replied Goff. 'We've watched one of her school friends getting into trouble with the police, several others mixed up in drugs, and many more facing all kinds of unhappiness and danger and we often wonder just what it was that the Lord saved our Barbara *from*.'

'So you never had any problem with acceptance,' I pressed them.

'Well,' hesitated Ruth, 'Acceptance isn't something you just do once, it's a continuous struggle. I'll suddenly see a young mum pushing a pram and I'll think, "that could have been my Barbara". Then I have to give her to God all over again, right on the spot.'

## It is never too late for acceptance

That story may be worrying someone whose reaction to suffering was not so immediately accepting as that of Barbara's parents. Perhaps that is why God allowed me to meet Jan, just a short while after they visited me.

She too, once sat next to her daughter in an intensive care unit, but she felt nothing but outrage when she saw so many children all around her suffering so cruelly.

'Under my breath I snarled, "Go away God, You cosmic sadist! Following you makes life too difficult." For nearly three years after that I felt a total absence of God, no church, no prayer, no hope. I thought God had taken me at my word and gone for good. As my husband and

---

*Being able to acknowledge that He knows what He's doing in the midst of difficulty, that is a goal worth striving for, it is precious to Him when we trust Him through some difficulty.* June Dickie

friends kept on praying for me, I slowly began to yearn for God again. Gradually I came to accept that our daughter will be permanently handicapped and at last I was free to recognise the good things in the situation.'

## When we cannot forgive God

What is it that keeps us hanging over the edge of our 'black hole', unwilling to trust God and fall into his arms? I think it is that we cannot forgive God.

Of course He never engineers tragedies, but when God sees something is about to hurt us He could easily step in and stop it. But often He does not because He knows He can use it for our benefit. Satan, other people or we ourselves may have caused our misery, but it is God who takes the final responsibility. He is the supreme ruler of the universe. To say that He is powerless to protect us is to say He is less than God.

I used to think that it is always God's will for His children on earth to be whole physically and to live problem-free lives. I must have been wrong, because:

* There is not one Christian in all the world who is ever one hundred per cent healthy. Everyone has something that is imperfect.
* None of us goes through life without problems.
* We all die in the end.

So is God's will thwarted in us all the time? If it were, He would not be God. No, Jesus said we would have trouble in this life (see John 16:33), but in Heaven at His

---

*Let us see God's hand in all events and let us see all events in God's hand.* Matthew Henry

right hand are pleasures for evermore. (Cf. Psalm 16:11)
If God had intended us to be exempt from the natural
problems of all human beings He would have made us
into angels.

## We need to forgive God even though He has done no wrong

'I could accept that I'm disabled more easily if I did not
believe in God's ability to heal me!' snapped Diana. The
day she was packing to leave for medical school she had
been involved in an accident which has left her crippled
and badly disfigured.

For three hours one morning she told me about all the
different people who were to blame for the accident.

'Even the surgeon removed more of my damaged brain
than he should,' she finished angrily.

'But God could have prevented the whole thing.' I put
in quietly. 'Do you believe that?'

'Oh yes,' she said impatiently. 'I even remember
praying for safety as I got up that morning!'

'Then surely it is God who takes the final responsibility
for the accident. If a human being causes us pain, grief or
hardship our relationship is broken until we forgive
them. If I chanced to be standing behind the door when
Tony suddenly opened it, I would probably be furious
with him for my bleeding nose and headache. In my hurt

*He has not created me for naught. Therefore I will
trust him. Whatever, wherever I am . . . He does
nothing in vain. He knows what He is about. He
may take away my friends . . . make my spirits
sink, hide my future from me, still He knows what
He is about.* Cardinal Henry Newman

and rage I might blame him, even though he had done me no wrong, he simply opened a door. I would have to forgive him before our relationship could be restored.'

Diana was looking at me with a growing expression of horror on her scarred face. So I hurried on to explain what I meant.

'There has to come a time when we say, "Lord, I forgive You. I know you have only allowed this for my ultimate good, but right now I am hurting – badly!"'

'Forgiving God!' gasped Diana, 'That's blasphemy!' and she swept out of my room and slammed the door. I spent a terrible few days feeling I had permanently destroyed her faith in the love of God, yet when I looked in my dictionary it said forgiveness means: 'ceasing to blame, giving up resentment against'. Could Diana ever manage to do that to God?

Two days later she was in my room again, a different girl.

'I did it,' she said quietly. 'I told God I forgave Him for not preventing the accident that day, and I asked His forgiveness for blaming Him.' Then she added with a sudden smile, 'and I said to Him, "I don't know what you're doing, but I know *You* know, and I trust You." Now there are no more nasty shadows between us.' Yes, as Amy Carmichael affirms, peace really does lie in acceptance!

---

*Prosperity is the blessing of the Old Testament, and adversity is the blessing of the New Testament.* Francis Bacon

# 6
# THE 'BEFORE' AND 'AFTER' DESERTS

---

When He has tested me I shall come forth as gold.
*Job 23:10*

---

The huge marquee resounded with joy as thousands of people praised God unanimously. This was the last night of a great Bible Week, and many people had received a wonderful new blessing.

'Thank you for filling me with Your Spirit,' gasped Louise, 'Now I love You more now than anything or any one.'

'What's gone wrong?' demanded the same girl, eleven months later as she stormed into her vicar's study. 'I was on cloud nine after last summer. I thought I'd feel like that for ever, but now everything in my life keeps going wrong, and God's not doing anything about it. I'm beginning to wonder if that experience was phoney, just mass hysteria.'

The vicar tried to speak, but Louise continued without taking breath. 'I've read so many books which describe dark patches that people go through, but then they are baptised in the Holy Spirit and the books imply that all their troubles were over – "she married the prince and lived happily ever after". Why hasn't it worked out like that for me?'

'My dear,' commented her vicar at last, 'don't forget that God only tests those who are really precious to him.'

'In that case,' snapped Louise, 'I'd rather not be that precious!'

The new blessing that Louise had received at the Bible Week was real all right, more real than life itself. She was simply in:

## The 'after' desert

So many deserts seem to happen *after* some great new blessing, *after* receiving a new spiritual gift, a revelation or vision for future service, even after a deeper personal commitment to God. Just when we feel we ought to march out in triumph to take the world for God by storm, we find ourselves floundering about in a desert.

Perhaps we feel as badly 'let down' as Louise, yet is this not exactly what happened to Jesus? He was baptised and heard God's voice speak to Him from heaven affirming that He was His own Son. Did He stride straight off to Jerusalem and start telling everyone He was the Messiah? No He was 'led of the spirit into the desert to be tested'. There Satan tried every way he knew to make Jesus doubt His deity and God's plan for His life.

All new things have to be tested. Before an aircraft is licensed to carry passengers it is subjected to tests of every kind and in an 'after' desert our 'new blessings' are being shaken and rattled like a VC 10 in a wind tunnel.

It is easy to love God in the blazing sunshine of a mountain top experience, but can we go on loving Him as we grope about in the dark valley which so often follows?

> *Though God doth visit my soul with never so blessed a discovery of Himself, yet I have found again and again that such hours have attended me afterwards that I have been in my spirit so filled with darkness that I could not so much as once conceive what comfort was with which I have been refreshed.* John Bunyan

As Louise sat facing her vicar she had to decide how important her new blessing really was to her. Would she cling on to it tenaciously, or shrug her shoulders and find something else to fill her life?

## The dark night of the soul – God's test for love

Five hundred years ago a monk we now call St John of the Cross described deserts as 'The dark night of the soul' and he stated that they are God's way 'of purifying the soul of everything that hinders its close relationship with God and ability to serve Him'. Many Christians are quite content to jog along happily as solid church-goers with God in one department of their lives. Probably they will never be troubled by the 'dark night of the soul'. A smaller group of Christians want to love God with everything, not just a part. Their path will undoubtedly lead through deserts because God will have to discover if their love is pure of any taint of self-interest.

'Souls begin to enter into this dark night when God draws them out from being beginners,' says St John. A desert is a sign of Christian maturity, not of failure!

In the marquee Louise told Jesus she loved Him more than anything or anyone else. When the feeling of spiritual ecstasy died out of her Christian life Jesus was asking, as once He asked Peter, 'Louise do you love me more than these? More than the fun of meeting your friends in church? More than you enjoy My power to do supernatural things? More than the excitement of having your prayers answered?'

---

*What is a religion worth which cost you nothing? What is a sense of God-worth which would be at your disposal?* Frederich von Hügel

Of course God does not want our lives with Him to be a harsh grind, and in time He gave Louise back all her enjoyment but with an added depth. God wanted to be loved for Himself, and not just for his gifts. He wanted to be more important to Louise than the excitement of being a charismatic Christian.

## After some great achievement for God
Many people told me that their desert came almost as a reaction;

'After I gave my testimony at our church carol service.'

'I worked so hard helping with our church mission that afterwards I felt a bit like Elijah after Mount Carmel!'

Martin Luther is remembered throughout history for his great trial at Worms, when he stood out against the power and corruption of Rome and launched the Reformation. Afterwards he was in such danger his powerful friends smuggled him away against his will and hid him in a lonely castle in the forest. For a year he was in a horrendous desert. All his life he struggled against frequent bouts of depression when he 'doubted that God is good and that He is good to me', but Luther's 'After Desert' was the worst he ever experienced.

As he lay on his damp bed unable to sleep, he would wonder if he had been right to say 'the just shall live by faith alone?' If he was wrong he would carry all his

---

*Give me Thine own self, without Whom, though thou shouldest give me all that ever Thou hast made, yet could not my desires be satisfied.* St Augustine

followers with him to hell. For a whole year he suffered mental agony, but when he eventually came out of hiding an eye witness described him as 'a man aflame with God, and twice the man he was before'.

## The 'before' desert

When someone is plodding wearily through a desert the last thing to occur to them is that God may be preparing them for some great work. Yet from the Bible down through church history, few people of God have *not* gone through a desert before embarking on a great work for Him.

Jamie Buckingham describes the desert as 'a scorching crucible that has burned from proud men both sin and selfishness until they have emerged pure and prepared for ministry.'

'I have tested you in the fire of suffering.' (Isaiah 48:10)

God told Joseph he was destined for greatness through a dream when he was still a boy. But years of rejection, exile, slavery and imprisonment had to come before he was ready to be the world statesman God needed.

David was a 'rosy-faced' shepherd boy when God told him he would be king one day. First he had to endure years as a fugitive hiding in the desert from the jealousy of Saul.

Moses was a proud, headstrong prince who sensed his job in life was to free three million jews from slavery. But

> *Hardly any outstanding champion of faith who has left an indelible impress on man's spiritual life can anywhere be found who has not won his faith and confirmed it in the face of trouble.* Harry Fosdick

he thought he could do it his way, and landed himself in a real desert with murder on his conscience. After forty years contending with a few scrawny sheep and an unhappy marriage, the Bible describes him as the most humble man on earth. He was ready for God to use him to accomplish a major assignment.

I have never met anyone in a desert who can possibly believe God will ever use them again! I felt infuriated with my friend – the one who poured tea all over the table – when she tried to suggest that my desert might be a preparation for something God wanted me to do. Yet she was right. As I look back, I can see it was not the end of the road, but the beginning of the completely new and exciting life that God had planned for me.

Probably we could all accept our deserts far more easily if only we could see them in the context of our whole lives. The most trying part of spiritual deserts is that at the time we never realise their significance!

*Never doubt in the dark what God said in the light.*
Arne Peterson

*A cricketer can never score runs unless he is bowled at.* Tom Rees

# THE DESERTS THEMSELVES

---

Now change your mind and attitude to God and turn to Him so He can cleanse away your sins and send you wonderful times of refreshment from the presence of the Lord. *Acts 3:19*, LB

---

## 1: THE DESERT WE CAUSE OURSELVES

In this chapter we are looking at the many things make us *feel* separated from God. The Bible tells us that the only thing that ever actually *does* separate us from Him is our own sin. There is one prayer which God always answers, 'Search me O God and know my heart. Point out anything you find in me that makes you sad.' (Ps. 139:23–24. LB). If your desert is caused by sin, God will certainly tell you. If you then ask His forgiveness and resolve to stop sinning in that way, *your sin is wiped out!*

### The unforgivable sin

Of course Satan may try to blind you to the fact that you can be so instantly and easily free. I have met three people this year who thought their particular sin was unforgivable.

I was whizzing through the park in my electric wheel chair when I first met Tess and her black labrador. We both admired each other's dogs and half an hour later we were still talking!

'You must get very bored, being disabled,' she said. 'Whatever d'you do all day?'

'Actually I'm writing a book,' I replied, feeling rather silly. When she pressed me, I told her it was about people who feel separated from God.

'That's me,' she replied turning pale. 'I used to love going to church more than anything, but of course I had to stop when . . .'

'When what?' I asked her gently,

'When I realised I'd once committed the unforgivable sin,' Tess whispered miserably. 'Ten years ago I had an abortion. We already had two children and wanted to educate them privately, so it seemed sensible at the time, but I have never regretted anything so much in my life. Going to church was a great comfort, until I heard someone on television say that abortion is unforgivable to God.'

'The fact that you are *worried* you have committed the unforgivable sin, is a sure sign you haven't!' I told her. 'No sin is unforgivable if you are willing to ask God's forgiveness. If Hitler himself had been genuinely sorry for all he did, and turned to God in repentance, we would meet him in Heaven one day.'

Tess gazed at me and then she said,

'You really mean it's possible that I could be free of this?'

When I next met Tess I could see by her face that she was finally free of Satan's lie.

## The mess that sin leaves behind

Another of Satan's ploys is to say, 'Look at the mess

> *Though I have fallen, I will rise, though I sit in darkness, the Lord will be my light.* Micah 7:8

you've made of your life. What's the point of having your sins forgiven when you'll still be helplessly enmeshed in their consequences?' He loves to remind you that the decisions you made when you were temporarily 'off the rails' have left you stuck in a difficult situation from which you cannot now escape.

'The results of my mistake are a constant reminder of the wreck I've made of my life,' said a man I met recently. 'Now I can never be a first-class Christian – I've spoiled all the plans God made for me.'

## God deals with our sins and their consequences

There is no such thing as a second-class Christian in God's eyes. When we are forgiven He sees us through Christ as if perfect. We may have surrounded ourselves with an ugly heap of rubbish which seems to trap and defeat us, but if we give it to Him, God will take delight in making something beautiful out of it.

Antique Eastern carpets were usually hand-knotted by apprentice boys. When the master carpet-maker came round to view their work he might discover a mistake they made days before. Yet he did not insist the whole carpet was thrown away, neither did he order hours of work to be unpicked. Because he was the designer, he simply incorporated the mistake into a new pattern, using it to create a unique effect.

'I look to the Lord for help at all times, and he rescues me from danger,' says David in Psalm 25 verse 15. If we keep concentrating on the Lord He will show us how to cope with our difficult situations, step by step. When

> *If God tells us to forgive seventy times seven, it stands to reason He will do even better Himself.*
> Thomas Bilney

David had confessed the sin of his adultery with Bathsheba and the murder of her husband (Ps. 51) they later
had a son, King Solomon, who was the wisest man who
ever lived. David had many wives, yet it was through
Bathsheba that Jesus descended. God made a very
special carpet out of that situation!

## The little sins that don't really matter
If Satan cannot crush us by making us feel our sins are too
big for God, he will make us think they are too small to
matter.

It is possible to be working happily for the Lord, full of
joy and power when, suddenly, into our lives creeps
something so small we do not even recognise it as sin. We
begin to feel drab spiritually but perhaps we put it down
to overwork. When our consciences begin to prick, we
think, 'That's impossible, God would never bother about
something as trivial as this.' Yet it is surprising just how
many little things the Bible tells us will destroy our
worship and prevent God from hearing our prayers.
Because they are often things we enjoy we reason away
to our consciences like this:

* Everyone else does it, it's our modern life style.
* God understands – He loves me and I've even prayed
  about it.
* We all have our little 'besetting sin'.
* Compared with other people round here, I'm a saint!

---

*Let not small and trivial sins be despised. With
little drops the river is filled. Through narrow
chinks in the ship the water oozes into the hold
and if it be disregarded the ship is sunk.* St
Augustine

Satan either makes us think of God as a punishing tyrant or he gives us the equally false impression of a jovial Father Christmas, distributing endless presents. When we sin we imagine God smiles indulgently and pats us on the head. But if He could treat our sin like that why did Jesus have to die in agony? He did not suffer just for the sins we think are serious – adultery, robbery, murder. He died because all sins are the same size in God's eyes and they all separate us from Him.

## Thoughts are as serious as actions

Outwardly Josie looked as if she was listening attentively to the sermon, but inwardly she was having sexual fantasies about the curate who was preaching. Josie would never dream of *doing* anything wrong, but Jesus tells us clearly in Matthew 5 that to *think* adultery is as serious in God's eyes as committing it outwardly. It is also as bad to feel bitterly angry and resentful towards another person as it is to commit murder!

Josie told herself that 'day dreaming' was all right because 'it didn't hurt anyone else'. But when she found it was interfering with her worship, she realised it was actually hurting both herself and God.

'But now I can't seem to stop. These thoughts just pop into my mind even when I don't want them and make me feel dirty,' she told me tearfully.

'Suppose a salesman knocked at your door,' I said, 'trying to sell something you can't possibly afford. You could say firmly, "No thank you", and shut the door. Or

---

*The steps of a good man are directed by the Lord. He delights in each step they take. If they fall it isn't fatal, for the Lord holds them with His hand.* Psalm 37:23–4, LB

you might ask him into the sitting room, make him coffee and read all his brochures.'

'If I did that,' smiled Josie, 'I'd probably find myself lumbered with his product!'

'Satan shoots darts into our minds constantly,' I continued, 'a lustful thought, a sudden surge of resentment, self-pity, a flash of doubt or envy. But a thought is not a sin until we entertain it. If we say "NO!" at once and turn to the Lord for help, we are not sinning. It is when we close our eyes and indulge ourselves in the thought that it separates us from God.'

After a few weeks Josie told me that Satan had soon become tired of his game of mental darts.

## Our attitudes can separate us from God

In the first chapter of Isaiah (verses 15–17) God says, 'Even though you make many prayers, I will not hear . . . wash yourself . . . Learn to do good, to be fair and to help the poor, the fatherless and widows.' (LB) In other words, God will not hear us if we are bullying someone who is in our power. Is there a pupil in your class, or a child in your family who always seems to get the rough side of your tongue? An office junior, an elderly relation, even your own husband or wife! God wants us to build people up with encouragement, not browbeat them by constant nagging or criticism.

Many people do not dare to do their bullying face to face, they prefer to destroy people behind their backs by niggling comments. I have come to believe that critical, cynical remarks and a harsh, unloving attitude towards

---

*If I had cherished sin in my heart the Lord would not have listened.* Psalm 66:18

other people are one of the most common causes of
spiritual deserts.

## We all know lies are wrong

We all know lies are wrong, but 'white lies make people
happy', we argue, 'half truths are kinder' and 'exagger-
ation makes a better story'. God must hate the smiling
masks behind which we hide our real thoughts from
other Christians.

## Spiritual pride

In Woolworths one day I overheard Mrs P talking about
Robbie, the girl mentioned on page 28.

'Fancy!' said this righteous pillar of the women's fellowship, 'I would never dream of going off with someone
else's husband!' Perhaps she would not, but she was
forgetting that pride is as bad in God's eyes as adultery.

Jesus told us about a really good man who went up
to pray in the temple – but God did not hear a word he
said because of his attitude towards someone else. The
Pharisee *did* nothing to the sinner hiding in the corner, he
did not spit contemptuously or stone the man, he simply
despised him mentally. (Luke 18:9–14)

When you think of your Christian friends, do you look
*up* at them with respect, or look *down* on them for being
less spiritual than you are? 'She can't speak in tongues
yet, poor thing.' Or 'How sad that they're all so shallow.'

> *But how can I ever know what sins are lurking in
> my heart? Cleanse me from these hidden faults.
> And keep me from deliberate wrongs.* Psalm
> 19:12–13, LB

The harder we strive after a holy life, the more likely we are to fall into the unholy trap of spiritual pride. 'Be humble towards one another, always considering others better than yourselves' (Philippians 2:3). When we cannot seem to give God worship, we need to remember that the kind He loves most is the offering of a humble, repentant heart. (Psalm 51:17)

## A rebellious streak

Some people are always slightly 'agin' the government of the day. They have to mock or criticise their vicar or church leaders and 'cut them down to size'. 'Obey your leaders and follow their orders,' says Hebrews chapter 13 verse 17. If you honestly feel you cannot follow and respect your church leaders then you are either separating yourself from God by a rebellious attitude, or you could be in the wrong church.

## Broken relationships

'I just can't seem to get through to God any more,' complained Yvonne, 'my Christian life's gone dead on me.'

'Have you asked God why?' I said.

Next Sunday Yvonne was sitting in church when verses 23–24 from Matthew 5 were read as part of the second lesson. 'So if you are about to offer your gift to God at the altar and there you remember that your brother has something against you, leave your gift there

---

*Our iniquities, our secret heart and its sins, (which we would so like to conceal even from ourselves;) You have set in the (revealing) light of your countenance.* Psalm 90:8, AMP

in front of the altar, go at once and make peace with your brother and then come back and offer your gift.'

Suddenly she realised that the beginning of her desert had coincided with a fierce row she had with Mrs P over the church flower rota. They had never liked each other and used the heat of battle to tell each other so – volubly.

'I *was* rather mean to the poor old biddy,' thought Yvonne as she realised just how much that argument had bothered her subconsciously.

'I felt like jumping up there and then and doing what the verse told me to do – putting matters right at once before I attempted to worship,' she told me later. 'But I managed to wait until Mrs P was pouring the after-service coffee before I told her I wanted to apologise.

'She slammed the kettle down and said, ''About time too, young lady!'' I was so upset. She just couldn't see that it was as much her fault as mine! But later in the day, I went for a long walk and realised I had done what Jesus told me to do, and it was not my fault if she didn't respond. I've felt close to Him ever since and I can worship again at last.'

If our relationships are wrong, and we owe someone an apology or need to forgive them for some damage they have done to us, we will feel separated from God until we do something about it.


## Thou shalt worship the Lord thy God and Him only shalt thou serve

It is terribly hard to keep that first great commandment in these days when most people worship 'things'.

---

*Conscious repentance leads to unconscious holiness.* Roy Hession

'In our first little rented flat we were so happy together and with the Lord,' said Catherine wistfully. 'Then we began using all our time and energy buying the perfect home. The most important thing in Ray's life was to get as high as possible in his firm, and for me it was to have the same 'things' as the others in our circle – a microwave oven, a dishwasher, a BMW car with a telephone, a size ten body and a foreign sun tan. Soon these things had become our bosses, but we did not realise we were worshipping them instead of God. We always went to church, unless of course it clashed with a golf match.

Then, suddenly, Ray was made redundant, and we got into financial hot water. In fact we looked like losing everything; even our marriage was falling apart. It was then that we remembered that Jesus said, "You cannot serve both God and money." (Luke 16:13) If ony we had put Him in the centre of our lives the job and the "things" wouldn't have become so important.'

It is not a sin to be rich. The Bible says the love of money, not money itself, is the root of all evil, but as Christians we need to ask ourselves who owns our possessions – us or God?

Because we live in this sin-filled world, we tend to absorb the attitudes and behaviour of the people around us. But if we ask Him, God will insert a completely new disk into our mental computer and reprogram all our thoughts. 'Do not conform yourselves to the standards of

---

*Jesus said: 'The seeds that fell among thorn bushes stand for those who hear; but the worries and riches and pleasures of this life crowd in and choke them, and their fruit never ripens'.* Luke 8:14

this world, but let God transform you inwardly by a complete change of your mind. – Then you will be able to know . . . what is good and is pleasing to Him.' (Romans 12:2)

## Addiction – the habit Satan says we cannot kick

'Mine iniquities have taken hold upon me, so that I am not able to look up . . .' (Psalm 40:12) That is exactly how we feel when we are gripped by a habit or addiction which keeps on trapping us in the desert.

'Satan's really got me by the throat this time,' we think miserably. But Satan is nothing but a beaten bully who likes us to remember verse 8 in 1 Peter 5, which says '. . . the Devil roams round like a roaring lion looking for someone to devour', while he prefers us to miss James Chapter 4 verse 7, which tells us that if we resist him he has to run away!

Fifteen years ago I was in a horrible desert and I felt utterly defeated by a habit I just could not kick. I knew it was wrong and God had told me clearly to remove it from my life. I would manage for several days and then give in to it yet again.

'Sorry Lord,' I would say and then I would get up from my knees and stagger on through the day, forgiven but feeling uncomfortable because I knew I was secretly looking forward to the next fall. My will wanted the enjoyment of the habit more than it wanted to obey God, and that troubled my conscience. Soon all I ever seemed

---

*. . . obeying God with deep reverence, shrinking back from all that might displease Him. For God is at work within you, helping you want to obey Him and then helping you do what He wants.*
**Philippians 2:12–13**

to say to God was 'sorry'. My comfortable relationship with Him was ruined. It never occurred to me to ask God to take possession of my will, as well as the rest of me.

## Vital fact

A very few fortunate people are cured of their addiction instantly to such things as nicotine, alcohol, drugs, over-eating or sexual wrong-doing. They are free as a result of just one prayer. Most of us struggle with our particular weakness all our lives. Far from feeling 'let down' by this, we need to revel in the fact that we grow closer to God when we have to rely on Him daily and even hourly for power to resist temptation. I did not know that then, so I felt annoyed with God for not making things easier for me.

One day, I went into a country churchyard to kill time while I waited for the post office to open. In a corner I discovered a life-sized crucifix and as I looked up into the Lord's face, I was horrified by the suffering and stark agony portrayed there. Perhaps it was a trick of the light, or the brilliance of the artist – or was it a vision? Suddenly the face was no longer a sculpture, it was real. I saw the drops of sweat, the bruises and the blood that trickled down from His crown of thorns. He had gone through all this to break the chains that bound me, yet I had been busy forging the links again with the sins and dis-

---

*So then, let us rid ourselves of everything that gets in the way, and of the sin which holds on to us so tightly, and let us run with determination the race that lies before us.*

*Let us keep our eyes fixed on Jesus.* Hebrews 12:1–2

obediences I had been treating so casually. My attitude mocked His agony and suddenly something inside me broke as I stood there in helpless tears of true repentance.

We come out of the deserts we cause ourselves when we realise just how intensely our sins hurt Jesus and how much He minds the loss of our company.

---

My mind and my body may grow weak, but God is my strength; He is all I ever need. *Psalm 73:26*

---

## 2: THE DESERT ASSOCIATED WITH PHYSICAL ILLNESS AND FATIGUE

Nothing can smother spiritual verve more rapidly than a cold in the head! So often, when we feel flat spiritually, we torture ourselves by unnecessary guilt, when all the time our desert has a purely physical origin.

We are made up of three parts: body, soul and mind. When our bodies are functioning below par, our minds may become depressed and our souls can feel far from God. Many spiritual problems actually stem from:

* Hormone imbalance
* Overwork or 'ministry burn-out'
* Vitamin deficiencies
* The side effects of a prescribed drug
* Prolonged stress
* Illness for which we should be receiving medical help

### Meet your body's needs first

When Jesus went into his desert, Satan waited until He was physically weak from fasting and dehydration, then he attacked. Satan knows that when the bodies of human beings are weak, their minds and souls are more vulnerable to him. Perhaps it is our bodies that need to be cosseted and prayed over before we begin to worry about our souls!

God knew that was Elijah's first need. He had just been through a huge time of stress on top of three years of scanty food when he ran away into the desert, lay down under a bush and wished to die. God allowed him first to sleep and then He sent an angel with some good food before He took the old Prophet away alone and gave him a fresh revelation of Himself. A holiday, with plenty of good food, fresh air and early nights, can often do wonders for the soul!

When we are at that initial stage of asking 'why Lord?' (see Chapter 2) it is often sensible to have a medical check up. One friend of mine felt her Christian life was disintegrating until she discovered she had a thyroid deficiency which her doctor easily remedied.

When we are ill, Christians have easy access to the best doctor in the world, Jesus Himself. Naturally, we turn to Him first – He may heal us miraculously, work through medical science or He may delay our healing completely for a time.

## Often while we wait for healing we go into a desert

Sometimes we feel closer to God when we are acutely ill than at any other time in our lives. He positively hovers over that hospital bed. It is when we grind on month after month never feeling any better that God seems far away.

> The menopause has a lot of deserts to answer for.
> Elizabeth Church

Perhaps we are told the illness is going to be lengthy or even a permanent part of our lives. 'Why doesn't He answer my prayer?' we ask miserably.

When we can no longer dash round for God or be busily involved in all kinds of Church work, we feel strangely devalued in His sight. That is just how a friend of mine was feeling when her brother Alan said something to her which literally changed her life:

> 'It is not what we do for God that matters
> but what we will allow Him to do for us.'

## 'My power shows up best in weak people.' (2 Corinthians 12:9, LB)

So when our arms and legs feel like cotton wool, it is then and only then that we discover the full extent of God's power. Satan tells us we are useless, (self-confidence always goes when we are ill) but it always seems to slip Satan's mind that we are actually no good to God when we trust our own abilities. It is only when we have to rely on God completely that we become useful to Him. The moment we realise that, Satan is defeated.

> 'A weak person who has nothing to rely on but the strength of God is one hundred times more powerful spiritually than an ordinary strong human being,' said Annette, who has multiple sclerosis.

If God had wanted to breed a race of supermen to be His earthly children, He would not have chosen

---

*When your liver is upset, your prayer life will suffer.* David Pawson 'what the world considers weak in order to shame the powerful'. (1 Corinthians 1:27)

## The healing epidemic

If I had become ill twenty years ago, I do not think I would have gone into a spiritual desert at all. It was only because I had been taught to expect healing on demand that I felt I had failed God and He had failed me. Since I wrote *Beyond Healing*, I have become increasingly concerned about the huge number of Christians who have gone into deserts because they have not recovered even when they had apparently fulfilled all the Bible's conditions for healing. I have received many letters like this one from Diane.

> I know God heals people, I've seen Him do it! I'm excited that the Church has rediscovered something that lay dormant for so long. When I became ill I was sure God was going to heal me, the whole Church prayed, fasted and the elders anointed me with oil, (James 5) but I still felt ill.
>
> 'Don't think about the symptoms,' they said, 'that's just Satan pretending', so I flushed my pills down the loo and told my doctor I wouldn't need them any more. I used every atom of my energy trying to convince myself and the world that I was well, I even told people lies.
>
> 'I'm fine,' I would say brightly. 'I'm perfectly fit now,

---

*I am most happy then, to be proud of my weaknesses, in order to feel the protection of Christ's power over me . . . For when I am weak, then I am strong.* 2 Corinthians 12:9–10

I've been healed.' But gradually it dawned on me that I was not. The pills I had flushed away were actually vital to my life. I was so embarrassed when the doctor was called out in the night, and I had to explain. I felt I had let the whole Church down, they said it was my fault and I didn't have enough faith or will power. I was so ashamed I left, but now I don't feel I fit into any Church somehow. I'm a complete failure.

How dare we do that kind of thing to our Christian brothers and sisters? Sometimes God has to allow a period of illness so we can discover certain of the more precious treasures of darkness. We are robbed of them when people cover us in condemnation.

I overheard a conversation at the supermarket check out the other day, 'Its only your health that matters', muttered one woman to her friend as they both looked at me in my wheelchair. A fly on the wall during some prayer meetings could be forgiven for feeling that Christians now agree with the world on the question of physical fitness. When we lay too much emphasis on the healing ministry, are we not denying the fact that the soul is permanent while the body is very temporary? Even Mr Universe and Miss World will be old age pensioners in a few years' time!

So, if you do happen to be ill, stop feeling guilty. Stop using so much energy agitating to be well that you have none left to dig for the gemstones down in those mines. The treasure God may want you to discover is that He still

> *For this reason we never become discouraged. Even though our physical being is gradually decaying, yet our spiritual being is renewed day after day.* 2 Corinthians 4:16

can heal miraculously. So go on believing in miracles, but keep digging in the meantime!

## Not 'one day at a time' – a day can feel like an eternity!

Even though God may not restore all our strength to us in one go, He never leaves us without enough for the things we really *have* to do. In his letter to the Philippians Chapter 4 verse 13 St Paul says, 'For I can do everything God asks me to with the help of Christ who gives me the strength and power.'

Recently I heard from my friend Clem who has been ill for many years. He has learnt to break his days up into short sections.

> God prepares parcels of strength and leaves them hidden behind every milestone along the way ahead. As we run out of strength during the day, we pray, and then pick up the next parcel.

How that helped me. Sometimes I will be sitting in my chair and I think, 'I just haven't the energy to get the supper tonight'. I have to bend down in prayer and pick up another parcel of strength which will carry me on to the next milestone.

---

*When we have exhausted our store of endurance,*
*When our strength has failed ere the day is half done,*
*When we reach the end of our hoarded resources,*
*Our Father's full giving is only begun.*
Annie Johnson Flint

---

'O God my Rock,' I cry, 'why have You forsaken me? Why must I suffer . . . O my soul, don't be discouraged. Don't be upset. Expect God to act! For I know that I shall again have plenty of reason to praise Him for that that He will do. *Psalm 42:9–11, LB*

## 3: THE DESERT OF DEPRESSION

'I wouldn't describe my depression as a desert,' said Janet, 'to me it felt more like a dark pit in the desert!'

'WHY do Christians always spiritualise depression?' demanded another friend, Pat. 'If I'd been in a general hospital half the Church would have visited me, loaded with grapes and chocolates, but because I was in the psychiatric wing, they only came near me to say I must be harbouring some unconfessed sin, or unresolved conflict. Someone even said, "self-pity is at the bottom of all depressions". It's funny how people who aren't depressed always know just what depressed people ought to do!'

There is nothing a human being can go through which is worse than severe depression. The Bible says, 'A man's spirit sustains him in sickness, but a crushed spirit who can bear?' (Proverbs 18:14, NIV) When you go through physical pain, grief or adversity, you can turn to God for support, but often one of the symptoms of depression is that you feel you have lost Him as well.

## Depression is not a sin, or a sign of failure
Depression is a normal part of human life from which

Christians are not exempt. Some of the greatest people of God down the centuries have suffered from bouts of depression. Jeremiah, David, Elijah, John Wesley and Lord Shaftesbury. Spurgeon was sometimes too depressed to climb into his pulpit on a Sunday, while Martin Luther, 'sobbed himself into his last sleep like a great wearied child'. William Cowper is alleged to have attempted suicide the day he wrote 'God moves in a mysterious way his wonders to perform,' and perhaps the greatest charismatic of our day, David Watson, also admitted he was frequently depressed. So perhaps it is time we all stopped feeling so embarrassed about an illness which is no more shameworthy than breaking a leg.

My trouble was I thought my problem was spiritual when in fact I was simply suffering from post viral depression. I battled away alone, too ashamed to admit how terrible I felt, even to my family. I thought if I went to my doctor he would label me as a 'nut case', and if I went to my minister he would think of me as a failure.

There are reasons why so many of us confuse physical illness with the 'dark night of the soul'.


## Symptoms of depression
The normal symptoms of depression make us feel:

* God no longer loves, forgives or accepts us.
* He no longer even exists.

---

*O my soul, why be so gloomy and discouraged? Trust in God! He will make me smile again for He is my God!* Psalm 43:5, LB

*Acute anxiety*
Anxiety often goes with depression and causes:

* Guilt about real or imaginary past sins.
* Fear of the future which robs us of our trust in God.
* Lack of concentration so we cannot read the Bible or pray.
* Fear of people which makes church impossible.

'Christians are the most difficult group of patients to treat,' explained the Christian doctor whom I consulted before writing this chapter. 'They find it so hard to admit they are depressed, particularly when the depression is not acute but long term or chronic. They, and their family, simply feel they have developed a naturally 'gloomy' personality. They may therefore function below their potential for years, feeling that their whole lives are grey and flat. They are always tired, lacking in enthusiasm and are unwilling to put much effort into life. Medical science could do so much to help them, if only they could be brave enough to go to their doctor, and receive his treatment as a gift from God.'

God really can heal the dark places in our lives and I am convinced that depressed Christians are closer to God's heart than any of His other children. I began to recover when I swallowed my pride and went to ask someone to pray for me. The healing took many months, but I know that day was the turn of the tide. Had I also gone to my doctor, his treatment could have been used by God as a supplement to prayer.

> *How long must I wrestle with my thoughts . . . ?*
> *How long will my enemy triumph over me . . . ?*
> *Answer me, O Lord my God; give light to my eyes*
> *or I will sleep in death.* Psalm 13:2–3

## The Lord dwells in clouds and darkness
## (2 Chronicles 6:1)

Whether we tackle our 'grey fog' with the ministry of healing, through modern medicine or through both, we will probably find our depression lifts much more slowly than we would like. How can we cope while we wait?

When Jane rang me she was right at the 'bottom of the pit'.

'I can't think why I'm 'phoning you,' she began, 'there is absolutely nothing you can say that won't irritate me. I love the Lord so much, yet He stands by and allows me to feel like this. Don't say anything,' she added hurriedly, 'there's no answer to that one either!'

'Surely there must be something that helps?' I said trying not to sound glib.

'John 1:5,' she snapped. 'That's what keeps me alive. "The light shines in the darkness and the darkness has never put it out." Often I feel in such darkness it almost chokes me, but I always know, deep down that the light *is* there, even if I can't see it and the darkness *has* never, *can* never and *will* never extinguish it.' Perhaps Jane was expressing her 'treasure of darkness' when she added, 'When you hurt so much that you feel you couldn't possibly hurt any more, your need for God is paramount. When you reach that stage you really know Him.'

## Pooh Bear was Janet's 'treasure of darkness'

'Just praise the Lord, dear,' someone said to Janet as she struggled with weeks of post-operative depression. She

> *The Lord is close to the broken hearted, and saves those who are crushed in spirit.* Psalm 34:18

reacted just like most depressed people when given such advice – she felt wild! It may be a biblical command, but it is one we all find practically impossible when we are acutely depressed.

'I really did try,' admitted Janet, 'but somehow I didn't feel He loved me any more. I always felt ghastly when I first woke in the morning and I remember once I sat up racking my brains, trying to think of something I could thank the Lord for, when I seemed to have lost all purpose in life.

'I heard the children down in the kitchen, could I thank Him for them? No! I wanted to be a bright cheerful Mum again, but I was letting them down by my gloom.

'Neil perhaps? No, I was being a rotten wife.

'My friends? No, I ought to ring them all and thank them for the cakes they had left on the doorstep, but I couldn't work up the courage.

'My bedroom then? No it was dusty and untidy. I ought to clean it, but I had no energy. I couldn't even decide what to put on that day. Surely there was something, just one small thing in all the world worthy of a 'thank you?'

'Then my attention was caught by the toy Pooh Bear we had bought for our niece's birthday. He just sat there on the dressing table, holding out his arms to be loved. He had no purpose in life either! He was useless really, but I couldn't help loving him.

"If I can love Pooh," I thought, "just because he sits

*Ye may yourself ebb and flow, rise and fall, wax and wane, but your Lord is this day as He was yesterday.* Samuel Rutherford

there holding out his arms to me, then surely God can love me, when I do the same to Him." Suddenly I found I could thank God for Pooh, as I hugged his furry body.

'It no longer mattered that I couldn't pray, God knew how I needed Him, even though I was as incapable as Pooh Bear of telling Him so.

'Somehow we never managed to give that Pooh away, because he was the beginning of my recovery. We had to buy another for my niece's birthday.'

There are no easy answers to depression. The one and only thing that helped me was the realisation that Jesus knows from bitter, personal experience just what it feels like. He cried out in His darkness,

'My God, My God, why have you abandoned me.' He told His Father just how ghastly He was feeling, and when I dared to do the same, I began to recover.

---

(As for me), I am poor and needy, yet the Lord takes thought and plans for me. *Psalm 40:17*

---

## 4: THE DESERT OF FAILURE AND WORTHLESSNESS

One of the earliest replies to my 'desert enquiries' came from a vicar's wife in London.

> *Thy love to me, Oh God, not mine, Oh Lord to Thee, can rid me of this dark unrest and set my spirit free.* Horatius Bonar

For years I have struggled with a crushing sense of worthlessness, of not feeling adequate. I always seem to make a mess of things, and feel sure God must think the same.

'How strange,' I thought, 'outwardly she always seems so successful, running the parish and a rambling old vicarage just like clockwork. While all the time, she secretly feels a failure.'

I used to think I was the only one who felt inadequate, but I am beginning to realise lots of us suffer from low self-esteem. Most of the time we manage to disguise it by flurries of Christian activity, but when something goes seriously wrong in our lives, the buried sense of inferiority bobs up to the surface again. We think, 'It's no wonder my husband left me – I lost my job – didn't get healed – I always was unlovable and unsuccessful.' Because we feel sure God must share the low opinion we have of ourselves, we go into a desert.

We live in a success-orientated world, and even as Christians we measure ourselves and one another by our achievements. We set ourselves impossibly high goals and feel useless to both God and man when we cannot attain them. When will we learn that God does not look at what we do, He looks at what we are?

I remember, years ago, standing at a sink full of greasy washing up and thinking, 'I'm nothing but a mess!' I had always dreamed of doing some great thing for God – being a missionary perhaps or an evangelist, but all I had become was an ordinary and very unsuccessful housewife. My cakes were always soggy, my children drove me

*Be patient with everyone, but above all with yourself.* Francis de Sales

up the walls and I couldn't even knit! I was fat, tired and defeated.

'Get out and meet other Christians,' someone had urged me. That made me feel worse. They all seemed to be so successful, praying out loud so beautifully, leading people to the Lord over the garden fence and having wonderful experiences, revelations and spiritual gifts. Nothing I tried to do for God ever worked.

*Have you ever felt like that?* I was certainly in a desert of worthlessness, and I escaped it by a chance encounter with a complete stranger.

One afternoon my mother-in-law had the kids to tea and I went into Tunbridge Wells in gorgeous solitude. I was browsing round the Christian bookshop, trying not to break my latest diet by visiting the cake shop near by, when I heard someone say,

'Ah! How perfectly lovely!' I had not noticed the elderly man standing beside me, we were both too absorbed in the books, so I jumped violently.

He was holding the newly published *Good News Bible* and suddenly he thrust it towards me, open at the book of Zephaniah. His gnarled finger was jabbing excitedly towards verse 17 of Chapter 3.

'The Lord your God is with you . . . The Lord will take delight in you and in His love He will give you new life. He will sing and be joyful over you.'

'What more do we want in life but to know that!' he exclaimed, and then, suddenly looking terribly British and embarrassed, he lifted his hat nervously, and scut-

---

*Jesus said, 'He has sent me to . . . deliver those who are oppressed . . . downtrodden, bruised, crushed and broken down by calamity.'* Luke 4:18, AMP

tled out of the shop. He probably felt a complete fool for the rest of the day, but when I arrive in heaven I shall tell him that his enthusiastic explosion caused scales to fall from my eyes. I stood gazing after him, positively quivering with joy.

'All right, so I'm a fat, spotty nobody, but God who made the whole universe takes delight *in me!* He even sings about me!' Other customers jostled round me, but still I stood there, as if bathed in God. Inside my head a voice said, 'You are the centre of the universe for Me. Nothing is more important to Me than your welfare. He who touches you, touches the apple of My eye. If you had been the only sinner in the world, I would still have been willing to be tortured, disgraced and killed, just so I could win you for myself.'

In those days I could still dance, and I have often wondered what people thought when they saw me waltz out of the shop! Whenever those old worthless feelings threaten me, as they still often do, I think of that day with joy and relief.

## Many deserts are caused by looking at other people

As a small girl I was once 'dared' to walk along the high wall that separated the senior and junior playgrounds – I did not dare at all, but even in those days my desire to be

---

*God loves each one of us as if there was only one of us to love.* St Augustine

---

*Oh Lord, You protect me and save me, Your care has made me great.* Psalm 18:35

accepted by the group overpowered my common sense.
As they hoisted me up someone whispered, 'Keep looking at the white gatepost.' I had no idea what she meant
until I was up on the wall and the world was spinning
round me. If I looked down at all the other children
jumping about and shouting their encouragement on
either side of me I would certainly topple to disaster. If I
looked at my own feet I was also doomed, but ahead of
me at the far end of my ordeal was the white ball on top of
the stone gatepost. Keeping my eyes fixed on that and
walking steadily towards it saved my neck.

Sadly, my hour of glory was short-lived. The head-
mistress had been looking out of her window. Yet I can
never read verse 2 in Hebrews Chapter 12, without
thinking of that day.

'Let us keep our eyes fixed on Jesus, on whom our faith
depends from beginning to end.' It is what God thinks of
us that counts, not how we feel about ourselves, or how
we compare with other Christians.


## The modern cult of 'love yourself'

Almost every Christian book you open these days seems
to tell you to love yourself and shows you how to build up
your self-esteem. For lots of us that is quite impossible.
We really do dislike ourselves because we feel we are
rather inadequate people. Trying to build your own
self-esteem feels like lifting a bucket you happen to be
standing in! The only way out of this self-hating desert is

> *Instruments that the world would have flung on
> the scrap heap with infinite contempt, have again
> and again in the hand of the Master worked
> wonders.* W. S. Watkinson

to look straight into God's face. It is not our *self*-esteem we should be building, but our *God*-esteem.

If you feel crushed because you have never been any good at anything, stop worrying about it! You are just the kind of person God wants. Jesus said it would be the meek and humble who would inherit the earth! He finds it harder to use people with many natural talents and glittering personalities. They tend to take His glory for themselves. He wants to show how powerful He is by using people who rely on Him utterly because they have nothing to be proud of in themselves.

Like a child on a high wall, we need to stop looking down at our inferiority complexes, or sideways at our successful friends and start concentrating all our attention on Jesus, revelling in what He can do for us and not in what we can do for Him. He says to everyone who feels worthless; 'I am the high and holy God, who lives for ever. I live in a high and holy place . . . with people who are humble and repentant, so that I can restore their confidence and hope.' (Isaiah 57:15)

---

*God says; 'The mountains and hills may crumble, but My love for you will never end; I will keep for ever My promise of peace.' Isaiah 54:10*

---

*So in my emptiness, waiting until,*
*I give my nothingness to be fulfilled,*
*Here, where no hand can touch, deep in my*
*    soul,*
*pours out His love divine, and makes me whole.*
Estelle White

## 5: THE DESERT OF DELAYED SHOCK

Everyone was shattered when Phil's husband left her and their three young children. It seemed unbelievable that their marriage could break up, when they had both been so involved in Christian activities. The whole church gathered round Phil protectively, and her radiant peace was a blessing to them all.

'That girl's a shining witness to the whole town,' said one of the elders. Then, suddenly, a few months later everything changed. Phil went into a desert.

'I think I was simply numb at first,' she told me, 'My mind wasn't working, I kept looking down on myself from above and thinking, "How wonderfully God is helping her to cope." But I didn't really feel it was *me*. I just floated along on the current of everyday events, I didn't try and swim. I suppose I was sure David would come back at any minute.

'Then one Saturday, I was out with the kids in the park. All round us were families. Families with Dads, and the shock finally hit me. It felt like being kicked in the tummy. David had gone. He was living with Sue. My kids would have to grow up without a Dad.

'Since then I seem to have lost my peace completely. I know I need help, but people have drifted back to their own lives, thinking I'm managing so well, but I'm falling apart inside.

'The memory of some cruel thing David did or said hits me unexpectedly when I'm right in the middle of doing

---

*He heals the broken-hearted and bandages up their wounds.* Psalm 147:3
*What wound did heal but by degrees.* William Shakespeare

something quite different, like peeling potatoes. Or perhaps I'll think, "it must have been all my fault. I ought to have lost some weight, been more appreciative, cooked better". Wherever I go, whatever I do, these thoughts keep on coming at me, like a swarm of bees buzzing in my head night and day. I can't pray because of them, or settle to read the Bible because these bitter thoughts make me feel so guilty. Why should all this happen to me *now*?'

I minded for Phil desperately, but I felt quite out of my depth so I suggested we prayed about it.

'You pray,' she said miserably, 'I'll listen.' As we sat there together before God, something wonderful happened. Phil saw a picture in her mind of a deep, sombre lake, and one by one up to the surface floated sodden logs of wood.

'I think this is a sign that you are getting better,' I said when she told me about it.

'*Better!*' she almost shouted, 'I've never felt worse in my life!'

'Look,' I said awkwardly. 'All the things you've been feeling are perfectly natural human reactions. When ghastly things happen to us, at first God protects our sanity by this numb feeling – rather as a doctor protects a gaping wound with a dressing. But you can't keep a dressing on a wound for ever. God has to remove it some time and allow all these reactions to come to the surface so He can heal them. He knows it would be too much for us to face them at the beginning, while we are still reeling from the initial blow.'

'I'd rather they'd stayed buried,' Phil complained.

*God is nearer to us than we are to ourselves.*
St Augustine

'But God wants you whole,' I replied, 'and He can't heal things until we admit they exist, and give them to Him.'

Two weeks later I rang Phil. She was still coping with what she called her 'Loch Ness monsters' as they broke the surface of her 'lake', one by one.

'Thoughts are so difficult to manage,' she said, 'They're so abstract. But when I suddenly think . . . "David took the cassette player and I paid for that!" I write down the way I feel on a piece of paper. Sometimes I have quite a struggle, I almost want to hug the hurt to myself. There's a crooked kind of enjoyment in feeling sorry for yourself. When I feel able to relinquish the pain to God, I go out into the kitchen, set light to the paper and flush the ashes down the sink. It is such a cleansing feeling.'

Phil's desert is quite a common one. As Christians we often get through horrific experiences on the crest of a spiritual wave, or 'floating on a lilo of other people's prayers'. We nurse our child through a terminal illness or keep our heads during a major crisis, but when the pressure is suddenly off, and no one is looking on any more, bang! We are hit by the devastating effects of delayed shock.

## Confusing shock with deserts

Don't confuse the natural symptoms of shock with a desert. We have already seen that doubt was a natural

---

*It is one thing to go through a crisis grandly, but another thing to go through every day, glorifying God when there is no witness, no limelight, no one paying the remotest attention to us.* Oswald Chambers

reaction for Ann when she lost her baby in a cot death. (Page 59) Other painful feelings are also part of the grieving process, such as anger, depression, guilt or loss of reality and even of God Himself. As Christians we feel so guilty about having these feelings, we are ashamed to look God in the face, but they are simply normal stages of human grief. Far from cutting us off from God, they can bring us even nearer to Him because: 'Surely He (Jesus) has borne our griefs – sickness, weakness and distress – and carried our sorrows and pain.' (Isaiah 53:4, AMP) No one can help us when we are laden with parcels and bulging shopping bags, unless we are willing to let them. Jesus longs to carry our griefs and sorrows, but we do have to hand them over to Him as the numbing effect of shock wears off and they come up to the surface one by one.

---

Answer me now, Lord! I have lost all hope. Don't hide Yourself from me, . . . Remind me each morning of Your constant love, for I put my trust in You. *Psalm 143:7–8*

---

## 6: THE DESERT OF UNANSWERED PRAYER

'I prayed night and morning for five years,' wrote Debbie, 'but God just didn't answer. What did I do wrong?'

---

*God can do wonders with a broken heart if you give Him all the pieces.* Victor Alfsen

For a Christian the problem of unanswered prayer can be sheer agony. As we beat on the prison walls of our circumstances we know without doubt that God could change them, but Heaven seems hard-bolted against our prayers.

'What did I do wrong?' asked Debbie, and of course the Bible clearly shows us that if we hold on to sin deliberately (Psalm 66:17–18) or persist in disobeying some specific instruction, the Lord cannot hear us. He says, 'Because they did not listen when I spoke, I did not answer when they prayed.' (Zechariah 7:13)

Yet, even after Debbie had given her life a thorough spring-clean, the answer to her prayer was still 'No'. Why? Seven 'principles of unanswered prayer' will help us to see a meaning behind the disappointments.

## First principle – 'no' is not a punishment

* David said to God, 'Answer me quickly, O Lord, my spirit fails. Do not hide your face from me.' (Psalm 143:7)
* Job said, 'Why won't God give me what I ask, why won't He answer my prayer?' (Job 6:8)
* Paul said, 'Three times I prayed to the Lord about this, and asked Him to take it away. But His answer was: "My grace is all you need."' (2 Corinthians, 12:8–9)

These men lived as close to God as anyone ever has, and yet they still did not have their prayers answered.

> Delayed answers to prayer are not only trials of faith but they give us opportunities to honour God by our steadfast confidence in Him under apparent repulses. C. H. Spurgeon

Even the man Jesus described as 'the greatest man who was ever lived'. His own cousin, John the Baptist, received a definite 'No' to his prayers.

When Herod's dungeon door slammed, John probably did not worry at first. He knew Jesus was the Messiah. Hadn't he seen the spirit of God descending on him by the river Jordan?

He knew Isaiah had foretold that the Messiah would not only make the blind see and the lame walk, but He would also set the captives free (Isaiah 61). 'I'll be out of here in no time!' John must have thought.

Then the weeks and months began to grind slowly by and John's prayers for freedom were not answered. It was torture being shut up in four walls after a lifetime in the wide expanse of the wilderness. Surely Jesus would come for him soon?

**Delayed hope is the hardest test of faith.** John began to doubt when God's promise appeared to be delaying.

'Are You the one we are waiting for, or should we be looking for some other man?' was the message he finally sent to Jesus.

Gently the Lord reminded him of Isaiah's prophecies which were being fulfilled as the lame walked and the blind received sight; yet for some reason He left out the one vital phrase about the release of captives, the only miracle that mattered to John in his prison.

Why? Jesus could so easily have burst that prison wide

> *When our hearts are turned to fear, rather than to faith we must hand over to God the mysteries of life's imbalance between good and evil. I find that if I mull too long over the things I don't understand I lose the things I do understand.* Jean Darnall

open. He sent an angel and an earthquake to rescue his friends Peter and Paul. Why leave his own cousin to face a sordid death at the whim of a dancing girl and her vindictive mother?

## Second principle – we might have wrong expectations of Jesus

John knew Gabriel had spoken to his father before he was born, and said that his life's work was to help the Messiah establish His earthly Kingdom. He thought that meant Jesus would give him the status of Prime Minister. Actually Jesus wanted to give him something far more important, the everlasting throne of a martyr. (Revelation 20:4)

Deserts often occur because we assume we know the will of God. We feel 'let down' because we want something so very much that we confuse our will with God's will.

Debbie was convinced God wanted her to marry Robin, because she loved him so much. He was always friendly when they met at church and occasionally he asked her out, but to him Debbie was just one of a whole crowd of single girls in their thirties. Yet she would happily have died for Robin. Desperately she clung to several promises she felt God had given her and prayed earnestly that Robin's feelings would become as deep as her own. There was nothing wrong with her faith, she went on confidently believing God would answer her

---

*Thousands follow Christ when He gives them what they want, few follow Him when He confronts them with what He wants.* Selwyn Hughes

prayers right up to the day he married her best friend –
then she went into her desert.

'I am trusting the Lord for healing – trusting Him for
that job – for that house,' we say firmly, but are we
trusting Him for *anything*? Even if that 'anything' is not
*our* will, ambition or desire?

'Lord,' we so often pray, 'I'll do whatever you ask, but
I just cannot stay – childless – single – ill or poor. You *must*
answer this one prayer.'

The love that Jesus has for you and for me is so absolute
that He allowed no earthly desire of His own to stand
between us, not even his own life. He longs for us to
return His love with the same single-minded quality. Yet
so often, there is something we want more than we want
Him. Prayer can be our way of manipulating Him to gain
our own desire. All the time we are nagging Him, He
does know what is the very best for us, and how much He
must long for us to realise that fact.

## Third principle – God never promised to make this life easy

'I thought,' continued Debbie's letter, 'God would be
on my side if I kept close to Him and did my best. I
thought He'd make everything easy and reward me
with a happy, trouble-free life.'

Yes, God has promised us an eternity of happiness,
health and prosperity, but for a brief time down here He
tells us things may be tough. Jesus told us the truly happy

> *For this world is not our home, we are look-
> ing forward to our everlasting home in Heaven.*
> Hebrews, 13:14, LB

people are the poor, the hungry, the down-trodden, the grieving, the hated 'because a great reward is kept for you in heaven.' (Luke 6:20–23) He also promised, 'In this world you *will* have trouble.' (John 16:33)

No one knows why Jesus did not rescue His cousin from prison, but one thing is certain, it makes no difference whatsoever to John now! The fact that he spent a few uncomfortable months in jail down here will be as unimportant to him now as the blink of an eye. I remember once feeling furious with Paul as I read; 'This small and temporary trouble we suffer will bring us a tremendous and eternal glory, much greater than the trouble'. (2 Corinthians 4:17)

'Small! Temporary! My foot!' I fumed. 'Paul's troubles may have seemed like that, but he ought to try mine!' When I descended from the ceiling I managed to read on; 'For we fix our attention, not on things that are seen, but on things that are unseen. What can be seen lasts only for a time, but what cannot be seen lasts for ever.' (2 Corinthians 4:18) I realised I had been feeling trapped and crushed by my circumstances, because I was looking at them with human eyes. When I imagined myself standing, millions of years into eternity, I could look back at myself stuck in a wheelchair and think, 'why ever was she making such a fuss?'

**What is God to us?** Of course God could make us all healthy and wealthy in this life, but if He did, people would follow Him simply for what they could get out of Him – right now.

---

*Many people want to direct God, instead of resigning themselves to be directed by Him, to show Him a way instead of passively following where He leads.* Madam Guyon.

When we are facing unanswered prayer we have to ask ourselves; 'Do I see God as an adjunct to my life, a lucky charm to grant my every wish, or do I see myself as an adjunct to Him as I kneel before Him and say "Master, what do you want me to do for you?"'

## Fifth principle – God always answers prayer

It was a bottle of fruit juice that helped my friend Fran to understand that 'wait' is just as valid an answer as 'yes'.

She had been grappling with an unanswered prayer for over a year, so I was surprised when she came to see me one day smiling broadly.

'Yesterday evening I was in the kitchen when Joy demanded a drink,' she began, (Joy is thirteen months old).

'Ju! Ju! Ju!' she squealed. Immediately I began the routine that getting her a drink entails. Boiled the kettle, then cooled the water, fetched bottle and teat from the steriliser, found the juice, measured a spoonful, collected a clean bib – it all takes so long and Joy was getting frantic, holding on to my ankles and hampering my efforts to help her. She was far too young to understand that at her age she has to have boiled water, and it would scald her if she drank it right from the kettle. I was doing all I could, as quickly as I could, but in her baby mind I was simply not caring about her thirst. I suddenly realised that quite probably God has the answer to my problems in the pipeline, but my human mind is too infantile to understand heavenly

> *What matter in eternity the slight awkwardness of time?* Robert Murray M'Cheyne

procedures. I've been like Joy, holding on to His ankles and slowing Him down.'

Fran found the answer 'wait' a lot easier to cope with than the resounding 'No', which Debbie received.

## Sixth principle – 'No' can be the best answer

Jesus once prayed, 'Father, save Me from this hour.' But the answer He received was, 'No'. His Father could have stopped the crucifixion, but He did not, because He knew that it would save mankind and glorify Jesus for ever. There are times when God's love for us will allow us also to suffer, and not answer our prayers by removing the pain. Paul, who three times received the answer 'No' to his most earnest prayer was able to say, '*In* all these things we have complete victory through Him that loved us.' (Romans 8:37) *In* them, not *by* having them removed.

I don't know why your child died, why you never had the baby you wanted so much, why you go to bed lonely every night of your life, why God has not healed me yet. No human being is wise enough to answer the question 'why doesn't God prevent suffering when He has the power?' In our pain and confusion we just have to reach out and say 'Father I do not understand you but I trust you.'

---

*One of the hardest things in our secret prayer life is to accept with joy and not with grief the answers to our deepest prayers. It was a long time before I discovered that whatever came was the answer. I had expected something so different that I did not recognise it when it came. And He doesn't explain, He trusts us not to be offended, that's all.*
Amy Carmichael

**Seventh principle – God always gives us strength**
'In the day when I cried, thou answeredst me, and strengthenedst me with strength in my soul,' says Psalm 138 verse 3. AV. God always answers our prayer *the split second* that we cry to Him; when the answer has to be 'wait' or even 'No', He always gives us strength, deep inside to carry us through, if only we will turn to Him for it.

Ridley said to Latimer as they were about to be burnt at the stake, 'Be of good cheer brother, for God will either assuage the fury of the flames, or else strengthen us to abide it,' God always does one or the other. He never leaves us alone in the fire.

---

I know how hard you have worked . . . but . . . you do not love Me now as you did at first. *Revelation 2:2–4*

---

## 7: THE DESERT OF PRESSURE AND OVERWORK

'I've got three kids under four. I love them, but a mountain of dirty nappies seems to be separating me

*Dear brothers, you are only visitors here. Since your real home is in Heaven . . .* 1 Peter 2:11, LB

*If contentment were here, Heaven were not Heaven.* Samuel Rutherford

from God; and coping with a hundred and one jobs all at once is making me too tired to do anything about it.'

There do seem to be definite periods in our lives when the sheer weight of unavoidable activities crowds out the things of God for a while. Working for exams, rebuilding, redecorating or moving house, starting a business, embarking on a new career or nursing elderly or dying relatives. In fact, I had more letters from people talking about the deserts caused by small children than any other, and I am not surprised either, having had six of my own!

Satan likes to use these 'pressure patches' to separate us from God, but I believe there are four ways we can prevent him from doing so, if we remember that:

## Under such pressure we may forget God

We may feel we have lost God behind a 'mountain' of hard work, revision – or even dirty nappies, but He wants us to know that He is with us on our side of the mountain.

It does not matter if, for a while, we have to curtail our church activities. God is not only to be found in the Wednesday prayer meeting, He is standing beside us continuously as we work.

In 1660, there lived a monk called Brother Lawrence. He became deeply upset when his work in the monastery kitchen crowded thoughts of God from his mind, so he developed this coping strategy which has blessed busy

---

*He will keep in perfect peace all those who trust in Him, whose thoughts turn often to the Lord.*
Isaiah 26:3

Christians ever since. He visualised God there with him in the hectic kitchen continuously, both watching him and enjoying his company. Soon 'I could not pick up so much as a straw from the ground without doing it for Him. The time of business does not, with me, differ from the times of prayer, and in the noise and clatter of my kitchen, while several persons are at the same time calling for different things, I possess God in as great a tranquillity as if I were upon my knees at the blessed sacrament.'

## A few moments each day for God

'Our duty to God,' said William Temple during an address at Oxford, 'requires that we should, for a good part of our time, be not consciously thinking about Him. That makes it absolutely necessary (if our life is to be a life of fellowship with Him,) that we shall have our times which are worship – pure and simple.'

That is easier said than done when you are a mother, working a twenty-six-hour day! But here are a few tips that might help.

'I always kept my *Daily Light* on the edge of the bath. Over twelve years I got through several copies, I kept dropping them in!'   (Ginny)

'All I wanted was to be alone with God, but Mums never *are* alone. So I kept a Bible in the loo. It may sound irreverent, but I used to read another verse

*For the eyes of the Lord range throughout the earth to strengthen those whose hearts are fully committed to Him.* 2 Chronicles 16:9 NIV

every time I went in there and it became a real place of sanctuary for me over the years.'    (Madeleine)

Mrs Billy Graham, the mother of five, and a housewife with a constantly open home, describes how she took her Bible round the house with her from room to room, and dug into it as she stirred a sauce or waited for the kettle to boil.

My own grandmother had seven children, and they can all remember her, kneeling beside the sofa, deep in prayer while they all played around her and two small boys bounced on her back.

In these days of cassettes in cars and kitchen, and even personal stereos in rush hour trains, we can all listen to the greatest preachers in the world, or the finest actors reading the scriptures. Many postal tape libraries are even free of charge.

## Our attitude is the key

'I always wanted children,' Madeleine told me, 'but when they arrived I was astounded by my reaction. I resented them. They interfered with what I thought of as "my ministry", playing the church organ and training a large choir. My husband was the vicar so he was always out serving the Lord, while I felt trapped behind cot bars – useless to God. Then one day I visited another clergy wife and over her kitchen sink I saw this notice:

*Think not of a holy life, for that will crush you by its immensity, think rather of this moment, and spend it for God. A holy life is but a series of holy moments.* Lindsey Glegg

HERE I AM, SERVING GOD,
JUST WHERE GOD WANTS ME TO BE,
DOING WHAT GOD WANTS ME TO DO,
UNTIL GOD TELLS ME TO DO SOMETHING ELSE.

That had a profound effect on me. I realised I was out of touch with the Lord, because I wanted to serve Him in a more exciting way than just looking after kids. St Paul, stuck in prison, wrote, "I have learned the secret of being content in any and every situation . . . I can do everything through Him who gives me strength. (Phil. 4:12–13 NIV) God wanted me to learn that secret too.

One night something happened which I suppose you would call my treasure of darkness. I was reading Matthew 25 verse 40, in bed. "Whenever you did this for one of the least important of these brothers of mine, you did it for me." As usual I was up and down all night long to the children, till I was almost at screaming point. Then as I was giving yet another drink to Timmy, I remembered the verse I had read, and realised that it was *Jesus* Himself who was thirsty – Jesus in Timmy. I did not need to run meetings or train choirs to serve Him, I could simply love Him as I cared for the children.' (Mark 9:37)

## We need to get back to God

'Suddenly my dear old mother-in-law was safe in Heaven, and I had time again. *Time – beautiful time!*'

*Nothing done for Christ is lost. The smallest acts, the quietest words, the gentlest inspirations that touch human souls leave their impress for eternity.* J. R. Miller

said Jean. 'Should I take up pottery, join the golf club or do a part-time job and earn some pin money? How easy it would have been to fill the vacuum with pleasant little interests, all perfectly all right in themselves, but I remembered in time that when I had been young, and without responsibilities, how much I had enjoyed spending my life doing things for God. I have watched too many of my friends drift into a middle-aged desert caused by ease and prosperity.

There's an old Arabian proverb which says, "All sunshine makes a desert."

I am so busy now in God's service I hardly have time to breathe, but I simply could not be happier!'

*May we be refreshed as by streams in the desert.*
Psalm 126:4

*Is my gloom, after all,*
*Shade of His hand, outstretched caressingly?*
Francis Thompson; from *The Hound of Heaven*

We do not know what to do, but we look to You for help. *2 Chron. 20:12*

## 8: THE DESERT OF ACUTE ANXIETY AND CHRONIC WORRY

Much has been written about worry, and most of it is thoroughly irritating! 'If you worry you don't trust, if you trust you don't worry.' That is the cliché placid, easy-going people love to quote, but if a stressful situation is causing you acute anxiety or you happen to be the nervous kind, worry becomes something you cannot remove, however much you try.

Once I was sitting on a tree stump in a wood reading an Agatha Christie novel, when I chanced to look up and see a rabbit only a few metres away from me. It was motionless, frozen by terror, as it looked at the swaying body of a weasel which was about to spring at its throat. The rabbit could run much faster than the weasel, but it was no good preaching that fact to the rabbit, who was totally paralysed by fear.

Worry can do the same thing to human beings, making our minds go into a state of spasm.

'I've got to have a major operation . . . sit an exam . . . start a new job . . . could this be cancer? . . . what if I die?' As paralysed as that rabbit, we feel unable to move towards God for His help.

### Vital fact
We don't actually have to move towards Him, because He is with us, on our side of the worries.

When I was about ten I went on the Sunday School outing to Hastings. While our teacher slept on the beach, we crept off to sample the forbidden delights of the pier. The ghost-train fascinated us.

'I dare you go on that all by yourself,' they said and like the 'sucker' that I always was, I swallowed the bait. Never in my life can I remember being so terrified. There I was, propelled at speed away from the sunshine and happy seaside noise into the sulphurous darkness of the tunnel.

As I sat helpless in the little car, gruesome apparitions reached out towards me. Blood-stained hands, evil faces, skeletons and cold, clammy things that brushed against my face. I couldn't move, I could not even scream for help, I just looked up in the general direction of Heaven and a miracle happened. Suddenly a window opened high above and light streamed down into the darkness. A face with a pipe in its mouth grinned at me, it was the man who controlled all the switches and levers and who was in charge of all the horrid apparitions that frightened me so much.

'Get me out of here,' I wailed.

'It's all right luv,' he replied, ''cos I'm 'ere wiv yer.' At the flick of a switch he could have stopped the train and transformed the darkness into light, but he did not need to do that. Just knowing he was there in control made all the difference, I almost enjoyed the ride after that.

Sometimes events, or the fear of what might happen can seem like those ghost train 'nasties' coming at me from every side. No one understands because I cannot explain how terrible I feel. But my treasure of darkness is to remember that the 'man who controls the switches' is

> *Oh Lord, may I be content to know that goodness and mercy shall follow me without wanting to see them in advance of me.* George Matheson

there with me, even when I can't see him through the darkness.

'I have set the Lord always before me; because He is at my right hand I shall not be shaken.' (Psalm 16:8)

## God is not only with us, but He does something to help

God tells us not to worry 365 times in the Bible – 'fear not', once for every day of the year but there are two ways of saying 'don't worry'.

I remember standing at my cooker one day while the sweat positively poured off me, the potatoes needed mashing, the table was not set and the mound of dirty saucepans was overflowing the sink. Any minute all my in-laws would be arriving for a birthday meal and I was behind schedule.

'Don't worry,' said a friend, who had 'just popped in' 'Why ever are you working yourself up into such a state?' she added as she lay back in the comfortable arm chair and slowly lit another cigarette. I felt like killing her!

'It's easy to say "don't worry" when she has no

> *Worry on the part of God's children is uncon-scious blasphemy, when we fret we are saying, 'God, You aren't in control of this situation'.* David Watson

> *Anxiety is the natural result when our hopes are centred in anything short of God and His will for us.* Billy Graham

intention of lifting a finger to help me,' I fumed as the custard boiled over the stove.

Just then my husband arrived home and as he walked into the kitchen he said,

'Don't worry.' What a difference! He intended to help me. 'I'll take over in here,' he said calmly, 'You go and set the table.' When God says 'don't worry' to us, He says it in the way Tony did. 'Don't worry because I'm not only here with you, but here to help you.'

## Transferring the worry

The thing I find so hard is the actual transfer of the worry from my head (or should I say stomach?) into the Lord's hands. I can pray about something at great length and then get up and go on worrying about it all day, while I burn the toast, forget appointments and generally render myself useless. I find I have to make that transfer a practical, visual thing. So I keep my mother's old Bible permanently open in my workroom. When a worry even looks like swamping me I write it down on a piece of paper and I place it on the open page of the Bible. Then pointing to it I say;

'There it is Lord, lying in your hands.' As I turn my back on it and go away I find I can leave it behind me mentally as well. Of course the old familiar butterflies keep coming back because I am the worrying kind, but I have to keep on fighting them every time by saying, 'Lord, that worry is now your responsibility.'

---

*And the peace of God which transcends all our powers of thought, will be a garrison to guard your hearts and minds in Christ Jesus.* Philippians 4:7 Weymouth

## Distraction helps

While the worry is lying there in God's hands the best way I have found to fight the 'butterflies' is by doing something else which is physically and mentally absorbing.

Martin Luther was constantly engulfed by anxiety and the depression which can go with it. His coping strategy was this:

'When I am assailed with heavy tribulation, I rush out among my pigs rather than remain alone.' On another occasion he said; 'I exorcise the devil when I harness the horse and spread manure upon my fields.' Fortunately most of us will not have to do anything quite as smelly as that, but turning out drawers, cleaning the car, or weeding the garden might be just as effective.

## Why doesn't God make all Christians placid and easy going?

Of course God could easily do that, but He has a special love for nervous people. Remember Gideon and Timothy? While God's strength shows up best in weak people (2 Corinthians 12:9, LB). His peace shows most in born worriers! It has never been the easy-going, self-confident people who have 'cut much ice' in the Kingdom of God. It is the temperamentally nervous and deeply sensitive people who often know God best. We meet God at our weakest place, and if you are the kind of person who always ruins today by panicking about the tiny details of tomorrow, that is the weak place where

---

*Jesus said 'Fear not', therefore it must be possible and is* made *possible by acting as though one were not afraid.* Basilea Schlink

you will meet God constantly. Placid people only worry over the big traumas of life, so they do not feel the need for Him so often.

Successful worriers can train themselves to turn to God frequently as each worry hits us, and by doing that we learn to know his special consolations. 'When anxiety was great within me, Your consolation brought joy to my soul,' says Psalm 94 verse 19, NIV. The Psalmist's joy came through meeting the Lord *in* his anxiety, and not by having it removed.

---

I am the Lord, I do not change. *Malachi 3:6, LB*

---

## 9: THE DESERT CAUSED BY OTHER PEOPLE

'I went to work on the staff of a Christian Holiday Centre, and was horrified by the way 'senior' Christians behaved when they weren't 'on show'. If knowing Jesus doesn't really change people all the way through, I felt there was little point in continuing to be one.'

'Our lovely Church was split apart by a silly human power struggle. People I thought were my friends

---

The worst evil one has to endure is the anticipation of the calamities that do not happen, and I am sure the thing to aim at is to live as far as possible in the day and for the day. Lord Beaconsfield

suddenly took sides and said bitter things about each other. We haven't known the Lord for long and we were horrified that Christians could behave like this.'

'When I discovered that the friend who led me to the Lord, and our (married) vicar were in love and seeing each other a lot, my faith was shattered.'

These are what I call 'deserts of disillusionment', and I have come across a tragic number of them this year. Perhaps the trouble is that we have extremely high expectations of our fellow Christians. It is easy for us to accept that we sin and can be forgiven ourselves, but we find it almost impossible to forgive other Christians, especially when we admired them greatly and have moulded our lives on their influence. We tend to think our leaders must be supermen, treat them with awe and put them on pedestals but when we discover they were only human after all, we feel disillusioned.

'Don't put your trust in human leaders', says Psalm 146 in verses 3–6: 'No human being can save you . . . Happy is the man who . . . depends on the Lord His God the Creator of heaven, earth and sea.'

We have lived through a revolution during the last few years. For many of us, Church is no longer a place to visit for an hour on a Sunday, it has become our close family circle. We rely on each other, share our deepest feelings and submit to authority in a way that would have been unimaginable a few decades ago. That is wonderful, and how Jesus wanted his Church to be. Yet taken to excess, it can be dangerous. Men have always found it easier to

---

*Nothing has ever come to me, nothing has ever gone from me, that I shall not be better for God by it.* A. B. Simpson

worship something they could see than to follow the invisible Jehovah directly. God cannot tolerate idolatry and when we put our Christian friends and leaders higher in our estimation than our God, that is idol worship.

## Church splits

Many Churches are splitting these days. The pain can only be appreciated by people who have been unfortunate enough to live through the experience, but there are 'treasures of darkness' even in this agony. Division often leads on to growth, not only in cells and border plants but also in churches. God allows these painful experiences to teach us to trust Him alone. Could *your* desert have been caused because you were relying on a human being more than on God Himself?

'Several of us decided to leave our Church when we felt the Leaders simply wanted to dominate people's lives like power-hungry sharks,' said Liz and Mike, 'but we felt so lost we didn't know where else to worship. So for a while, we met in our house, but it soon developed into a "grudge-sharing" session.'

They felt they had lost their identity when they left their church, their status in their community, friends, security and even their opportunity for Christian service. But they had not lost God Himself. Discovering that was their 'treasure of darkness'.

---

*I have a problem with pedestals, I tend to put people on them, when God wants to be there alone.* Hester Dain

Before Liz and Mike could settle peacefully into a new church they had to ask God to help them forgive the people in their previous fellowship, and also to give them the courage to ask forgiveness for the pain they had caused them by leaving.

## Whose fault was it really?

'Nothing anyone can do to us can injure us, unless we allow it to cause a wrong reaction in our own spirit,' says Amy Carmichael. Sometimes we feel our desert was caused by the selfish cruelty of someone else. The driver who drank too much and killed our child; the man who elbowed us out of the job we so much enjoyed; the husband who left us to cope with the family alone. These people may have caused our misery, but secretly we know they did not cause our desert.

## Our inability to forgive

It is our inability to forgive which separates us from God. 'If you forgive others the wrongs they have done to you, your Father in heaven will also forgive you. But if you do not forgive others, then your Father will not forgive the wrongs you have done.' Matthew 6:14–15

Margot's father was a tyrant who clouded her childhood in misery and his malevolent influence followed her into her adult life. When he died, he left his affairs in a cruel trust that shackled her permanently to her old home so full of unhappy memories.

---

*Whoever says that he is in the light, yet hates his brother, is in the darkness.* 1 John 2:9

'I felt chronically angry with him as the years went by,' she told me, 'always my resentment of him was at the back of my mind. I carried on going to Church on a Sunday, but gradually all the joy and reality of my Christian life died. Inwardly I knew I had lost God. One day a friend said something to me, quite out of the blue, which made me furious.

"You'll have to forgive your father, you know, this anger is destroying your life." I totally ignored the comment and "dropped" the friend completely. Some years later I was persuaded to go on a Church pilgrimage to the Holy land at Easter. I only went to please someone I was very fond of at the time. Something strange began to happen to me on Good Friday. I stood watching the pilgrims from all over the world carrying their heavy crosses up the Via Dolorosa and the tears just streamed down my face. The thought of Jesus struggling along the same road broke something inside my heart. If He could forgive such cruelty, why could I not forgive my father? At long last I was willing to be made willing to forgive, but somehow I just couldn't do it by myself. On Easter Sunday I was standing by Lake Galilee, and I actually met the risen Jesus. I didn't see Him, but I know He literally confronted me, and I asked Him to forgive my attitude and help me to forgive my father for damaging my life. I have never been the same since, and my relationship with God is now the centre of my existence.'

Perhaps from time to time, it would do us all good to ask God to help us make a list of anyone we need to

---

*She could have loved them if it had occurred to her to ask for the grace of God.* Elizabeth Goudge. From *The Rosemary Tree*

forgive. 'Get rid of all bitterness, rage and anger with every form of malice. Be kind . . . to one another, forgiving each other as in Christ God forgave you.' (Ephesians 4:31–32)

## Persecution

'My husband didn't seem to mind when I first became a Christian. He said it was only a craze that would pass, like jogging.' Christine told me. 'But when he realised how important it was becoming to me, he started poking fun at me all the time, making negative little comments about my Christian friends and criticising the Church. I'm beginning to see things from his angle now, and I wonder if Christianity is really worth the hassle.'

'The Bible says you must be glad about this,' I told her. 'Because it makes you one of the élite group of Christians and you'll have a special reward waiting for you one day.'

'What do you mean?' she demanded.

'You are being persecuted,' I replied. 'Not thrown to the lions or burnt at the stake – dramatic persecution like that often strengthens people marvellously. It is far harder to live permanently with subtle persecution, as you are.'

When you are surrounded by people who constantly pour scorn on your faith and Christian involvement it is very hard not to go into a 'desert of doubt'. It is tough never to feel accepted in the group at work, school or college and to be the butt of every joke. An even more

---

*It has always been easier for Christians to be thrown to the lions than to be laughed at.*
Tom Rees

difficult situation to handle is persecution by other Christians.

'When I was baptised in the Holy Spirit,' said Kevin, 'people at church felt I had been carried away with new-fangled ideas. I could feel old friends pulling back from me. I was even asked to stop teaching my Bible Class. It was easy at Spring Harvest to be bubbling with joy, but after a few months back in our Church, I was beginning to think I had made rather a fool of myself until I suddenly realised I was caring more about what people thought of me than what God thought.'

## Persecution is never pleasant
The Bible says:

* We must expect to be persecuted. (Matthew 10:22–23)
* Be glad about it because of the reward involved. (Luke 6:22–23)
* We have to pray for those that persecute us (Luke 6:28)
* and express our love to them in practical ways. (Luke 6:35)

## Coping with cruelty
One day I received a letter from Kelly who was really suffering at the hands of other people. Her boss brow-beat her, her elderly mother-in-law (who lived with them) bombarded her with constant irritating comments and:

---

*God teaches men through suffering and uses distress to open their eyes.* Job 36:15

My husband criticises everything I do, and disagrees with everything I say. We don't argue verbally, but our spirits clash all the time. It's my inner reaction to all this that bothers me. I'm always simmering with silent rage, and that makes me feel guilty when I come before God.

I spend my time grovelling on my knees asking God to forgive me and then almost at once their comments 'get to me' yet again.

I sat in front of my keyboard for a long time wondering whatever to say in reply, and feeling sure I would fail totally in trying to cope with a situation like this. Then, suddenly I realised it was three o'clock, my favourite time of the day. Each afternoon I get into my electric wheel-chair and go off to meet Richard from school. That day, however, it was so stormy that the rain seemed to be hitting me horizontally! If it had not been for my storm cover I would have been drenched. It is a huge water-proof Red-Riding-Hood cloak that envelops me and my wheelchair completely.

I had been reading Psalm 18 verse 2 that morning, 'The Lord is my protector . . . and with Him I am safe, He protects me like a shield; He defends me and keeps me safe.' As I battled along I thought to myself grimly, 'I need more than a shield like a dustbin lid to keep me safe in this storm.' Then I realised that in fact my storm cover was far better than an old-fashioned shield; it wraps round me completely, just as God enfolds me. I knew then how to answer that difficult letter. After a hot cup

---

*In the shelter of Your presence You hide them . . . in Your dwelling You keep them safe from accusing tongues.* **Psalm 31:20**

of tea, I did my best to describe my storm cover to Kelly.

'When we let Jesus envelop us completely, the unpleasantness of others falls upon Him, like the rain, but it cannot get through to damage us.' I wrote, and then added a quotation by R. Leigham which says: 'What can harm thee when all must first touch God, with whom thou hast enclosed thyself?'

Kelly replied a few weeks later, saying; 'When they all start on at me now, I put God between myself and them, and it works wonderfully.'

---

For I am overwhelmed and desperate and You alone know which way I ought to turn. *Psalm 142:3, LB*

---

## 10: THE DESERT OF UNCERTAINTY

These are horrible deserts, with no roads or signposts, just irritating goat paths that look promising at first and then peter out into an empty expanse of sand.

'God has blocked the way and I can't get through, He

*One day, in my distress, I prayed fervently . . . Then all of a sudden, it was as if the finger of God was pointing not at the other person, who was causing me such distress, but at me. 'You are the one who has to change.'* Basilea Schlink

has hidden my path in darkness.' says Job in Chapter 19 verse 8.

I met about ten people this year who were lost in a desert like this:

> I feel as if the secure structure of my life has crumbled away, leaving me vulnerable and emotionally homeless. People who know where their lives are going and what God wants of them can say such maddening things from their position of security. All our friends have different opinions on what we should be doing but only the Lord really knows and for some reason, He just isn't saying.

Brian Woodgate describes these deserts as, 'walking the plank blindfolded. Every time you reach the end and think you're going to plunge into disaster, you find the plank has lengthened a few more inches.'

I shall never forget Beatie's pinched, white face as she sat opposite to me, trying so hard not to cry.

'We were sure God wanted us in full-time Christian service. We had the green light through several verses from scripture as well as the opinion of mature Christians. God could so easily have stopped us, but we sold our house easily and found a lovely new one near the Missionary Society headquarters. The four kids were all settling happily into new schools when everything went wrong. Working in an office with Christian people was not what my husband thought it would be, personalities

---

*I will lead my blind people by roads they have never travelled. I will turn their darkness into light . . . these are my promises and I will keep them without fail*. Isaiah 42:16

clashed, and after three months he had to resign. That's when my desert began. I kept wondering if we had mistaken the Holy Spirit's guidance in the first place?

'We don't know what to do now. We can't afford the mortgage to stay here and anyway my husband can't find another job, so we felt we were supposed to move to a cheaper area to be near our parents, but again – no sign of a job, and this house has been on the market for over a year now. What is God playing at with us? I could understand all this if we had wilfully gone against the Lord like Jonah, but we only wanted to serve Him.

'The one thing that helps is this verse someone gave me. I've stuck it on my dressing table mirror. The Lord says, "I will teach you the way you should go. I will instruct you and advise you." (Psalm 32:8) That's a promise and I know God never broke one yet! But I have to confess,' she added grimly, 'It's taking me all my time remembering that!'

## Don't forget the battle of the super powers
Satan and God are both trying to do something different in these agonising deserts. God wants to teach us to trust Him in the face of human reason. He has a perfect plan for our lives, organised in detail before the world began. It is His responsibility to reveal it to us, but He never does that all at once, just step by step because He wants to teach us to walk 'by faith and not by sight'. We cannot know, love or please God until we have learnt to trust

---

*Faith is a poor thing if we cannot trust in the dark, whether we understand or not.* Canon Guy King
*It is the darkness which makes faith a reality.* Bramwell Booth

Him in the dark. Until He tells us what to do next we must do as George Macdonald suggests and 'Fold the arms of faith, wait in quietness until light goes up in the darkness.'

Another of God's objectives is to develop patience in our lives, but the only way this fruit is ripened is by adversity and frustration. 'Dear brothers, is your life full of difficulties and temptations? Then be happy for when the way is rough, your patience has a chance to grow. So let it grow, and don't try to squirm out of your problems. For when your patience is finally in full bloom, then you will be ready for anything, strong in character, full and complete.' (James 1:2–4, LB)

*Satan on the other hand is working hard* to use all this confusion and frustration to hurt God badly. He knows that if we panic, and begin to doubt God's ability and desire to care for us, God will be deeply hurt. In this desert Satan can also indulge his favourite hobby – condemnation.

'You must have got it wrong as usual,' he says. 'God didn't really tell you to move . . . change your job . . . come to this college . . . marry that man. How presumptuous of you to think God Almighty should guide a worm like you.'

The very first time we read about Satan in the Bible he is trying this game on Eve.

'*Did* God *really* tell you not to eat fruit from any tree in the garden?' He sneers. He did it to Jesus too, in His desert. '*If* you are the son of God . . .' in other words, 'you could be wrong'.

*The only way to survive Satan's constant battering* is to do

---

*Thou camest not to thy place by accident – it is the very place God meant you for.* French

as Jesus did. He simply met Satan's sneers with scripture.
'If . . . ?' said Satan.

'It is written,' replied Jesus.

Beatie was doing just that when she stuck that verse on
her dressing table mirror and clung to her promise
against her earthly common sense. One man I heard
about recently wrote out on a large piece of paper the
promise God gave him from the Bible and 'took possession' of it each morning by standing on it before he got
dressed.

*We can rely on God to prevent us from making a mistake*
when we genuinely want to walk the path He has
planned for us. If we keep on trying one little goat track
after another He will certainly stop us every time we set
off in the wrong direction. 'The Lord is compassionate
and when you cry to Him for help He will answer you . . .
If you wander off the road to the right or the left you will
hear His voice behind you saying here is the road, follow
it.' Isaiah 30:19–21

## What happened to Beatie?

My mother had a favourite little ditty which went: "The
God who taught me to trust in His name, would not thus
far have brought me to put me to shame.' I could not help
remembering those words when I had a letter from Beatie
recently.

Eventually they *did* sell their house and found a new
one right in the heart of the country. Her husband *did*
find a job and the children all settled into excellent
schools.

---

*If we are desirous of living in God's will, He will not
allow us to get out of it by a small mistake on our
part.* Fred Mitchell

'Best of all is our new Church,' she writes. 'We have always been a bit traditional in our worship, but this Church has recently come into renewal, and the people have a joy and a freedom we knew we wanted the moment we walked through the door . . . We feel as if our outward shell of Christianity has been smashed by all the trauma we went through and inside we are now warm pliable putty in the hands of God. This experience has changed our whole lives and all the misery and confusion has been worth it, just to be here.

One Sunday night in our new Church I reflected how nearly I had given up on God. But inside my head He said, "would I so lightly give *you* up?"'

## Chaos at the airport

I once discovered a wonderful Treasure of Darkness in a crowded airport terminal. We had to meet a friend who was coming to stay with us during a very unsettled and confusing patch in our lives.

'This place looks like I feel,' I remarked rather crossly. Fog had delayed flights and caused utter chaos. People were swarming anxiously in all directions, not knowing what to do next. I saw one poor man dashing round behind a trolley piled high with luggage, the perspiration was running off his face, but on his back in a carry-seat his baby slept peacefully, oblivious of the pandemonium going on around him.

'It's all right for some!' I smiled, then I remembered a verse I had read that morning, 'Let the beloved of the Lord rest secure in Him for He shields him all day long

> *God's deliverance does not come from trouble, but in trouble. He offers victorious living, not whimpering back door escapism.* Dr Crossip

and the one the Lord loves rests between His shoulders.'
Deut. 33:12. That baby trusted his father to get him home
on the right plane and to satisfy all his other needs, but I
had God for my father, He knew the way He was taking
us through the shambles of our lives. We did not need to
strive and wrestle with our problems; we could rest
between His shoulders and relax. As Corrie ten Boom
said, 'Don't wrestle, nestle.'

---

Jesus said; 'But the time is coming . . . when you
will be scattered . . . leaving me alone. Yet I will not
be alone, for the Father is with me.' *John 16:31–32,
LB*

---

## 11: THE DESERT OF LOSS – LONELINESS AND BEREAVEMENT

'I went into a desert when I lost . . .' so many of my letters
start like that.

'All my children seemed to leave home about the
same time, making me feel redundant.'

'We moved house and I missed the support of my
friends at church, especially my prayer partner.'

Others mentioned the loss of a job or a responsibility.

---

*The Lord Himself will lead you and be with you. He
will not fail you or abandon you, so do not lose
courage or be afraid.* Deuteronomy 31:8

'Without a job to get up and go to, I felt devalued and I thought God must feel the same.'

'We had to watch the vision we felt God had given to us destroyed by other Christians.'

Some people mentioned the loss of their health, youth and good looks – the middle-age crisis, or the emptiness that retirement can create. Some even felt they had lost something they had never actually possessed.

'I wanted to be married, have a home and kids, but it never worked out, and I feel bereaved.'

'People thought I was silly grieving for a baby I had never actually held in my arms.'

The most poignant letters of all were from those who had lost people they loved through rejection or death. Any kind of loss can leave us staggering under a deep sense of desolation which also destroys our self-confidence and makes us feel unsure of where we fit into the universe. The joy has gone out of our lives, which easily leads us to imagine that God has left us too.

## What is really happening above our heads?
Satan likes to see us lose the people and things that we love. When we feel shattered, rejected and empty, he hopes to encourage us to feel bitter as well. His one fear is that we might fill the gaps left in our lives by a deeper relationship with God.

---

*I depend on God alone; I put my hope in Him. He alone protects and saves me.* Psalm 62:5–8

*On the other side*, God is *not* gloating over our misery, He yearns to be allowed to pick us up in His arms and comfort us. Naturally He never snatches other things away from us but when, through the normal course of human life, they go, He longs to fill by His love the emptiness they leave behind. So often these people or activities have actually been more important to us than God, so He waits anxiously to see if at last we will make Him the centre of our existence.

'My husband was such a wonderful man,' said Ivy wistfully. 'So good at knowing what to do, and he was such a good Christian too; he had the faith for both of us. When he died I was knocked for six. For months I was in one of your deserts and it had no signposts, paths or landmarks. Then I gradually came to realise that for years I had had no need of God at all. I hadn't looked to Him to provide for our needs. It was Tom's good job and clever investments. It was not God who guided us in our major decisions, it was Tom's common sense. Suddenly I was alone, all the decisions were mine to make, and I had no ability to make them, I *had* to trust God, for perhaps the first time in my life, and turn to Him over every detail.

'When Tom was there I didn't need God's company either, now I'm alone I hate having no one there to hear me say, "I think I fancy a nice cuppa." So I started chatting to the Lord instead. Oh, if only I could describe the joy I've found in coming to know Him as a friend.'

---

*Sometimes He takes away that which is most precious so that into the void of a life that is utterly broken He may pour the glory of His indwelling love.* Dr Alan Redpath

It sounds trite to say 'fill the gaps with God', but when that advice comes from people who have discovered the truth of it during the worst moments of their lives, it makes you feel it is worth taking.

When the police came to tell me Jack had been killed, the silly thing was that all could think about was a couple of lines of a hymn. 'From the best bliss that earth imparts, I turn unfilled to thee again'. The words kept ringing in my ears for days, and somehow they showed me in which direction to run – towards God.

'God is actually the only person we can be perfectly sure we shall never lose,' wrote Elizabeth who lost her husband and small daughter in a car crash. 'Everything and everyone else in life can fail you, leave you or let you down, but God – never!'

## Danger! desert hazard

Beware of filling the gap with something else. Pascal, the philosopher once said, 'In every human being there is a God-shaped hole that only He can fill.' When we try to fill that void with something or someone else we stay in our desert.

Perhaps the loneliest woman I know lost her husband about six years ago. In her grief she turned all her attention to her teenage son.

'She worships that boy,' people used to say, and they were right, but her possessive need of him smothered the boy entirely and he could not wait to leave home. He hardly bothers to keep in touch now.

*Thy presence fills my solitude.* Longfellow

Cardinal Wolsey worked for Henry VIII with all his energy, but when he was a frail, frightened, old man who expected to be executed at any moment, he said, 'if I had served my God as I have served my Prince, He would not have left me thus.'

There is nothing wrong in enjoying the people or activities God sends to enrich our lives, but if they become idols, greater in importance to us than God himself, our happiness is in jeopardy. So often the harder we cling on to people the more likely we are to drive them from us in the end. Clinging to God brings everlasting security.

## The secret sorrow you cannot share

Hilary never really minded being single. She had a close friend with whom she shared hobbies, holidays, and shopping expeditions, yet there was always the privacy of her home to enjoy. It was a happy relationship.

Then, for some unexplained reason, Hilary's friend drifted away, found another companion with new interests and the relationship died abruptly. Hilary felt completely desolate. She had relied on her friend for spiritual support and strength as well as fun and companionship. If it had been a husband who had left her, people would have rallied round and comforted her, but this was a private grief she could not share.

'One day,' she told me, 'I realised I had reached a crossroads, I was certainly in a desert, but there are

> Can I be fully the person I should be while remaining single? I decided I could be – otherwise God is not God. He chose my circumstances and must mean them for my good. Hester Dain

always crossroads in the desert, you can decide to go towards God or away from Him into secret bitterness. I chose to go towards Him, even though, since the loss of my friend He had become so cloudy and dim. The old Authorised Version of the Bible seemed dry and unhelpful, so I went out and bought myself a new translation. It was so refreshing, it bought the whole thing to life for me. Suddenly I found myself in the middle of a springtime love affair with the Lord Himself. It was indescribable. Strangely, a short while later, He sent along a replacement friend, but since then my deepest relationship has always been with Him.'

## Sorrow and bereavement

It seems from my letters that bereaved Christians are more vulnerable to the tactless blunders of other people than any other desert traveller – and most bereaved Christians do go into a desert at some point within the first three years.

I would hate to add to the stack of trite sayings, because so far this desert has not been one through which I have had to go. So I will let these people speak for themselves.

'Time heals', everyone tells you, but it doesn't, you just learn to live with it.

You feel oddly angry when birds sing, people laugh and flowers still bloom, your world has stopped, how can the rest of the universe be so insensitive?

---

*Let me not be afraid to stand alone, for if only I will turn from other people and look for You, You are always there.* Mary Hathaway

When my son died, at the age of ten, I felt furious with people who tried to comfort me with little texts. They all seemed to be in the future tense.

'He *will* suddenly remove the cloud of sorrow . . . *will* destroy death for ever . . . *will* wipe away the tears from everyone's eyes.' Is. 25:7–8 All those future *'wills'* were no help to me, when it was *now – this minute* that hurt so much. Believing in a future Heaven does not save us from the pain, grief and tears of this present life. So it is useless for us to try and pretend that death is not an outrage, however prettily we dress it up by calling it 'resting in peace', or 'going home'. It certainly *is* all that and infinitely more to the Christian who dies. To those of us who are left without them, it is nothing but an agonising experience of loss, when it brutally drags away from us someone we love and *need*. However close we may be to God we cannot really expect to recover from the pain of that blow in this life. All we can know for certain is that we shall recover one day when God finally destroys death.

One day a card arrived with a verse written inside which actually was in the present tense at last. 'Even though I walk through the valley of the shadow of death, (in the deepest darkness) I will fear no evil for you *are* with me.' Psalm 23:4. Now I just hang on grimly to those words, 'you *are* with me', and gradually I am discovering that He comforts *now* as wells as in the future.

---

*When I look beside me, I see that there is no one to help me, no one to protect me. No one who cares for me. Lord I cry to You for help, You Lord are my protector.* Psalm 142:4–5

One day I was sitting in the armchair in Brian's old study, surrounded by his books and missing him unspeakably. Because he had been the vicar, I felt I lacked someone whose responsibility it was to comfort me! Brian was always so loving towards widows. Idly I picked up a book and noticed it was called *Pastoral care of the Bereaved*, and I almost dropped it again in disgust. Then, suddenly I noticed a passage that Brian had marked heavily. It had obviously been so important to him that I looked at it more closely.

As I read these words I felt Brian himself was speaking to me, saying the very things he would want me to know if only he had been here. Needless to say, I found them indescribably comforting.

'There is NO getting over sorrow, but there is getting into it, and finding right in the heart of it the dearest Human Being – the Man of Sorrows Himself. I pray that you will never get over it, but through it, right into the heart of God.'

---

*All Your waves and billows have gone over me, and floods of sorrow pour upon me like a thundering cataract. Yet day by day the Lord also pours out His steadfast love upon me.* Psalm 42:7–8

> And He (Jesus) is the head of the body, the church
> . . . so that in everything He might have the su-
> premacy. *Colossians 1:18*

## 12: THE DESERT ASSOCIATED WITH LIFE IN A CHURCH COMMUNITY

It might surprise Church leaders to know how many
people feel their deserts are caused directly by the
Church itself. Some people wrote to tell me they felt their
church was either too cold, lukewarm or just too hot for
comfort.

### The cold church

This letter comes from Vivian, who was delighted when
her family moved to a cottage in the country, but:

> There is no alternative to the Parish Church. It's very
> picturesque, but the people all go along because it's the
> thing to do – a village institution. It smells of musty
> hymn books, woodworm killer and damp plaster. The
> services are dreary and divorced from everyday living,
> and all the congregation seem to care about is who's
> allowed to do the flowers or clean the brass.
> When I read about other Churches where people
> actually expect God to intervene in their lives, I feel like
> a child outside in the cold, looking through a window
> at someone else's party.

> *Jesus turned water into wine, sometimes the
> Church manages to turn wine into water.* David
> Watson

Because there is absolutely no alternative for Vivian, I suggested that perhaps God wanted her there, in that situation, to show people that God is very much alive. By the same post I received another letter from someone I greatly admire and I sent a copy of it to Vivian.

> I have attended our Parish Church for thirty years now and never once have I heard the gospel preached from the pulpit. I have wept, fasted, prayed, stumped round our fields with the dog or knelt in my prayer cubby hole – nothing, no change. But I have not died of thirst. Psalm 84 verse 6 says, 'As they pass through the dry valley of Baca, it becomes a place of springs'. My 'springs' in the desert have been the books I read, magazines, and tapes I listen to, conferences we attend and the little prayer group in the next village. I know I am where the Lord has put me, so I can trust Him to keep me going. G.

Vivian found that letter very helpful.

## The lukewarm church
This is what Gordon said about his church:

> Actually neither of us wants a Charismatic Renewal, but we've begun to feel oddly frustrated by our Church. I look round at them all on Sunday mornings, good solid evangelicals, steeped in Bible knowledge

---

*Forget the former things, do not dwell on the past, see I am doing a new thing! Now it springs up, do you not perceive it. I am making a way in the desert and streams in the wasteland. Isaiah 43: 18–19*

and thoroughly worthy activities. Living on the religion of our godly parents or basing our existence on some blessing we received long ago in our teens. But everything happened 'yesterday' and I catch myself feeling, 'surely Christianity isn't supposed to be this dull'. Some of our friends have left and gone to a more adventurous Fellowship ten miles from here. Naturally their names are mud round here, but we can't help privately thinking how alive their faith has suddenly become. We don't really know what makes this other place tick, and we are not sure yet, if we have the courage to go and find out.

When the Jews had walked right over their desert they stood looking across the Jordan at the Promised Land. It was still only a few months since they left Egypt, but they were too scared to march into a new situation. Sadly God had to allow them to wander back into their desert for forty long weary years. If your pillar of cloud is leading you on, into a new land, do not be too frightened to follow. Edward England once said, 'By holding onto yesterday's adventure, we miss what God has for us today.'

### The church that feels too hot

Gayle, who is a very shy, quiet person said this:

I tried very hard to enjoy the House Church that my family and all their friends attend, but I felt exposed

> We try to domesticate the Holy Spirit and use Him like the house cow, we like to confine Him inside the walls of our Church, for our own benefit. Jim Graham

and embarrassed. When I went to university I found an Anglican Church and I discovered a new peace in contemplative prayer. I have always found it easier to worship through classical music, so I love the organ and choir, the order and dignity of the traditional services and beautiful surroundings make me feel safe. I know the folk in our fellowship at home think I have gone into a desert, but really I have escaped from the one I was in for so long!

## God has given us a choice

Recently we spent a day in Kew gardens which contains the world's biggest collection of plants. Some flourish in hot humid greenhouses, like steaming jungles, others bloom in dry desert heat, some like marshy bogs and plenty of shade, others prefer the cool rocks of the alpine house. All the plants do well at Kew because all their different needs are met. Just the fact that they are all plants does not mean they should all blossom in the same environment. Just because we are all Christians does not mean one type of Church is right for us all.

We feel upset by the many denominations into which Christ's body is split, but I am sure He has allowed it in order to provide us with different ways of worshipping to satisfy our varying temperaments. I happen to like spontaneity, exuberance and a good beat to the music, but the services I like would deafen Gayle's spirit. Deserts begin when we try and force ourselves to stay in the wrong kind of environment, simply because we have always gone there to please other people.

## Why do we find it so hard to change churches

Perhaps, like Gordon you genuinely feel that your Church is holding you back from God, yet you find it hard to think of moving to another.

'I couldn't possibly leave this Church,' you say, 'I might lose my friends.' But are your friends more important to you than getting out of your desert and restoring your relationship with God?

'I don't want to upset and hurt people.' God might need them shaken before they will start to realise something is missing in their lives with Him.

'I've been a member here for so long, it's a question of loyalty.' The church is the body of Christ world-wide. Of course we owe our loyalty to that body, but it is not contained exclusively in one little building down our road. By staying, you may be bolstering up something that is not honouring to God, a group of people from which His spirit has departed, but they are far too busy running their organisation to notice.

## Danger! Desert hazard

Beware of becoming a spiritual nomad. Some Christians spend their lives wandering aimlessly from one Church to the next in search of the latest excitement to liven up their dry souls. Nomads are doomed to a lifetime in the desert because God wants us to settle down and be committed and submitted to one identity group. Often it is responsibility that nomads are trying to escape. They look for a Church that will do something for them – provide a well organised social programme, excellent music, comfortable buildings – it never occurs to them that God might be asking them to give, as well as receive. Many Churches are crying out for people to man their Sunday Schools, visit and care for the sick and elderly and organise support for missionaries. It is often by

*Do not trouble about anything but loving Him, never mind if you cannot see Him.* Francis Malval

doing something for God that He becomes real to us again.

## Desert of stagnation
The Dead Sea is a lake in the desert full of impurities and chemical deposits. Why? Because the river Jordan flows in at one end and nothing whatever flows out of the other. It is the lowest point on the earth.

We can listen to sermons, read Christian books, attend Bible studies and conferences, but if nothing ever comes out at the other end we are in a desert of stagnation.

## Ministry burn-out
'I suffered from a chronic inability to say the word 'No'.

'I dreaded Sundays. By the time I'd dashed round madly fixing someone to do the crêche on Wednesday morning, nabbed people to make quiches for the Harvest Supper and organised lifts for the Youth Group outing, I was too harassed and exhausted to worship.'

'I saw a programme on television about Africa. A certain tribe had over-farmed their land, never giving it time to lie fallow or feeding it fertiliser. They had produced a desert. I thought, that's me! I'm too busy to listen to God, my prayer life is nothing but a series of gasps for help as I gallop to the next assignment and I only read the Bible in order to work up talks for other people.'

> *No amount of activity in the King's service will make up for the neglect of the King Himself.*
> Robert Murray M'Cheyne

If our christian activities are becoming more important to us than God himself, perhaps it is time we gave them up.

Could your desert be caused by:

* too much giving and not enough receiving,
* too much talking and not enough listening,
* too much doing, and not enough being?

Has God taken you into this desert to say, 'Be still and know that I am God?' Psalm 46.10.

## Working for the wrong boss

I wonder if God ever feels like asking, 'Who are you doing all those jobs for – yourself or Me? Amy Carmichael says, 'Are you doing your chosen work for God, or His chosen work for you?' There is a very big difference. When God asks us to do something for Him, He also gives us the strength and ability. When we do something just because we think we might do it rather well, or we feel it is expected of us or simply because it needs doing, it can become the burden which causes a desert. A need does not constitute a call. God would rather *not* have a job done than see you in a desert because of it.

## Professional Christians

Many Christians become too heavily involved simply because everyone wants to feel valued by others.

> *If you are never alone with God, it is not because you are too busy, it is because you don't care for Him, don't love Him and you had better face the facts.* A Ghazzali

Perhaps we are secretly quite proud of the many jobs we do so tirelessly for God, our success makes us feel like a better Christian. It was not always like that, of course. We might have felt helpless when we first took over the Youth Group, but we prayed earnestly for God to help us in our utter weakness, and He did! In fact He helped us so much we began to think, 'Really I'm quite good at this, I've got a real gift with these youngsters, look how big the group has grown since I took it on.'

'You're doing a wonderful job,' people tell us admiringly, but when we allow professionalism and self-confidence to rob God of his rightful glory we sentence ourselves to a secret desert of which no one else is aware.

One of the nastiest deserts in the Bible happened to Nebuchadnezzar. He stood on his roof garden and gloated over his beautiful city of Babylon.

'I have conquered the world,' he thought, but he refused to admit it was God who had made him great (Dan. 4:24–37). His pride caused seven years of mental illness. No psychiatric hospital for him, Nebuchadnezzar was driven into the desert, where his hair grew long and wild as did his finger nails, like the claws of a bird. It was not until he 'praised the supreme God and gave honour and glory to the One who lives for ever' (Dan. 4:34) that he escaped from his desert.

Of course God wants us to take on responsibilities in His Kingdom, but it is His power that achieves the success, so when we fail to give Him the honour He might well withdraw that power and leave us looking very small and silly. Deserts are terribly humbling places, as Nebuchadnezzar discovered.

> *If Satan cannot make us lazy or sinful Christians, he will make us proud of the fact that we are neither!* Tom Rees

## The real reason we go to church

There is no such thing as a perfect Church this side of Heaven, but real worship has nothing whatsoever to do with the other people in the pews, the buildings, or the form of worship.

Once when the Church we attended was right in the middle of a most unpleasant patch of squabbling and upheaval I found myself wondering, 'whatever do I go to church *for* anyway?' It took a great big plumber with a ginger beard to show me my treasure of darkness. He was a neighbour of ours and every evening he came lumbering home, down the crowded street, clutching his tools and his lunch box. His little three-year-old daughter would watch from their window, and as he turned the corner she ran down the busy pavement like a rocket on short, fat legs.

'Daddy!' she would shout, 'I found you a caterpillar, for your tea'. As he knelt down and enveloped her in his arms, they were both oblivious of everyone else, locked together in a private world of happiness and all the time she talked about the little happenings of her day she had a delightful way of stroking her father's cheek.

I thought of those two when I heard David Pawson preach on a tape from Zechariah Chapter 7 verse 2. He told the story of the men of Bethel who came to Jerusalem 'to pray for the Lord's blessing', He told us that the Hebrew for that phrase actually means, 'to stroke the Lord's face'. In Church, I worship God by coming eagerly into his presence, like that little girl, so that I can be close

---

*So then stand where you are and you will see the great thing which the Lord is going to do.* 1 Samuel 12:16 *Don't just do something, stand there.* Jamie Buckingham

enough to 'stroke His face'. It is simply a fusing together
of my soul with God's spirit, regardless of other people or
anything else.

*Set my spirit free that I might worship Thee,*
*Set my spirit free that I might praise Thy name.*
*Let all bondage go and let deliverance flow,*
*Set my spirit free to worship Thee.*

Author unknown. From *Songs and Hymns of*
*Fellowship*, Kingsway

# 8

# DANGER IN THE DESERT

---

The Lord will make you go through hard times, but He Himself will be there to teach you and you will not have to search for Him any more. If you wander off the road, you will hear His voice behind you, saying 'Here is the road. Follow it.' *Isaiah 30: 20–21*

---

Poisonous snakes, scorpions, and running out of petrol are some of the hazards of life in the Sahara. Spiritual deserts also have their classic dangers.

## Spreading your desert

'They were driving me mad,' said Jeremy, 'sitting round on the floor, Bibles open on their laps, smug smiles on their faces. Christian jargon spouting all round the room. I wanted to shake them out of what I suddenly felt were their cosy delusions, so I waited until our House Group Leader asked if anyone had anything to share, and then I let them have it. I suppose I

---

*When any fit of anxiety or gloominess or perversion of mind lays hold upon you, make it a rule not to publish it by complaints but exert your whole care to hide it; by endeavouring to hide it you will drive it away.* Dr Johnson

exaggerated my negative feelings for dramatic effect, but I was sick of being a hypocrite – pretending everything was still all right when it wasn't.'

When we are suffering in our desert the desire to shock other Christians can be very strong. We want to use our pain as a weapon to make others suffer, and because we are so angry with God we want to hurt Him by destroying the faith of people He loves. While it can be a huge relief to talk in public about our deserts, we are actually in danger of doing Satan's job for him by spreading our doubts far and wide. If you catch 'flu it is always kinder to go to bed than to breath your germs about in the cinema. Doubts are just as catching as 'flu, and often just as short-lived. Jeremy, the 'angry' young man in that House Group was fine again after a week at Spring Harvest, but three of the people who heard his outburst that night never came back.

Of course we need to talk openly to someone, we badly need prayer, love and advice. It is *who* we talk to that matters. A small group of mature and prayerful Christians can literally carry us through our desert and they will not relax until they see us safely out at the other side. We must talk honestly to them, but it is never fair for us to relieve our feelings in front of weaker Christians, if by doing so we jeopardise their faith.

### There is no need to lie

'So what am I supposed to say when people at church ask, "Are you all right?" Do I invent a lie?'

No – you could be much more subtle than that. Say, 'The Lord is doing wonderful things with my life. I'll tell

---

*Don't cherish your doubts.* Douglas McBain

you all about it soon.' You may not believe what you are saying, but it does happen to be the truth.

## A desert in the family

Some of the most tragic letters I have received this year were from people whose husband or wife is going through spiritual desperation.

> 'He's moody, snappy with the kids, and nothing I say or do seems right,' wrote Fanny. 'You walk in through the door and a thick cloud of gloom hits you in the face.'

Of course when we are really clinically depressed we probably cannot help ourselves, but when we are merely 'feeling down' we must fight constantly not to allow our 'moods' to lower the joy temperature of those around us. We have no right to pull them into the desert of despair with us. I found a prayer by Dr Leslie Weatherhead which has often helped me on gloomy days.

'Help me O Lord so to strive and so to act, that these things which cloud my own way may not darken the path which others have to tread, give me unselfish courage so that I am always ready to share my bread and wine, and able to hide my own hunger and thirst.'

## Beware of decision making in the desert

> 'I'm feeling drained by all these Church responsibilities, I think I'll just chuck the lot.'

---

*Never act in a panic, be still, wait upon God until He makes known His way. So long as that way is hidden it is clear that there is no need of action.* Dr F. B. Meyer

---

'I'm a hypocrite, being a House Group leader when I feel so far from God.'

In a desert we feel like quitting everything, and Satan loves our letters of resignation. Perhaps we are ever more drastic, 'I'm getting out of this job,' we say, 'selling this house,' or 'leaving my wife'.

## Stop! Danger!
Satan would love to make the desert an opportunity to curtail our work for God and ruin our lives permanently. The basis of our decision-making as Christians is our trust in the Lord and close contact with Him. If for some reason we have lost those, we might easily make a mistake if we do something hastily while we are still in the desert.

Duncan was two when I lost him in Woolworths. We kept missing each other as we ran round searching among the counters. After that day we made a rule that if he was lost, he was to sit down on the floor and wait in the place where he last saw me. Unless circumstances force us into action we are better to stay quietly in the place where we last saw the Lord.

Of course the mature Christian, who is counselling you, may insist that you take a temporary break from Christian leadership in order to receive ministry yourself. You may well need space for a while, but avoid permanent, life-changing decisions.

## The irrevocable change
About seven years ago I remember talking to a friend of mine, a minister who I now realise was in a desert.

---

*Faith is a willingness to trust God when the pieces don't fit.* Katie Wiebe

'How can I stay in the ministry when I suddenly can't believe a word I'm preaching?' he demanded miserably and resigned. When I was researching for this book I asked him if he still felt he had made the right decision. He looked at me sadly and replied,

'If only I had realised then how short these wretched patches are! I regained my faith very soon after I had gone into secular work, but by then we had lost our home and changed our whole way of life. I should have stuck my head down and sweated it out and I would have come out at the other end with a renewed and strengthened vision. I feel as if I have been wandering aimlessly ever since.'

'Wouldn't it have been wrong to pretend you were all right when you weren't,' I ventured.

'I could have put other people "up front" whose enthusiasm was high, and simply kept pegging on in the background quietly,' he replied. 'Because I admitted I had doubts so publicly the faith of many people I had led to the Lord was shaken or destroyed. Perhaps most people who work for God have bad patches but I would advise them to stay put and wait for the storm to pass, because it does.'

## A recipe for hypocrisy?

'If we are in trouble and we do not feel we have enough faith to meet it, we should *act as if* we did.' Those words were written by Pascal the seventeenth-century mathematician and theologian and at first sight they look like gross hypocrisy. Should we act the part of a Christian, even when we don't feel like one?

Hypocrisy means pretending to be something which

---

> *You can't feel your way into actions, but you can act your way into feelings.* Selwyn Hughes

you are not, and however you happen to feel just now, you are still a child of God, so you are being honest when you act like one. If one of the Queen's sons became mentally ill and secretly thought he was a tramp, it would not be hypocrisy for him to go on living in Buckingham Palace, launch a ship or open a new hospital. However he feels inside cannot alter the fact that he is still a Prince. It may be an 'act' to act as if we are a Christian but is it not an 'act' of faith?

It began to worry the young John Wesley that he was a busy clergyman while inwardly he had no real faith in God's salvation. He was advised to:

'Preach faith until you have it, and then because you have it, you will preach it.' Pascal's 'Act As If' method certainly worked for John Wesley.

'Good spirits which are first simulated become at length real,' says Sir Walter Scott.

## The hazard of synthetic praise

'My dear,' cried a friend as she breezed through my door one morning, 'I have a word from the Lord for you.' My heart sank, I was deeply depressed and sick of people with hot lines to Heaven. 'Your attitude is negative,' she beamed, 'start praising and thanking the Lord for this situation.' I did just manage to stop short of murder. 'What right has she to say that?' I fumed, 'her life's not shattered.'

People will probably have told you to start thanking the Lord, too, or peppered you with books on the power

> *How God rejoices over a soul which surrounded on all sides by suffering and misery does that upon earth which the angels do in Heaven, namely loves, adores and praises God.* G. Tersteegen

of praise. Actually, not many people in the Bible thanked God loudly until *after* their trouble were over. Elijah wanted to die in his desert (1 Kings 19:4). When David's baby son was ill, the king refused all food and spent the nights lying face downwards in prayer on the cold floor of his bedroom (2 Samuel 12:16). Job complained bitterly and Jeremiah acidly enquired, 'Do you intend to disappoint me like a stream which runs dry in the summer?' (Jeremiah 15:18).

Of course when we can thank God in and for our troubles, miracles begin to happen – Jonah's fish deposited him safely on the beach and Paul's prison was demolished by an earthquake. However, for most of us, exuberant praise is not an automatic reaction under stress.

Over the last decade, perhaps many deserts have been caused because people felt crushed by guilt and condemnation when they were unable to praise God loudly in the face of tragedy. God knows we are human beings, and it is not a sin to feel sad when our child dies or when we are badly hurt. He does not expect us to thank Him glibly for allowing it, He only longs that we will turn towards Him in our pain and by doing so enable Him to bring good out of ugly situations. Jesus wept for Mary as she stood by her brother's grave, He did not condemn her for not saying 'thank you'.

Paul and Silas certainly praised God loudly in their prison, but Peter went quietly off to sleep in his, yet he too, escaped. When we put our hand into God's hand and trust Him silently for an impossible situation, that is just as much a form of praise as singing hymns loudly.

---

*Praise is not so much thanking God for what has happened, as trusting Him for what is going to happen.* John Sherrill

## The danger of turning to idols

The Jews had reached the most ghastly point of their desert. Moses had left them. It was over a month since he had walked up that great rumbling mount Sinai and disappeared in clouds of thick smoke. He was certainly dead by now. Here they were – stuck! They'd be killed if they went back to Egypt and killed if they went on to Caanan, stay here and they'd die too – of thirst and starvation. All those fairy stories about God! Moses must have made them all up!

It was no wonder they were miserable, and what did they do? Just what we do when we are tense, depressed, bored, or generally 'fed up'. They looked for comfort.

'We need a nice pretty god we can see, touch and enjoy, like the ones they had in Egypt,' they said, and made a golden calf.

When we feel we need a way of escape we 'drown our sorrows' by over indulging in whatever is our congenital weakness. Food, drink, smoking, sex (either in reality or vicariously through video nasties, porn, sexy books or

---

*I cannot say, beneath the pressure of life's cares today,*
*'Joy in these';*
*But I can say that I had rather walk this rugged way*
*If Him it please.*
S. G. Browning

---

*Happy are those who trust the Lord, who do not turn to idols or join those who worship false gods.*
Psalm 40:4

trashy television). Of course we do not really find comfort – like the Jews in their desert, we only add guilt to our misery.

God has not abandoned us any more than He had left the Jews. It is to Him we need to keep on turning for comfort when life feels shaky, and not to the idols of this world, however attractive they may appear.

## The hazard of crowds and noise

When God is trying hard to tell us something we do not want to hear, it is easy to hide from Him in a crowded church or a busy home. We can even keep our minds so busy with the noise of modern life that He has no chance to reach us. We have a television set in the lounge and bedroom, a radio in the car and cassette player in the kitchen, but are we drowning out God's voice by constant noise?

God had to take Elijah away alone into the Desert of Sinai before He could speak to him in His 'still, small voice'.

If you are the kind of person who tends to take life as it comes, accepting people and situations as they are, without trying to change everything, deserts can be very dangerous. As the folk song says, 'I've been down so long it seems like up to me'. We can get used to feeling flat and dull and accept without thought a less than satisfying Christian life. Sometimes we have to shake off that lethargy by doing something drastic.

---

*The dearest idol I have known, what e'er that idol be,*
*Help me to tear it from Thy throne and worship only Thee.*
William Cowper

Many people who wrote to me described the turning point of their desert as a definite time when they went away alone with God, with the firm intention of 'sorting themselves out before Him'.

'I packed a picnic,' said Betty, 'and I said, "Lord, I don't care if you speak to me or not, I just want to give you my undivided attention for once." I didn't really pray, but I thought through the whole of my life as I walked over the Downs. It was that day which got me out of the wretched limbo I had been floating about in for so long.'

Other people escaped their deserts by attending Bible weeks, conferences or pilgrimages. 'I booked two nights in a bed and breakfast,' said one person, while others went on a supervised retreat in a community, with counselling, fasting, and silence.

Time is our most precious possession, when we are willing to give God our day off, a weekend, even our precious annual leave and go away in order to listen to God in silence, we are saying, 'I care *this much* for our relationship, I want to get it right again'.

## The danger of forgetting other people exist
'Stop feeling so sorry for yourself and start thinking of other people for a change.'

'*Ouch!*' Doesn't it hurt when well meaning people say that? I don't know about you, but my own misery became

---

*We need to find God, but He cannot be found in noise and restlessness. God is the friend of silence. The more we receive in our silent prayer, the more we can give in our life.* Mother Teresa

like a hood that settled over my head blinding me to the needs of others.

'Don't tell me your troubles, I've enough of my own,' says the folk song, and really when we are staggering under the load of our own problems we feel someone else's would certainly be the last straw which flattens us. Yet the Bible tells us that is not so.

> If you give food to the hungry and satisfy those who are in need, then the darkness around you will turn to the brightness of noon . . . your wounds will be quickly healed . . . you will be like a garden that has plenty of water, like a spring of water that never runs dry.   (Is. 58:10–11)

Have *you* ever felt surrounded by darkness? Wounded? Or dried up like a garden in drought? God's promise is to all of us who feel like that, but the condition is that we divert our attention from our own misery and start caring for other people.

This is actually how Jesus Himself coped with the agony of His crucifixion. He healed the lacerated ear of a man who came to arrest Him, he cared about the women who watched Him struggling up to Calvary and as He hung on His cross He arranged for His mother's future, and the comfort of His best friend John. He even had time to reassure the dying thief beside Him.

Job pitied himself for more than thirty chapters of his book, but when at last he was able to pray for his irritating, friends, God released him from his desert. (Job 42:10)

---

*We are never so near to God, as when we are telling someone about Him.* David Pawson

Peggy is a farmer's wife from Somerset and her desert was long and dreary.

I noticed a remarkable thing. Every time I was filled with despair, doubts or a sense of inadequacy, the Lord reminded me of someone even more in need than I was. When I could manage to pray for them, I began to feel better. If I popped in to see them, or asked them round for a coffee, I found myself talking about a faith I do not feel as if I felt it, and a God who seemed far away as if He was as close as ever. I got all excited about the things I was telling people and as I listened to myself talking I came away feeling far more cheered and comforted than they were. When I use people as a waste paper basket for my fears and doubts the problems seem to grow bigger.

I did not dare to write to Mother Teresa and ask her if she had ever been in a desert! If I had, she might well have reminded me of something she once said;
'We all long for heaven where God is, but we have it in our power to be in Heaven with Him right now – to be happy with Him at this very moment. But being happy with Him now means; loving as He loves, helping as He helps, giving as He gives, serving as He serves, rescuing as He rescues.
'Be a living expression of God's kindness; kindness in your face, kindness in your eyes, kindness in your smile.'

---

*There may be times when you cannot find help, but there are no times when you cannot give help.*
George S. Meniam

# 9
# DESERT SURVIVAL

---

My whole being follows hard after You and clings closely to You, Your right hand upholds me. *Psalm 63:8, AMP*

---

In desert warfare, if you can manage to cut off or jam your enemy's lines of communication, you can relax and leave starvation and dehydration to do your work for you. No one survives in a desert without fresh supplies. Satan is a cunning 'desert rat', so the first thing he always tries to do is stop us communicating with God. He makes church uncomfortable, Bible reading boring and prayer virtually impossible. But are we going to let him? This chapter is mostly a collection of the ways some people managed to keep in contact with God even 'under fire'.

## 'The Bible is boring'

'There's no point in reading the Bible, when you don't get anything out of it,' says Satan, but God has told us that the Bible is:

---

*My teaching will fall like drops of rain and form on the earth like dew. My words will fall like showers on young plants.* Deuteronomy 32:2

---

* More important than our daily bread (Deuteronomy 8:3)
* It is a lamp to light our path (Psalm 119:105)
* More precious than all the money in the world (Psalm 119:72)
* The sword with which we defend ourselves (Ephesians 6:17)

Duncan, our son, had mumps extremely badly! I did not insist he ate steaks and suet-pudding, I gave him just a few mouthfuls of something nourishing every couple of hours.

'This milk-shake tastes like sawdust,' he complained.

'Never mind,' I replied, 'You must swallow it down however it tastes, because it will give you the energy to fight the germs.' A desert is really an illness of the soul, just as mumps is a physical illness. Naturally we cannot take huge chunks of Romans or long chapters from Revelation, but our spiritual 'milk-shakes' are vital.

'After our little Hannah died,' wrote Carol, 'I couldn't cope with my usual daily Bible reading notes, it felt such a grind. So I just went to certain passages I know and love, bits of the Bible that fitted my feelings at the time. When I was at my worst I just managed one verse a day.'

Carol's letter gave me the idea of making a collection of short passages that might help people in various deserts. You will find them at the back of the book under 'Desert Rations' (p. 205). It is of paramount importance that we

---

*If your law had not been the source of my joy, I would have died from my sufferings.* Psalm 119:92

keep on listening to God daily through the Bible even when He appears not be to saying anything to us at all.

'I couldn't read for myself,' wrote Joan, 'but Phillip would read aloud to me, and then give me one verse to hold on to all day; he used to write it on a card, which I propped up on the mantelpiece.'

Another coping strategy came from Sandra:

I bought one of those tear-off calendars from the Bible bookshop with a text for each day. I had it in the kitchen, somehow it made me realise God can speak to me even while I do the ordinary jobs of every day.

## When Church is impossible

'The first reaction to any wilderness is withdrawal,' says Jamie Buckingham and most of us would agree with him.

'The hymns bring back too many memories.'

'I used to feel part of the "in crowd", now I feel at the very back of the "out crowd".'

'If you don't leap for joy in the aisles in our church they all want to take you apart and dissect you. I just want space.'

These are a few of the comments I have heard and the Psalmist adds, 'I am like a wild bird in the desert, like an owl in abandoned ruins.' Psalm 102:6. Whoever heard of a flock of owls?

> *When we feel least like going to church, that is the time when it is most vital to go.* Tom Rees

As we have already seen in Chapter Two, Satan loves to separate us from other Christians. If you slice off your finger it can be stitched on again, provided you arrive at the hospital quickly. Leave the thing lying around for a few days and no surgeon in the world could help you! As Christians we are part of a body, and like the finger we can survive a short separation from formal Church services but never a long one. The gap between our deciding not to go and the withering of Christian life is short. Here are some ways people coped when acute depression or trauma made Church impossible for a while.

'Church was too full of sympathetic people, but our little Tuesday evening prayer group was my lifeline,' said Alice.

Ruth told me, 'I made myself go to Church after Denis died, but I never went there on Sundays! I crept in during the week when no one was about. I knew I needed God, but He was so maddeningly intangible, I had no assurance that He was there, but I was in a consecrated building that had been used by generations of people who needed Him, so I used to sit there in a pew, not praying, just sitting there in God's house. It helped so much that, after a while I managed to stay for the small Wednesday morning Communion Service. Again, no feeling of comfort, but going forward to the Communion rail and holding out my hands to receive the symbol of Christ's body was like a physical joining. I needed something concrete like that. I'm a practical, down-to-earth person.'

> *Sometimes when things are at their worst, you simply have to grind through, step by step, clinging to the Lord as hard as you can.* Maggie Boon

Sylvia said, 'After we lost our son, formal worship was impossible for a while, so I spent a whole summer of Sundays going on long rambles alone with God. I poked around under the stones in a stream and watched all the tiny creatures He made in such perfect detail, or sat on top of a hill looking into the far distance. It made me see my own problems in perspective. If God could make all this, He could certainly help me with the small and the large things that frightened me so much. Worshipping Him like that mended the parts of me that had been damaged and when the winter came I was happy to go back to church again.'

## What the Bible tells us about Church

* We are commanded not to 'give up the habit of meeting together, as some are doing. Instead let us encourage one another.' (Hebrews 10:25)
* As Christians we need to follow the example of Jesus. 'On the Sabbath day he went as usual to the synagogue,' (Luke 4:16)
* God wants us all to feel we 'belong'. 'He sets the lonely in families.' (Psalm 68:6, NIV)

If we go on going to Church even if we don't feel like it, we are at least being obedient. If we decide to give up and watch a video instead we are less likely to hear God's voice.

---

*How clearly the sky reveals God's glory! How plainly it shows what He has done!* Psalm 19:1

Martin Luther, who frequently suffered from bouts of depression, wrote in his diary; 'At home in my own house there is no warmth or vigour in me, but in the Church when the multitude is gathered together a fire is kindled in my heart . . .'

## Praying when prayer is impossible

So much has been written about prayer, that it amazes me that most of us still find it so difficult! Few great men are as honest as David Watson when he says, 'There are times when I almost give up the battle of prayer altogether and have to trust God's grace and faithfulness. When I am in these seasons of depression the Lord seems a million miles away.'

Praying in the desert can feel impossibly hard. How many of us have felt like saying this to God?

If I try to pray my words bounce back off the ceiling and I feel embarrassed at talking to myself. Sometimes I do not want to find You, it's too disturbing. But God, you would rather I brought the turmoil of my thoughts to You than use them as an excuse not to pray. Whether I want to or not I must find You, for without you life has no meaning and I cannot rest until I reach You.

I found that prayer in a book written by Mary Hathaway, who lives in constant pain. (*Peace Be Still* – Lion Publishing)

---

*The essential act of prayer is to stand unprotected before God. What will God do? He will take possession of us. That He should do this is the whole purpose of life.* St John of the Cross

Are we all trying too hard? Perhaps we think we have to work through a spiritual aerobics routine every morning when all God wants us to do is to sit for a while and listen to Him.

## Prayer does not always need words
Recently I was watching 'Songs of Praise' on the television, when a vicar allowed himself to be interviewed, just two weeks after his wife had died of leukaemia.

'During your wife's illness did prayer help?' he was asked.

'Yes,' was his reply, 'but not in the way you might think. At a time like that prayer is more an attitude to life than a recitation of set words at the same time each day. It is just resting on God – taking Him for granted.'

Here are a few extracts from the letters I received.

'Praying feels like talking to a man who is watching a cricket match!' said Denise.

'I didn't want to pray when my husband died,' said Maureen, 'and no words would come, but I made myself sit in my chair for a while each morning. I wasn't confessing, praising or begging, just sitting there with God. I used to breathe very deeply, and tell myself I was breathing *out* all my tensions and worries and breathing *in* God and all His peace.'

We live in days when the emphasis is on extempore prayer, but when our own words fail us, here is some

> *But as for me, I will pray to You, Lord; answer me God, at a time You choose . . . because of Your great love, because You keep Your promises to save.* Psalm 69:13

good advice from Sister Margaret Magdalene from her book *Jesus: Man of Prayer*. 'Liturgy comes to our aid in times of great spiritual darkness and aridity, when we can dredge up nothing from inside ourselves. It enables us to jump into the great river of prayer that flows ceaselessly to the Father and be carried along in it, when we do not feel like praying at all.'

## The more difficult prayer is the more precious it is to God

Satan says, 'your silly little prayers aren't doing you or anyone else any good, why not get on with something useful?' Yet seven hundred years ago Mother Julian of Norwich wrote; 'Pray inwardly even though you find no joy in it, for it does good, though you feel nothing, yes, even though you think you cannot pray. For when you are dry and empty, sick and weak, your prayers *please Him* though there be little enough to persuade you. All believing prayer is precious to God.'

So prayer is something we can do for God's benefit, and Sister Margaret Magdalene adds to this idea by saying; 'Prayer is an offering to God and it is the offering that matters not whether we enjoy making it or not.'

Max Harper had been suffering from such severe depression that he had not been able to work for several years when he wrote to me:

I suppose when people praise God out of the overflow of their hearts, because they are happy and blessed that pleases God, but the praises of a sick

---

As a deer longs for a stream of cool water, so I long for You, O God. I thirst for You, the Living God. Psalm 42:1–2

and depressed person are far more precious to Him
because they are so much harder to give.

## Change your routine
'I have always prayed first thing in the morning,' said
Rachel, 'but for months after the business failed I would
wake in a panic. My mind would fizz like a catherine
wheel, I knew I needed to pray, but prayer was totally
impossible, in fact it made things worse. Activity of body
helped the mental fizzing, So I used to get straight up and
on with the jobs. Strangely I often found myself praying
quite easily when the vacuum cleaner was going full
blast.'

Perhaps Isaac Watts would agree with Rachel's discovery when he says 'little and often' is the answer to
prayer in the desert. 'Do not affect to pray long. God is
not the more pleased with prayers merely because they
are long. It is much better to make up by the frequency of
our devotions what we lack in the length of them.'

Records and cassettes of hymns and praise songs can
grate on the nerves badly in some deserts, while other
people find listening to sacred music is the best way to
communicate with God.

## Jesus prays for us
When we cannot manage to pray ourselves, Jesus does it
for us. Perhaps that is the most comforting fact when
prayer is being hard. 'He lives for ever to plead with God

---

*But I am in pain and despair . . . I will praise God
with a song; I will proclaim His greatness by
giving Him thanks.* Psalm 69:29–30

for them.' (Hebrews 7:25) Have you ever wondered what Jesus does these days? He is praying for you.

'If I could hear Christ praying for me in the next room,' wrote Robert Murray M'Cheyne, 'I would not fear a million enemies. Yet distance makes no difference. He *is* praying for me.'

## Danger don't miss the oases

Deserts are never totally dry, every now and again you always find an oasis. We might be sitting in church, our mind a bored blur, when one phrase from the pulpit rivets our attention. A friend could make a remark or something we read may suddenly give us fresh hope.

'I'm out of this at last!' we think happily. Then a week later, when we feel just as dry as ever, we wonder whatever it was that made us so excited. 'If only I'd written it down' we think crossly.

Bedouin and their camels have the sense to preserve the water they draw from these desert springs and carry it carefully with them back out into the desolate sand dunes. Here are two ways of doing the same thing.

'I bought a little notebook,' Anna told me, 'and every time anything made any sort of sense I wrote it down with the date. When I felt bogged down in the "slough of despond" I would flip back through the pages and realise God had been speaking to me surprisingly frequently.'

Brenda said, 'I'm always at my most depressed in the kitchen, trying to cope with the jobs I can't really

---

*The life of prayer is just love to God and the custom of being ever with Him.* St Teresa manage any more. So I write on cards any special promise God gives me and stick it on the kitchen wall. Now after two years we can hardly see the wall for my promise cards!'

There certainly seem to be more ways of keeping in contact with 'HQ' than I ever imagined a year ago, but sometimes even these helpful ideas will be useless in the face of extreme suffering. During the terrible depression that Barbara experienced after the tragic death of her son on his motorbike, she confessed to a friend that she could neither read her Bible, pray, nor go to church. The friend replied,

'Don't you think God is big enough to cope with that? Can't He put His arms round you and hold you even when you cannot hold on to Him yourself?'

---

*When I am surrounded by troubles, You keep Me safe . . . You will do everything You have promised. Lord Your love is eternal, complete the work that you have begun.* Psalm 138:7–8

---

*He hath more ways of hunting for our love than one or two.* Samuel Rutherford

# 10

# THE HIGHWAY TO FREEDOM

---

When My people in their need look for water, when
their throats are dry with thirst, then I, the Lord, will
answer their prayer, I the God of Israel, will never
abandon them. I will make rivers flow among
barren hills and springs of water run in the valleys.
I will turn the desert into pools of water . . . *Isaiah
41:17–18*

---

'For a long time I didn't even miss the Lord,' said Jan,
'then suddenly I couldn't stop thinking about the sheer
ecstasy I had known when I first met Him at university.
Verse 4 in Revelation Chapter 2 seemed to haunt me: 'But
this is what I have against you; you do not love me as you
did first'.

'One day I had this burning desire to recapture what
I had possessed then, so, on impulse, I parked the
children, hopped on a train and went back to Exeter for
the day. Nothing had changed as I walked round the old
familiar streets and parks, all the memories came
flooding back.'

'And did you find your first love again?' I asked her.

'I did,' she laughed, 'but I discovered I didn't really
want it any more, it had been nothing but pink, fluffy
candy floss which hadn't stood up to the pressures of
my life. I knew I needed to find a new, more durable
relationship with God. What I have now, makes my
desert worthwhile.'

I hope by the time you read this chapter your desert
will be slipping into history. Perhaps you are in that

strange 'No Man's Land', between two worlds. The
activities and patterns of thought that were once your
life, have been rocked to the foundations, leaving you
wondering, 'where do I go from here?' The important
thing, according to my friend Jan, is not to go back to
where you began. It is not your old faith and love for God
you need to regain. He wants your desert to be a prelude
to something even better.

## Beyond the desert lies a new blessing

One day God's Spirit took Ezekiel into a forgotten valley
and showed him heaps of old, dry bones scattered about
on the ground. 'These are my people,' God told him,
'They say that they are dried up, without any hope and
with no future.' (Ez. 37:11)

Is that how you have been feeling? Just a dried,
shrivelled skeleton of the Christian you once used to be?
Picked clean by the vultures, useless and forgotten in the
scorching heat of a desert valley? God is speaking to you,
just as surely as He spoke to his people through Ezekiel.

'See I am going to make you live and breathe again, and
cover you with skin. I will put breath into you and you
shall live and know I am the Lord.' (Cf. Ezekiel 37:6) 'I
will give you a new heart and a new mind. I will take
away your stubborn heart of stone and give you an
obedient heart. I will put my spirit in you and I will see to
it that you follow my laws.' (Ezekiel 36:26)

As Ezekiel watched in amazement, God made those
dry bones into living soldiers and they marched out of
their arid valley in triumph. Are you prepared for Him to
do something just as miraculous for you?

---

*I will . . . and make Trouble Valley a door of hope.*
Hosea 2:14

'But I don't feel like a triumphant soldier,' perhaps you are thinking. None of the rest of us rode proudly out of our deserts – with polished boots and a gleaming white charger. We staggered out in blood-stained tatters, but that does not mean we lost the battle. The soldier with the battle scars wins the war medal. We win when we lose our pride, sin and self-reliance and come to depend on God in complete humility. A tragically high proportion of Christians never come out of their deserts simply because they don't want to. If you have managed to crawl this far, you have won, however battered you feel!

Of course even Ezekiel's soldiers needed a road on which to march home. We too had to build ourselves a way back to God through the 'trackless wilderness', and for many of us it was very hard work.

'Comfort my people,' says your God '. . . her sad days are gone . . . make a road for the Lord through the wilderness. Fill the valleys, level the hills, straighten out the crooked paths and smooth off the rough spots in the road.' (Isaiah 40:1,3–4, LB)

In our deserts we realised just how crooked our lives had become, and with God's help we had to straighten them. We filled in the valleys of omission (by adding good things that were missing). We had to remove mountains by the faith God gave us and smooth the rough attitudes that were obstacles in our pathway back to Him.

'There will be a highway there, called "The Road of Holiness". No sinner will ever travel that road; . . . Those whom the Lord has rescued will travel home by that road.' (Isaiah 35:8–9)

> *You have put us to the test, God; . . . we went through fire and flood, but now You have brought us to a place of safety.* Psalm 66:10–12

Of course we are all sinners, for whom Jesus died, but there is no way out of a desert if we are not willing to leave our sins behind us, buried for ever under the sand.

## How am I going to feel now?
The simple answer to that is – different. As I said at the beginning of this book, the desert is an experience you walk through from one side to the other and you come out on the far side a different person. 'You have . . . enlarged me when I was in distress.' (Psalm 4:1)

As I look back over my life I can remember feeling angry with God on several occasions on behalf of friends who seemed to be going through far more than their fair share of life's problems.

'Why should God allow such nice people to suffer like this?' I have so often thought. Then, perhaps years later, I meet them again and suddenly they are not just nice people any more, they have become special people. A subtle and indescribable change has taken place in their whole personalities and the way they look at life is just not of this world. Job lost everything in his desert, but after he had prayed for his irritating friends and apologised to God for his rude behaviour, God gave him back a double quantity of all he had before. Therefore, I suppose it is not surprising that God has made some of my friends into twice the people they were when I first met them.

'Jesus returned . . . the power of the Holy Spirit was with him,' says Luke 4:14. Returned from where? From His desert.

---

*Give us now as much happiness as the sadness You gave us during all our years of misery.* Psalm 90:15

## Are you willing to march the whole way?

After forty years wandering in the barren wilderness, some of the tribes of Israel were so pleased to see a few patches of green grass they settled down and lived in a partial desert instead of crossing the Jordan and making right for the heart of the Promised Land. (Numbers 32) Few spiritual deserts end abruptly. Things begin to improve gradually and it is tempting to relax too soon and settle down to life in the suburbs of Little Blessings, instead of marching right on to claim the Big Blessing that awaits us.

## Preserve your treasures of darkness

When the rest of the Jews finally crossed the Jordan into the Promised Land, God told them to pull out from the river bed twelve great stones and set them up as a monument, to remind them for ever of all God had done. Perhaps we too, need a monument of some kind.

On my wall I have a poster, a picture of footprints disappearing into the far distance and the famous poem in which the writer asks why, if God had promised to walk with him always, there was only one set of footprints behind him? God told him that through the worst patches of his life He had *not* walked beside him, He had actually been *carrying* him! To me, that poster is a constant reminder of my desert. I also thought God had left me to walk alone, and whenever I am tempted to feel like that again, I go and look at my poster.

Naturally we want to forget our nasty experiences, but the 'treasures of darkness' we discovered are things we

---

*That which had lain desolate in the sight of all who passed by . . . has become like the garden of Eden.* Ezekiel 36:34–35

definitely want to preserve for ever. Could you write down the positive things you feel you have gained through this experience and keep the list in your Bible? Maybe you realise now what caused the desert in the first place. If you made a note of that too, it could work like an early warning system to help you escape, if ever you saw another desert looming on the horizon.


## God even uses our deserts

One morning I was typing away at my keyboard, trying to take down everything my visitor was telling me about his desert, when suddenly his voice trailed away in mid-sentence. When I looked up I saw tears trickling from behind his glasses. 'I hate remembering it,' he said at last, 'it was all such a waste of precious time . . . time I could have spent with the Lord . . . time I should have been telling others about Him.'

So many of us feel as he did; perhaps that is why God put a special verse of encouragement into the book of Joel, just for us. 'I will restore for you the years that the locust has eaten,' Joel 2:25. A swarm of locusts can strip the harvest fields as bare as a desert, but God wants us to know He does not see our deserts as wasted, barren years, He is going to make them 'blossom like a rose'. God used Job's experience to bless him profoundly and He has also been using it to bless the rest of us ever since!

Many people who contributed to this book did not find

---

*What a wonderful God we have . . . who so wonderfully comforts and strengthens us in our hardships and trials . . . so that when others are troubled . . . we can pass on to them this same help . . . God has given us.* 2 Corinthians 1:3–4

it easy to do so, but we wanted God to use our pain to help others. He will use yours too, if you give it to Him.

To show you what I mean, here are a few final extracts from letters I will value all my life.

'Pride may come before a fall, but you are a much nicer person afterwards! There are few people more useless to God than those who have never tripped over and therefore pride themselves on their consistent rectitude. William Shakespeare rightly says, "He jests at scars who never knew a wound". I came from a very sheltered background and really did tend to look down on other people. Now that my "knees" are still hurting from my fall, I understand how people feel. No one is ever going to get trite, glib little answers from me again. I've learnt to say, "I just do not know why God does or doesn't do certain things. But I do know that He knows why and that's enough for me."' Sherry

'I am beginning to see now why God allowed me to be ill for so long . . . I hope to take on a ward sister's post in the autumn and I feel a new affinity now with suffering people. I did not know what it was like for them before, and shudder when I remember how I treated certain patients. I shall never be the same Again.' Maggie

'The experience stripped us of everything else except God. It put our priorities right. The endless

---

*Don't you think that some of us must know the trials of misty weather if we are to be enabled to understand when others are in the mist?* Amy Carmichael

paraphernalia of modern life suddenly seems terribly unimportant.' Joy

'When I was going through the mill, I suddenly realised that Jesus also knew what it was like to be hassled by Satan, pressured by a family business, misunderstood, criticised and then even rejected by the people He loved best. Perhaps worst of all, to watch His life's work apparently lying in ruins. Since those things happened to me I really have come to know Him in a new and deeper way, by sharing "in His sufferings".' (Philippians 3:10) Michael

'You ask, what have I learnt through all this? Well I've discovered that happiness depends on happenings and my happenings haven't been very pleasant recently so I felt cheated. But I came to realise that happiness was not what Jesus promised us, it was joy. Like David in Psalm 51, I asked Him to 'restore unto me the joy of my salvation', and He answered that prayer as I discovered that it is possible to have joy right in the middle of unhappy events, simply by realising that God loves me, understands, and has everything under control!' Bill

'In my utter weakness I am having to lean very heavily on the Lord's arm,' wrote Peggy, 'You never learn how strong someone's arm really is, until you have to lean your whole weight on it.'

Perhaps of all the letters I received, that last one sums up the desert experience best: a time when we learnt just

In the end *we shall see that what seemed so hindering does not hinder, but helps*. Amy Carmichael

how strong God's arm really is. 'Who is this coming up from the desert, leaning on her beloved?' says the Song of Songs (8:5). Actually there is no other way to get out of the desert than by leaning on Him, and no greater 'treasure of darkness' than to discover the full strength of His arm. Through Solomon God says to us now:

The winter is over, the rains have stopped; in the countryside the flowers are in bloom. This is the time for singing; the song of doves is heard in the fields. Figs are beginning to ripen; the air is fragrant with blossoming vines, come then my love, my darling come with me. Song of Songs 2:11–13

*You have changed my sadness into a joyful dance, You have taken away my sorrow, and surrounded me with joy. So I will not be silent I will sing praise to You, Lord, You are my God I will give you thanks for ever. Psalm 30:11–12*

# APPENDIX 1
# DESERT RATIONS

When Jesus was in His desert He said, 'man cannot live on bread alone, but needs every word that God speaks'. It is through reading the Bible regularly that we gain strength to survive our deserts and eventually discover our escape routes. Yet, so often, when we are facing emotional trauma or physical illness, we simply cannot face reading long irrelevant passages. Here are a few of the best loved 'mini meals' to sustain you each day.

## DRY, DULL PATCHES

Psalm 107:4–9
Isaiah 35:1–4
Jeremiah 17:5–10
Deuteronomy 8:2–10
Isaiah 55:1–3

Psalm 63:1–5
Psalm 36:5–9
Habakkuk 3:17–19
Psalm 42:1–5
Isaiah 55:6–11

## WHEN GOD SEEMS VERY FAR AWAY

Psalm 139:1–6
Isaiah 41:9–10
Jeremiah 31:2–4
Psalm 22:1–11
Hebrews 13:5–6

Psalm 139:7–12
Romans 8:31–39
Jeremiah 29:11–13
Matthew 28:20
Isaiah 59:1–2

## FAILURE, DISAPPOINTMENT AND WORTHLESSNESS

Psalm 37:3–7
Psalm 40:1–3

Psalm 31:14–22
Isaiah 50:9–10

1 Corinthians 1:26–31        2 Corinthians 4:8–9
Psalm 131:1–2               Psalm 119:81–84

## STRESS, ILLNESS AND GRIEF

Psalm 143:4–8              Psalm 91:1–6
Psalm 91:14–16             Psalm 94:17–19
Psalm 73:23–26             Psalm 62:5–7
Psalm 46:1–3               Psalm 25:15–18
Psalm 23:1–6               1 Peter 1:3–7
1 Peter 4:12–14            Matthew 11:28–30
Romans 5:1–5               Psalm 121:1–8
Psalm 34:17–19             Isaiah 40:28–31
Isaiah 43:1–5              John 14:1–3
2 Corinthians 4:16–18      2 Corinthians 5:1–7
Lamentations 3:19–26       2 Corinthians 4:8–10
1 Peter 5:6–7              Psalm 71:1–8
Psalm 69:29–33             Psalm 71:19–21

## WHEN WE FEEL WE HAVE CAUSED OUR OWN DESERT

Jeremiah 15:18–20              Hebrews 4:14–16
1 John 1:8–10                 Isaiah 54:7–8
Psalm 130:1–6                 Psalm 107:10–16
Psalm 103:8–14                Psalm 25:4–7
Psalm 25:8–12                 Psalm 51:1–5
Psalm 51:6–13                 Romans 5:6–11
Romans 7:24–25 and 8:1–2      Psalm 37:23–25
Isaiah 1:18–20                Isaiah 53:4–6

---

*In Your goodness You told them what they should do; You fed them with manna and gave them water to drink. Through forty years in the desert you provided all that they needed.* Nehemiah 9:20–21

---

# APPENDIX 2

## GUIDE BOOKS FOR DESERT TRAVEL

Backhouse, Halcyon (ed.), *Cloud of Unknowing*. London, Hodder & Stoughton 1985.

Backhouse, Halcyon (ed.), St John of the Cross, *Dark Night of the Soul*. London, Hodder & Stoughton 1988.

Billheimer, Paul E., *Don't Waste Your Sorrows*. Alresford, Christian Literature Crusade 1983.

Billheimer, Paul E., *The Mystery of His Providence*. Eastbourne, CLC/Kingsway 1983.

Buckingham, Jamie, *A Way Through the Wilderness*. Eastbourne, Kingsway 1984.

Carmichael, Amy, *Candles in the Dark: letters of Amy Carmichael*. London, Triangle 1981.

Christenson, Evelyn, *Lord Change Me*. Amersham, Scripture Press.

Cowman, Mrs Charles E., *Streams in the Desert*. Basingstoke, Marshall Pickering 1985.

Green, Wendy, *The Long Road Home*. Tring, Lion Publishing 1979.

Hathaway, Mary (comp.), *Peace Be Still*. Tring, Lion Publishing 1987.

Hession, Roy. *Calvary Road*. Alresford, Christian Literature Crusade, 1950.

Hurnard, Hannah, *Hinds' Feet on High Places*. Eastbourne, Kingsway, 1982.

Julian of Norwich, *Enfolded in Love*. London, Darton, Longman & Todd 1980.

Lloyd-Jones, Martyn, *Spiritual Depression*. Basingstoke, Marshall Pickering 1985.

Magdalen, Sister Margaret, *Jesus: Man of Prayer*. London, Hodder & Stoughton 1987.

Marshall, Catherine, *Meeting God at Every Turn*. London, Hodder & Stoughton 1981.

Schaeffer, Edith, *Affliction*. London, Hodder & Stoughton 1984.

Schlink, Sister Basilea, *The Hidden Treasure of Suffering*. Basingstoke, Marshall Pickering 1985.

Sjaastad, Egil, *In the Shadow of the Cross*. Basingstoke, Marshall Pickering 1987.

Warren, Ann (ed.), *Facing Bereavement*. Crowborough, Highland 1988.

Wiersbe, Warren W., *The Bumps Are What You Climb On*. Leicester, IVP 1986.

# Beyond Healing

Jennifer Rees Larcombe

HODDER AND STOUGHTON
LONDON SYDNEY AUCKLAND

British Library Cataloguing in Publication Data

ISBN 0 340 62136 2

Typeset by Hewer Text Composition Services, Edinburgh
Printed and bound in Great Britain


Hodder and Stoughton Ltd,
A division of Hodder Headline PLC
338 Euston Road
London NW1 3BH

# Foreword

Faith, pushed beyond limits, may be forced to cry, 'Why?'

Still, if God chooses to remain silent, faith is content.

Why was so choice a servant of God as Amy Carmichael of India required to spend the last twenty years of her life in bed and frequently in pain as the result of an accident? It was during those years that she wrote books that have become priceless classics to those who know and love them.

Why did George Matheson have to lose his eyesight? Yet what would we do without the hymn born out of his suffering, 'Oh Love that wilt not let me go . . .'

One could well question the incomprehensible sufferings of Job. Yet how many down through the centuries have had their own faith strengthened in the face of insurmountable trials, by Job's unquenchable faith?

Suffering can be a hideous thing, frustrating, debilitating and apparently wasteful of useful, fulfilling lives.

And yet God, in His sovereignty, still permits illness.

The pressure to seek healing can lay heavy burdens of guilt on the ones God does not choose to heal.

Like the Psalmist in Psalm 55:6, many of us are pressured to pray, 'O that I had wings of a dove then would I fly away . . .' (or 'Let me out of here!') while others wait patiently on the Lord and find their strength renewed as He promised in Isaiah 40:31. So there is the choice: 'away' or 'up'.

Here is a book for us all, written by one who knows whereof she speaks. Jen has been a dear friend for years, as her parents were before her. If anyone deserved to be healed it

5

was Jen. But it could be that Jen, like God's medal of honour heroes in the last of Hebrews 11, will not receive the promise of deliverance, 'God having some better thing for us.'

I look for the book to be a part of that 'better thing'.

Ruth Bell Graham

## Preface

It was nine years ago that I wrote the preface for the first edition of this book – and I wrote it in a hospital bed. I'm writing this new preface in the departure lounge of a Canadian airport. Life seems to have changed quite a lot for me since then.

You'll see from the first chapter of the book that it was always my desire to travel round the world telling people about the Lord Jesus. When I became ill in 1982 I thought that dream was shattered for ever and I felt as if the Lord had tossed me away, abandoned and useless. During the eight years which followed I was amazed to discover that it was my friendship and company which were far more important to the Lord than any service I could ever render to Him. Everything else became unimportant in comparison with the piercing joy of that discovery. Then, five years after I finished writing this book, He healed me suddenly and most unexpectedly, but I do not want to change a word of what I wrote then. I still believe that physical cure is not as important as the healing of the real person inside.

Back in 1984, while I was wondering if I should write this book or wait until I had some of the answers to the suffering we were facing as a family, I met a girl called Maisie. Her family was suffering too as they struggled to adjust to the fact that one of their daughters had been born severely handicapped. 'Write the book now,' she told me, 'because we're all sick to death of books written by Christians who went through horrible experiences so long

7

ago they've forgotten how much they hurt at the time. They give the impression they sailed through everything, oozing joy and triumph all the way. You write about what you're living through now, while you're right in the middle of it, *and be honest about how you really feel*!' I'm so glad I took her advice, because when you look back it is easy to see only the mountain peaks and forget the valleys in between.

All the people who so nobly allowed me to write about them are still our close friends and our children have not regretted their willingness to be 'exposed to public view'. In their own individual ways they have all come to know and love the Lord Jesus for themselves. I would not want to have to live through those years of illness again, but I would not want to have missed them either, because it is not until 'the crunch' comes that you know for sure whether your Christian faith is worth anything or not.

May 1994

## Chapter One

The telephone rang as it always does at the most incon-
venient moment possible – just when lunch was ready. My
husband Tony was at the furthest end of the garden where
men go when you want them to carve a joint, so I gave the
saucepans an irritated shove to the back of the stove and
picked up the receiver. It was Eunja, a Korean Christian
friend of ours, and she sounded upset.

'Jen, I just don't know whether I should have rung you or
not,' she began, 'but Charles and I have prayed so much this
morning and we feel that I should tell you something.' She
sounded as if she was crying, but my mind was still with the
Yorkshire puddings – my watch told me that in just four
minutes they would start to burn.

'What's up?' I asked, trying not to sound hassled.

'Well,' she began, 'God often shows me things in dreams.
Last night, I had a terrible dream about you. I dreamt you
were going to die soon.'

I felt as if someone had kicked me very hard in the tummy
and I sat down heavily on the bottom of the stairs.

'It probably doesn't mean anything,' she added quickly,
'but do pray about it, won't you.'

That was doubtless very good advice, but I did no such
thing. As I put the phone down I felt very angry. 'God
doesn't frighten people with forecasts of doom,' I raged to
myself, as I watched the custard boil all over the stove. 'All
this is a load of spoofy codswallop!'

'God used dreams a lot in the Bible,' said a small voice

9

inside my head, but I refused to listen, and was very bad-tempered with the children for the rest of the day.

All the same, I was badly frightened by that telephone call. It had come much too soon after a horrible nightmare of my own. Just a few nights before I had dreamed that something terrible was going to happen to our family, but I had woken in a cold sweat of terror before finding out what it was. I'd been so frightened I'd had to creep down to the kitchen and put the kettle on. As I had sipped my tea a wave of relief swept over me. It had only been a silly dream after all. Nothing was going to spoil the life I enjoyed so much.

I had every reason to be happy and I was. We lived in an idyllic Sussex village where I knew everyone. They all knew me as 'that mad fat woman with herds of kids', for not only did I have my own large family but I was a foster mother and also 'minded' several other children on a daily basis. Our home was down a little lane, surrounded by woods and fields. We kept hens, grew our own vegetables and made our own bread. I cooked cakes for every village function and dashed happily round the district doing things for people whether they really wanted me to or not.

Looking back I am horrified at how irritating I must have been! There can be something vaguely unsympathetic about Christian families apparently living in permanent sunshine, and we certainly appeared to have everything. Our marriage and home were secure, our children were healthy, Tony's job as a teacher adviser was reasonably paid and we were involved and appreciated at our little local church. It was the sort of lifestyle that others might envy, but I was so happy and busy that the idea never occurred to me.

I never even thought of the dream when I woke next morning with the feeling that something nice was going to happen. I'd had the morning marked in my diary with a large red cross for days. I was going to Firtoll Woods, and I had a very special appointment there. In a few months I was going to be forty, and by then Richard, our youngest son, would be at school all day. I had the delicious assurance that something exciting was going to happen.

After fourteen solid years of motherhood I felt I was about to reach a new beginning and was convinced that child-rearing was only a prelude to the real business of life. What did God want to do with my time: surely not spend it just cleaning loos and peeling potatoes and looking after other people's children?

I was beginning to get a number of invitations to speak at coffee mornings and lunches run by Christian women who wanted their friends and neighbours to hear about what God has done for us. It would be fun driving off in the car and meeting lots of new interesting people after years of baby talk, but was it right to do that and be a mother?

Before I said 'yes' to any more of these invitations, I really wanted to talk the whole thing over with God and ask Him to tell me what to do, but I had to go out if I wanted to do that. I knew only too well that if I knelt down to pray at home, I would think: I could be doing the ironing, or Why don't I knock up the dough before Richard comes back from play-group and 'helps' me. The phone would ring or a friend would pop round for a coffee. No, if I wanted to be quite alone with God, I had to go out.

A few minutes after waving goodbye to Richard at the playgroup door, I was happily pulling on my wellingtons and gloating over the memory of the wonderful times I had enjoyed with God in this lovely wood. I remembered the pungent scent of the bluebells, the way the sunlight flickered through the beech leaves and dappled the water in the little stream. It had been so easy to communicate with God amongst such beauty.

But I was in for a nasty shock that morning. Of course, I really couldn't expect bluebells in late February, and the once lovely leaves lay rotting and mouldy on the ground, smelling of death and decay. It was a dark, dismal morning and the rain splashed down on my soggy hat through the bare branches. I splashed miserably along by the muddy

11

stream dictating what sounded like a shopping list of requests to God who felt too far away to hear anyway.

At last I sat down on a crumbling tree stump and gave up even trying to pray. But then God spoke to me instead. I didn't hear a voice or see a vision, but I knew He was speaking all right. The first time that had ever happened to me I had been skinning a tomato and I was so surprised I dropped it – splat – on to the kitchen floor! When God is really speaking to me, there is no doubt whatever in my mind that it is His voice I can hear. If ever I think, That's just my imagination, and I do not have that clear certainty, I know it *is* only me talking and not God at all.

This time it was unmistakable.

'Your life has been like this wood was in the springtime,' He said. 'If it became bleak, lifeless and wintry could you still praise Me?'

'I don't know, Lord,' I replied out loud, feeling rather startled.

'In Heaven,' He continued, 'your life will always be like the woods in May time.'

That was *not* the kind of thing I wanted to hear. I had expected some great commissioning from Him. Whenever I scrubbed the kitchen floor I imagined myself as a female evangelist popping on and off jet planes to address vast conventions of women all over the world. After all, both my parents had been evangelists, and I felt sure I would be called to be one as well.

But as I sat hunched on my damp tree stump I suddenly remembered my dream of the night before, and felt very cold. The memory of the 'terrible thing' that was going to engulf us made me shiver and I went home rather hastily to put the kettle on, and write down exactly what God had said in the little black diary I have been keeping for the last few years.

'I don't understand you, Lord,' I muttered as I hurtled into the car to meet Richard, but as I shot down the lane I found myself singing a chorus we have sometimes at

12

church. It's just a few verses from Habakkuk set to a bouncy tune:

> Although the fig tree does not blossom
> and there be no fruit on the vine,
> The produce of the olive fail,
> and the fields yield no corn,
> The flock shall be cut off from the fold,
> and there be no herd in the stall,
> Yet will I rejoice in the Lord,
> and I will joy in the God of my salvation.
> (Based on Hab. 3: 17–18)

As usual, I was disgraced by being 'last Mummy' at the playgroup, but yet again Richard's huge bear hug showed me he had forgiven me and I was soon caught up in the whirl of the rest of the week and forgot my dreams and fancies – until Saturday morning and Eunja's telephone call.

Fear becomes bigger and bigger when it is not faced and as I tried to run away from mine, I was forgetting that when God provided us with armour to protect us from attacks by the enemy (Eph. 6: 10–13) He gave us none for our backs, so we deserve all we get when we panic and run.

The next few days as I spring-cleaned the house and did loads of unnecessary washing, I knew full well I was just being busy on purpose. When Tuesday evening came and I realised I would be alone because Tony was away at a conference for maths teachers, I surrounded myself with a huge pile of long-overdue mending, and turned on the television very loudly. But it was no good. My stomach was churning, I had reached the end of the road.

'I must talk this over with someone,' I said, as I hurled a half-darned sock across the room, 'but who can I ring up this late in the evening?'

How can it be that a person who has known and loved the Lord for as many years as I have, when faced with a problem always thinks, Whose advice can I ask? or What book could

13

I read for help? When will I learn to go straight to God Himself, for whenever I do that He either removes the problem, changes my reaction to it, or sends along just the right person to help. Fortunately, it *was* far too late to ring anyone that evening, so I got down on my knees among the mending and said, 'Lord, I must talk to you, I'm terribly frightened'.

'Are you *really* frightened of dying?' was His instant reply. I thought that through carefully and then replied, 'No Lord, I definitely am *not* frightened of being dead because I know I'll come straight to Heaven and meet you there.'

There was no doubt whatever in my mind about that. It might sound rather presumptuous, and I once deeply shocked a neighbour of mine by saying that to her as we stood in the queue for fish at Heathfield market.

'How can you possibly be sure you're good enough to go to Heaven?' she had demanded.

'Well I know for certain I'm *not* good enough and never will be,' I replied over the fillets of plaice, 'and all the wrong things I do *should* separate me from God completely. That's why Jesus came to earth and died on the cross to be blamed and punished for my sins, and because I've accepted what He did for me I know for sure I'll make Heaven.' She looked so shocked that I could not help adding, 'If Heaven was going to be full of "goodie goodies" who felt they had a right to be there because of their good behaviour it would be so boring I'd rather go to the other place!' Quite horrified, she ordered sole instead of her usual coley – we have often laughed about it since.

But I wasn't laughing that Tuesday evening. No, I was not frightened of *being* dead, but the actual dying bit bothered me. What would it feel like? And then I remembered Tony and the children. Like all mums I thought I was quite indispensable. It was our foster daughter Janie who worried me far more than the other five. Both her mother and father were dead, and we had looked after her as part of our family since she was seven. Watching both her parents die had given her a terror of illness, and I only had to sneeze for her to

14

panic. Once when the central heating broke down and I crossly said I was sure I'd die of the cold, her two little hands clutched my woolly jumper like clammy starfish for the rest of the day. Her little life had been so shattered that it had taken nearly five years to piece her together with prayer. Surely, I thought as I knelt among the mending, God couldn't allow a third tragedy to envelope her.

'You can trust me for yourself,' the Lord seemed to say, 'why can't you trust me for the children?' It is strange, but that always does seem harder to do.

I picked up Tony's half-darned sock and hoped he'd marry again quickly. I knew just the right person, and had a sneaking suspicion that she'd make him a far better wife anyway. Should I write him a note to point out her obvious virtues? That started me giggling – what if I didn't die after all and he found the note one day, what a fool I'd look. I laughed so much I felt loads better, and when I had committed the whole thing to the Lord, I went off to bed in peace.

A very wonderful thing happened to me two days later at our House Group meeting. Although we met at the home of our pastor, Brian Hill, the group was open to anyone, and not confined to our church members. So there was Dr Jordan from the parish church, Mr and Mrs Burton who were very elderly Strict Baptists, and Brother Tom – a Roman Catholic monk and the cook in a small community in our village. Once a bad-tempered old man with a habit of swearing loudly and frequently, he was now one of the most joy-filled people I have ever met, and all because of a remarkable encounter with God in his cell one night.

Those Thursday evenings were the high spot of the week as about a dozen of us met to read the Bible and pray. Because we all came from such different backgrounds, we enjoyed discovering the many important areas where we agreed. Mrs Burton's incredible knowledge of the Bible, gained by eighty years of close study, amazed Brother Tom – while she was equally intrigued by his accounts of what the Lord said to him while he cooked in the monastery kitchen.

15

'Surely, God only speaks to us through His scriptures,' Mrs Burton said one night. 'You talk as if He chatted to you all day long,' she added rather wistfully.

'So He does, dear Mrs Burton,' replied the old monk, his eyes twinkling. 'He would never contradict His holy scriptures, but why should He not speak to me direct, as I can speak to Him?' The two of them had many heated arguments about speaking in tongues and the Virgin Mary, but they both loved the Lord they recognised in one another.

During a quiet period of prayer that particular Thursday evening, I was startled to hear Brother Tom speaking my name. I had told no one except the Lord and my black diary about the fears I had faced that week, but suddenly Brother Tom said, 'Jen, the Lord tells me to say that you are released from your fear!'

I was overcome with relief and joy. So I wasn't going to die after all. It had just been a test to see if I did trust God in death as well as life. I could live on to a ripe old age, and knit for my grandchildren. Looking back now, I realise that was not what Brother Tom told me. I was released from my *fear* of death only, and I was certainly released from that. 'Through his death he might destroy the Devil . . . and in this way set free those who were slaves all their lives because of their fear of death' (Heb. 2: 14–15).

Later that evening something else rather special happened. I suddenly found myself saying something that I had not thought out beforehand. It just came into my mind as I went along. I suppose it was a prophecy, but we usually left that kind of thing to Brother Tom! I wrote it down as soon as I got home. Because I wrote it at a time in my life when I was utterly happy and fulfilled – and yet it has such meaning for me in the light of what has happened since – I would like to copy it down here:

February 1982
    I am training a special people to be my companions throughout eternity, to be my heart's delight and joy. You

will be able to praise and worship me so easily when you see me face to face, but I need you to learn how to do it now, down here. I do not want automatic praise which costs nothing. I want you to learn to praise me when you are depressed, downtrodden, being tempted or not having your prayers answered. That is when your praise and worship mean something to me. Learn it now, it will matter in eternity. I did not promise you ease and comfort. Remember that the more difficulties you have now, the more real Heaven will become to you. All I want is to live in you and use your body, personality and circumstances to show my reality and power.

I did not realise that night that God was gently and kindly trying to prepare me for what was to come; almost to explain His reasons for allowing it. I tucked the piece of paper away in a drawer where it lay forgotten for two years. It did not seem significant to me then. I was not 'depressed or downtrodden' and life was fun. I could not see why things could not be pleasant down here *and* in Heaven. Surely a God of Love could arrange that. If only I had stuck that paper up on the wall I could have saved myself so many hours of doubt and misery and God Himself the pain of my misunderstanding Him.

By the following Thursday, I had gone down with a violent attack of flu. Well, not exactly 'gone down with' because mothers of six children are so important that they never 'go down with' anything – or so I thought. If I had possessed a thermometer it would probably have registered around 104 degrees, but no way was I going to miss a precious Thursday House Group meeting. Anyway it was the only time in the week when Tony and I went out, just the two of us. I did feel a bit guilty spreading all my germs round that precious little collection of people, so I sucked antiseptic sweets, and sat as far away as possible from old Mrs Burton. But my conscience pricked me so badly that when Brian, our pastor, broke into a time of prayer by saying, 'I feel there is someone here who

needs prayer for healing,' I did not want to admit to having
flu. Anyway, I hate the embarrassment of 'being prayed for'
in public.

But my sneezes and coughs gave me away and soon
Brother Tom and Dr Jordan were firmly laying hands on me.
I actually felt my body temperature dropping, and even my
streaming nose dried up.

How wonderfully powerful God is, I thought. He said we
could pick up snakes without being bitten, and we don't even
have to suffer flu.

I felt so well I stayed up half the night! But the next
morning I felt dreadful. I had read enough books on healing
to know that when you have been prayed for, you *are* healed
even if the symptoms still remain.

I must *hold on to my healing*, I told myself firmly as I went
down to cook the breakfast bacon. This is only a test of faith.
I only *feel* ill – really I'm living in health.

All that day I stalked round the house confessing that I
was well. I had just read the book by Dr Paul Yongai Cho,
*The Fourth Dimension*. What you say with your lips becomes a
reality in your life. However by teatime I felt awful and my
faith (and temper) were failing badly.

As I perched on the side of the bath watching Richard
(four) and Duncan (six) splashing happily in the steam and
bubbles I felt still more confused. Tony and I had come to
believe firmly in the supernatural power of God to heal the
sick. As Duncan sailed his boat round the treacherous waters
of the bath, I remembered that it was only a miracle of
healing that had saved his life five years before when the
doctors could do no more for him. When you see something
like that in your own family experience you cannot possibly
doubt the reality of it. Yes, we knew then, and we know now,
that God still heals.

At that time I was also convinced that it is never God's will
for one of His children to be ill, yet that flu just would not go
away. The sore throat stayed for three months. My arms and
legs ached incessantly and became increasingly weak, while

the pain in my head and eyes spread down my neck and spine.

'I am well, I am well, I am well!' I repeated as the Easter holidays arrived. I so love having the children and all their friends around the place, and the time of year is so busy in the garden, that there is just no time to be ill. It never entered my head to go to the doctor. Tony and I didn't bother much about illness; we thought that if you pretend you are not ill, you find one day that you aren't any more. Anyway, I was quite sure that most of the ill people I knew were only hypochondriacs wanting extra attention.

It was not that we disapproved of doctors. It was just that we were such an irritatingly healthy family, we rarely needed one, and believing in God's gift of healing I should have felt like a hypocrite dashing to the doctor before I had given God time to work. So instead of a visit to the surgery I steeped myself in tapes and books on healing.

When I became so giddy that I began falling flat on my face, the children thought it was a huge joke.

'Don't you dare tell Daddy about this,' I would say firmly, knowing that if he guessed how ill I really felt he would probably ring the doctor at once. Tony is a marvellously tolerant man and very easy to live with because he never seems to notice things. I'm sure that if I dyed my hair pink he would make no comment!

'Christians do not need to have problems,' boomed a well-known preacher's voice from my cassette player, as I struggled to wash up the dishes. 'Jesus said we could remove mountains by faith. The problems in our lives can seem like mountains, but we can all be problem-free people, perpetually living life to the full.' A cup fell from my hand, which was beginning to feel oddly numb, and shattered on the kitchen floor. 'Where am I going wrong?' I sniffed, as I fumbled awkwardly to pick up the pieces.

When Eunja came over for coffee I unleashed all my confusion upon her.

'You're doing too much,' she said in her forthright way,

'being a Sunday school teacher and dashing round speaking at coffee mornings. Why don't you just settle down and enjoy being a mother, instead of using up your energy doing Christian work outside the family? While they are so young they must be your number-one spiritual responsibility, so enjoy them – you'll only have them for such a short time.'

Perhaps she was right, but if that was all God wanted me to do, why did I have this burning desire to tell people about Jesus, and do some great work for Him? Could He not give me the supernatural energy to do both jobs? But soon I began to realise that I was becoming too ill to do either!

As I attacked the tide mark round the bath one morning, I experienced a devastating feeling of panic as I realised my body was just not under my control any longer. At that 'happy' moment the door bell rang – it was Rosemary from up the lane, a leading light in the local Red Cross. She watched in silence as I struggled to make us some coffee and then demanded, 'Why for Pete's sake don't you go to the doctor?'

'I don't like to bother him,' I protested. 'Anyway, I had a lifetime's share of the medical profession when I was younger.' Pride (and I believe it was pride by this time) comes before a fall, and as I jumped up to answer the phone the vertigo was so severe I fell flat on my nose at her feet.

'That does it!' she said indignantly. 'I'm coming tomorrow morning to take you up to the surgery.'

I knew I was very ill by then and needed proper help quickly, but I still felt God wanted to heal me without bothering the National Health Service. So when Tony came home I said, 'You know that bit in James 5 about he that is sick calling the elders to pray for him?'

'Yes,' answered Tony from behind the *Daily Telegraph*.

'Well,' I continued, 'do you think you could ask Brian,' – our Pastor – 'to pop round and pray for me? I haven't felt really well for months.' The *Telegraph* collapsed like the walls of Jericho. After years of being surrounded by so many

20

children and so much activity, we had almost lost the art of talking to one another and we were certainly both ostriches when it came to ignoring anything unpleasant.

'Why ever didn't you tell me?' he enquired. 'I'll go and ring him at once.'

But Brian was in London and his wife promised he'd come the following evening. Next morning in the doctor's waiting room, I really did feel I was going to waste his time. I was so totally convinced that when Brian came everything would be all right, that when the doctor told me to go straight home to bed and not to move until he came to see me the following day, I felt a terrible fraud. Brian was coming that evening, so I'd probably be out digging the garden when the doctor arrived.

But Brian did not come. He was unavoidably detained in London and rang to say he'd come the following morning. None of us knew there was any need for urgency. I also believe that God actually prevented him from coming at that stage. It's as if God sometimes allows things to get worse for His own purposes, which we can't understand at the time. When Jesus took so long to reach Bethany in John 11, was it so that a greater miracle might be done?

That last evening that I was to have at home for so many months has lodged in my mind like a video recording. Naomi, who was then nine, and Richard cuddled into my bed and I read aloud *Rainbow Garden* by Patricia St John. Something odd was happening to my speech, and I sounded as if I had drunk several glasses of whisky. But they did not seem to mind, and I felt Richard's little warm body relax as he fell asleep in mid-chapter. Duncan, a hyperactive six-year-old, was far from warm and cuddly, and insisted on using my bed as a trampoline. At last my head would stand it no longer, and Sarah, our eldest daughter who at fourteen was very much my deputy, marched him firmly off to bed. At ten o'clock our son Justyn, then thirteen, padded into my room with the portable television. The Falklands war was at its height, and he and I had watched every news bulletin, but with a great feeling of guilt because Tony is a pacifist and did not approve of our patriotic fervour.

In the middle of the night the pain in my head and spine was so appalling I could not keep it from Tony any longer.

'I think you've got encephalitis again,' he said, and his voice sounded strange and thin through the darkness. I realised suddenly that it had not only been pride or faith which had delayed my visit to the doctor. It was buried fear. All the strange sensations I had been experiencing were not new to me. They were like the repeat of a horror film I had seen nearly twenty years before.

## Chapter Two

Tony and I first met in the early sixties through my father. He was Tom Rees, and he worked full time as an evangelist, travelling around the country telling people about God. At that time the Beatles and the Rolling Stones were at their height, and my younger brother Justyn was 'Stonestruck', and had just bought himself an electric guitar. He had a good singing voice and began to compose his own songs about God which he and I used to sing together raucously while we helped with the washing up.

'Why don't you two form a group to sing at the young people's rallies in the winter?' Father suggested. Not a very revolutionary idea you might think in these days when guitars are almost as common in churches as organs are. It wasn't like that twenty-five years ago. After our first performance in the City Temple Church, Holborn, Father received shoals of letters from shocked Christians, outraged by the sacrilege.

'It would not have been so bad,' wrote one vicar's wife, 'if they had used wooden guitars, but all those wires and amplifiers!' The drums were too shocking for her even to mention.

Father was a very wise man, and replied, 'We must move with the times. Young people today are far more likely to listen to someone telling them about God if they hold a guitar in their hands.'

There were six of us, five boys and me, and we called ourselves the Peacemakers. Tony was one of them, and it was a case of hate at first sight. We loathed each other.

Not all the Christian world disapproved of us, and although we were one of the first groups of its kind we were soon being asked all over the country to lead youth services, Christian Union meetings, Sunday school anniversaries and even weekend missions.

Our parents were both well-known preachers, and I'm sure Justyn and I only got the invitations because our name was also Rees. But we were painfully aware that the ability to speak in public is not necessarily handed on in our genes, and we were both shy, diffident people with no great personalities to project as our parents had. The group had been formed simply to accompany singing, but suddenly we found we were both expected to preach to packed churches or even town halls. We were scarcely out of our teens and both suffered from massive inferiority complexes, because we constantly compared ourselves to our gifted parents.

'I can't stand up in front of a church full of people and tell them about God,' I protested to the first vicar who had invited us to his church. 'I'm much too shy.'

'Just open your mouth, and let Him do the talking,' he replied simply.

That night was probably the most important of my whole life until then. I could feel God standing behind me using my voice to tell people that He loved them and wanted to make them happy and whole. I could see as I looked at their faces that they were responding to God. It was not me talking: I could feel the power of God surging through me. Labelled as 'backward' at school because of undiagnosed dyslexia, I had withdrawn into a private world of failure. Suddenly I realised that God did not only use superstars like my parents, he could even use *me*, and I knew that all I wanted to do for the rest of my life was to stand and watch God at work.

The three years that followed were the most hectically enjoyable years of our lives. We were all working or studying in the London area. Tony was at teacher training college, Justyn was doing hotel management, and I had a job in a nursery school. I can't think how they ever managed to pass any exams, because we met up most evenings to pray and practise and then set off every Friday afternoon to travel anywhere in the land, wedged into our ghastly old van between the amplifiers and drums.

Sometimes we slept on newspapers and other times we were entertained like royalty, but each weekend we saw God changing people's lives.

Tony and I argued and quarrelled all the way until we realised we could not manage without one another. It dawned on me that being a housewife and even a mother need not prevent me becoming what I most wanted to be – an evangelist.

Somehow, in all the happy rush of life, we never found time to buy an engagement ring. Then suddenly one evening when we were setting up our musical equipment the world began to swirl around me, and a few days later I was in the National Hospital with viral encephalitis.

Practically unable to speak, see or move I lay wondering how Tony would feel about me now. Many young men would have fled, but he strode firmly down the ward full of people in wheelchairs, and said, 'Until we manage to buy that engagement ring, I want you to keep this instead,' and taking the cuff link out of his shirt he put it into my hand, closing my limp fingers around it. If I lost my engagement ring today, I'd be quite cross, but if anything ever happened to that cuff link, I'd be heartbroken.

His love gave me the will to live and his encouragement helped me to fight the effects of the disease – which is an inflammation of the brain. It took two years of determined effort to get completely well, but finally we were married in 1966 and with our travelling days behind us we settled down to life in the Hertfordshire village of Sarratt. I shelved my ideas of becoming an evangelist, and tried to force myself into the mould of a perfect housewife.

'But you can't have encephalitis twice surely?' I protested, as I tried to make myself swallow the cup of tea Tony had kindly made me long before first light.

25

'Viruses can lie dormant in the body for years,' he replied gloomily, 'and then just flare up again. Look at your symptoms – they're much the same as last time.'

I'm not going to have encephalitis again, I told myself firmly. After all, the healing ministry was almost as unusual as guitars in those days. Brian had promised to call that morning, before going on holiday, so he just *had* to make it before the doctor. I felt it was my last chance, but the doctor came first, and I heard him and Tony making serious noises in the room below.

'We're getting you into hospital, Mrs Larcombe,' the doctor told me brightly. 'Just for some tests.'

'I know,' I replied crossly, 'a lumbar puncture, thanks for nothing.' He was a very nice man really. It was not his fault he was a doctor!

It was not a playgroup morning, and we felt Richard might be upset seeing me whisked away in an ambulance, so Tony took him off with him to work, and I felt quite alone and rather frightened as the ambulance lurched along the country lanes I loved so much. I had missed Brian by half an hour.

As the mother of so many energetic children, I had spent hours in the casualty department of the Kent and Sussex Hospital with endless scalds, cuts, broken bones and even a small tummy full of junior aspirin. But there were no long hours of queueing for me that day, and as I was whisked through the corridors on a trolley I thought how funny people looked upside down!

'You can always squeeze something to laugh at out of every situation,' my grandmother used to tell me, but as I was abandoned in a lonely little cubicle to wait for the doctor, my sense of humour deserted me. I cursed myself for forgetting to pull something out of the freezer for the children's tea, and remembering that the first thing they all do as they come in is shout 'Mum!' I wondered how they would feel when they got no reply.

'Lord, let them remember You're there with them,' I

implored, 'and help me to do the same.' Suddenly that tiny room was totally full of His presence. It was as if He took the whole load of all my worries and poured His peace into the hole where they had been. I lay there smiling up at Him – positively basking in His nearness.

Opening my eyes suddenly, I saw looking down at me the most beautiful pair of grey eyes I have ever seen. They seemed to be floating above a medical white coat, but surely no one with a smile like that could possibly be a doctor! He was Polish, and even if I could remember his name I would never be able to spell it. It took hours to piece together my medical history, but he never became impatient when I got muddled or ran out of breath. He was just about the only doctor I had ever known who treated me like a sane human being, and explained what he was doing as he examined me. Finally he sat down beside me and said, rather as one might discuss the weather, 'I think you have an inflammation of the brain, and the fluid round it, which goes down your spinal column. I think the casings of your nerves are also inflamed, and the lining of your heart, and you have probably got some clots in your lungs. Does all that worry you?'

I am quite sure it would have, before God had cushioned me with that supernatural peace. Many people had told me before about that special grace He gives His children in sudden crises, but He never gives it in advance, so we only fully believe it as we experience it. He had taken away my worries so I could quite genuinely reply, 'No, I'm not frightened at all, because I am sure God knows what He's doing.'

He leant forward, suddenly interested. 'You believe in God then?' he asked almost wistfully.

'Oh yes,' I replied. 'What about you?'

'I did once, and I loved Him deeply – my parents are devout Catholics, but since I began my medical training I've seen so much suffering, I don't feel so sure any more.

'Anyway,' he continued, standing up rather suddenly,

'We've got plenty of time to talk about that later. I'm sending you up to the ward now, and when I've had my tea, I'll come and give you a lumbar puncture.'

I knew from bitter experience that having a needle stuck into your spine to tap the spinal fluid is not a pleasant experience, but that lumbar puncture was almost enjoyable compared to the first one, many years before, because that young doctor just could not stop talking about God – quite regardless of the two nurses who were assisting him.

'What possible reason could God have for letting you be here like this, with all those children at home missing you?' he demanded as he stuck extravagant quantities of sticking plaster all over my back.

'I don't know yet,' I replied with as much dignity as someone in that position could muster. 'But I'll tell you when we meet in Heaven.'

It was supposed to be a feeble attempt at a joke, but he stood looking down at me very searchingly before he said, 'Lie flat and don't move for twenty-four hours,' and he was off down the ward, leaving me with nothing to do but to pray for him.

Naturally Tony could not come and see me that night, he was far too busy putting everyone to bed, but the Lord sent me the only other person I really wanted to see just then – my brother Justyn. I nearly died of surprise when he appeared beside my bed. I had not expected to see him again for years. He was just leaving to take on a church in Canada, and we had said our tearful goodbyes some days before. Within two minutes of his arrival he had me laughing and he had brought me something very precious: a card from our cousin Max Sinclair.

A few years before, Max had broken his neck in a car crash, and had spent many weary months in Stoke Mandeville patiently regaining some use of his limbs. Justyn read me what he had written: 'Sue and I just want you to know we're praying for you. We know only *too well* what you and Tony are going through just now. The next seven days are going to be tough, but here's a verse to help you through. We've broken it down into a tiny phrase for each day.

> 'Fear thou not
> For I am with thee
> Be not afraid
> for I am thy God
> I will help thee
> yea I will uphold thee
> with the right hand of my righteousness
> (Isa. 41: 10 AV).'

I got through the next week simply by repeating the tiny phrase for each day, over and over again. I was far too ill to cope with long passages of scripture or even whole verses, but I could cling to three or four words. How well Max understood that.

After Justyn had gone, I lay holding the little card for a long time, thinking about Max, and a great feeling of shame spread over me. Clearly I remember the day he had his accident, and we heard he was completely paralysed. How angry I had been! We were on holiday in Devon and I had stamped up and down the cliff tops raging at God. How could He let a thing like that happen to Max who had given up his career to serve the Lord full time at Hildenborough Hall? 'What a useless waste!' I stormed.

But it had not been a waste, and I realised how much more God had been able to use Max since his accident. Because he knows what it feels like to suffer, people with many kinds of problems feel they can trust him, and when he tells them about Jesus they listen in a way they might never have done when he was fit and healthy. His love and prayers meant so much to me that night simply because he did understand.

'Sorry, Lord,' I whispered, and I wish I could say that I drifted peacefully off to sleep. But pain in my head and back reached a terrifying level, and I bit my tongue so hard it bled. Across the ward a woman was having a violent attack of asthma and making a great deal of fuss. None of the nurses took any notice, probably for some very good reason, but it seemed to me quite useless to ask for help, as no one would care.

'Lord, send someone to help me!' I pleaded. In my semi-conscious state I had no idea of the time, but when it seemed like the middle of the night, I suddenly found the Polish doctor standing by my bed.

'I thought you might be feeling a bit uncomfortable,' he smiled.

'How did you know?' I asked.

'God must have told me.' Was he mocking me? I didn't really care, for my opinion of doctors reached an all-time high as he stuck a needle full of heroin and morphine into my arm.

Next day, I think I must have been much worse. They moved me into a darkened side ward because I could not stand any light, movement or sound. The next thing I remember is a night nurse trying to make me drink some tea out of a cup with a plastic spout, and saying brightly, 'It's Sunday morning.' Sunday meant church to me, and I felt so lonely for all our Christian friends. Then I remembered that hospitals have chaplains who bring round communion. That would be so lovely, but he would probably only go into the main ward. He would never find me in this dark little cupboard. Desperately I prayed, 'Lord please work a miracle, let the chaplain come in here.'

I had hardly finished praying that when a very dear and familiar face floated over my bed. Of course! George Swannell who had been our friend for many years was chaplain of the Kent and Sussex! He is more like Jesus than any other man I know; in fact during muddled moments during the next few weeks, I often mistook him for Jesus himself as he sat by my bed, sometimes for hours on end.

His view of illness was quite different from many of my friends'. He was often quoting Samuel Rutherford, who lived some three hundred years ago and did not seem to feel that illness was a sin or a work of Satan when he said, 'Blessed is the fever that fetcheth Christ to the bedside.'

Christ certainly came to my bedside that Sunday morning, wearing George's body.

It must be terribly easy to think that people who look unconscious cannot actually hear what is going on around them. Actually they can, and I am sure I heard far more than people intended I should. Over the next week the virus that was causing the inflammation was gradually winning, as one by one my body's systems went out of action. Tubes were pushed into all kinds of embarrassing places. My arms and legs wouldn't go where I wanted to put them, and I couldn't see because the darkened room spun round. Soon I began to have difficulty in swallowing even soup and fruit juice through the plastic spouts. I kept forgetting how to breathe and gasped in terror like a fish on a marble slab. They put cot sides up round my bed because of convulsions, and I was convinced they piled goats, geese and turkeys into this 'cage' with me. In spite of these hallucinations, part of my brain remained totally clear and alert to everything and everyone around me. I was literally hanging on until Brian came back from holiday. Then I knew all would be well.

31

## Chapter Three

In comparison with what Tony was going through, I was having a holiday. It is always far harder to watch the illness of someone you love than to be ill yourself. He longed to be with me, and I needed him, but he had the awesome responsibility of so many children. He did not go to work for the first week, and he also had the support of my brother and his wife Joy who, bless them, delayed their flight to Canada.

But he had to make plans for rather a bleak future. His job as a teacher adviser not only takes him to schools all over Kent, but also to places as far away as Devon and Scotland. He needed reliable cover for his absences. Countless people offered to take some or all the children off his hands, but he had been a teacher long enough to know that children cope better in a crisis in their own familiar surroundings and routine. He tried to be father and mother rolled into one, as well as visiting me, so he constantly felt torn in two, and the phone never stopped ringing.

Naturally my friends and relations wanted a daily progress report and they wanted to talk to Tony himself. It was only their loving concern which prompted them to ring, but every time a bedtime story reached its climax or the fish fingers went into the pan, the phone rang, and Tony had to go over the same depressing details which lowered his spirits a notch every time.

Many people rang to say, 'Tell us what we can do to help.' How often I have done that in the past. But Tony was suffering from shock and he says his mind just used to blank out. He knew he needed help badly, but he just could not think what help to ask for. 'Well, just ring when you think of something,' people would say. Strangely, when you are in the middle of a crisis you hardly ever do that. You either feel you will be a burden or you are so paralysed by shock you cannot pluck up the mental energy.

Everyone reacts differently to stress. Some people need friends around them all the time, and constant phone calls reassure them, while others can only cope in privacy. Tony is the private sort. Our little church longed to surround him by physical and tangible expressions of their love and concern, but he just could not bring himself to go to church. The singing and sympathy made him feel emotional. I was visited by one well-meaning lady weeks later who said, 'What a pity your husband has lost his faith, we haven't seen him in church since you left home.'

Actually Tony's faith deepened and matured greatly, but he needed to be left alone. Perhaps we expect other people to react to a crisis in the way we would ourselves, and it is easy to be baffled, hurt or even shocked when they seem to need a different kind of help. I am sure the Lord can and does give us wisdom to know what people need when we ask Him specifically.

Tony became more and more independent, and sensing people's disapproval, he withdrew further and further into his shell. The friends who helped him the most were the ones who just did things without being asked. For many weeks Grace, a busy house mistress at a nearby boarding school, 'broke' into our house each morning and scooped up from the floors, beds and drawers all the dirty washing, returning it next day, washed, ironed and prayed over. Several people deposited whole meals on the doorstep, foil-wrapped and complete with vegetables and gravy; such a lovely change from fish fingers! Some people would arrive unexpectedly and take the children off for a picnic or a trip to the sea. If they had rung the day before, the children, who had become rather clingy, might not have been brave enough to commit themselves.

Poor Tony also had to cope with Janie who reacted to my absence by rejecting him utterly, and withdrawing from the family into her own little icy world. She would not even address a remark to him and would say, 'Sarah, will you ask Dad to pass me the salt?' Many men would have been baffled and frustrated by that, but Tony realised that Janie had been hurt too many times, and was just protecting herself from future pain.

Tony longed to shield the children from as much suffering as possible, so he did not tell them how ill I really was. Recently both the two older ones, Sarah and Justyn, told me how angry and hurt they felt because of that.

'Dad just kept saying, "Mum's fine, everything's all right," but we could feel he was keeping things from us,' said Justyn, while Sarah commented, 'If only Dad had got us all together and told us straight out every single thing we would have felt safer and been able to help him more.'

It is so easy to look back and think what people should or should not have done. When you are drowning, you have to keep swimming hard and there is no time to think about psychology. Perhaps Richard and Janie could not have coped with straight talking like that, even if the others would have felt happier knowing the truth. Probably children are like adults and only the Lord can show us how to treat them in the individual way that they each need.

When I had been in hospital for just over a week I discovered a very important doctor hanging over the side of my cot. I guessed he must be important because he wasn't wearing a white coat!

'We've decided to move you to a hospital in London, Mrs Larcombe,' he shouted. (Why do they always shout? Just because a person is ill or foreign does not mean he is deaf!) 'They have more advanced equipment up there,' he added.

'All right,' I grunted. 'But get this goat off my legs.' He turned and said something to Sister that I was never intended to hear: 'We're probably too late to move this one,' and for the first time since Brother Tom's pronouncement in

34

February, I remembered I was supposed to be going to die. But I had been definitely released from the fear of death, and I felt nothing but joy at the prospect.

All that day I felt life slipping away behind me, rather as the land recedes when you float out to sea in a boat. But there was something I knew I had to do urgently. Tony must not feel guilty about marrying again, but when he came to visit me I was not brave enough to bring up the subject. So, with the help of a friend I wrote that pre-planned letter to him, and gave it to George, saying, 'I'm off to Heaven, can you give this to Tony when I get there?'

'I certainly will!' he replied with a beaming smile. How often we can rob people of the joy of looking forward to Heaven. George looked really pleased for me, but he told me weeks later that the letter felt like lead in his pocket for days.

They gave me a nurse all to myself that day, and Sister and the Polish doctor seemed to be constantly in the room. I felt so safe and cared for, the last thing I wanted was a trip to London the next day. The pain was so ghastly that even the thought of moving was terrible and to leave my dark room and face the daylight would be shattering. I profoundly hoped I would die in the night! But long after visiting time was over, suddenly there was Brian with his wife Penny. They had dashed home from their holiday, straight to the hospital. Sister herself showed them in; I suppose she thought they had come to bring the last rites!

'I'm going to Heaven,' I managed to say.

'We know that,' Brian replied gently, 'but we've come to pray for you. I'm not sure how to pray, so I'm just going to start, and see what happens.'

I still don't know how he prayed; all I could hear was his voice as he and Penny sat either side of my cage holding my hands through the bars. His voice grew fainter and fainter as I began to have difficulty in breathing.

So this is what dying is like, I thought as I began to float above the bed. The pain was stopping at last, and suddenly over my left foot at the end of the bed a soft gentle light began to glow. I knew it could not be in the room because it did not hurt my eyes – nothing hurt any more. It was the entrance to Heaven, and I could not wait to get inside! God was there waiting for me, and any minute now I would see Him face to face. And then He spoke to me.

'What do you want me to do for you, Jen?' This was not quite what I had expected. Before me lay all the freedom and glory of Heaven, the Lord Himself, and so many other people I loved. Back down in the darkness behind me was pain and discomfort.

'I'm too tired to choose, Lord,' I said fretfully. But He seemed to be waiting, and through the darkness I saw Tony and the children standing in a little group.

'Well,' I said rather ungraciously, 'if you're giving me the choice, I suppose I had better go back to be with them.'

Very gently, He said, 'Very well, from this moment you will begin to go back. It is going to be a struggle, *but I will give you my strength*.'

Suddenly I could hear Brian's voice again still praying on, and I interrupted him rather rudely.

'It's all right now, you can stop praying. It's all been done, I'm healed.'

'Amen,' finished Brian hurriedly, and they kissed me good night and went home. Later that week I dictated a description of all that happened that night to my friend Rhoda and months later I stuck it into my black book.

How wonderful that Brian had been prevented from coming until I had been allowed the privilege of looking right into Heaven. I know now that I shall never again be afraid of dying – it is the loveliest thing that can happen to a Christian: total, utter and complete healing.

When Brian and Penny had gone, I felt desolated. Heaven never seemed further away. I was convinced that God had healed me, but the pain was back, and tomorrow was only a few hours away. If the healing was not going to be instant I felt I would rather not have had it at all.

It might just have been the hallucinations, but I felt

36

horribly conscious of the powers of evil that night. They seemed to surround my cot – above me and below, angry, menacing, vengeful. Wherever was God, I wondered, as I lay shaking in terror. Suddenly a white shape loomed over the bars. It seemed to have no head, but it spoke to me.

'Mrs Larcombe, are you afraid?'

'Yes, very,' I squeaked, 'but you can't hurt me, I belong to Jesus.'

'That's great, so do I!' and a large, strong and very human hand gripped mine. The dim light from the porthole in the door revealed that the apparition was only a white coat worn by a very tall black man.

'My name is Mr Jones, and I am the Senior Nursing Officer,' he told me. 'I am in charge of this hospital tonight, and I came to tell you I shall be taking special care of you. As I walk round the wards and corridors, I want you to remember I shall be praying for you, all through the night.'

I shall never know if it was the beginning of the healing process or Mr Jones's prayers, but I never had another hallucination – no, not one single goat. Just when I thought God had deserted me, He sent along one of His most special servants to reassure me.

Long before the night staff went off duty, Tony crept unnoticed into my room. He had not been able to sleep either, and had spent the time digging around in Philippians.

'Look what I've found!' he said gleefully. It had blessed him so much that he had decided to make the twenty-mile round trip to Tunbridge Wells to share it with me before the children woke up. 'For you have been given the privilege of serving Christ, not only by believing in Him, but also by suffering for Him . . . Your life in Christ makes you strong – that's your bit, Jen, and this bit's for me – and his love comforts you' (Phil. 1: 29, 2: 1).

'We've had such fun serving the Lord together, haven't we?' he went on. 'In the Peacemakers, at church and with the children. All that was so much easier than serving Him in this way, but it's just as important to Him.'

Of course I could not read the verses he was showing me, but he underlined them so hard in my Good News Bible I can't miss them now. We held hands, and thanked God together for these lovely little gifts to us both.

'Serving Him has been fun,' I said as he sat quietly beside me. 'But *knowing* Him is more important. I wish I knew Him better.' That sent Tony rummaging further into Philippians 3: 10: 'All I want is to know Christ and to experience the power of His resurrection and to share in his sufferings.'

I did not have much breath, and words were still very hard to bring out, but I told Tony as best I could that the evening before I had really experienced the power of His resurrection. But we could not understand what sharing in His suffering really meant. Later that day I began to understand.

Before he left Tony gave me a pair of extra-dark glasses to help me through the journey, then the door swung closed behind him as he dashed home to get the children up and off to school. But I really did not have time to miss him, I was so completely surrounded by love and care. My own nurse gave me an extra-special blanket bath and packed my few belongings into a grey polythene bag.

'Don't worry about the journey,' she said. 'I'll be coming in the ambulance with you.'

The Polish doctor came in, full of enthusiasm for the visit to this country of the Pope, which was just finishing. Not only had it inspired his Roman Catholicism, but it had restored his faith in Jesus Christ.

'Don't worry about the journey,' he said. 'I've laid on a special modern ambulance for you – so smooth you won't know you're moving.'

I had to laugh when Sister came in at that moment and said, 'Don't worry about the journey, I'm going to give you a huge injection just before you leave.'

I was so spoilt and cosseted, I never realised it was going to be the worst day of my life.

## Chapter Four

The neurological department of the large teaching hospital where I was taken is famous throughout the world for its high standards, but everyone can have an off day, and I just happened to arrive on one of them. The ward was divided into glass cubicles, and the first thing I remember was piercing light attacking me from all four sides at once. My own nurse was gone and in her place, writing at a small table, sat a female dragon in a white doctor's coat.

'Please,' I whispered hoarsely, 'would you mind drawing the curtains?'

'No,' she replied shortly, 'I have a great many notes to make and I can't write in the dark.' I thanked God for the small help of Tony's dark glasses and gritted my teeth.

'Come along now, Mrs Larcombe, wake up!' she rasped in a hectoring tone, 'we've got work to do.' The Polish doctor had asked me all the same questions but had left me still feeling like a human being. After an hour with her, I was reduced to the status of an imbecile animal. She bullied, shouted and banged the table in exasperation when I got muddled over the dates of my pregnancies – even in full health it's hard to remember so many! The more she cross-examined and accused the more stupid I became, as I tried to keep telling myself she must have had a row with her boyfriend or been on duty far too long. But over the next few days I heard her shouting at elderly and often simple-minded patients, some of whom were immigrants with very little English, so perhaps it was just her particular bedside manner.

'I am going to examine you now,' she said. 'So take off those ridiculous glasses and open your eyes when I'm talking to you.' Sister had packed my ears that morning with wads of cotton wool to keep out the pain of sound, but with a revolted snort she pulled them out and threw them on to the floor.

'Follow this pin as I move it,' she shouted. But I could see two pins at least.

'How many fingers am I holding up?' I felt even she could not have eight on one hand! Then she discovered my plastered back.

'What sort of an imbecile put all this stuff on?' she roared, and as she ripped it off I felt like Poor Old Michael Finnigin in Richard's nursery rhyme book, who 'took off half a yard of skin (agin!)'. But when she finally tripped over my catheter bag, she really lost her cool.

'Staff Nurse!' she bellowed. 'Come and take this ridiculous thing out at once. Mrs Larcombe will use a bedpan or else . . .' The staff nurse – who I later learned was deeply concerned about this woman – replied coldly, 'Only the night staff remove catheters in this ward, Doctor.'

'Well, I've a good mind to yank it out myself,' she replied, and stormed off to Sister's office. I was told later in the week she had put her feet up on Sister's desk and said, 'Well, that one's for the cabbage patch for sure,' meaning I was so hopelessly brain damaged, I would never be any good again. It was only her first term in neurology, and how was she to know the Lord was beginning to heal me?

I sighed with relief, thinking she had gone for good, and it was then that I realised how wildly thirsty I was. I had been so frightened of being sick all over the ambulance that I had purposely not had anything to drink that day, and as swallowing had been difficult the day before, it was probably over twenty-four hours since I had had a sip of any liquid. Suddenly my tormentor was back.

'They are ready for you in the EEG department, so we're sending you straight down there for an electroencephalogram.

After that you'll go straight for a brain scan and then a chest X-ray.'

'Please,' I begged, 'could I have a drink of water first?' She looked annoyed and glanced at my locker. 'They haven't been round with the water jugs yet,' she snapped, 'and we can't keep the technicians waiting. They're very busy, so you'll have to wait.'

I managed to make no comment, but then to my horror I saw a wheelchair being pushed through the door. When you have done nothing but lie completely flat and still for nearly two weeks, even sitting in a comfortable armchair for a few minutes is a great shock to the system, but this was no comfortable armchair! The steel back bit into my painful spine and there was nothing to support my head which lolled about ridiculously.

'Please,' I begged, 'couldn't I go on a trolley?'

'Trolleys take two porters,' she replied firmly, 'and we're very busy today. But we'll send a nurse with you.' The nurse was male and looked very bad-tempered.

All this sounds as if I am grumbling horribly, but actually I learnt more of the pure love of God that terrible day than I had done in thirty-nine years before it, and I could not have learnt some of those lessons any other way.

As we rocketed off down the corridors, up ramps and round corners, the severe vertigo made me feel I was on a speeded-up version of the looping star at Margate fun fair! The pain in my head and spine was quite terrifying, while behind me the porter and nurse chatted away to each other amicably. Had they understood what vertigo is like, they would have supported my flopping head or at least put a hand on my shoulder.

I became aware of someone screaming like an animal in a trap, and was deeply humiliated to discover it was me, who had always prided myself on having five babies without a whiff of gas and air! The men behind me were laughing; I am sure it was at some joke they were sharing, but I felt they were mocking me in my humiliation. Then suddenly before my tightly closed eyes I saw Jesus. He was hanging on the cross. *He* felt totally humiliated as well, mocked by uncaring professionals, hurt by the utter indifference that allowed them to sit and watch Him there (Matt. 27: 36). For the first time ever I realised a tiny fragment of His awful pain, and yes, human terror. I knew He understood just how I felt. He was right there with me in it, minding for me and hurting with me. Then it dawned on me suddenly that He had gone through His worst hours separated from the comfort of His Father's presence, utterly forsaken and alone, because He was not only being punished for my sins, but was actually being blamed for them, and all because He loved me so much.

But *we* never have to face anything this life can throw at us, without His presence and support. When we are really suffering physically or through bereavement, rejection or loss, it does not help to think of Jesus sitting in triumphant ease, enthroned in Heaven. It can almost feel as if He watches us writhe and squirm while going through the nasty trials He has planned to test our faith and build our spiritual character.

'Seeing' Him there on the cross at one of the most horrible moments of my life showed me that when we suffer, He suffers too. Nothing happens to us that does not deeply affect Him as well. It is not just that He remembers His own sufferings – He *feels* ours with us. When we are Christians He lives in our human bodies (I Cor. 6: 19). So naturally He feels every pain and grief with us because we are part of Him, and (incredible thought!) He is part of us.

Naturally I did not think all that out clearly at the time; I was hardly in a fit state for deep theological thoughts! But I have been convinced ever since that because He is so near us in our blackest times, one of the greatest of all the sufferings of the Lord Jesus must be to see people He loves reject Him and turn away from Him when they are hurting and needing Him most.

I can laugh now (but I couldn't then) at the very ordinary

42

prayer that I uttered at such a sublime moment in my life. As I realised I was going to faint and fall forwards out of the wheelchair (pulling all my tubes with me) all I could say to the Lord was, 'Please don't let me lose Tony's sun glasses.' They had become to me then what his cuff link had been nearly twenty years before.

When I came round, crowds of people seemed to be milling around far above my head, poking oxygen masks, stethoscopes and needles at me, while an authoritative voice thundered, 'A patient in this condition should never have been in a wheelchair; fetch a trolley at once.' I had a fleeting glimpse of my male nurse looking crosser than ever. And my dark glasses were gone.

The next thing I clearly remember is lying on a narrow bench having the electrodes glued to my head for the EEG. I had had one nearly twenty years before, so I knew they were quite painless, except for the horrid bit at the end when they flash lights into your eyes to measure how quickly your brain reacts. It was so lovely lying still at last, I might have been happy if I had not felt so thirsty. The technician sat behind a glass partition, but I was conscious of not being alone. Somewhere to my right, I felt the glowering morose presence of the male nurse. During a break in the proceedings, I plucked up all my courage and asked him for a drink of water.

'They don't have any down here,' he snapped. 'Wait until you get back to the ward.'

That could be hours, there were still the brain scan and X-rays. What a perfectly horrid young man! I thought. He shouldn't be a nurse at all! Hating him took my mind off the thirst quite marvellously, but then to my dismay I discovered God had another lesson for me to learn that day. (Life with Him is not always pleasant but it is never boring!) Suddenly I 'saw' the cruel callous soldiers hammering nails into those kind work-worn hands that had never been used for anything but good. How desperate would have been their punishment in eternity for such bestial cruelty, if Jesus had not prayed,

43

'Father forgive them, they know not what they do.' That same Jesus had said earlier, 'Pray for them which despitefully use you' (Matt. 5: 44 AV). He practised what He preached.

'No, Lord, that's going too far,' I said firmly. 'Why should I pray for this vile young man who laughed at me, let me fall out of a wheelchair and can't even be bothered to get me a drink?'

'But he needs you to pray for him.' So (very crossly) I gave in and began to pray, and almost at once I *knew* why he was in such a bad mood. Without really thinking what I was doing I said to him, 'You're very worried about something, aren't you?' He had been slouching in the chair, his head down on his chest, hands deep in the pockets of his white overall, but when I spoke he sat upright, like a puppet jerked by strings.

'How did you know that?' he demanded.

'Well,' I replied nervously, 'God just told me while I was praying for you.' He almost sprang across the room towards me, pouring out a great torrent of words. He *was* desperately worried and frightened about something that was going to happen to him the following day, and he was almost crying as he told me all about it.

'Do you really believe in prayer?' he finished at last.

'Yes, I really do,' I gasped. 'I'll pray for you specially tomorrow, and I *know* God will help you, to prove just how much He cares about you.' As I drifted off into another faint, I remember saying to the Lord, 'I'm trusting You for a miracle – it's Your honour that's at stake.'

High above my head I could see water. A whole cool jug of it. Was it another hallucination, I wondered. No, I was back in the ward, brain scans and X-rays just a dim nightmare I had slept through. The jug stood on the high locker beside my bed. The late afternoon sun blazed at me through the wall which was one huge window, and my glasses were gone. Could it really only have been that morning Tony had given them to me? What a whole world away Tony seemed. My thirst was urgent now; I had to have a drink. But even the

44

male nurse seemed to have gone off duty, and I was far too weak to lift a glass, let alone that jug, even if I could have reached it.

'I'll suck my flannel,' I thought, not caring how soapy it might be. Then I saw my grey bag of possessions far across the other side of the room. Even if they had not had time to unpack it, they might at least have left it within reach. I was much too frightened to ring a bell, even if I found one. Never have I felt so alone, and broken in my life. 'This is a God-forsaken hole,' I muttered. Then a wonderful thing happened. In a hopeless gesture of defeat, my hand flopped against the side of the locker and hit something metal. I did not have much feeling in my fingers, but I knew there was some kind of bracket there. With quite indescribable joy, I realised it contained a little Gideon New Testament. Some Christian member of the Gideon Society had taken the trouble to place it there, and had probably prayed for everyone who would lie in that bed. I fumbled it out of its brass pocket and fell asleep holding it in my arms. I could never have read it, but it represented a tangible proof of the presence of God there with me. I wonder how many other desperate people in prisons, hotels and hospitals throughout the country have been blessed by those Bibles, as I was that day. Above all, it taught me that there is no such thing as a God-forsaken hole.

Some time during that evening I remembered a sermon I had once heard, and had thought was rather silly! The preacher had said that thirst must have been the worst part of the cross for Jesus; the heat of the sun, the salty taste of blood and each breath a gasping effort. When he said, 'I thirst,' it was not like the fretful complaint of a feverish child, but a desperate, agonising need – he was dehydrating.

You have to experience real thirst before it is possible to know how horrible it is. All that I experienced then was only a minor pin-prick in comparision to all His suffering for me, but in my comfortable, protected, happy life I had never really suffered anything. Before that day Jesus had been

45

someone to be served, followed and prayed to, but I never really *knew* Him until I could identify with Him in His humiliation and pain, discovering also that He was identifying with me.

His suffering was voluntary; I had no choice. At any time He had the power to stop that pain, and summon legions of angels to scorch off the face of the earth all the people who hurt Him, mocked Him or ignored Him. Only His faithful steadfast love for me, and sinners like me, kept Him there to the bitter thirsty end.

## Chapter Five

Not often in a lifetime is one woken first thing in the morning by a stark-naked man doing a war dance round the bed! It was my first experience of being in a modern mixed ward, and it certainly made a change from goats and geese. He was hustled away by two sweating night nurses and I later learnt that the poor man had a brain tumour. When he had gone, I could not help wondering what else might befall me that day.

I need not have worried. Sister returned from her holiday and all the confusion of the previous day was forgotten, as she unleashed upon the ward the highest possible standards of care. I was not even allowed to sit up in bed and went for further tests on a trolley. Under her efficiency the world felt safe again, and all the scowling nurses started smiling while their cockney wit was better than any medicine. Even the 'mocking' porter of the day before padded into my room with my sun glasses, which he had found under a radiator. How good the Lord is to care so much about little things. He *did* work a miracle for that male nurse, and we became such good friends, he even brought his wife and baby to wave at me through the glass wall on his day off.

My feelings about mixed wards were – mixed! It is hard enough trying to use a bedpan without being held on one by a man, and when the nice old chap next door died and was rolled away in a huge metal box on wheels by two hilarious porters just before lunch, I secretly hoped he might be replaced by a nice, fully clad female.

47

But it was not a feminine face that I saw beaming at me through the glass when I woke from an afternoon nap. That man just has to be a Christian, I thought. The same idea occurred to him as he saw my Bible lying on the still impossibly high locker. He pointed to it, waved and positively jumped up and down with excitement. However, the beginning of a promising conversation was firmly nipped in the bud by the appearance on his side of the glass of the Female Dragon to take his case history. His face looked like a pricked balloon as it disappeared suddenly from view.

Much later in the evening he paid me a proper visit, looking subdued but not entirely crushed. He had recently had a wonderful new experience of God, after having attended the same very dull church all his life. He was now 'Heaven bent' on turning the whole place upside down, and said with shining eyes, 'Things are really happening now in our church – I never knew being a Christian was supposed to be such fun!' It was so kind of the Lord to bring him with his infectious joy and exuberance.

I told no one about that first terrible day in London (Tony might have been arrested for woman slaughter if I had!) because the next day the Lord told me very definitely that I had to forgive, as an act of will, everyone who had made it so unpleasant, and you cannot forgive unless you also try to forget. That sounds a bit odd when I have written it all down like this, but I learnt so much from that day, it would be less than honest to leave anything out. It was perfectly easy to forgive the porter and male nurse, but every time I heard the rasp of the doctor's voice down the passage, I broke into a cold sweat, and I still have nightmares about her now. Forgiving seems to be impossible for me without God's help, so I started praying for her every day. I think it must be working, because I can laugh about her now, even if my subconscious is still sweating!

The first experience of that glass cubicle might have been hellish but the rest of the time I spent there was nearer to

Heaven than I thought it possible to be while still earth-bound. Justyn brought me a present of a personal stereo so I could listen to tapes of hymns and Christian songs through the earphones. I could not read, but God just reached into my soul through the music. I lay there basking in the presence of God.

I had been brought up in an age when the emphasis was on serving God. Every ounce of strength and each moment of time must go into working for Him. 'Let go and let God' was a scornful way to describe a lazy Christian. Then the worship explosion had hit the church and I found that new and refreshing. It was great to feel all the inhibitions going as the wonderful new church music bathed my soul.

But I could never get away from a deep feeling of doubt. Was this more active form of worship really coming from inside me, or was it something I was supposed to do because everyone else did? Was it becoming just another liturgy most of the time?

What I was experiencing there in hospital was something quite different. It was the source of a river bubbling out of me to meet with God; it was not something I was working up or putting on. I could not have stopped it if I had tried.

It cured one secret fear that I have always had. Being such an active person, I have always had a sneaking feeling I might get terribly bored in Heaven, but I realised once and for all in that cubicle, that eternity itself will not be long enough to enjoy the full loveliness of God.

The news from Tony was better. Mrs Ashman, a Christian friend in the village who had run the playgroup where our children had been so happy, offered to be a stand-in mum for several days a week. Dear old Gom, my old nanny, promised another day a week, and Richard was happy to stay with a friend on the remaining day. He has nothing but happy memories of those months, due, I am sure, to so much prayer and the kindness of Christian people.

But my deep mother-hen instinct needed to be *doing*

49

something for my children, so I felt I should be praying for them. Strangely that is very hard to do when you are ill. People say, 'Aren't you lucky having all that time to lie in bed and read the Bible and pray?' But you cannot concentrate. First I felt guilty about it, then I used to imagine taking each one by the hand in turn, and leading them to the throne of God. I did this frequently throughout the day, watching the clock for their 'vulnerable' times – the hassle of getting off in the morning, dinner break at school, coming home to no mum, and bedtimes. It was such a lovely peaceful wordless way of praying, but some days when the pain was very bad, I could not even manage that much. Then I would just say, 'You pray for them, Jesus.' 'He ever liveth to make intercession' (Heb. 7: 25 AV).

The first Sunday that I was in London, a very wonderful thing happened to me. The chaplain came and gave me communion about eleven in the morning during a gigantic thunderstorm. When he had gone, I was quite overcome by the joy of the Lord. What I did not realise was that all over the country and even across the Atlantic congregations of Christians were praying for me in their Sunday services. How good of them. Mostly they did not even know me, but I have had the privilege of meeting some of them since. As they closed ranks, I was wafted up on the strength of their prayer.

Poor old Eunja, and a friend of hers called Gill, had been fasting for days ever since Eunja heard I was in hospital. She told me she felt personally responsible! That Sunday the Lord told her to stop – all was well.

As I lay there I had a vision. I know it was not just another hallucination like the goats, because it later came true. Rhoda came to see me that afternoon and I got her to write it down for me, and it is now pinned into my black book.

I saw God as a tall strong father striding through a deep dark valley. The rocky walls were so high they almost blocked out the sky. Behind huge menacing boulders lurked evil monsters, waiting for a chance to grab me, but I was perfectly safe, because God was carrying me. I looked like I did when I was about two, golden curls and a pink smocked dress. My chubby arms were round His neck and we were talking and laughing happily together. Green slimy rocks were under His feet, but He never stumbled or dropped me. We were utterly enjoying each other. Then suddenly we came to a small sinister valley leading off the one we were in, and at the entrance stood Satan, mocking me.

'She's just loving all this attention you're giving her,' he sneered. 'You're making it too easy, send her down this valley alone. It's called depression. If she can't feel your presence she'll soon lose her faith.'

The one thing I have always feared is depression. I believe it is the worst thing a human being can go through.

'Lord,' I implored, 'I'll take any amount of pain or disablement, so long as I feel You with me, but please – not depression.'

He looked down at me so kindly and said, 'We must prove Satan is wrong, just as I had to with Job. I will *always* be with you even if you cannot feel Me. I have promised My presence with you for ever, but I never promised you would feel it. Your trust in Me will never grow in a perpetual state of joyous feelings. It *is* going to be a dark valley. But I will be there even if you don't *believe* it.'

I had to struggle very hard to accept this, and when at last I did, I expected to go straight into a deep depression. But the God 'who will not let you be tempted beyond what you can bear' knew I was not ready for that experience yet (1 Cor. 10: 13 NIV).

## Chapter Six

When you are lying flat on your back alone all day, the truth about your damaged body does not really hit you. There is no one to see you or to compare yourself with. But when I was moved back to the Kent and Sussex Hospital into a general medical ward, I became acutely conscious that I was a physical wreck. My arms and legs were impossible to control and they twitched and shook, while my eyes blinked and winked embarrassingly. When the physios came round and tried to stand me upright, the vertigo crashed me to the floor.

I hated the humiliation of wheelchairs. Have you ever realised that when you are in a wheelchair you are not considered a person by most people? No one ever addresses a remark to you, they only talk to the person pushing you! I was determined to lurch and reel around the ward on my own, however silly I looked, but I had to travel down to the physio department each day in a chair. To discover that you cannot control your body is an enormous shock to the system, but the Lord was good enough to meet me even in that.

One Sunday morning George came into the ward for early communion. I had made an awful fool of myself by falling over in the loo just before, and was still shaking from shock and rage. But as he handed me the wafer dipped in the wine he said (quoting Jesus of course), 'This is my body, broken for you.' I felt the tears of joy trickling from the corners of my eyes as I inwardly replied, 'and this is my body broken for you, Lord. Paul said, present your bodies, as a living sacrifice (Rom. 12: 1 RSV), so here you are, have mine.'

I could not think what He could possibly want with a broken, twitching body like mine, but I felt unutterable joy in giving Him something even as useless as that. However, as the days went by I have to admit I often felt it can be much harder to be a living sacrifice than a dead one.

Being ill gives you an entirely different perspective on life. I found myself noticing things much more and becoming acutely aware of how people react. It was as if my own suffering had given me an insight into other people's.

I learnt how small things can so easily increase an ill person's misery; things that I had done without thinking in the past. I was determined that I was going to learn from having been on the receiving end.

Lying watching other patients with their visitors showed me how people so often pretend to be better than they really are so that friends and relations don't go away feeling miserable. I saw patients lie quite still and quiet all day until their visitors arrived. Then they sat up and laughed, talked and generally put on a good impression, only to collapse with exhaustion when the bell was rung to clear the ward.

Visitors, however lovely, are a strain. When people come from a long distance they feel they must stay as long as possible. A three-hour visit is probably fine if you only have a broken leg, but when you have been very ill your span of concentration is only about five or ten minutes at the very most. The worst thing of all is having several people who don't know each other sitting on different sides of the bed. The effort of communication with them all, while turning your dizzy head from one side to the other, is devastating. One at a time and never for more than a few minutes, is going to be my future rule when any friend of mine is ill.

Tony and I are devoted to one another, but we are very different. I needed my friends round me, and their love carried me through and reassured me I was still a person. But it was hard on Tony, who is a very private person. Sometimes he just longed to have me to himself to let off steam about the children, but he could not get near the bed for people who were too insensitive to see his needs and leave us alone together.

We very carefully planned Richard's first visit to me one afternoon, and I had lots of little parcels ready under the bed clothes for him to find and a story to pretend to read from a book. That first meeting was crucial if we were to begin to rebuild our relationship after so many weeks. But no sooner had he settled down and begun to relax slightly, than three visitors arrived. Tony tried to explain to them, but they irately said they had come a long way, and had another train to catch, and surely Richard could come any time. Richard could not tolerate my divided attention and behaved so badly Tony had to remove him in haste, leaving me to the visitors and a lump in my throat the size of a turkey egg. Tony never risked bringing him again, but my yearning for him was a physical pain.

Visitors brought me so much wonderful fruit that if I had eaten it all I would never have left the loo, and the boxes of chocolates were gorgeous, but not much use when I was too nauseated to manage more than dry bread! I liked best the visitors who said, 'I haven't brought you a present, but when I come next time what would you like me to bring?' The nail file or envelopes you really need are worth all the exotic presents you are too ill to appreciate.

It is lovely when a visitor reads a verse from the Bible, but better still if they also write it out on a card so if you have failed to concentrate at the time you have it to chew over later. Short, quiet prayers are wonderful, but when visitors kneel down, or worse still raise their arms in loud praise, it is rather difficult to live in the ward after they have gone home!

It is also desperately embarrassing when visitors break ward rules and insist on coming out of visiting hours. One friend of mine was always turning up in the morning. She managed to time her visit to coincide with Sister's coffee break and she strode confidently in remarking to anyone who noticed her that she was a *hospital visitor*! They must have thought she was some kind of a social worker, for she always got away with it.

There is always a very quiet patch in a ward between the violent activities of bed-making and washes, and the serving of lunch and pills. It was into this deathly hush that my friend always insisted on reading several long chapters from obscure parts of the Old Testament in a very loud penetrating voice. But it was worse still when she began to pray for me and my very personal needs, while the whole ward listened in – eyes popping with interest!

The best hospital visitors are people who have been very ill themselves, but not the ones who make your stomach turn by a recital of the horrors they suffered, or encourage self-pity by getting you to talk about your own. You just want to be treated like a person again, but some people cannot help talking to the handicapped in an odd voice reserved also for small children and imbeciles.

I received many letters while I was in hospital and my reactions to these also changed my preconceptions about how an ill person can be best helped. All the letters were well-intentioned and full of sympathy, but some were so gloomily spiritual that I felt more in need of comfort at the end than I had before I started reading! Illness, like bereavement, can make people extraordinarily sensitive to tactless comments. It was very hard for people to get it right!

This was never the case with the letters I had from my mother's youngest sister, Geraldine. She seemed to know instinctively how I was feeling but never probed or patronised. Instead she told me all the funny things that kept happening in the remote Scottish village where she lived, recounting them so vividly that I would cry with laughter. She wrote frequently, on a battered old typewriter, and I would re-read the letters over and over again. Through Auntie Gerry's letters I rediscovered the humour in everyday happenings, as I started looking out for funny things to tell

55

her. The joy of the Lord started becoming a positive thing again; I was no longer just getting through the day but relearning to enjoy the small things that make up life.

Occasionally she would write about spiritual things, but she did so by way of discussion – sharing her own thoughts and inviting my response. She didn't write in the sort of charismatic or evangelical language that so many Christians slip into without realising, but in a direct and personal way which didn't give me that horrid feeling of always being on the receiving end. It was exactly the sort of help I needed; profound and yet practical.

Then there were the healers. Naturally the Christians who came to see me prayed I would get better, but sometimes people would come with a strong burden to lay hands on me. That was lovely, but I felt convinced I *had* been wonderfully healed, and I accepted the healing was going to be a slow and gradual process. I felt I should only be thanking God for what He *was* doing.

'But it is *never* God's will for us to be ill even for one minute,' said one earnest friend. 'You must be harbouring some secret, unconfessed sin, or you could walk out of here now.'

All that night I could not sleep, as I went back over a lifetime that seemed to contain nothing but sin. By the time the early tea came round, I had reached the conclusion that if God was punishing me for all or any of that, it was a wonder I was not in the hospital mortuary!

That afternoon, after a long hard session in physio, when the only thing that had kept me going was my desire to get better quickly to see my children again, it was rather lowering to be told by another visitor, 'Your trouble is, you're just accepting this, and not fighting. Satan has possessed your will.'

George told me that as a hospital chaplain he sees some Christians who expect God to heal them instantly, and when He does not, their faith is shaken. So they lose the comfort He longs to give them and they blame themselves. The resulting guilt and depression rob them of their natural human will to fight their diseases, so they are hurt spiritually, mentally and physically. Fortunately for me, I had the memory of looking right into Heaven and I clung to the certainty that I had been healed.

Guilt is a weapon Satan can use very easily in illness. Endless people said, 'You brought all this on yourself, you know, you've been doing far too much.' I have heard that said so often to people who have had heart attacks, strokes or nervous breakdowns, but what is done is done, and piling guilt on top of suffering does not help.

Having said all that, it is vital to add that the love and company of all those visitors really gave me the will to fight back towards the real world. Hospital visiting is one of the most special jobs a Christian can do.

I realised how much I was helped by them all when after a few weeks back at the Kent and Sussex, I was isolated again in the side ward. A bad relapse and a complication of the disease had set in.

# Chapter Seven

I was utterly shattered. Where was the healing God had promised me? Or had He promised it at all? Had He just given me back my life and told me it would be a struggle? The pain was sometimes worse than I felt it was possible to live through; I felt angry and desperate.

Suddenly the double swing doors of my cubicle were thrust open and in strode the neurologist from London. I peered at him in terror, fearing he had brought his assistant with him – but fortunately he was alone. He came over and stood looking kindly down at me.

'Well, Mrs Larcombe,' he said, 'they tell me you have developed complications.' I apologised profusely and assured him I had worked extremely hard at my physio.

'Much too hard, I'm afraid,' he smiled. 'You want to run before you can walk.'

He produced the inevitable red-headed pin that all neurologists wear in their lapels like a badge of high office, and proceeded to stick it into every part of my body. I didn't mind at all; I couldn't really feel it because my skin had begun to feel like the thick hide of a hippopotamus.

'Can you smell this?' he asked, producing a tiny bottle from his pouch. I had to admit I could not even smell the gorgeous flowers that filled my room or taste my toothpaste. He seemed quite put out when he could not reduce me to helpless giggles by scratching the soles of my feet and when he had done all the things neurologists always do, he sat down on the end of my bed.

'We must have a little talk, Mrs Larcombe. What seems

to be happening is that the inflammation is now damaging the actual nerve casings, so that messages from your brain are taking longer to reach other parts of your body. That's why you have to concentrate so hard even to manage small simple actions. The nerves that affect your heart, breathing mechanism and temperature control are all affected. You see double and your eyes hurt because of damage to the optic nerve, and you feel seasick and giddy because the nerve controlling the body's balancing mechanism is faulty.'

'How long will it be until the inflammation dies down again?' I asked.

'We just don't know that,' he replied while his kindly smile slipped away. 'You must face the fact that you might be left permanently damaged.'

'You mean I'm not going to get completely better,' I faltered.

He did not answer, but turned away and did something that I had no idea important consultants would ever demean themselves by doing. He bent down and pulled my bedsocks back on!

'Rest,' he said quietly, 'that's the best thing you can do,' and the swing doors of my room flapped shut behind him.

Rest! For me that was a rude four-letter word. I lay and gazed bleakly at the wall. Had I really understood what he was trying to say? What was that going to mean to the life I had so carefully organised for myself?

I longed to talk to Tony about it, but when he came to see me that night he looked completely exhausted – drained of all strength like someone who has had a haemorrhage. I wondered if Sister had told him what the neurologist had said; somehow I just could not bring up the subject. If he looked that bad when I had only been ill for a few months, how could he face living with a permanently disabled wife – no longer attractive or able to cope at home? Would he go on loving me?

For the next three nights I had a recurring dream. I had always lost something and was desperately, hopelessly searching for it. I wondered if I was mourning the loss of my own body and strength. Our whole happy lifestyle was threatened. We could not go on living deep in the country if I could not drive the children to all the places they needed to go. What about the home-made bread and cooking our home-grown vegetables? A handicapped mum could never run that house and garden, and if I could not walk into the woods and fields, how could I escape from the pressures of life at home to communicate with God? I really panicked, and all that fretting and churning gave me such severe headaches, I felt life was intolerable.

I decided to have a talk to George about it all, and I had plenty of time to do so because he came every single day. When the pain was at its worst, he just sat and held my hand like my father always did when I was ill as a child. The test of a real friend is when you *don't* have to talk and silence is relaxing and not awkward. I sensed he understood completely how I was feeling, but he cared too much for me to soothe me with trite words of sugary sympathy. Instinctively he realised the danger I was in, and firmly pointed out the trap that self-pity and doubt can be.

'I think our old enemy Satan is having a go at you,' he told me. 'Why not use your sword and fight back?'

'Sword?' I faltered.

'The sword of the Spirit which is the word of God' (Eph. 6: 17). 'If I give you a verse, do you think you could go on repeating it to the Lord, to yourself and to Satan until I come back later?'

How much I gained through his spiritual discernment. So often our Christian friends just rub us with soothing ointment, when really we need spiritual castor oil! George gave me Romans 8, from verses 31 and 32: 'If God is for us, who can be against us – He gave us His son, will He not also freely give us all things?'

I felt such a fool repeating that over and over again, and old Satan sat on the end of my bed and laughed at me.

'I'm still fighting,' I told George weakly when his head popped round the door later in the afternoon.

'Keep it up!' he said. 'Maureen (his wife) and I are really praying you through this.'

It was late in the evening and that horrid time of the day in hospital when you long for sleep, but have to force yourself to stay awake for the sleeping-pill trolley to come round! I was still 'doing my homework' and wondering why the Lord was not dealing with Satan, when it suddenly and finally dawned on me: *God was for me!* So Satan could *not* prevail against me. God was not going to deal with Satan *for* me. He had delegated that authority to me. 'Resist Satan and he will flee from you' (James 4: 7 RSV). So I told him firmly in the name of Jesus to go, and he did!

As well as giving me Jesus, God was going to freely give me all things. I nearly shouted with the joy of it. Did the 'all things' mean healing, or courage and endurance to cope with a new life, and could not the God who made everything in the world be trusted to take care of one man and six children?

I was so excited and released, no amount of sleeping pills acted on me that night. About three in the morning I was listening to some riotous choruses on my headphones, but what I did not realise was that I was singing loudly along with the tape. I could not hear myself, but suddenly an enraged night nurse burst in.

'What do you think you're doing?' she demanded. 'You'll wake the whole ward.' Even my embarrassment could not spoil my joy, and later that night, or probably the next morning, I was conscious of Jesus sitting at the end of the bed, where I had felt Satan to be, so recently.

'What is it that you really want me to do for you?' He asked. I was overcome with a deep sense of awe and also a certainty that this was one of the most important moments in my life. My first instinct was to say, 'Heal me, Lord, and I'll walk right home.' But I waited a moment to give myself time to think. I felt His power was so present, I must not bungle this precious interview with the King of all Kings. What *did* I really want most? Well, I am a mother, so it was **obvious**.

61

'Lord,' I replied at last, 'most of all I want *all* my children to grow up to know, love and serve You, and marry people who love You too.' He seemed to be waiting, so I dared to add, 'Please give Tony a massive dose of Your strength and blessing, I love him so much.'

'And what about *you*?' He said at last. 'What shall I do for you?'

If He had asked me that nearly twenty years before, or even twenty months, I would have replied, 'Lord, let me do something really big and important to serve you.' But something had changed inside me, and it was unthinkable that I should just go back to being the same person I had always been before. This deep worship relationship with Him had become so precious to me that I really did not care what else life held or did not hold for me, so long as I could keep that.

'Lord,' I began rather diffidently, 'I've always had this hang-up about worshipping You. I've put on worship like a Sunday hat for church or House Group, but it's been so different here in hospital. Please couldn't I spend the rest of my life worshipping You day and night like Anna the prophetess in Luke 2: 36? Please give me a continuous secret relationship with You – like Brother Tom has.'

Now here I have to confess something, because I am writing this in the presence of God. I did not ask for bodily healing, because I was convinced He would heal me anyway! After all, the Lord asked Solomon what he wanted and when he asked for wisdom rather than riches, the Lord was so pleased with him, he gave him both! I thought the same rule would apply to me!

I drifted happily off to sleep, and in the morning I might well have been tempted to think the whole thing was just a dream, if the Lord had not given me a very special proof of its reality.

On the very day that George and Maureen were so specially praying for me, a farmer's wife in the back woods of Somerset pulled on her wellingtons and splashed down the muddy farm track to post a letter in the box half hidden by the overgrown hedge.

Peggy Darch had known God all her life, but recently her relationship with Him had 'come alive' in a new way, and she found He was giving her the gift of composing spiritual poetry as she helped her husband Ken with their dairy herd or made the clotted cream. The letter she posted reached me that morning, and here is an extract from it.

'Some weeks ago, the Lord gave me a poem – not one bit of it is for me, but I suddenly felt I should send it to you:'

I am with you in the pain
    I am with you in the sorrow.
In the heartache of today
    and all that comes tomorrow,
I will never leave you.
    I have promised to be near,
so lift up your head rejoicing,
    be delivered from your fear.

I will hold you close beside me
    as we walk along together.
Take my hand and dance along
    in the sun or stormy weather.
Do not ever let a cloud or fear
    fall across your lovely face,
for I've made you to be beautiful
    and I've done it all in grace.

I love you dear to walk with me,
    your company is sweet.
I love your quiet listening
    when sitting at my feet.
Please do not feel inferior,
    I love to hear you sing.
Stay close beside me always,
    my dear daughter of the King.

Peggy knew nothing of how I was feeling when she wrote that, and only God's perfect timing could have caused her to post it on just the right day. As I lay there clutching it that morning, I knew it was a tangible confirmation of all that had happened in the night.

One morning a few days after this, the ward domestic came into my room at 7.30 to mop the floor as usual. She had to do it three times every day, once with a dry mop, once with a wet one and once, I believe, just for luck! Her cheerful, uncomplicated friendship meant a very great deal to me, but that morning she was looking far from cheerful and her huge round face was all blotchy with tears.

'What's up?' I asked. Dropping her mop, she plonked her enormous bulk down on the end of my bed.

'Do you believe dreams mean anything?' she began. I grinned ruefully and said I was beginning to think that they did.

'I lost my dad a few months back,' she continued, 'and last night I went and dreamt I saw him in Heaven.'

'But surely that was a very nice dream, wasn't it?' I asked, puzzled.

'You don't understand,' she wailed, as the tears trickled down her round cheeks. 'That means I'll never see him again, and I loved my dad.'

'But why will you never see him again?' I insisted.

'Don't tell anyone, will you,' she pleaded with a sniff, 'but I just can't help shoplifting – oh, I've never been caught,' she added fiercely, 'but God wouldn't have a shoplifter in Heaven, so you see I never will see my dad again, will I?'

I fumbled into my locker for a tissue for her, and prayed hard for wisdom. She blew her nose and went on rather shyly, 'I felt you were the kind of person who might know how I get to Heaven.'

'I *do* know how you can get to Heaven,' I said, praying Sister would not look through the glass porthole in the door. 'And what's more, there'll be lots of shoplifters up there, and murderers as well.'

Her eyes opened in amazement.

'I thought only good people got to Heaven,' she said.

'No,' I replied, 'only bad people who admit they're bad and ask Jesus to come into their lives and change them.'

'Is that *all* I've got to do?' she asked, as a great beam spread across her face. 'Don't I have to get the vicar to do a special service for me in church?'

'Well, you can if you like,' I replied, 'or we could talk to the hospital chaplain about it, but there is nothing to stop you doing it right here and now.'

'I will!' she said. 'Before Sister catches me.' We shut our eyes and prayed together surrounded by her mops and buckets. I told George all about her when he came in, and later that day he talked to her and gave her a copy of John's gospel and some simple notes to help.

About a year afterwards, I was shuffling painfully through Tunbridge Wells feeling rather low, when something huge hurled itself at me from behind. It was my friend, the ward domestic.

'I've so wanted to see you again,' she beamed, positively jumping with excitement. 'I wanted you to know I've left the Kent and Sussex, and me and my husband are in Hailsham now, but we go to church every Sunday, and the vicar's so lovely, and,' she added, suddenly dropping her voice to a confidential whisper, 'I've never pinched another thing since I had that dream and learnt the way to Heaven.'

## Chapter Eight

'I'll go mad if I don't get out of this place soon,' I sniffed, as I hid in the loo for some privacy. I had reached a point where the hospital could really do no more for me, apart from providing rest, painkillers and physiotherapy. I longed to go home, but the doctors were adamant that I needed at least two more months of total rest.

'What you need is a good dose of Burrswood,' said Marilyn, an old school friend of mine, when she came to visit me later that day. Marilyn was the very first person I ever led to the Lord, and I still feel weepy now, thirty years later, at the memory of the joy of it. We were sitting up in bed having a midnight feast one summer holiday, when she was staying with us, and she asked Jesus into her life between two chocolate biscuits! Now she was the housekeeper at Burrswood, a beautiful country house set in magnificent gardens.

It was founded by a remarkable woman called Dorothy Kerrin. When God gave her a gift of healing, she opened Burrswood as a nursing home where religion and medicine could work hand in hand to care for and heal the whole person — body, mind and soul.

It is strangely moving to see the chaplain and the doctor working together in the services of healing in the beautiful chapel. For many of us who live in the district, Burrswood has become a place where we can retreat from the world for an hour or even a day, just to sit in the garden or pray in the chapel. There is a sense of the Lord's presence that seems to hover over the place. I could not think of anywhere, except home, where I would rather go.

I do not know who paid my fees for all those weeks, and I am still too embarrassed and grateful to enquire, but the afternoon I arrived at Burrswood, I really felt I must certainly have made it to Heaven this time.

Dorothy Kerrin believed people mend best amongst beauty and comfort, so the house is furnished exquisitely with antiques and restful colours, while quantities of flowers fill and surround the place.

Marilyn pushed my wheelchair into the most luxurious bedroom I have ever had, and produced a tray of china tea served in delicate cups. As I sat in my comfortable chair looking over the gardens, I felt all the bustle and pressure of the busy ward receding like a nightmare. However well run hospitals are, they are very impersonal and so noisy that sleep is almost impossible. Nor can you ever be perfectly sure that someone is not going to come at you with a needle or 'tear you off a strip' for not moving your bowels for ten days! I sat and cried for at least an hour just with sheer relief.

But after a few days of wallowing in luxury something rather odd began to happen. Everything was *too* comfortable and the staff were too loving. A terrible feeling of guilt set in.

Why should I be having all this lovely care while Tony and the children seemed to be going through hell? Everything was going wrong at home. Mrs Ashman's father had a stroke, so she could not help any more, the other friend who was looking after Richard had to stop because of a family crisis, and most other people had returned to their busy lives feeling, quite rightly, that Tony preferred to be independent. Even the social services were overloaded in that area and could offer no help.

Sarah had to stay at home from school for the last few weeks of term, and for a fourteen-year-old she did a remarkable job, but suddenly something broke inside her, and seeing no end to the tunnel of hard work, her anger and resentment against me, with its resulting guilt, boiled over and made her unco-operative and moody. She remembers actually wishing I had died. 'At least,' she said, 'we would have known where we were then.'

67

Jane's inner tensions made her unhelpful and withdrawn, but Duncan was worse than I dare describe him. Until I left in the ambulance, he had been quite an ordinary, lively six-year-old, but that summer his teacher at school told Tony she was completely baffled by his behaviour. He rudely rebuffed every overture of friendship anyone made towards him, and was so horribly naughty no one could possibly put up with him, except one very frail neighbour – Ann Frost, who, even though she was in constant pain from a disease of the spine, met him each day from school and let him lose himself in her garden until Tony came home from work. Poor Duncan, even the cat ate his beloved blue budgie.

Justyn was in very strict training for the National Swimming Championships. His training programme required Tony to do the twenty-mile round trip to the pool in Tunbridge Wells early each morning before getting the children's breakfast, then back to Tunbridge Wells and his office, home to get tea and put the younger children to bed, and finally back again to the pool with Justyn for a further session. The strain was almost too much, but he did not want to let Justyn down by failing to help him.

'Kind' friends came to see me and told me how appallingly Duncan was behaving and how worried they were that Tony was on the point of a breakdown. I could see for myself how exhausted he was, his mind and body totally overstretched. Then one day he dropped a bombshell on me.

'I've put the house on the market,' he said, 'and I've found us somewhere in Tunbridge Wells.'

I was completely horror-struck. I know I had been wondering how we would cope in Mayfield, but the actual realisation of leaving it was devastating, and surely it was unnecessary, because the Lord was healing me.

'Everything would be easier if we lived in town,' Tony claimed, but I wanted the security of my familiar and much-loved home, and the tranquillity of the country around me was a physical need. Even more, I felt I needed the people. In Mayfield I had an identity – I was a person everyone knew. I did not believe I had the ability to make new relationships. Self-confidence is totally destroyed by a serious illness, and I felt I could not get better without the support of my loving Christian friends at church.

Of course I was being selfish – digging my toes into country soil. Tony, in his love for me, realised that I would not be the same person when I went home, and a new life would be less painful for me than discovering how much of my old life was now impossible. But I would not see it from his point of view.

'What about the children,' I stormed. 'They're insecure enough already without making them all change schools and church.'

I thought he was beyond thinking rationally, and he knew I was pig-headed! The last thing we both wanted to do was pray about it, but when at last we did, we settled on a compromise. We would leave the house on the estate agents' books until September, and then if it had not been sold by then, we would take it that the Lord wanted us to stay where we were.

But a horrid shadow lay between us, which did not help either of us. He became even more tense and strained, and something went wrong with my heart beat, so I had to be put on rather powerful drugs which gave me side effects and my physiotherapy had to be cut down.

As my anxiety about Tony and the children increased, I began to pray in an urgent, desperate fashion, but my prayers were becoming nothing more than an expression of worry – a faithless nagging at God, an endless repetition.

One morning as I sat in my wheelchair at the healing service, I felt God say to me, 'Lovest thou me more than these?' (Perhaps it's because I grew up with it that God often seems to speak to me in the Authorised Version.)

'What do you mean by "these" Lord?' I asked.

'Your house in the country,' He replied, 'do you rely on beauty and peace to feed your soul rather than Me alone? Your reputation in the village? Your status at the church? You enjoy people talking their problems over with you, it boosts your ego. Suppose I took everything away from you, would you still trust Me?'

I struggled like mad; He had broken my body, why did He demand everything else as well? I was sure Tony was wrong and I was right, but something inside me argued that if I really meant what I had said in the Kent and Sussex Hospital that night, that I only desired to worship the Lord and live in the sanctuary of Praise, it really did not matter where I lived or how few people I saw.

At Burrswood most people go up to the communion rail for the laying on of hands, but Father Keith Denerly always came first to those of us in wheelchairs. As he put his hands on my head that day, I offered my house, possessions, friends and psychological needs to the Lord, and asked Him to forgive and heal me from my pride and self-centred attitude. Afterwards I felt a lovely glowing feeling. I had reached a spiritual milestone – passed a test. I was to discover how wrong I was! If only we did not have to learn the same lesson so many times over!

That afternoon a kind friend brought Naomi over to visit me. Most people who brought the children to see me quite naturally stayed with us, but that made it hard for the children to relax and talk to me. This wise friend, Ann Frost, understood that and took herself off into the garden and Naomi and I were alone together for the first time since I had left home. As usual she set herself diligently to cheer me up, by telling me all the things that filled her nine-year-old world. She had won the silver cup at sports day, her mouse had nine more babies, and Mrs Frost's pond was full of baby frogs. But I could see she was struggling to fight back the tears, and was desperate not to let me see them.

'It's not right to bottle things up,' I said at last. 'Can't you tell me what's making you miserable? How is it at home?'

'It's fine really,' she replied with a gulp. 'It's just when we come home from school and no one's there to talk about the day.'

'But there's Daddy, surely?' I encouraged. She looked at me in helpless misery.

'Daddy's not quite all right at the moment,' she managed at last. 'He's all wound up like an alarm clock.' The tears were beginning to win and poor Naomi was panicking. If that dam burst she might never get back into control again. Just at the crucial moment, a glorious butterfly flapped in through the open window and rested on her shaky little hand. Naomi shares my deep love of country things, and it totally delighted us both by its utter perfection. No sooner had it flown away through the window, than we caught sight of a baby rabbit cheekily nibbling grass right by where we sat. We were so captivated we forgot to be sad, and Naomi whispered, 'Mum I think they were both really angels, sent to cheer us up.' Her calm was completely restored by the time she went home, and she looked quite supernaturally happy as she waved to me through the window. I believe angels can wear many disguises.

But I was in a turmoil that evening, terrified of what might happen if Tony cracked under the strain. What would happen to the children? I began my agitated anxious praying until someone knocked at my door. It was Father Keith himself. Spiritual counselling is as important at Burrswood as medical treatment. No one ever forces you into 'baring your soul' if you do not wish to, but there was the chaplain just when I needed him. God has never let me down.

'Oh, do please help me,' I pleaded, dissolving into tears. He slowly drew up a stool beside the comfortable armchair where I always sat overlooking the garden, and I was struck once again by the utter stillness of this man. He never moved a muscle as I told him of my concern and anxieties, and even confessed how I had concealed all my food in a polythene bag the day before so I could fast as well as pray. A crazy thing for a woman to do who had just rapidly lost four stone in weight. At last he said very gently, 'Naturally this illness is far harder for your husband than it is for you, and I think he and all your children need God's healing.'

71

'Yes of course,' I replied impatiently, 'but we'd never get them to a healing service – they'd never sit still long enough.'

'They don't have to come to a service,' he answered quietly. 'They can have the laying on of hands by proxy.' I was not perfectly sure what he meant, but he produced a little jar of consecrated oil from his pocket and said, 'Give me your hands.' Mystified, I watched as he rubbed the oil into my palms, but my mystification turned to horror when he knelt on the floor by my chair and bent his head.

'You lay hands on me,' he said, 'and I will represent Tony and the children.'

'I can't do that,' I protested, 'I haven't got a ministry of healing, and you're a priest.' He looked up and smiled at me.

'When I lay my hands on the heads of sick people, it isn't my hands that heal them, but the power of Jesus flowing through my hands. He can just as easily use your hands as mine. None of us are ever worthy to be used by God.' Then he bent his head again, and I had to get on with it. After I had prayed aloud and expressed everything to God we remained in silent prayer for a very long time – me leaning back on my pillows, and he kneeling motionless beside me. At last he said, 'I feel God has begun something special today, but you must leave Him to finish the job in His own way and His own time. He knows exactly what He's going to do and how He's going to do it. You have committed all your worries to Him; now by an act of the will you must leave Him to take care of them. These days we often demand instant healing from God, like instant coffee or mashed potato, but God's timing is perfect and He sees us from the other side of eternity where only the soul endures.'

When Tony next came to see me he was utterly different. He looked ten years younger.

'It's funny,' he said, 'but I feel I've been living in a nightmare recently, but it's suddenly beginning to lift, I can't think why.' I could think just why, but I did not dare to tell him, not just then.

The summer holidays were approaching – always a relief

for any teacher, but Tony had another problem to solve. We had planned our holiday that year back in January, long before the first rumblings of my illness. Through a Quaker friend, we had booked up to spend a week in a Quaker youth hostel in Yorkshire. My hopes of going with them had died long since, and Tony did not feel he could cope with a self-catering holiday all on his own. He was heartily sick of fish fingers. Then Ann Frost's daughter, Sarah, who was then eighteen and just about to go up to Oxford, offered to go with him and be a substitute mum. I wrote an urgent letter to our Sarah imploring her to see Dad had a real rest. She really took it to heart, bless her, and the two Sarahs firmly marched everyone off for long all-day rambles over the moors, disregarding Jane's grumbles and carrying Richard most of the way. That gave Tony time on his own with his Bible and the Lord to mend inside. He has never looked back since. How good the Lord is.

I thought I might feel rather flat with them all away on holiday without me, but it actually turned out to be one of the most eventful weeks of my life.

## Chapter Nine

'Have you ever heard that some physical illness can actually be caused by traumatic events in childhood or unresolved conflicts?'

Rosemary Anne, one of the Burrswood counsellors, had come to see me. I replied that I had never given it a thought, so she fixed me with her rather penetrating eye and said, 'Have you ever considered that you might need a form of treatment called the healing of the memories?' I couldn't help laughing.

'Not me,' I said, 'I had a wonderful and privileged childhood. Surely that kind of thing is only for people who've suffered horrible things.'

'I feel you should pray it over,' she said ominously. 'Lack of forgiveness and resentments can impede healing. I'll come back tomorrow.' As she went out of my room she turned, with her hand on the doorknob. 'We don't want to leave any stone unturned, do we?'

If I could have got better by turning every stone on Brighton Beach, I would willingly have done it, so if she was prepared to give a couple of hours of her valuable time each day, who was I to quibble? But I still felt a terrible fool, and dreaded her coming into my room for the first session. How could things that had happened to me years ago possibly be responsible for my succumbing to a virus? Anyway, I was embarrassed about letting another human being into the secret places of my life.

I need not have worried. During that week I often forgot

she was sitting there beside me. It was simply Jesus walking through my experiences with me, helping me to see people with His eyes, giving me the power to forgive, and also His forgiveness where it was needed. The complete atmosphere of other days surrounded me all the time, not just during the set times with Rosemary Anne. The smells, sights and feelings, things I thought I had totally forgotten, became more real than my bedroom. Gently my counsellor encouraged me to see Jesus in every event – actually to picture Him present. I realised He wanted me to be a whole person, with no hang-ups or chips on my shoulder. He needed to explain to me why certain things had happened, why people had acted as they did, and lovingly to show me where I had gone wrong.

The most exciting thing of all, however, was to see how He had actually healed me as I went along. I believe, after the experience of that week, that children from Christian homes, who are prayed for frequently, have a unique experience of being continually healed. They are not shielded from the traumas of life – in fact, they often seem to suffer more than most children – but if they are bathed in prayer, and are themselves willing, Jesus heals the wounds as they occur, and uses them for good. So although the concept of 'healing of memories' does sound a bit weird and way-out, it did teach me this wonderful truth of God's continuous healing for me all through my life.

It astounded me how fiercely we can relive past emotions. During the first session, I was quite overcome by a total feeling of rage. I saw the world through a red haze of hurt. I was three years old and being bathed by the new nanny. Suddenly I hated her so violently, I tore at her fat wet arms with my fingernails until her blood ran into my bath water.

'Oh God!' she screamed, flinging herself down on to the loo, 'help me to manage the dreadful child.' Then she burst into tears, but I did not care, and the next day I bit her.

My world had fallen apart, and I was bewildered and furious. My life had been spent in utter happiness in a tiny

75

cottage in a country village. Father was away most of the time preaching, and Mother wrote books and painted pictures. She had a heart condition and was so totally undomesticated anyway, that Molly, a girl from the village, did everything for me. Together good old Molly (known as Gom) and I fed the chickens, pummelled pastry, and muddled along together. Mother was always there, and I could hear her typewriter clacking, even if I must not speak to her, and so break a mysterious thing called her chain of thought.

Then everything changed, it seemed to me, overnight. Through his huge campaigns in London, Father was leading hundreds of young people to God. In those days, just as the war was ending, regular church life had been disrupted; there were no cassettes, and few Christian books were being published. Nor were there any conference centres or great holiday celebrations as we know them today.

'It is not enough for people to turn to God, they must follow on to know the Lord.' That was the great burden both my parents shared, and it was then they received their vision of a peaceful country mansion – a centre for evangelism, teaching and rehabilitation.

That was why I was so cross. They exchanged our little cottage, climbing roses and all, for a huge dilapidated mausoleum surrounded by thirty-two acres of jungle that had once been a garden. Of course they could imagine how it was going to look, but I certainly could not. We arrived at Hilde:borough Hall on a cold foggy day in November, and I trotted around the vast empty rooms, festooned with cobwebs, the walls crumbling with damp, while our few familiar pieces of furniture looked ridiculously tiny scattered around the neglected parquet floors. Father and Mother were naturally totally absorbed in materialising their vision, with the help of a willing army of (to me) strangers.

It might not have felt so desolate if I had still had Gom, but Mother was pregnant again, and it was felt that a real properly trained nanny should be engaged to take charge of me. Gom refused to desert me completely, and cooked for the community, but the terrible starchy creature who came to take her place did not like our relationship and established 'her' nursery in the old housekeeper's room behind the green baize door that had once separated the servants from the family. I was the wrong side of that door, and I could never find my parents when I needed them.

Gently Rosemary Anne brought me back to the present, praying for healing and forgiveness, and helping me to see those experiences from my parents' and Nanny's point of view.

'When our lives are shattered,' she said, 'as human beings we want to blame someone for it – ourselves, other people or God. When we blame ourselves we suffer guilt, and then often depression. If we blame other people, our personalities can be poisoned by resentment. If we blame God, we are worst off, because we cut ourselves off from our source of comfort and help.'

I blamed poor Nanny because really I knew my parents both loved me greatly, and minded about how I felt. They must have prayed a lot for me, and their prayers were answered, because I can clearly see now that three things happened to help me.

Justyn was the first. I know all the books would say that the arrival of a baby brother should have been the final end to my damaged security, but actually it was the beginning of my salvation. I loved Justyn from the moment I first saw him, and felt we were both in the same leaking boat together. All Nanny's crackling efficiency was unleashed upon his helpless body, and he was not even equipped with teeth to bite her! I was not alone any more.

Then, some time during that first year, I encountered God for the very first time. I must have become a terribly nervous child, and I was dreadfully frightened of the dark. The night nursery was down a long gloomy corridor and I was always terrified by the creaking noises the old wooden floors made as they contracted or expanded. One night I woke in a panic – I was sure I could hear footsteps creeping menacingly down the parquet floor outside my room. I was paralysed with fear, too frightened to call out even if anyone would have heard me.

'God,' I pleaded, 'do something to help me.'

He did. Out in the garden beyond my curtains a bird began to sing. Then another joined in, two cuckoos held a conversation, and suddenly the whole world was full of wonderful music. I know now that it was only the dawn chorus, but I'd never heard it before, and felt God had put on a concert just for me. I remember feeling, as I listened in utter delight, that if God could do a miracle like that, just because I was frightened, then all I ever wanted to do in my life was to know Him better and better. He totally healed my fear, and I have never minded the dark since.

I suppose it must have been because of that desire to know Him that the other thing happened which finally trans-formed me into a happy child again. A lot of people don't believe children can, or should be encouraged to, commit themselves to God, to become indwelt by Him, until they are old enough to know exactly what they are doing. But when I was about four, I clearly remember sitting in a car in Jermyn Street in London with my mother. We were waiting for Father to see a man in an office, and I can recall so well the smell of the real leather seats of the old car, and see the feathery hat Mother was wearing. It was so lovely to have her to myself once again, that I asked her, 'Why do we have to live in that horrid big house with all those people?' (There were at least a hundred and twenty guests each week, plus a resident community of about thirty.)

'Because we want them to know Jesus, and ask Him into their hearts,' she replied simply.

'Why should they want to do that?' I persisted.

'Because Jesus can make them happy, and help them to be good.' Now I desperately wanted to be happy, and under-neath my rages, I really did want to be good, so I asked her if I could do it too.

She could have said, 'Yes dear, when you are old enough

to grasp the whole concept of God.' But I desperately needed Jesus right then, and she understood that. I remember her praying a tiny prayer, which I repeated after her: 'Come into my heart, Lord Jesus, come in today, come in to stay, come into my heart, Lord Jesus,' and He did, right there in Jermyn Street.

It made a profound difference. I can see from old photos that my whole face changed from that day. I lost the frantic hunted look of anxiety, and became normal and smiling again, and I can remember myself the feeling of peace that stayed with me for days. I have seen the same thing happen so often with other troubled children. Once they open themselves up to God, He plants His own peace where there was fear, joy where there was hopeless depression, and self-control in very aggressive children.

Certainly I began to enjoy life from that time, and became excited by the miracle that was taking place around me. The house had been decorated before the first guests arrived, but it was the gardens that I really loved. I watched German prisoners of war dredging a bullrush swamp into a huge magical lake; ploughed fields were levelled back into the velvet lawns they had been before the war, and bramble thickets were discovered to contain rhododendron walks which I could easily imagine were fairyland. The resident community went into action producing their own vegetables, eggs and fruit, not to mention cream from Jersey cows, and I had the fascination of watching baby turkeys swelling into Christmas-plump gobblers. All this was very necessary in those days of ration books, when people had hardly seen cream or a freshly laid egg for years.

I also discovered that living in a busy community can feel very safe for a child. Whenever I could escape from Nanny there was always someone to talk to or watch. They were all working there because they loved God, whether they peeled potatoes or cooked them, made the beds or preached in the seminars. Father and Mother lived completely within the community, having only their bedroom and the study where

79

Father counselled people. Everyone had one single aim: to show the guests whom they served the pure love of Jesus.

Father and Mother both became spiritual superstars in their generation. Father filled the Royal Albert Hall more than fifty times and they both preached and broadcast all over the world. Through them I met many famous Christians. One of my favourite memories is of one day when I was out for a walk with Nanny and we met Father. He was deep in conversation with a young man in a real cowboy hat. 'This is Dr Billy Graham,' said Father, as I looked up into a pair of amazingly blue eyes. 'He has come over from America to help me tell people about Jesus.'

Of course I did sometimes resent the fact that my parents spent so long helping other people that they didn't have much time for us. But I think they must have realised that, because they both made a point of carving out time for us in their busy days. After lunch Nanny always took me to the study for half an hour with Father (or the Boss as everyone called him). Perhaps that was the only time I saw him, but during those thirty minutes he gave me his undivided attention and our relationship became one of the most wonderful things in my life.

Father always got up early to pray alone in his study, but Mother sat up in bed with her Bible on her lap and she never minded us snuggling in beside her. She never had to force us to have a time with God ourselves each day, we both just caught the habit.

She always sat in the nursery at meal times, telling us stories. She really made the Bible come alive, and Joseph, Moses and David were far more popular than Winnie the Pooh or Peter Rabbit.

I laughed ruefully as I thought of the hectic whirlwind our meal times are at home.

'I must be a terrible failure as a mother,' I told Rosemary Anne. 'But I suppose Mother did have Nanny there to shovel cereal into Justyn, and cut me toast soldiers. Nanny must have had some uses, but at the time I could never see any!'

Rosemary Anne and I had quite a bit of praying to do at the end of that first day's session. So much of Duncan's behaviour was now explained to me. Just as I had been angry with Nanny because she was not the person I had lost, so was he furious with everyone because they weren't his mum.

I had never accepted Nanny, and I must have made her life very hard. But I knew perfectly well that she disliked me as much as I hated her. 'But,' I finished, 'I suppose there is not much I can do about that now because she's dead.'

'But it's not too late,' said Rosemary Anne. She went on to explain that it is perfectly possible – and very necessary – to forgive and release people even after death.

When I reach Heaven I won't feel embarrassed about meeting poor old Nanny now, but I do wonder if she has forgiven *me* yet for spitting so often into her hat!

When we started the next day's adventure, I was almost suffocated by a devastating feeling of failure. I saw myself standing outside a huge white building – my school. I knew without a shadow of doubt that I could never go back inside it again. Human beings can only take a certain amount of humiliation before they crack, and I knew my cracking point had been reached.

Unfortunately for me, dyslexia had not then been widely recognised. I was just labelled as 'backward'. Everyone else in my class of eleven-year-olds could read perfectly, so why couldn't I? My mind was full of ideas and stories, but if I tried writing them down teachers fell about laughing at my spelling, and often shared the joke with my derisive classmates. I might not have been so far behind them in subjects where dyslexia does not matter, if I had not spent every winter off school with pneumonia, rheumatic fever or bronchitis. I had no friends at school since Marilyn had left, and worst of all Justyn had been sent away to boarding school.

As Mother drove into the school drive to collect me that day, I opened the car door, and quavered, 'I am never ever going to school again.'

I never did. School phobia is also well recognised now, and backward or disturbed children are often withdrawn into small groups with special teachers. I know, because part of Tony's job is caring for these children, and I can tell him just what it feels like to be one of them! My parents had no support like that, but they were brave enough to do what needed to be done, and in the face of fierce criticism from family, friends and authorities, I stayed at home. A Danish lady called Marrianne came to be a nanny and governess rolled into one, and I loved her. Learning to read even at twelve can be great fun when no one is laughing at you. But the feeling of failure has never left me. Maybe that is why I am always striving to do something big and important just to prove myself.

Not going to school was wonderful at first, but then everything went terribly wrong. Father decided to move Hildenborough Hall to an Edwardian hotel on the sea front at Frinton. I missed the garden and the countryside quite desperately. There was nowhere to go for escape; even on the beach I felt spied on by hundreds of lace-curtained bathing huts. Marrianne hated it too, so she left and my home-based education was continued by a stream of retired school teachers. Frinton positively crawled with them. I was too terrified to go back to school, but I was also deeply ashamed and embarrassed because I didn't go.

Suddenly that day at Burrswood I looked back through the years and saw a revolting sight. Myself – a grossly overweight teenager stuffing herself with food behind the locked doors of her bedroom.

I ate because I was miserably lonely, but I dared not leave my room in case people would laugh at my hideous shape as well as my lack of ability. I was a total physical, mental and emotional mess, and I hated and despised myself.

'You were not alone in that room,' said Rosemary Anne gently, 'and even if you hated yourself Jesus was there loving you all the time. He understood how you felt. Let's picture Him there with you now, as we ask Him for His healing.'

As we did that, I suddenly realised how He *had* stepped into my life and rescued me.

'Everyone is good at something,' I remember 'the Boss' saying one day. 'Except me,' I had replied gloomily.

The modern theory of child-rearing is that parents must build their child's self-esteem by encouraging them in something they are good at doing. Mother and Father knew that without reading any books, and they must have worried about the state I was in, and prayed so much for wisdom. Father arranged music lessons and bought me a piano which he let me have in my bedroom. Considering his room was next to mine, and he spent many hours a day in it at that time, praying and studying the Bible, it was no small act of love on his part. He said he loved to hear my playing through the thin partition, and I actually believed him! He took a passionate interest in every new piece, and praised my discordant efforts. Because of his encouragement, in three years I was working for grade seven.

Mother played her part in my reclamation, by buying me a set of golf clubs and booking me a series of lessons with the local pro. At first I was almost too fat to see the ball, but soon I was a fully fledged member of the golf club, and when I was not playing the piano, I was endlessly hitting balls on the practice fairway. Suddenly I found I was the Essex Junior Champion, and poor Mother was hurtling me all over the country to national and international competitions. I had to keep fit to play well, so I lost weight, and travelling round to county matches and tournaments gave me self-confidence at last. What I hadn't realised before though, was how hard both my parents had to work to help the Lord answer their prayers!

Finally another miracle happened: even though I hadn't passed any exams, I got a place to train as a nanny. Though I still don't know how I had the cheek after the way I'd treated mine!

'Children of parents who are great achievers often feel guilty for just being normal,' commented Rosemary Anne.

'I don't think you'll dare to relax until you have lived up to your parents.'

So we prayed about that together and gave God the inferiority complex I had lived with ever since, and I know now that I am free of it.

But training as a nanny didn't prepare me for dealing with my second child, Justyn. After four years of hyperactive hell, I can remember standing in the middle of complete chaos, screaming hysterically.

I had spent all day preparing the house for special visitors, and gone upstairs to change just before the door bell was due to ring. When I came down, four-year-old Justyn had shaken scouring powder over the velvet suite, made flour castles on the carpet and squeezed toothpaste and washing-up liquid all over the carefully laid out tea. I knew from that moment how easy it could be for children to be battered. If it had not been for the grace of God, I would not have stopped short of murder!

Every theory of child-rearing Tony and I had learnt while training as teacher and nanny had been smashed. I could not take Justyn out because he had tantrums in supermarkets or bit other children we visited, and no one wanted to come to see me! As I stood there screaming, I really hated him, and felt he was spoiling my life.

I was in such helpless tears when the friends arrived that the wife took me upstairs to calm me down, while everyone else did the spring cleaning.

'I hate him, I think I have ever since he was born,' I sobbed. 'I thought mothers are supposed to love their children automatically. He's such an impossible child, do you think I should take him to a child guidance clinic?'

'I think Justyn's troubles stem from your relationship with him,' this very wise friend told me firmly. 'He doesn't need a psychiatrist, he just needs you to love him.'

'Love!' I exploded. 'But that's just what I can't seem to give him.'

'But love is not an automatic emotion,' she told me, 'it's an act of the will. Let God's love pour through you to him.' I must have looked a bit unconvinced. My knowledge of God had all retreated to my head by that stage in my life, leaving my heart very empty.

'Try a week of emergency prayer,' she encouraged.

'I haven't got time to pray for an hour, let alone a week!' I almost shouted.

'I realise that,' she said, 'but why not set the timer on your cooker to ring every half hour. When you hear it, stop whatever you are doing and lift Justyn up to God, and then re-set the timer for another half hour. God understands how exhausted you are.'

Even before the week was up, Justyn had changed completely, and even more important, I had relaxed and started to feel differently about him. It was not long afterwards that he was playing in the sandpit and suddenly asked if he could ask Jesus to come inside him.

He was certainly one of those troubled children I watched Jesus change. He is still hyperactive as a teenager, but all his energy goes into his many sports, hobbies and interests, and now I totally love him.

I wish I could say that incident brought me back to God again. It is so easy to turn to Him in a crisis and then drift away again when He answers our prayers and life improves. We still went to church, but our faith was all rather on the outside, until suddenly one morning I woke up and found I just did not believe anything any more.

It was a devastating feeling. Father had just died very suddenly, leaving my brother Justyn to take on the work of Hildenborough, and I suppose my relationship with God and my father were too closely bound. I just could not believe the world no longer contained him and now I had lost my faith, I could not believe Heaven existed to contain him either.

But God rescued me yet again; this time by a dream. On the night that should have been the Boss's birthday, I had gone to bed in a low state of misery. I was in mourning for

God as well as my father. Suddenly our bedroom door opened and in he walked, looking fit and well, and he sat down on the end of my bed as he always did in life.

'I've come with a very special message for you, Jen-Jen,' he said. 'Heaven *does* exist, and it's a lovely place. I want you to know that I am wonderfully happy there. But I also want you to realise that how you live on earth affects the way you enjoy it up here. Don't waste your life. Remember, "Only one life, 'twill soon be passed, only what's done for God will last!"' Then he was gone.

In the morning I desperately wanted to tell Tony about it but my throat felt as if I had swallowed a hard-boiled egg. I tried again to tell him as we were undressing for bed, but I was still too choked with grief. Tony is a very easy man to live with, and he never questions people about their private, deep feelings. He merely remarked as he got into bed, 'I've had such an odd day, you know how you can get a tune on the brain, and you keep singing it all the time until you're sick of it. Well, I haven't had a tune, but a kind of jingle, like a record over and over again. "Only one life, t'will soon be passed, only what's done for God will last." I can't remember hearing it before, have you?'

That finally broke me, and I told him the whole story. A few days later my brother was sorting through some papers, when he came upon a letter written by the Boss to Justyn and me some ten years before he died. I know this quote by heart.

'When you have finally got rid of me, don't ever forget this. There is "only one life, t'will soon be passed, only what's done for God will last". The world says eat, drink and be merry – we only have one life to enjoy, but a Christian knows that life is only a tiny, quickly passing fragment of his real existence, and pleasing God is the *only* thing worth doing with it.'

## Chapter Ten

When you are unmarried, you get into the habit of chatting to God as you dress, listening to Him talking through the Bible in a leisurely quiet time, and then falling asleep at night talking over the day's events with Him. But when you are married you talk things over with your husband instead. Soon you are dashing up in the morning to feed the baby, make breakfast for the children, sort the lunch boxes and find the PE kits.

I suddenly realised as I looked at Rosemary Anne what Paul meant in 1 Corinthians 7: 34: 'An unmarried woman concerns herself with the Lord's work because she wants to be dedicated both in body and spirit; but a married woman concerns herself with worldly matters, because she wants to please her husband.' From that moment I have always known that people who are called by God to be single are highly favoured by Him and very precious in His sight.

For although Tony and I had worked together in the Peacemakers and were equally dedicated to God, once we were married we didn't seem able to share Him. We tried to have our quiet times together each morning, but it just didn't work. We were so much in love we didn't want to go into different rooms, yet we felt inhibited praying with someone else in the room.

As baby followed baby in rapid succession, our times with God became shorter and shorter until they petered out completely. The church we attended was peacefully dying in its sleep, and spiritually so were we. It is terrifying how our

Christian lives can atrophy: as the practice goes, so does the desire. Nor can we live on past experiences; there is no such thing as 'spiritual capital' – it has to be a daily income.

Grinding on as a dutiful Christian was wearing me down, yet I couldn't help noticing that exciting things were happening to some of my friends whom I had known from Peacemaker or Hildenborough days. God was doing something new in people's lives – reviving them and giving them power and gifts I thought had gone out with the early church.

I was so intrigued that I spent nearly all the week's housekeeping money on books about this wave of blessing. But I got a nasty shock. Tony saw them lying on the kitchen table and he was furious.

'I'm not having books like that in the house,' he fumed, 'go out and burn them right now!'

Unfortunately for me, I had just read a book by Larry Christenson where he said that the wife's duty is to submit to her husband, thereby submitting through him to God. So off I trotted to the bonfire with *The Holy Spirit and You, They Speak in Other Tongues*, not to mention *Nine O'clock in the Morning*. As I watched the whole lot go up in flames, I couldn't help thinking sadly how many groceries their price would have bought!

Submission is easy enough on the odd occasion; but soon I was forgetting all about it, and beginning to feel that I should not let Tony 'hold me back'. He'd always been so easygoing that I had really become the dominant one – rather bossy really. I so desperately wanted a deeper relationship with God, that I mentally pushed him aside. I wanted this new excitement and power too much to wait any longer.

So I made a terrible mistake. Instead of praying earnestly about Tony's reaction, and then going to him and asking him if we could reconsider all these things together – which I'm sure he would have done – I never discussed it with him again, and it became a taboo area for us. It must already be obvious that Tony and I had a communication problem in our marriage. A shy person living with a very gregarious one must often have difficulties.

So, because I just would not wait, one day I put baby Naomi into her pram and pushed her off to a local park, and sitting by the lake I said, 'Lord if there is such a thing as Baptism in the Holy Spirit, and You think I need it, please do it for me now.'

Nothing seemed to happen, so rather drearily I went home to wash the nappies, but the next morning I felt completely different; a bit like someone who has always watched a black and white TV and then suddenly buys a colour set. I read the whole Bible through like a novel, suddenly it was a completely new book to me. At first when I tried to pray in tongues, I felt a complete idiot but as the embarrassment faded, I found this new form of prayer was refreshing to my whole being as it still is today. Sometimes I even found I knew just how to pray for people or what to say to them by supernatural knowledge, and once when I was visiting a little girl in my Bible class who was desperately ill with a painful and incurable disease, I felt compelled to place my hands on her and she began to get better.

But I kept it all a secret from Tony – I felt he would not approve of this new supernatural Christianity. I met masses of new charismatic friends in Tunbridge Wells where we were living then, and the gulf between Tony and me widened as I dashed from prayer meeting to praise group. We were no longer friends: I had excluded him from the most important area of my life. He was very absorbed in setting up a team teaching system in his school, and began to spend longer and longer in the company of other teachers and less and less time at home. They gave him the acceptance, companionship and friendship that I had effectively withdrawn.

I felt I had joined the ranks of the Christian elite. With all this wonderful new power, perhaps I could do the great work for God I had always longed to do. I felt it was my ministry to fill the house with crowds of people who needed help. So whenever Tony did come home he fell over women having nervous breakdowns or marriage problems. I became so absorbed in my rosy little spiritual life that Tony and my responsibilities as a wife disappeared behind the horizon.

Spiritual inferiority complexes are rife in Christian homes. Women at home with small children have so much more time to grow in the Lord through prayer and Bible study groups, while the men are out at work, that it can cause terrible tension. I thought Tony was unspiritual; he thought I didn't need him any more. We were drifting apart at a frightening pace and our marriage was disintegrating.

I realise now that God would never have allowed me to be 'held back'. I am convinced that if Satan cannot stop new waves of blessing, he tries to cause people to become spiritually proud because they have received new gifts, then he manages to bring divisions in churches, friendships and families. If only I had shared everything with Tony and let us move on together, we would have been saved so much unhappiness.

Finally, God rescued us by allowing sorrow and stress to come our way. As Samuel Rutherford wrote, 'God hath more ways of hunting for our love than one or two.' We had not planned a fourth baby – I didn't want to disrupt what I saw as my 'ministry'. (I have come to loathe that word used in its present-day form. It sounds so arrogant; Jesus sends us to serve, to be slaves for the gospel and not superstars!) But Naomi had been such an easy child after the horrors of Justyn, that I wasn't too worried when I found I was pregnant again. In fact, I thought I was a pretty good mother by then; God certainly has used Duncan to topple my pride!

I knew there was something badly wrong with him by the time he was five days old, for he was in constant pain. He was born with a rare disease of the digestive system, and everything shot through the poor little chap, virtually unprocessed. He hung on to life somehow for several weeks, and then the consultant said, 'I am very sorry, but there is no more we can do.' It is a terrible feeling looking down into a hospital cot and realising your baby is dying, and no human can do anything about it.

Tony and I sat in the little cubicle with Duncan, and I remember gripping the radiator, feeling I wanted to shake it off the wall.

'I was reading the Beatitudes this morning,' said Tony, and his voice was coming from hundreds of miles away. 'Happy are they that mourn for God will comfort them.'

'I don't want to be comforted,' I stormed, 'I just want my baby to live.'

That evening Trevor Deering was preaching in Tunbridge Wells at a healing service. 'I'm going to that,' I said, 'you stay here with Duncan.' It was a huge meeting, packed to the doors, and at the end I went up and asked Trevor Deering to pray for Duncan. But when I got back to the hospital Duncan looked just as white and lifeless as he had when I left him.

But the next day something happened. The consultant came round again, and told us they were going to have one last try, feeding him with a new substance. 'So long as he eats nothing else whatever, it may just keep him ticking over until he gets stronger.' Valactin did that. It kept him alive – just – and for fifteen months we fed it to him through a bottle every three hours, day and night.

They were ghastly months. He developed breathing problems as well, so I had to do all my housework with him strapped in a carry seat on my back. Being upright helped him to breathe, and the warmth of my body soothed his tummy pain.

It was confusing. Why did God not fully heal him? I had laid hands on him in faith so many times, many people were praying and several with healing ministries visited us, but still I had to care for a little shrivelled wheezing monkey, hanging on to life by a thread. Why?

It could not be God's fault, so it must be mine. One evening after a desperate day when I really had had enough of his wails and wheezes, there at the door was our vicar, Donald Eddison – one of the most gentle people I have ever known. The look of sympathy in his eyes broke me down finally.

'He'd get better if I only had more faith,' I wept.

'No, no,' replied Donald gently. 'Never have faith *in* faith, it's only *His* faithfulness that counts.' Suddenly all the guilt and blame slid from me, and I was smiling as I showed him out of the front door later.

'Wait for God's time,' he said, as he stood on the doormat. 'It's always perfect.'

Because we had to wait fifteen months for His Perfect Time, Tony and I were drawn right back close together again, as we literally struggled for survival through the sleepless nights and exhausting days. We had time together at last because I could not be out at praise meetings, and the only people I had time to 'minister' to were my own four far from easy children.

Of course God didn't *cause* Duncan to be ill, but I think He does use the natural difficulties of life to bless us – and we really were greatly blessed by Duncan's illness.

Some time before Duncan was born I had managed to persuade Tony to come to a large charismatic gathering with me – I can't think how! We were met at the door by a well-meaning but massively tactless friend who beamed at Tony, and said, 'I didn't realise you had been "filled".' Tony was filled all right, but unfortunately it was with rage and not with the Spirit, and he vowed never to go near anything like that again.

So when Juan Carlos Ortis came to Tunbridge Wells I did not for one minute expect Tony to come with me. But it had been so many long months since we had been out together, that we trusted Duncan to Gom, just for once, and decided to go. We were both deeply blessed that night, and when Juan Carlos asked anyone who wanted to rededicate their lives completely to God's service to take off their coats and tie them around their waists as a sign that they would serve God in any and every way He desired, Tony's jacket came off before anyone else had their buttons undone.

92

Tony does not talk much, everything happens inside him, but two days later he said suddenly. 'The difference between consecrating one's life to God and receiving the Baptism of the Holy Spirit, is that when you *give* you can be proud that you were willing to give that much, but when you *receive* you can only feel humbled at receiving such an enormous amount.' That is all he ever said, but we were together again walking side by side, and right from that time we have actually enjoyed praying together daily.

It is a strange thing, but the week we moved into the peace of the country in Mayfield, Duncan was due to go back into hospital for a biopsy and other horrid tests (they thought he had cystic fibrosis among other things). He was just beginning to crawl, and while I was preoccupied with the hassle of moving in, he got into the larder and went through a box of groceries which lay on the floor. When I realised what he had eaten I was horrified. Even a tiny spoonful of the different foods the hospital had tested him with periodically had caused a violent reaction. Now he had gorged biscuits, sugar lumps, a cheese triangle, silver paper and all, and taken several bites out of an onion. When you have never actually eaten anything in your life, that is quite a lot!

'Good,' said the hospital when I rang them, 'as soon as he gets the reaction, bring him right over and we'll do the biopsy at once.' We are still waiting for that reaction, the next wheeze and the biopsy! God healed Duncan in his own perfect time and saved our marriage from foundering.

## Chapter Eleven

It was most humiliating for me to feel the same furious rage at the beginning of the last session with Rosemary Anne, as I had felt on the first, and this time I was not three, but well into my thirties. My only slight comfort was that I was pounding the walls of our lounge and hurting my fists instead of scratching to ribbons the person with whom I was really angry.

'Lord,' I heard myself pray, 'why don't You just take her to Heaven right now. She'll never be happy again down here, and she's driving me mad!'

It seemed terrible to pray that your mother would die, but I knew how she longed for Heaven.

When Father died she did not just lose a husband, she lost her work and her home. They had been together for so long, praying, working and uniting their gifts, that the shock of his death finally disintegrated her health. It was only right that she should leave Hildenborough to give Justyn and his wife Joy complete freedom to run the place in their own way, but when you have lived in a community for so long and are totally undomesticated, as well as having a rapidly deteriorating heart condition, you cannot really manage on your own.

She did not completely live with us, but we combined with Father's mother Lolo, and bought a house in the country big enough for us all to have a kitchen. It worked wonderfully well with Lolo, who was fit and well at nearly ninety, but with Mother it was a disaster. Her body may have worn out, but her mind still raced on, and she had no one now to organise but us! She rattled through a series of housekeeper-companions, becoming more and more depressed as her frustration grew.

Finally we just had to admit failure, and when we lost Lolo, we decided to split up and Mother began a life of private hotels and nursing homes in Tunbridge Wells. As her health became worse, senile dementia began to grip her mind and she was just not the same loving, outgoing person who had helped many thousands of people. In fact, her illness made her so impossible that she quarrelled continually with each nursing home and hotel, and Justyn, Tony and I constantly had the embarrassing job of moving her and her possessions on to the next place, until we almost exhausted even the vast list in Tunbridge Wells.

It was unbearable to see her like that, and Tony and I were constantly asking ourselves, 'What shall we do about Otty?' (as we all called her).

Of course we felt we should have her to live with us again, but my relationship with her had never been a very easy one. Her beauty, gifts and personality had always accentuated my own sense of inadequacy and I felt she despised me for just being a housewife and mother. Somehow, beside her I felt like a lumbering cart-horse next to a beribboned Derby winner.

'But when she had deteriorated physically and mentally, why did you still feel like that?' probed Rosemary Anne.

'Well,' I confessed, 'that irritated me just as much. With numerous small children of my own and fostering other people's, I had to live at a high speed, and her slowness infuriated me. And I never could cope with illness and handicap anyway.' Even as I said that, a cold feeling spread over me – if I could not cope with that in other people, how was I going to cope with it myself, and would my family feel as irritated by my incapacities as I had been by my mother's?

Vividly I remember the awful burden of guilt. We had her over one day a week, and I rang every day, but I still lived with the feeling that I was neglecting her. I knew she longed to come and live with us again and felt lonely and rejected, but I also knew I just could not cope.

When she had her stroke the whole thing came to a head. We realised it meant a geriatric ward or a full-scale nursing home after that, but I had visited such places, and heard the confused old people endlessly calling for the people they loved, and praying just to die.

That is why I started pounding our walls. Why could she not just die? I could not live with myself if I abandoned her to strangers, but she was only sixty-six and might live for years, and if she came to us what would happen to the 'work' I was going to do for God once the children were off my hands?

'What are you trying to do to me, Lord!' I raged, as I pounded the walls. 'Richard is only two, Jane needs so much time, and with the other four as well, how can you want me to look after a senile, incontinent invalid? Just take her home to Heaven, and solve everyone's problems.'

But He didn't. I'm glad now: He had so much to teach us. We were in our little church in Mayfield the following Sunday, and Sarah, who was then about twelve, suddenly passed her Bible along the pew, pointing vigorously to some verses in 1 Timothy 5. Hurriedly I read them, and felt my cheeks turning scarlet. 'But if a widow has children or grandchildren they should learn first to carry out their religious duties towards their own family and in this way repay their parents and grandparents because that is what pleases God. But if anyone does not take care of his relatives, especially the members of his own family, he has denied the faith and is worse than an unbeliever' (1 Tim. 5: 4, 8).

'Look at that, Mum!' said Sarah, in a hoarse whisper everyone in church could hear. 'We *ought* to have Otty to live with us.'

We went home and held a family council round the Sunday lunch table. All the childen agreed with Sarah, Tony was his usual easy self, only I knew I just could not cope.

'We'll pray about it,' I said weakly, but that afternoon as I did so, I saw a picture of myself hurtling at speed towards a brick wall on which I felt sure I would smash myself. But I knew the Lord wanted us to have her, and the children confirmed that conviction.

I don't think that *all* Christian families should care for their elderly relatives at home. The Lord must guide individually in each case. He knew I would not find it easy to cope, but He also knew I would not *have* to for long, so He gave me just enough strength and patience for the seven months more that she lived.

When she had her second stroke I was just about reaching cracking point, and the doctor said, 'Hospital I think,' when he looked at me. But I knew her one great fear was to die alone, so we decided to get private nurses to come in for a few hours each day, to give me a break.

'We're going to the sea, for some fresh air,' Tony said that Sunday, when the nurse arrived. It was so lovely after having been shut in the house for so many months. On the way home I was sitting in the back to keep the boys from fighting, and I suddenly realised I could not face arriving home. I just could not keep my mother any longer, my energy had run out. What shall I do, Lord?' I remember whispering, and then I saw that brick wall again, and I was still rushing towards it. The impact was imminent, and I braced myself for it, but as I reached that wall it just dissolved.

'I'll never test you above what you are able,' I heard the Lord say.

When we reached home, the nurse told us that Mother's condition had deteriorated suddenly. A few hours later she died, just as she would have liked to have done, with her son holding one hand, and me the other.

Looking after her like that to the end didn't exactly heal the guilt, though I am sure that's mostly why I did it. But guilt can't be dealt with by just doing positive things, and not letting God free us of the past. When she died the guilt about my feeling for her really set in hard.

One night I had a terrible nightmare. I was washing her in bed, as I had every day for all those months, but suddenly she was a skeleton. Only her eyes were alive, reproaching me for the way I was really feeling about her inside. I knew I needed help so I went straight round to my friend Rhoda, who had often prayed with me about things that troubled us both. Together we confessed my guilt to the Lord, and she asked Him for definite healing.

As she stood beside me, her hands on my shoulders, I saw that reproachful skeleton again, but as I watched, it fell away from me into a dark valley and I looked up to what seemed like a sunlit mountain top. There I saw Mother standing happily next to the Boss. She was wearing one of the feathery hats she always loved, and they both waved, reassuring me once again of their continued and happy existence in Heaven.

I did feel healed after that, though it never seemed quite fair to me that someone who had served God so faithfully should have been allowed ten such terrible years at the end.

That night, when Rosemary Anne had gone, I picked up Mother's worn old Bible from beside my bed. It had been such a joy to me at Burrswood. I could not read long passages, but I was fascinated by her heavy underlining of certain verses, which must have been very important to her. That night the tiny phrase 'But if not' caught my eye. It could hardly have failed to do so, seeing it was circled in red: Daniel 3: 18 (AV).

Suddenly I saw us at breakfast long ago, Justyn in his high chair, Nanny fussing round him, and me with egg on my face, while Mother told us the story of Shadrach, Meshach and Abednego so vividly that we could see the billowing flames, and feel the heat from that fiery furnace.

'What god is able to deliver you from me?' mocked the wicked king, while my egg grew cold.

'Our God is able to deliver us . . . but if not . . .' (Dan. 3: 17–18 AV) and I remember Mother actually crying with emotion as she told us that even though they knew God could deliver them from the flames, they were still prepared to trust Him even if He did not. In the margin and also in red Mother had added, 'Job said "If He slay me yet will I trust Him."' A little further on in her Bible I found this poem which must have dated from those last ten sad years.

> I thank you Lord for trusting me with pain
> That I should suffer loss, and so should gain
> Gold of experience tempered in God's fire,
> O Lord through suffering only we acquire
> Those priceless riches of Eternity,
> That soul enlargement, fellowship with thee.

I fell asleep with the happy knowledge that even if I did not understand why God had allowed her suffering and however muddled and agitated her mind had become, she had never lost her total love for the Lord. As soon as she stepped into Heaven, He would have explained to her *all* His reasons for allowing it! (2 Cor. 4: 16–17).

'I've found a verse for you,' I said when I saw Rosemary Anne next day – my last at Burrswood. 'Proverbs 20: 5: "A person's thoughts are like water in a deep well, but someone with insight can draw them out."'

She had done that so gently and so perceptively, and taught me what a wonderful form of healing this can be. I felt clean right through my whole being, and – yes – excited. I had looked back over forty years and realised He had been there to heal me in every crisis of my life, so He was not going to fail me now.

I left Burrswood full of hope, feeling healed spiritually, mentally and physically. I was growing stronger each day, and suddenly it was good to be alive again.

We did not go home straight away, but spent two weeks at Hildenborough Hall, where Tony was organising the children's activities at the family weeks Max was running. I stayed quietly in my room all the time on doctor's orders, but it was a wonderful opportunity to remake the relationships with Tony and the children without actually having to care

99

for them. They were all rather shy of me at first, but when one evening Richard climbed into bed beside me and said, 'Tell me a story,' I knew I was accepted again.

While we were there we had our wedding anniversary, and Tony took the day off and we went out together, just the two of us. It was one of those golden days that never fade in your mind. There was so much to talk about, and time to get it all said without the end of visiting hour waiting to cut us off.

There was something we badly needed to discuss. The doctor at Burrswood had called Tony aside before we left and said, rather ominously, 'Your wife will have to have completely full-time living-in help for at least eighteen months – no household responsibilities whatever, and she must spend most of every day resting.'

'We can't do that!' I protested in horror when Tony brought up the subject as we drove along the Kentish lanes. 'Our budget wouldn't even run to an hour's cleaning a week, let alone a full-time nanny/housekeeper/nurse/chauffeur – even if we could ever find such a paragon of virtue. And anyway,' I almost sobbed, 'I couldn't possibly have some strange woman running my house, I wouldn't have a reason for living any more.'

Cooking, washing and cleaning have always been my ways of showing love to my family and if I may have been 'just a housewife' at least that did give me some status in the world. '*And*,' I finished firmly, 'I'm being healed, and coping by myself will be good for my floppy muscles. You must *fight* illness, not sit about and rest all day!'

Tony understood, bless him, and said with a wry smile, 'I can always give you a hand, I'm pretty good with fish fingers now.'

We wanted to go into the little church in Otford where we had been married, at just that exact time sixteen years before, and as we knelt side by side at the rail we thanked God together that Tony had not had to face this day alone. We also thanked Him for preserving our marriage through some rough patches, and bringing us so close together, but there was something more we wanted to do. Certainly we wanted to thank the Lord for His steady daily healing, but we also felt we should ask for a definite leap forward, a speeding up, a big dollop of health as an anniversary present.

As we rose from our knees, I handed Tony my stick, 'I won't be needing that now,' I beamed, 'and I'll flush all my pills down the loo and leave the Lord to control my heart beat and do all the other things they're supposed to do. From now on I am *living in my healing!*'

When we reached the car we paused and looked at each other. 'I just know I am completely healed, so why shouldn't I drive up to Hildenborough?' I said.

Tony gulped, as faith and common sense fought each other, but faith won, and he handed me the car keys. He is always tense being driven by anyone, so that journey must have been terrifying for him, but five minutes later we landed safely, and as I pulled on the handbrake a wonderful thought struck me.

'Now I'm healed, we won't have to leave our lovely home and garden – we can stay in the country and live happily ever after!'

'We promised the Lord and the estate agent we would leave it till September,' replied Tony doggedly. 'We must keep our word.'

But our house had once suffered badly from subsidence, and everyone who viewed it threw up their hands in horror when they saw the cracks in the walls. By September no one had shown any interest in buying it. I could not help feeling a bit like Abraham when he found the ram in the thicket, and did not have to offer up his beloved son Isaac.

God had given me back my home – I had asked Him for a continuous joyous relationship with Him, but He had also healed me!

101

## Chapter Twelve

I was positively bubbling with excitement as we left Hildenborough. 'Lord make me an instrument of thy peace at home,' I wrote in my black book that morning, but several weeks later, I notice, I added a bitter little comment beside the entry: 'Ha blooming Ha!'

Selwyn Hughes says it is only too easy for Christians to confuse faith with presumption and it only took a few hours of being home for me to realise I was a cripple in body and mind. In hospital, at Burrswood and even in my room at Hildenborough, I had been sheltered from the real world of healthy people. Now they swarmed round me like ants in a disturbed ant heap.

I shall never forget Richard's first morning at school. I was determined to go with Tony and take him, even though I had not been out 'in public' before. As we reached the school gates I felt pierced by the stares of other children and their mums. They gazed at my suddenly emaciated body as it twitched and shook and reeled across the playground like a drunkard's. Some looked at me with pity in their eyes, which I hated, while others I had known for years turned away and pretended I was just not there.

Cooking was a nightmare. I hardly had the muscular strength to put a dish in the oven, and no feelings in my hands to tell me it was dangerously hot when I took it out. The vacuum cleaner became a monster with a will of its own, and without my stick I fell frequently because I could neither balance nor feel my feet. The family's recurring gag became

'What did you break today, Mum?' as my fingers, which would not grip, daily sent our china crashing to destruction. But it was my speech which caused them the most hilarity. I became increasingly unable to express what I wanted to say, and no one will ever forget the day I told Duncan to eat his clothes before putting on his cornflakes! My mind felt like a house gutted by fire – a burnt-out wreck. My ability to think was gone, and I could not even remember how long fish fingers take to cook.

The utter frustration and weakness made me terribly bad-tempered. I felt the children had run as wild as the garden in my absence, and soon I was constantly nagging about tidiness and table manners, and foolishly over-reacting to muddy footmarks and unbrushed hair. They must have wished I had never come home.

'You can't go on like this!' said my friend Penny (Brian's wife) when she discovered me one day, trying to do the ironing in a cold sweat of weakness. 'We'll organise a rota of church members – we'll take everything over from you. It will be a wonderful way to demonstrate to the whole village the ministry of caring.' But in my pride I did not want to be on the receiving end of anyone's 'ministry'.

'No thanks,' I said firmly, 'I couldn't bear the house full of people all the time, I just want to be left alone to get on with it.'

She was hurt, and I did not deserve friends like that. But I just wanted to run away from people because I was not the glowing Christian witness I felt I ought to be – I was too tired. Nor could I stand people seeing how mutilated I was. I was brain-damaged, and I could not even speak clearly enough to hold a conversation. So I locked the doors to prevent people popping in as they always do in the country, and if I heard someone ring the bell, I hid. They soon got the message, and stopped coming. How I thank God that Grace had already learnt how to break into our house. She continued to do so every morning, insisting on taking the children to school, and having a quick time of prayer with me before they left. She has suffered many things in her life, and I felt she accepted me as I was, and never made comments or offered sympathy and advice. We have prayed together regularly ever since.

One evening Tony found me standing at the window gazing helplessly over the garden. The apples needed picking, the vegetables were ready to go down in the freezer, and everywhere needed an autumn tidy-up, but I did not even have the energy to open a tin of baked beans.

'That's why I wanted to move, darling,' he said gently. 'Starting a new life would have been easier than not being able to live the old one.'

'But I *will* get better!' I stormed repeatedly, as the chaos mounted around us. I had once been so proud of my spotless house – how ridiculous that seemed now.

Two of my mother's sisters were so concerned in the end that they paid for us to have someone in to clean several times a week, or I really think the children might have become ill from living in unsanitary conditions.

I did not mind Melody coming in because she was paid to do so, but I was not going to sponge on other Christians. I seemed to have forgotten all the joy I had received from cleaning other people's houses, and cooking them meals in my old 'Martha' days. All I managed to do was to make myself bitterly lonely, and hurt a lot of people as well as robbing them of the blessing God would have given them for helping us. It *is* much more blessed to give than to receive, and also much more pleasant for the ego!

The inevitable consequence of my pride was a relapse. The doctors had warned me that if I did not rest the inflammation would begin to increase again. Soon the pain in my spine and head was quite indescribable. The high-voltage painkillers did not help the vertigo, and I was soon too nauseated to eat. The slightest thing sent me into a panic, but still my pride would not let me admit defeat and rest was still a rude word.

Quite the most devastating thing of all was that I seemed to have lost the closeness of my relationship with the Lord.

For years I had looked forward to Richard going to school so I could have time on *my own* to study the Bible and pray. Now he was out all day, I missed him desperately and felt redundant and lonely, while prayers seemed never to penetrate the ceiling and the Bible felt just a boring jumble of meaningless words.

'You are not playing fair, Lord,' I burst out one morning as I struggled to scrub the egg from the breakfast plates. 'I asked You that night in hospital for a *continuous* close relationship, but I couldn't feel further away from You if I was Judas! I thought You'd healed me, but in fact I am getting worse!'

But He did not answer me, and so I muddled on with the help of quantities of painkillers until, quite suddenly, I went into the dark valley. Of course, I had forgotten about the vision He had given me in London, warning me of the depression to come, so I was completely devastated.

By then I was just beginning to be able to concede that it might be possible for God to allow a Christian to succumb to a physical illness for several good reasons, but it was quite impossible for a Christian to be depressed. That, in all the books I had read, was caused by inner conflict or buried sin, and I had just spent a whole long exhausting week having my memories healed. If I had gone to the doctor he would have told me depression hits most people after such a serious illness. But I wouldn't go – I thought he might label me as a mental case. I did not mention it to Tony, Grace or anyone else, I was too deeply ashamed, but a terrible black cloud descended over my head, tangible and suffocating.

No pain or illness is as bad as depression, and you cannot believe it will ever end. In all other forms of illness, distress, bereavement or suffering of any kind a Christian can feel conscious of God's presence, but one of the symptoms of depression is the loss of joy in the Lord, the assurance of His love, and often the belief in His existence.

I have to confess that I had always been slightly irritated by depressed people, feeling sure that their problems were brought on by their own self-centred attitude – all they needed to do was to stop thinking about themselves and start praising the Lord. I sense that quite a few Christian people think like this – until depression hits them as well! Proverbs 25 verse 20 says, 'Singing to a depressed person is like taking off his clothes on a cold day, or rubbing salt into a wound.' I quickly learnt the truth of that verse, and could not go near church or even Burrswood for months. After all, God had not healed me, so He could not really love me.

The black cloud was always worse first thing in the morning, and if I had managed to sleep at all it hit me as I woke, feeling more like a ton of wet sand than a cloud. However could I face another day?

I would have been far worse off without the children. Because of them I *had* to get up and see them off to school complete with lunch boxes, and although the lethargy of depression made me want to lie in bed all day with a pillow over my face, I had to cook a meal for them all in the evening, and that often took me three or four hours at least!

Of course I had deliberately cut myself off from people, but another symptom of depression is feeling no one cares about you any more, and I was bitterly lonely, after always living in a house full of people. Now the phone and the door bell never rang, and each day seemed like a week.

Somehow I could not bring myself to address the Almighty direct, but communicated with Him through my diary. I am embarrassed to read it now, and only comforted by the fact that Job, when he was ill and depressed, expressed his feelings to God in much the same rude fashion. I must have gone on reading my Bible each day and heavily underlined and positively wallowed in such passages as Psalms 42, 69, and 102, not to mention Lamentations Chapter 3.

I am one who knows what it is to be punished by God. He drove me deeper and deeper into darkness and beat me again and again with merciless blows. He has left my flesh open and raw and has broken my bones. He has shut me in a prison of misery and anguish . . . He rubbed my face in the ground and broke my teeth on the gravel. I have forgotten what health and peace and happiness are . . . my hope in the Lord is gone.

(Lam. 3: 1–5, 16–18)


Only a few months before, the Lord had been everything I wanted my life to contain. His love had been a constant hourly joy; now He was a brutal punishing tyrant. What had I done to lose His company and comfort? I missed Him unutterably.

One entry in my prayer diary says, 'Lord, these pages are full of requests, which You never seem to answer, how come?' A few days later: 'All right Lord, so You don't care about me any more, but You might at least help me to be less bad-tempered with the children! All this must be hell for Tony.'

However horrible depression is, I think it must be harder to live with depression than to *be* depressed. Tony just thought I was in severe physical pain, but I could see his spirits drooping, just when he was becoming happy again after my experience with Father Keith. I exhausted myself by making frantic efforts to lift the gloom I knew I was creating, only to be cut to the heart one day at tea time, when Sarah remarked, 'We never seem to laugh any more these days.' How responsible a mother is for the atmosphere of a family!

Looking back on it all now, I can see how good God was to give me that vision in London of the dark valley, and gently to explain to me His reasons for allowing me to go through it. That helps me now to understand that depression, but strangely it did not help me at the time. Never once during those dark months did I look backwards in my diary and recall that vision. I suppose if I had I would never have learnt one of the main lessons He wanted me to learn through that experience. When we belong to Him, He *is* with us whether we feel it or even believe it. All through that dark valley His 'everlasting arms' were beneath me (Deut. 33: 27 AV), even when I did not *realise* it. His presence with us does not depend on our feelings or our faith, it just happens to be a fact!

I can see from my diary how serious things were becoming when I read entries like, 'I am lost. Life is quite hopeless. Why didn't I just die on June 2nd when I had the chance? Tony and the children would all be happier without me. I am just a useless zombie. Perhaps I should destroy myself before I damage my family any more.' What would the village say? I thought cynically as I lay in the bath one night. I have spent years gossiping about how wonderful God is, they'll hardly believe me when I'm found hanging.

It was only a kind of game at first – planning my suicide, but one day I discovered an old bottle of my mother's sleeping pills and stood in the middle of my bedroom holding them in my hand for a dangerously long time. I could take them all, and then stagger into the wood, so the children did not find me when they came home. How easy it would be. With a shudder of horror I threw them back into the drawer, but the idea stayed with me night and day. Suddenly I realised that I needed help urgently. It was my pride I needed to swallow, not a bottle of Mogadon.

I had to go to the Kent and Sussex for one of my boring out-patient checks, so very nervously I made an appointment to see George on the same day. I was literally shaking with fright as I knocked on the door marked Hospital Chaplain.

'I'm terribly sorry,' I apologised, 'but I seem to have gone into a depression.' To my relief he did not seem to be shocked or even surprised. He did not need all the gory details, nor did he probe into the reasons or try to detect the 'root sin'.

'You must not feel guilty about this depression,' he said gently. 'You are feeling absolutely ghastly, and when Jesus felt like that on the cross He told His Father just how He felt, and cried out to Him in the darkness. So He understands *just* how you are feeling now. We are going to do just what He did, but we're also going to ask the Father to take this depression away.'

There was no oil, or laying on of hands – no 'going down under the Spirit' – he just asked God to take it away and God did, and suddenly I felt that cloud lift off the top of my head.

I really cannot say I 'went on my way rejoicing' because when you have been depressed for a long time your mind gets into the habit of it, and has to be reprogrammed. But the next morning I woke waiting for the now familiar weight to drop, and it did not. That night I recorded in my diary, 'Felt groggy physically all day but not *one bit depressed*!'

Being George, he had not let me off scot free! 'Take one verse from the Bible each day,' he told me, 'and repeat it over and over as you work round the house, but each time emphasise a different word:

> *My* grace is sufficient for you
> My *grace* is sufficient for you
> My grace is *sufficient* for you
> My grace is sufficient for *you*.'

It is just as well that our house was right out in the wilds, because if any of the village gossips had looked at me through my window and seen me muttering, 'I *can* do all things through Christ,' while watering the house plants, and setting the table while shouting, 'My strength is made perfect in weakness,' the village grapevine would have had me certified!

But at the beginning there was one verse I just could not manage – 'The joy of the Lord is my strength' – because I had to re-learn what joy was.

It is extraordinary how healthy and happy everyone else looks when you are feeling depressed. Even television adverts are irritating! When a friend gave us tickets for the opera *Fidelio* in Eastbourne, I felt deeply threatened by all the laughing faces around me, and did not enjoy my evening out until the house lights went down and the curtains rose.

During the wonderful scene when the prisoners are led out of their dark dungeon into the light of freedom, I whispered, 'Lord, I've been in captivity like them, I know I'm coming out into the light now, but I've lost all my joy.'

'Have mine then,' He replied through the glorious crescendo of music.

It's all very well saying 'have mine', I thought as we drove home through the fog and rain, but practically speaking, how can I get it?

As usual, I knew the answer in theory. *It is the act of praise that brings the joy, not the joy that brings the praise.* That night I looked up two of my favourite 'depressed' passages, and was suddenly struck by the antidote to depression the Bible so clearly gives. Psalm 69 was so full of gloom that I had loved it, but the sudden change comes between verses 29 and 30. 'I am in pain and despair, lift me up O God, and save me!' How often I had pleaded with Him, seemingly in vain to save me, but verse 30 gives the answer: 'I will praise God with a song, I *will* proclaim his greatness by giving him thanks.' Then I looked up Lamentations 3: 19–24: 'The thought of my pain . . . is bitter poison, I think of it constantly and my spirit is depressed, *yet hope returns to me* when I remember this one thing: the Lord's unfailing love and mercy still continue . . . the Lord is all I have, and so I put my hope in him.'

Somehow it had to be an act of will on my part to praise Him when nothing seemed to be going right, and trust Him when everything else seemed to have vanished. I found many other passages in the Bible with this theme, but I still firmly believe that this cure for depression cannot be forced on to a depressed person. Had George told me, when I went to see him in depression, 'The Bible says just praise the Lord and everything will be fine,' I might well have hit him! What comforted me then was to know that Jesus really did know how terrible I felt, and through George's prayer for me the Lord Himself opened my eyes to the Bible's way out of depression.

'But I don't know how to praise you, Lord,' I gulped as I

110

weakly looked round the bomb site which is my house after the children have left for school. Even with Melody's help with cleaning there was still a terrifying amount of tiny little jobs that made up my day. I would stand and sweat with panic as I faced the mountain of clean washing which had to be sorted into eight different piles, and lunch boxes were a nightmare, trying to remember seven various likes and dislikes.

I started to force myself to see each little job as something actually done for God. I implored His help at the beginning, imagined Him watching me as I did it as an offering for Him, and finally thanked Him with relief when it was finished, and before I started to panic about the next job. I did not feel like praising Him, and I often had to do it through clenched teeth. But at last one day I remember cleaning some mud-encrusted hockey boots, and shouting, 'The joy of the Lord *is* my strength!'

Slowly it began to take effect – I can actually see the entries in my prayer diary changing in nature. At first they were screams for help and deliverance, then endless little personal requests like, 'Lord, show me what to wear today,' and 'What shall I cook for tea?' People in depression are totally turned in on themselves. They cannot help it; it is a symptom of the illness, like spots with measles, but after a while I found myself praying for Tony and the children. Then as I forced myself to make contact again with other people, I began to be concerned for their needs and prayed about their problems, a sure sign I was on the mend. Finally one morning I wrote, 'Lord I seem to come to You each morning with a list of things *I want You to do for me or others*. Please help me to ask You first what You want *me* to do for *You*.'

Through that depression – ghastly as it was – I learnt a new reliance on the Lord. If I had never reached the point of utterly devastating inability, I might never have realised how much I need His help in the little things as well as in the big things of life. I had asked Him that night in the Kent and Sussex Hospital for a continuous relationship of worship.

Dimly I began to see that He could be worshipped through the ordinary little jobs of every day just as easily as He can be in church on Sundays.

When that landmark of the fortieth birthday arrived, and it dawned on me that I probably never would achieve any great world-shaking work for God, it was a deep comfort to realise that the two words for worship and serve are the same in Hebrew. Just as I could worship Him while I washed the dishes and made the sandwiches, I was also serving Him when each tiny act was done for Him. I do, however, have to admit that it would be much happier for the ego if one was called to do something for the Lord that other people noticed as well!

## Chapter Thirteen

'How are you?' beamed a Christian friend one day as I struggled round the village supermarket.

'Fine!' I lied as I contorted my face into what I hoped was a 'good Christian smile'. Actually I felt ghastly, but other Christians expect you to be problem free and constantly victorious, and I felt I had to live up to their expectations or I would let the Lord down.

'You're coping all right then?' she continued, in the tone of voice that demands only the answer yes.

'Melody does the things I can't manage,' I told her.

'How wonderful,' gushed my friend. 'She will see such a grand Christian witness in your home.' I gulped and my smile slipped a bit. Right between the shelves of baked beans and biscuits it dawned on me that I was living a double life; putting on my Christian smile like a hat when I went out. At home Melody did not see a patient Christian nobly putting up with trials, but a bear with a sore head – the grizzly kind!

As I crawled home, I felt the size and shape of a slug. Suddenly my mind went back to the days of the Peacemakers, and I remembered one of the group called George. He had many problems in his life. 'Christians should always be happy and cheerful whatever they go through,' he was told. 'Then I can't really be a Christian after all,' he said hopelessly, and hanged himself in despair.

George was more honest than I am, I thought, as I felt once again the shock of his death.

I have observed Christian friends going through terrible

crises and bereavements, and their radiant witness to the world builds your faith in the reality and loving kindness of the Lord. But when the acute stage is over or if their problems are long term, a very human reaction can set in – just when their Christian friends feel they should be 'getting over it'.

This is just what happened to Job. At first he coped with his trials in triumph, saying, 'The Lord gave, and the Lord has taken away, blessed be the name of the Lord' (Job 1: 21 RSV). But when his illness had dragged wearily on for months – if not years – he started behaving very badly saying the most outrageous things. Yet God still loved him, and it was in those dark times that Job said, 'Though He slay me, yet will I trust Him.'

At least Job was honest with his friends, even if he did shock them. But in these days of stereotypes we feel Christians should be perpetually joyful, and if we don't feel like that, we force ourselves to pretend. But aren't we forgetting that we are human beings? We must allow ourselves and one another to hurt sometimes, and we have to keep remembering that we all react to things differently. What may be an enormous trauma to one person is only a slight annoyance to another. God sees us as individuals – when will we learn to do the same!

'I'm a hypocrite!' I confessed to a friend later that day. 'But everyone I meet says, "How are you?" so what *am* I supposed to say?'

Betty grinned at me over her coffee cup. 'Just say, "I've got lots to thank the Lord for." It's always true, however ghastly life may be, and it also honours God.'

Of course it is wrong for us to grovel around constantly moaning about our problems; the more we talk about them the bigger they seem. But I have become convinced that we need to be more honest with each other. Someone came to see me the other day who has recently lost her husband, her home and almost everything else she valued.

'I am baffled and hurting,' she told me. 'But I know the

114

Lord will help me through.' I felt she was so much more genuine than I was when I went about wearing a fixed smile and saying 'I'm fine, I haven't any problems.'

The wonderful thing is that although I felt so embarrassed about my bad witness to Melody, she still found the Lord, though in spite of me and not because of me. When she answered my advertisement in the sweet-shop window, she was already searching for God because her sister had recently found Him, and had started to pray for her. She began asking me questions about God as she scrubbed the floors or cleaned the windows.

'You Christians always seem so happy,' she said one day, and I nearly died of surprise. Perhaps joy is something we have whether we actually feel it or show it. We don't have to put it on – it is there underlying everything when Jesus lives in us. Happiness depends on happenings, but He promised us His joy no matter what we have to go through.

Melody became such a good friend, it seemed like the end of the world when she said she had to leave because she was moving house. But as always the Lord helped us, though He certainly sent the help in an extraordinary package.

One night at the House Group meeting, Brother Tom told us about a wonderful dream he had had several nights before. He was in his kitchen, he told us, when suddenly Jesus Himself came to the door. I'll make Him the best meal I've ever cooked, Brother Tom thought ecstatically. In his dream he set to work and soon placed before the Master a plate of grilled fish covered in cheese sauce, fluffy white potatoes and green peas. 'But,' finished Tom sadly, 'I woke up before I saw Him enjoying it.' Mrs Burton's face was a study, but Tom had not finished. 'Two days later, I had just taken my brothers their meal in the refectory, leaving my own in the oven. When I came back to fetch it, I heard a knock on the back door, and outside in the rain stood a very smelly tramp, who asked for a meal.' Communities like Brother Tom's are obliged by their rule to give hospitality, but there was no food left, except Tom's own plate in the oven.

'So rather crossly I served him with it at the kitchen table. But as I watched him begin to eat, I realised it was grilled fish in cheese sauce with potatoes and peas. I was so overwhelmed I had to start washing the saucepans to hide my tears.' 'As much as ye have done it unto one of the least of these my brothers, ye have done it unto me' (Matt. 25: 40 AV).

It so happened that John, the tramp, had recently been converted and baptised by a wonderful man, Pastor Lywood, who works tirelessly among gipsies and men of the road. Dear old John could praise the Lord even louder than Brother Tom. While he stayed on with the brothers, he started to come to our church in Mayfield. But John had a bad drinking problem, so the community had to ask him to leave, and he began sleeping rough again round the village, sheltering in farm buildings and even under hedges. Of course he did not need to, with the welfare state and many private charities, but he had been a tramp for so long, he hated the thought of being restricted.

One very cold Sunday as he sat stinking in the pew in front of us, Naomi whispered, 'Mum, let's ask him back for lunch.' We did, and he stayed with us for the rest of the day while everyone breathed through their mouths, and not through their noses, trying hard to keep remembering Tom's dream. It was easy enough for me – I'd lost my sense of smell!

When it was late and we began to make 'final noises' in John's direction, Naomi drew me into the kitchen and said, 'Mummy, you can't let us sleep in warm beds while John freezes under a hedge.' We had no room in the house so we made him a bed in the shed at the bottom of the garden where Tony hides when he wants to write a book.

'You're welcome to stay here tonight, John,' we said, and he took up permanent residence!

What a good story it would make if I could say that John reformed and became a member of AA, but sadly John likes drink too much to be delivered from it, and still frequently disappears for a few wild days, always returning repentant and needing a bath. He likes being a tramp, and also he did not get his nickname, Burglar Bill, round the village for nothing. But he has given us far, far more than we could ever have given him – a few old clothes, a shed, and his food. If we had paid him for the hours of work he does for us, Tony's salary would not be adequate. He hacked the garden back into shape, mended the drive, cleaned the car, and then quietly came along behind me doing all the things he knew by instinct I could not manage – peeling potatoes, polishing furniture, scrubbing floors and vacuuming the carpets.

'You sit down, Mrs Woman,' he would say, 'I'll do that, while you have a cupacoffee.'

The village looked at us askance and our friends gave us lectures on bad influences on the children. Even the village policeman warned us to be careful, but we just do not deserve the pure unselfish love John still gives us to this day. The Lord sent him along to be my lost strength and energy, and to teach us that 'Our God *shall* supply all our needs', even if He does so in rather unconventional ways.

## Chapter Fourteen

Once I heard a preacher say, 'Come to Jesus and all your problems will be solved.' I'm glad for him that his life was so easy, but I am beginning to think it is more a question of: 'Come to Jesus and your problems will increase but you will have Him there to help you in them.'

It was spring, and old familiar friends were beginning to reappear in the overgrown garden. The depression had gone, the Lord's presence was a reality again, and I was stronger physically as well. Everything in the garden (and the house) should have been lovely, but as I emerged from my self-centred cocoon, I realised what a hammering the children had taken over the previous year.

Duncan was now the terror of the village, the despair of his teacher, and so difficult in Sunday school that Tony had to teach him in a separate private class all on his own. My handicap embarrassed him terribly.

'Don't ever come into school,' he told me, 'I couldn't bear my friends to stare at you.'

Later when I needed sticks again, he hid them constantly. I lost five in a row and the physio department were going mad. His love of sport and vigorous movement was outraged by my lack of co-ordination.

Jane still could not seem to forgive me for deserting her, and did not want to start relying on me again – she could no longer trust me. She was as rude and morose as any teenager could be, and was also in very serious trouble at school. But Sarah was worse than any of them! She can talk about it

118

now quite frankly, but at the time I was just baffled by her behaviour.

'When you were in hospital Dad relied on *me*. We made all the decisions together; I was in charge. I missed you, but when you came back you were not my mum any more, you were more like my great-great-grandmother. You never appreciated all I had done, you just grumbled because the kitchen was reorganised. I wanted you to look after me again, but every time we came near you it was "pick up that for me" or "reach this down". I felt guilty inside because I hated the way you looked and how I felt about you, so I freaked out.'

She certainly did! Withdrawing herself from the closeness of the family, she started mixing with a wild set of friends, going out with a non-Christian boyfriend and attending rowdy parties. She did no work at school whatever. Thank God it was not her O-level year, but the end-of-term exams were important because they decided which subjects she would be taking.

I have discovered since, from the teenage children of terminally ill or suddenly handicapped parents, that all these reactions are quite normal. But it was a real anguish at the time. I could feel them drifting away from us and from God. Tony and I prayed earnestly for them all, with fasting. 'Lord,' I cried, 'have You forgotten that night in the hospital when I said all I want is for my children to know and love You?'

We long for the very best for our children – easy, carefree lives with success and achievement – but strangely that is not the best soil for growing character or dependence on God.

I heard recently that horticulturists have discovered that causing stress to tiny seedlings by touching them regularly appears to have an effect on their growth. The plants that receive this 'harsh' treatment initially appear to be stunted. However, by the time they are ready to be planted out, they are far more sturdy than the seedlings raised in 'untroubled' conditions.

I am convinced that the same rule applies to humans.

James 1: 2 in the Living Bible says: 'Dear brothers, is your life full of difficulties and temptations? Then be happy, for when the way is rough, your patience has a chance to grow. So let it grow, and don't try to squirm out of your problems. For when your patience is finally in full bloom, then you will be ready for anything, strong in character, full and complete.'

Of course no parent wishes disaster on their children, and it is a real agony when *you* are the cause of their lives being unsettled. I struggled daily with a deep feeling of guilt – it was my fault that they were suffering and *I* was the reason they were behaving so badly.

Many other parents I have talked to, who are having a rough time with their teenagers, share this deep feeling of guilt. As parents we are all constantly making mistakes and failing our children in countless ways, so when they appear to go off the rails, we despairingly blame ourselves. It's this feeling of guilt that causes us to try to 'make it up to them' by being soft, which only makes matters worse. We have to ask God to deal with the guilt; I can't think why I didn't do that at the time.

In May Sarah caught a bad dose of flu, and for a week or two I put her depression down to 'post-flu blues', but as time passed I was horrified to observe her going through the ghastly experience from which I had so recently emerged. When she 'couldn't face going to school' and locked herself in her room for hours, crying, I wasted no time. I had learnt my lesson.

First I went straight to Burrswood. Sarah refused to come with me, which lowered me a notch, and then worse still, I was late for the healing service. I wanted to catch Father Keith before it began so I could tell him about Sarah, but they were singing the first hymn when I finally lurched in.

This is just a waste of time, I thought in agitation. If I could have explained to him first, he could have prayed for Sarah when he lays hands on me.

As I knelt that morning at the communion rail, something

120

wonderful happened. Father Keith put his hands on my head and prayed as usual for me and for those for whom I prayed, and then he paused, as if listening to God, then he said, 'Fear not, I am in control of this situation, it will bring Me glory, and My blessings will not cease.' I knew that was a word straight from God for us, and I went away clutching it, like a rope thrown to a drowning person.

Our doctor was marvellous. He said it was post viral depression, coupled with the strain of my illness. I felt Sarah should go straight back to school, knowing from my own past how hard it is to go back once you stop. He would not hear of it, and she spent the rest of the summer fruit-picking at a local farm.

As I have already said, living with a depressed person is terrible. I knew only too bitterly well what she was going through, but she did not want to share her world with me – she was a teenager. Jane's school troubles were escalating alarmingly, and she and Sarah were both so rude and aggressive at home, life was almost intolerable! I could not say the right thing to either of them, or to Duncan either for that matter. As usual I knew how to cope in theory, but in practice I did all the wrong things, and became just as rude and bad-tempered as they were.

'Why am I such a failure as a mother, Lord?' I wept at the kitchen sink one morning, when I had lost my temper with one of the children yet again. 'They were all so lovely when they were little, now they have rejected me utterly.'

'You said you wanted to share the fellowship of my suffering,' He replied. 'The day they dragged Me to Calvary I looked like the greatest failure of all time, and the rejection of "My own" when they received Me not, was a greater suffering than the pain of the whips. Only parents who admit they are failures and so rely on Me are successful in My sight.'

That was a real turning point. Just knowing that Jesus understands what it feels like to be rejected helped. Over the last three years, although Tony and I have been conscious so often that we have failed, we have clung to the promise in James I: 5: 'If any of you lack wisdom let him ask of God' (RSV). We have seen all those three children changing wonderfully, and each one having a definite encounter with God. As parents we long to do everything for our children, but sometimes the only thing we can do is step out of the way and let God act in their lives – healing them of consequences of our own mistakes and inadequacy.

Sarah went back completely happily to school that autumn and discovered the enjoyment of working really hard for her O-levels, but she still would not go to church with us.

'Our church bores me, and I hate sitting in the pew like all the other good little Larcombes.'

'Well, why don't you choose a church of your own, and go there as a person in your own right?' I replied. She looked slightly amazed, but replied, 'I might just do that. I'll go with Lois to her church – they have dancing in the aisles and drums there.'

She went to church with Lois, and was deeply blessed, and soon she had dragged along most of the wild set she had been mixing with earlier in the year, and one after another they found the Lord. Yes, we did miss worshipping as a whole family together, but it was only our pride that liked to see all our children with us on a Sunday. I genuinely would not mind if they all went to different churches, so long as they are all growing in the Lord.

Perhaps Jane needed to get herself into deep trouble at school in order to test us. When she discovered we loved her whatever she did, and were prepared to stand by her, she relaxed and her behaviour problems ceased. All the same, I still found her rudeness and unhelpful attitude at home often made me so angry I did not even want to pray for her. When I told the Lord about this, He said, 'Don't pray for her any more then, just praise Me for her.' That was far from easy at first, I can tell you, but as it became easier He showed me that my negative, critical attitude to her was destroying our relationship.

'But, Lord,' I said, 'there's always something to be negative and critical about.'

'You can praise *Me*, so now praise her,' He replied. Well, that was even harder, but as I exaggerated my thanks and positively buttered her with appreciation every time she did anything that was even remotely helpful, she became a great deal more responsive. The other children looked rather aggrieved at all the unusual fuss I was making of her, reminding me of the prodigal son's older brother. Meanwhile Jane blossomed with this encouragement, and has developed into a marvellous cook and a real help and joy to us, while our relationship with her is closer now than we have known it before. God is also answering our prayer for Duncan – people meeting him for the first time would never believe he was once the local terror!

By summer I felt wonderfully better, and once again we began to believe that God was healing me. That bad patch when I had first arrived home was surely just a satanic attack on our faith. Our family increased when Gom retired and came to live with us. Our house had elastic sides and fortunately she loved John as much as we did. Strangely, they have a lot in common. They both derive the maximum enjoyment from the little things of life, and they neither of them care one jot for their own comfort. Between us we ran the household, and made a blissfully happy team.

We went back to the same hostel in Yorkshire that summer and it seemed hardly possible that a whole year had gone by. I could walk without a stick and I felt positively drunk with the beauty of the scenery and the joy of feeling well.

'Next year, we'll walk the whole Pennine Way together,' I promised the family, and we bought maps and guide books in anticipation. I went into training and as soon as we got home I started a get-fit campaign. I became a complete health-food addict, and even tried to force my unco-ordinated body to jog.

That autumn was the happiest time in my whole life. The children were peaceful and settled again. Tony looked ten years younger, and because John and Gom did most of the work, I was free to do something I really wanted to do. I had written several children's books some years before, but I longed to try a novel for teenagers. My fingers could not hold a pen but in my reclusive teenage years I had taught myself to type, so I locked myself in my bedroom and tried to make a start. But it was completely impossible to write a word in our house because John and Gom never stop talking, or should I say shouting, because they are both rather deaf! I had to drive myself into the middle of a field and type on my knee in the back of the car. I used to cry with joy over the beauty of the golden leaves as I walked through the countryside with our little dog Minty. It was so easy to praise the Lord that autumn, and even the book was accepted.

Then one day I caught a little snuffly cold from the children. It was not even bad enough to keep them off school, but the effects on me were devastating. The joy of banging your head against the wall comes when you stop, but if you start again it is far worse than the first time, because you know what is coming. Once more the pain, giddiness and fatigue clamped down on me as the inflammation flared up again, and I was sent back to the neurologist I first met in London.

'Your condition seems to have reached the chronic stage,' he explained in his usual patriarchal manner. 'You now have persistent inflammation of the brain, menenges, nerves and muscles. There is nothing we can do to cure this, or reverse the damage it will do. You have been unusually lucky over the last few months, but you must expect the condition to have periods when it worsens – we call them relapses. If you keep away from infection, and really rest, you will have fewer relapses.' That struck me as a hilarious thing to say to a mother of six young children!

'Learn to enjoy the better times,' he said graciously as he showed me to the door.

How odd, I thought as I staggered out of the neurological department. 'All I can do is laugh! For sixteen months I've

124

believed the Lord was healing me gradually. Now I find He's doing no such thing, and I don't even mind. Perhaps that is a greater miracle than my healing.' That numb feeling lasted for weeks, but it was only the mind acting as a thumb does when you hit it with a hammer. The pain is delayed, but it has to come in the end.

During that numb patch I felt almost euphorically happy. I still had my lovely peaceful home, I could see the woods and fields even if I could not walk in them, and I was carried along on the love and prayers of our little church and all our Christian friends who had become all-important to me again, since I came out of the depression.

But one Sunday afternoon a huge bombshell fell and exploded my peace completely.

## Chapter Fifteen

'I can't stand it any longer!' burst out Tony one day, as we sat on a seat while the children swarmed over the ruins of Pevensey Castle.

'Stand what?' I said blankly.

'Stand living in Mayfield, we just have to move back to Tunbridge Wells.' In my dazed state I had failed to see how worn and tired he was looking. His mind had not been numbed by the shock – he saw into the future all too clearly.

'I really cannot spend my whole life driving between Tunbridge Wells, Wadhurst and Mayfield. It's not just the swimming now, they've all got their hobbies and interests and they can't go anywhere now unless I take them. And let's face it, this house is quite unsuitable for you now, and we'll never cope with the garden again.'

'The Lord sent us John to help over that,' I put in.

'We can't rely on him,' said Tony crossly, 'he'll get himself run over one night when he's drunk.' I remembered the reason our house had not sold before and clutched at a straw.

'We'll never sell the house with all the cracks.'

'We'll have a jolly good try,' answered Tony mulishly, 'and what's more, I need a bigger church.' We had attended huge Anglican churches in Paddock Wood and Tunbridge Wells and I knew he felt happier in a larger, less intense atmosphere, but I flourished in the intimacy of something more like a house church.

We drove halfway home in silence. I was too stunned to speak. I had offered my home and friends up to the Lord at

126

Burrswood that day, but I had been so relieved when He had given them back.

'Look, we must pray about this,' I said at last, secretly hoping that God would listen to my side of the argument. We did pray, and we asked the Lord for a definite sign.

After tea that day our neighbour Charles popped in to the kitchen as we were washing up. The houses were semi-detached, but because of years of enlargements our side was much bigger than theirs.

'We were wondering if you would object to our building an extension,' he said, 'we are feeling rather cramped now with three children.'

'Don't bother to do that,' said Tony, wiping his hands on the tea towel. 'Buy our end.'

'What about the cracks?' I said desperately.

'Oh, our side has them too,' beamed Charles, 'they don't bother us, we won't even have this surveyed.'

'But you'll never sell your side if it's subsiding,' I went on doggedly.

'I'm an estate agent,' smiled Charles blandly, 'don't worry about that.'

If that wasn't the sign we had asked for, what was? But I still locked myself into the loo and cried for half an hour after he had gone.

'There is only one house in Tunbridge Wells I could ever bear to live in,' I sniffed when finally I came out, 'and that is Sally's house.' We had been to dinner with Sally some years before, and although her house was at the end of a Victorian terrace, it overlooked from every window a lovely park full of old mature trees. Next morning Tony went into an estate agency on his way to work.

'We do have a house with six bedrooms,' they said. 'Just coming on to the market today.' It sounds like one of those stories sometimes told in sermons that sound too neat and perfect to be believable, but I shan't feel the same lack of conviction now when I hear of such happenings. For that house actually *was* Sally's house! We had asked God for a sign, but he seemed to be giving us two. Tony dashed home to fetch me, and we went straight round to see it, but I was determined not to like it this time.

'It's in a road, I'll feel I'm living in a goldfish bowl,' I complained.

'We've got nothing to hide,' Tony pointed out, as we treated ourselves to a cup of coffee in a local café.

'It's wrong to move the kids, now they've just settled down.'

'Moving schools might do them all good,' Tony said firmly, and I realised we were at a complete deadlock for the first time in our married lives. There was no compromising this time. What happens when a Christian couple have this experience – who's right and who gives in?

'Look,' I said, gripping my coffee cup for support, 'Colossians 3: 15 says, "The peace that Christ gives is to guide you in the decisions you make," so surely a Christian couple like us ought to have peace over a big thing like moving house?'

'We need to pray this over with someone right away from Mayfield or Tunbridge Wells,' Tony replied. 'Let's go down to Southampton, and see Hugh and Ginny.'

Hugh O'Connor had recently given up a dental practice so that he and his wife could both devote all their time to biblical counselling. As we drove down through the fog of a November morning, I felt sure they would make Tony see reason. We prayed with them, explained our dilemma and prayed again, and then the worst happened! It was *me* who had to see reason.

'When you reach a head-on crash like this,' explained Hugh, 'it is the wife who must submit to her husband and trust God to guide them both through Him. He is answerable to God for the welfare of his family.' I had known all that for years, but it was the actual doing of it that was so hard.

'It is difficult for a man to adjust to living with a disabled wife, so you must make things as easy as possible for him.

128

Physically and spiritually, he would be better off in Tunbridge Wells.'

'But I need the peace of the country,' I burst out.

'No, Jen,' replied Ginny. 'All you need is Jesus.'

We went home and finally 'clinched the deals' with Charles and Sally. With my conscious mind I had submitted to Tony, but every single day I got myself out on two sticks to the nearest wood, and cried as if I had been bereaved.

Brother Tom discovered me in tears one day, and had no sympathy whatever.

'I'd live in a sewer if Jesus wanted me to,' he said cheerfully. That helped me so much I was fine for a few days and then drifted back into self-pity.

One sparkling frosty morning, when every dead leaf and bare twig in the wood looked as if it were covered with diamonds, I shouted out to God, 'How can You expect me to live in a town? Don't you realise all this beauty *is* You to me, not just Your creation, but a see-able feel-able *You*. I can't seem to worship You without it.'

'I know that,' He replied, 'and I made it all for you to enjoy, but now you must learn to see Me in people, not lonely beauty – in the old, sick and lonely, the depressed and tired, and love them just as you love these frosted branches.'

I wrote it all down as usual, and reading it each morning helped me for at least a month. It would not have hurt so much if we could have gone quickly, but the Lord's timing is always perfect and I really think I learnt more during the following months than at any other period of my life.

In a large church it is possible for a Christian to hide and suffer in privacy. That I think is why Tony likes a big church – he needs privacy if he is suffering. Our church was so small that there was no way we could suffer without hurting everyone else as well. When we announced that we were going to move they found it hard to understand, and some even felt we were rejecting them and all their great love and kindness to us. Tony was an elder and we had both been involved in the large Sunday school for years. Why did we have to go? Having submitted to Tony by allowing the move to be put into the pipeline, I felt it was not really playing fair not to support him in word as well as deed. So I would say brightly to my friends, 'We feel we shall all be better off in town, now I can't drive the car, and the house and situation are just not suitable now I'm disabled.'

But yet again I felt a terrible hypocrite inside for not saying how I really felt. The hammer on the thumb effect was rapidly wearing off. The shock of being permanently disabled came to me slowly, but it had to come. It is harder for a Christian to accept than it is for a person with no belief, because we know God *can* heal, so why doesn't He? I have met many disabled people over the last three years, and it is sad to note how much better-adjusted and peaceful the ones who have no faith in God so often are.

I felt deeply that our moving house was a public capitulation to the illness – a final laying aside of hope and faith, and I knew that some of the local Christians did too. I could not tell Tony how I felt after that day with Hugh and Ginny, so the hurt inside became resentment, and bitterness made communication between us virtually impossible.

Tony himself was going through a very bad time just then. In many ways it is harder to adjust to living with a disabled person than it is to be disabled yourself. The enormous physical burden of looking after six children is sometimes enough to crush two parents, but to face it alone with the added care of an invalid, and a responsible job to hold down, must sometimes feel terrifying. And then there was the frustration. For a man who has always thought and acted at high speed, it must be terrible to be chained for life to a slow-moving tortoise. I remembered what it had been like caring for my mother as well as a herd of high-speed children, and I knew how he felt, but was powerless to help.

It is also extremely hard living with someone in almost constant pain. Apart from their bad temper, they are either floating away on their painkillers or desperately trying to do without them. You can't just hug them when you feel like it in case you hurt them – though actually we would rather be hugged and hurt than not hugged at all. It's doubly hard within a marriage because it means the whole physical side can become a source of tension rather than release.

'I don't know how to help you!' Tony would explode sometimes. He could see I needed assistance dishing up a meal or pouring out the tea, but if he took over and did it for me, I felt threatened – crushed and more useless than ever. I knew without him telling me that my illness revolted him and he was frightened of how he might react in the future if it became even worse. Because I knew, I pulled away from him, hurt and humiliated, and as always when suffering he retired into a morose, silent shell that I could not penetrate. It was not that he had stopped caring about me, but both of us were imprisoned by the walls we had set up around ourselves, and we could not express our love. Once again our relationship was in very great danger.

Some time in those unhappy months I heard that Satanists are praying and fasting all over the country for the break-up of Christian marriages, and I realised suddenly that we were being attacked by the powers of darkness.

That Sunday in church someone told a Bible story for the children. It was all about how the Israelites, when they were slaves in Egypt, had to kill a lamb and paint the doorposts of their houses with its blood. The angel of death who was sent to bring destruction to Egypt passed over the houses where he saw the blood, and the families inside were safe. 'Jesus shed His blood for us, just like that lamb,' said the speaker, 'but we have to paint it on the doors of our lives if we want to be safe from the powers of darkness.'

'Perhaps we should do that for our marriage,' I said to Tony that night. We both realised we were in a state of crisis, so we knelt down and asked God to cover our marriage with the blood that Jesus had shed for us. Once under that protection we were safe from Satan's power, and although it did not seem to make any difference at the time, looking back I can see it as a turning point in our relationship.

131

## Chapter Sixteen

As my numbed acceptance of the disablement wore off, a desperate desire for healing and strength set in. I was beginning to fear that our family might break apart if I did not get better quickly, and I wondered how often Tony regretted giving me his cuff link. If God would only heal me all our lives could be easy and happy once again.

So I set out on a frantic search for healing. I read books, listened to tapes, visited healing services or people with a gift of healing, and of course we prayed earnestly ourselves.

Looking back, I think I stopped looking at Jesus and concentrated on my own body instead. I was forgetting that we must seek the Lord for Himself and not His gifts, or we block the very gifts He wants to give us. I wish I had remembered Oswald Chambers' words, 'God wants you in a closer relationship to Himself than receiving His gifts, He wants you to get to know Him.'

Many of our friends who attended different churches all over the district were uniting their prayers for my healing and the delay in signing the contracts for the house sale and purchase seemed to point to the wonderful fact that God did not want us to move and was going to step in and do something miraculous. But the weeks and months dragged on, and I seemed, in fact, to be getting worse.

'What's the hold-up, Lord?' I kept demanding. Could it still be Satan who was to blame? I knew from that experience in the Kent and Sussex that Jesus has given us the authority to oust him, so I went into action. I had realised some years before that evil spirits can penetrate weak places in our armour, and if unchecked can begin gradually to influence our lives. With earnest prayer and fasting I examined my life to see if there could be any spirit of infirmity, doubt or lethargy that could be causing my problems. Then, with the help of someone who has a deliverance ministry, we commanded all such enemies to be gone in the name of Jesus.

We also at that time ransacked the house for objects that could be causing harm. For some reason it was late one evening in a high wind when we finally made a huge bonfire at the bottom of the garden and Sarah threw into it all her cassettes and records made by groups who were openly Satanists. I put in books I had used for research on the occult for the teenage novel, and we even rummaged through the family museum and pulled out souvenirs from abroad such as devil masks and carved gods. I shall never forget John's incredulous face as he watched us through the window of his nearby shed – hoping no doubt that the wind would not change direction!

But still my condition was unchanged. My friends were puzzled. They could see the pain and weakness I was living with, and they had prayed for my healing, never doubting God could make me well. When He did not, they knew it was not their lack of faith or sacrificial prayer; it could not be God's fault, and so it must be mine. Many of the friends whose love and respect I depended on began to look at me oddly, and I felt them draw away from me, baffled. I suppose they felt they were wasting their time praying for me, while I continued to block my own healing. Unanswered prayer can seem very threatening to Christians.

'You don't have to suffer one more day,' beamed one friend whom I had led to the Lord a couple of years before. 'I've been reading this marvellous book, all you have to do is look to Jesus in faith.'

I could not dampen her enthusiasm by telling her I had read that book years before, and the effect of 'looking to Jesus in faith' was nearly driving me demented.

'You're a disgrace to the Lord, when you hobble round on sticks,' said another friend sternly. 'You should be demonstrating the Lord's power to make you whole.'

We went to church while visiting some friends and hugely enjoyed the free worship and lovely praising choruses, but as we left the church one of the elders came up to me and said, pointing to my surgical collar and sticks, 'You don't *have* to have those, you know.'

'I'd fall flat on my face without them,' I giggled feebly, but he was not laughing.

'Jesus could take them from you if you let Him,' he continued. 'Sometimes we cling on to illness as a way of feeling important and being noticed. Are you *willing* to be healed?'

'Am I willing, Lord?' I cried that night. 'Do people think I am some sort of hypochondriac? Perhaps I am one.'

As a child I had been delivered from school by having pneumonia or rheumatic fever; was I now escaping from life through illness again? But why should I want to escape from a life I loved so much? I could see clearly that a long-term illness could be very destructive to the personality. Was I enjoying too much the sympathy and attention I received?

I had positively shaken with rage after that man had spoken to me, but really he did me a great deal of good. That night I recognised the danger of the illness becoming the centre of my life, ruling me, becoming like an absorbing hobby.

'Lord,' I prayed, 'help me to put You in the very centre of my life, and then You can push the illness away to the circumference.' But still I could not get myself off to sleep that night. I kept thinking: Am I willing?

'Lord, I know I want to be well, but is my subconscious mind wanting to be ill? If my will is blocking your will, show me how to change it.'

Suddenly I simply had to laugh, and Tony groaned in his sleep and turned over. Worrying about your will is like trying to lift a bucket when you're standing in it, I thought. If my will belongs to the Lord, then surely it is His job to control it and make it line up with His own.

I slid cautiously out of bed and knelt down in the darkness. 'Lord,' I prayed, 'I want what You want. Please will You do all the rest.' I was soon drifting off to sleep repeating Philippians 2: 13 (AV): 'For it is God which worketh in you both to will and to do of his good pleasure.' It is not for us to 'will' and Him to 'do'. He's responsible for the whole thing, when we ask Him to be.

'I have a word from the Lord for you.' It seemed almost every day that someone came in, rang or wrote a note starting with those words. We became utterly confused because surely if they had all come from the Lord, they would not have been so contradictory.

One person said, 'The Lord wants you to fight harder.' Only the next day someone else rang to say, 'The Lord says, rest in Me, you are trying too hard.' Several people mentioned my will being the block, when both the Lord and I knew He was already dealing with that. I was beginning to feel rather hunted when another friend said, rather cryptically, 'It is your husband's attitude that is the hindrance,' but she refused to explain what she meant. When someone else waylaid me in the school car park, I really longed to be able to run away. 'It is your parents' sins that are being punished,' she said, as wintry sleet bit our cheeks. 'Or it might be your relationship with them that is causing physical harm.'

'I've had the healing of memories,' I told her tearfully, 'and my parents were the most godly people I shall ever meet. Of course they sinned, but God punished Jesus for that, not me.'

The last straw came when a Christian leader we know well and respect greatly, said, 'Jen, have you ever stopped to consider *why* so much prayer which has been offered for you has not been answered? You must search your heart.' I hardly had time to take breath before someone else came up to me and said, 'Jen, the Lord wants you to stop being so introspective.'

Job's comforting friends seemed to surround me, and I was beginning to want healing just to save my spiritual reputation! It was very good for my pride to know everyone was talking about me, each with their own opinion as to why I was not getting better.

The Lord certainly does give His servants messages to deliver to individuals. He was constantly doing that in the Bible, and He still does it now, but we have to make sure it is not just our own critical feelings we are voicing. God can also give us a burden to go and lay hands on someone for healing, but again we have to be careful it really is His prompting, and not our own enthusiasm, or untold damage can be done to the sick person's faith. When we feel the urge to speak or heal, it need not take hours of waiting on the Lord first, we only have to stop and mentally turn to Him for guidance. But if we ask the Lord to stop us from making a mistake, He most certainly will.

I wanted to be well so badly I twisted myself into mental and spiritual knots, trying to take all this conflicting advice. So it seemed a positive relief when someone said, 'Stop praying for healing – just praise the Lord.' Her face radiated confidence. I had read many books on praise, so when she added, 'Praise always brings results,' something pricked me at the back of my mind. I took her advice enthusiastically, but the pricking grew worse, until I faced the fact that praise, when used as a means to an end, becomes a ghastly form of flattery – buttering up God to get our own will done.

Surely, I thought in desperation, we should be able to praise God whether He brings us good or bad, and go on praising Him even when our circumstances do not change (Job 2: 10). Oswald Chambers said, 'We must not use God like a machine for blessing men.'

But the pressure to be healed increased both within myself and from the people around me, and when I was told that a young man from our fellowship had lost his newly found faith because God had not answered his earnest prayers for me, I felt miserable and condemned. The feeling grew when I realised the church youth group were giving themselves to prayer for me, and my healing was becoming terribly important to their faith.

My greatest comfort was the book of Job. I could identify with him perfectly. Like him, I had lost my possessions (home), health, relationship with my husband and my spiritual standing and status. Of course I should not have minded what people thought of me, but I did!

The strain of all this conflict was too much, and it erupted violently one Saturday morning. I was confined indoors when I would much rather have been in the woods with the children, facing a huge pile of ironing I did not have the physical strength to do. Tony made some bright remark about how convenient it was going to be living in town, and something inside me snapped. All the pent-up bitterness over the loss of my fields and lanes burst uncontrollably, and picking up my steaming iron, I flung it in his direction. Fortunately it missed, hit the wall and smashed, letting off steam as it died.

'It'll cost at least fifteen pounds to buy a new one,' remarked Tony with maddening detachment. Making sure the children were out of range, I really told him what I thought of him, giving vent to the torrent of words I had buried for weeks, but suddenly I was halted in mid-sentence.

'What's the matter?' I faltered in panic as I saw him huddled in his chair, clutching his chest, his twisted face a ghastly colour.

'It'll pass in a minute,' he gasped, 'they always do.'

'What do you mean, they always do?' I demanded, suddenly realising how very much I loved him. When he could speak again, he told me he had been having severe chest pains for some time, but had not liked to worry me with them. After a cup of tea he looked better, but I made him promise to visit the doctor on Monday.

I just had to be alone with God that afternoon, and I forced myself across the fields to the woods, but the heavy March rain had turned the path into a muddy bog, and soon my wellington boots were helplessly stuck and I burst into tears. 'This path is just what our lives have turned into,' I told the Lord as I sat down heavily in a puddle. 'It's just a squelchy mess.'

'I know,' He replied, 'but keep on remembering that I am right here in the mess with you.' The memory of that muddy path has helped me so often since.

Next morning in church I was still rocking with the shock and more desperate than ever to be healed. If Tony suddenly died of a heart attack, I had to be fit to care for the children. When all the Sunday school had gone out halfway through the service – and of course Tony with them, to teach his huge class consisting of Duncan – Brian suddenly said publicly, 'Jen, the elders and I would like to pray for your healing right now.'

'This is the moment at last!' I thought as I went happily to the front of the church. I was secretly pleased that Tony was safely out of the way. Watching my frenzied attempts to take everyone's conflicting advice had worried him – though typically, he had made no comment. His trust in God's ability to do what was best for us all was much greater than mine, but of course I did not realise that at the time. I just thought that if he was in church his apparent lack of faith might spoil the elders' prayer! As they gathered round me praying, I added silently, Lord, please heal Tony as well.

But by the following Sunday Tony had an appointment to see the heart specialist, and I was having such a bad relapse I could not even go to church, but lay in bed miserably wondering how many young people's faith I was damaging by this latest public failure.

That week there was a mini mission being held in the district by a very remarkable woman. Over the two years she had been a Christian, God had done wonderful things for her and she longed to pass them on. She happened to be visiting our church that particular Sunday. She was furious with Satan for his hold over me, and positively stamped round to our house straight after the service. For two exhausting hours

138

she prayed with me and drove out yet more spirits that might still be causing my defeat, while I tried not to hear the chaos of Tony dishing up the Sunday lunch in the kitchen beneath us.

During the week she was to hold two coffee mornings, and I was determined not to miss either. The first was on Tuesday, and the house where it was held seemed to be packed with people when I finally crawled in. She talked for an hour, and all she said about healing was right. She used verse after verse from the Bible and we all had it down in black and white before us.

'It is God's will,' she said, looking round the room with her compelling dark eyes, 'for *all* his children to live in health and financial freedom. In the Old Testament healing and prosperity always come after repentance and obedience, and ninety per cent of the ministry of Jesus was healing the sick.'

Deep down in my mind something nagged at me. We live in an age where health, physical fitness and financial achievements are worshipped. By laying such a passionate emphasis on the gift of healing and deliberately blinding ourselves to so much else that is in the Bible, are we not just following the world's obsession with bodily perfection? The memory of the face of an old lady we had recently met flashed into my mind. A beautiful face, but it had been etched by years of pain and suffering. 'Remember, my dears,' she had told us, 'look *forward* to your inheritance (1 Peter 1). He's keeping it for you carefully in Heaven, so be glad!' We had looked up 1 Peter 1 later, not really being sure what she meant. 'We look forward to possessing the rich blessings that God keeps for His people. Be glad . . . even though it may be necessary for you to be sad for a while because of the many kinds of trials you suffer. Their purpose is to prove that your faith is genuine. Even gold . . . is tested by fire; and so your faith . . . must be tested so that it may endure' (1 Peter 1: 4–7). I groped my way to the passage again, as my confusion mounted. How can our faith be tested if all our problems both physical and financial are removed from us – wouldn't we be like spoilt children?

'One of God's signs of approval is material prosperity, which of course includes health.' The voice jerked me back into the room again, back from a past generation who felt it was a privilege to suffer, right into the middle of a modern trend which was beginning to lay too much emphasis on only one side of the truth. Peter said we were assured of our inheritance in Heaven, but did that really guarantee material benefits down here as well?

'I believe God wants to demonstrate His power by physical healing this morning,' concluded the speaker, and suddenly I was conscious of everyone in the room looking at me. They all knew me and had prayed so long for me, and as I was the only ill person there it seemed obvious to them all that God's power was going to be demonstrated on me.

'I am going to put this chair here in the centre of the circle and, Jen, I want you to come and sit here while some of us lay hands on you.'

But suddenly I could not take any more. The elders of our church had prayed publicly for me not ten days before, the speaker had spent two embarrassing hours praying for me on Sunday, and I had had so many hands laid on me it was a wonder I was not bald!

Everyone sat round the room expectant and excited, but I just could not take another public humiliation.

'No,' I said, 'I won't.' A stunned shock wave circled the room.

'Don't you want God to heal you?' she demanded.

'Of course I do,' I almost wailed. 'But I feel completely confused. I agree with everything you have said this morning about God's ability to heal, but you've only quoted one side of what the Bible says. Paul had a painful physical ailment, a thorn in the flesh, but God did not heal him.'

'That is just a bad translation, he's talking of a spiritual thorn, not a physical one,' she replied.

'But Jesus said, "In the world *ye shall have* tribulation."'

140

'Yes, but that means persecution,' was the reply, 'not sickness.'

'What about Job then?' I quavered. 'God allowed him to be ill.'

'Job lived in a different dispensation.'

Everyone in that room was looking at me in dazed horror. I am still so embarrassed as I write about it, even my feet are turning red! I ought to have subsided, and just let them lay hands on me once again, but somehow the torrent inside me could not be dammed.

'Listen,' I was almost crying with rage by that time, 'the Bible says hundreds more things about suffering and healing, they can't all be contradictory. We can prove almost any theory we like by separate verses or illustrations. Surely each Christian must seek God's face separately to discover what is God's will for *him*. I am beginning to think that's what I should be doing instead of trying to force God to do what may only *seem* to be the best thing.'

I looked round at the shocked faces through a blur of tears.

'We can't use our faith like a demand note to wave in God's face. He treats us all as individuals, and even David Watson with all his faith and purity died of cancer!'

There is no way that you can leave with dignity when you walk like a drunken sailor, but I had hardly staggered down the garden path, when my rage died down into humiliation. How could I have lost my cool like that – all those people in that room must totally despise me. Perhaps they did not, but God allowed me to feel that they did in order to teach me that I valued other people's opinions more highly than I valued His.

As I made myself a cup of tea in the shelter of my own kitchen, I began to worry in case my negative attitude had prevented the Lord from doing for other people what he was fully able and willing to do. I felt so wretched I went back and apologised to the speaker and her hostess for ruining the coffee morning. They were very kind and loving but I still felt deeply embarrassed.

That night I was putting Duncan to bed and kneeling on the floor fumbling to undo a knot in his trainer laces. Seeing me on my knees, I suppose the Lord felt He could speak to me at last, and while Duncan put on his pyjamas, God said, 'You are blinded by arrogant pride. There are things in you that displease me. I must eradicate them at all costs, they are blocking your progress.'

Duncan got into bed and started drawing pictures, quite unconscious that I was still kneeling by the chair.

'Yes, Lord,' I said at last, 'do eradicate them, please, however much it hurts. I do love You and You know all I want to do is grow closer to You.'

The next day I was to have a very special treat. My friend Trish was recovering from a cancer operation. Leaving her seven children, she was coming to spend twenty-four precious hours with me. It was so good to have someone from the other side of London with whom to talk over the whole of my muddle, and better still to pray together. We sat comfortably either side of a roaring fire, talking to the Lord about our husbands and thirteen children in companionable detail, when suddenly I felt the Lord so close to us I just had to slide out of my armchair and on to my knees.

'Lord,' I cried urgently, 'show me the blockage You told me was there.'

'It is your rebellion towards Tony,' came the answer at once. 'You have submitted to him in word and deed, but not in your heart. Your rebellion has caused him actual physical pain, and you have also hurt Me by your lack of trust.'

With Trish's help I repented and asked God to change me, and as Trish and I wept and prayed together, I realised what a fool I had been to put fields and woods before my happy relationship with Tony. Worse still, I knew I had hurt the Lord.

'Whatever do I do now, Trish?' I said as we started on a new box of tissues.

'Well, you'll have to put things right with Tony,' said Trish.

'But he's away for a whole week, and I can't do that sort of thing over the phone,' I gulped.

'Let's have a look at James 5 and ask the Lord to show us why your elders' prayers were not answered.'

We both sat with our Bibles on our knees and looked at verses 14, 15 and 16.

'Look,' said my wise friend, 'it says you must confess your sins to one another, "so that you will be healed". If you were still rebelling inwardly, you were blocking the healing – and it says *you* call the elders, it is not for them to call you.'

'It would be a bit difficult for me to ask them to come here,' I admitted, 'because Tony is so fed up with the whole subject he won't even talk about it.'

'Look,' said Trish firmly, 'your body belongs to Tony, under God, and so you should never have consented to be prayed for without his presence and permission, and you tell me he wasn't even in church! That was part of your rebellion. It has to be Tony who calls the elders, and look,' she added, jabbing her Bible with an excited finger, 'it says there should be oil, and I'm also afraid it is quite clear that you have to confess your sins not only to Tony, but also to the elders.'

With this unpleasant thought she left me, and as I waved her away down the lane, all I could hear was my father saying, 'If you have to do something unpleasant – do it *now*!'

## Chapter Seventeen

I lay on my bed with the duvet firmly pulled over my face. I had cried for so many hours that night that even the duck down was soggy.

I had done the 'unpleasant thing' the previous evening, but if I had known it was going to be that unpleasant I would never have summoned the courage to go and confess to Brian the rebellion as Trish had said I must.

'I don't think it is only rebellion that is blocking your spiritual life,' Brian had said as I faced him over the polished expanse of his empty dining table. After half an hour with him seeing myself through his eyes, I felt like a snail without a shell. What he said would not have stung so much if I had not realised he was so painfully right! It cannot be much fun being a pastor and having the solemn responsibility of speaking the truth, but I shall be grateful to him for the rest of my life for those thirty minutes. As Psalm 19: 12 says, 'No one can see his own errors; deliver me, Lord, from hidden faults! Keep me safe, also, from wilful sins.'

For months I had been grappling with the 'wilful sins' but there are so many faults we hide under apparent 'good' things, that we even deceive ourselves, and only someone very wise and courageous can help us to 'see our own errors'. Brian had to use his surgeon's knife to reach very deep-seated poison, and he did me more good with it than any amount of soothing ointment. But as I lay there in the dark I was definitely suffering from post-operative shock! Reduced to nothing as I was in my own sight and other people's, however could the Lord go on loving such a failure? I wanted to run away and never again see anyone I had ever known.

Some time long before morning I poked my head out from under the duvet and groped for my black book. 'Whatever shall I do, Lord?' I scrawled right across the page. 'Everyone else has a word from you about my situation – except me!' Even as I wrote that I realised I had never taken the time to ask Him for one. I had spent months listening to other people's opinion and taking their conflicting advice, until I felt I had no personality or confidence left. Never once did I doubt the Lord's desire and ability to heal me. I felt it was all my own fault that I was ill.

As I saturated yet another tissue, I realised the Lord wanted to forgive and change me, if I would only give Him the chance. All this mental churning certainly was not His will; He had promised me His peace (John 14: 27). 'If only Tony was here,' I sniffed as I looked at his empty cold side of the bed.

Then I realised what a wonderful thing it was that Tony was away at a maths conference for the next seven days. Suppose I used that time to seek the Lord's face finally over this whole question? I wouldn't answer the phone or door bell, and only do the essential jobs in the house. I could even fast with Gom and Tony out of the way, so I would be more responsive to what the Lord would say.

As I slid out of bed on to my knees, I prayed the last two verses of Psalm 139. 'Examine me, Oh God and know my mind; test me and discover my thoughts. Find out if there is any evil in me and guide me in the everlasting way.' Suddenly I felt Him speaking to me through the lonely darkness.

'You have been like a tiny boat in a storm, buffeted this way and that by the opinions of others. I will make you like a firm rock in the ocean standing solidly against the waves' (James 1: 6).

That week would have been horrid enough without the icy March winds penetrating every crack in the house. I was so

145

cold without any food inside me, I spent most of the time in bed packed round with hot-water bottles – a woolly hat on my head, an open Bible on my knee and a pencil and note book ready to write down the blocks as the Holy Spirit revealed them to me. I laugh now every time I think of it, but I did not laugh then. I felt like a huge mountain with a cave running right to its centre. If I wanted God right there in the very middle of me, I had to allow Him to dynamite His way through the granite boulders that had blocked the cave, and those explosions hurt! But I knew great peace as He identified and removed them one by one, because of His wonderful power to forgive.

'But please reprogramme my personality, Lord; don't just let me slip back into being me again,' I implored.

'I shall go on doing that for the rest of your life,' He replied. 'We shall fight a constant battle with these lumps of rock.'

'But that means I shall never be ready to be healed,' I cried.

'You can't earn your healing any more than you can earn your salvation. Both are free gifts from Me,' He replied. 'You have no more right to healing than any of the other gifts I shower on you each day, most of which you never even notice.'

In spite of the cold and hunger it was a very wonderful week, rather like a major internal spring-clean and redecoration! It was not just asking for His forgiveness. I had some practical homework as well. There were relationships He wanted me to restore, and attitudes that had to be changed. The Bible on my lap was replaced by my typewriter, as I wrote many letters. I had drawn away from so many people because I felt they despised me, but that had not pleased God. I had to reopen the relationship by making the first move – just a friendly note or card. I also had to ask forgiveness of some people I had hurt and they responded so warmly and lovingly. I also had to forgive the people who had hurt me. I needed so much help from the Lord over that, but He showed me definitely that He could not forgive me unless I forgave them (Matthew 6: 14, 15). I certainly did not tell them I was forgiving them – that might have hurt them unnecessarily.

I felt massively better when all that was done, so I settled down to earnest prayer, asking the Lord how He really wanted me to pray. I knew it was no good pleading for healing and then tacking 'if it be Thy will' on to the end like a feeble failsafe. He wants us to pray specifically and with confidence. But we had never really taken the time to ask Him to tell us what He wanted to do.

'Lord,' I prayed, 'give me the gift of faith so that we can "ask in faith, nothing wavering. For he that wavereth is like a wave of the sea driven with the wind and tossed" ' (James 1: 6 AV).

I had to sit there and listen to God – which is probably the most important form of prayer anyway – but I am such a gas bag I'd never realised it before. But the Lord was strangely silent, so I began to search the Bible for what He wanted me to understand.

I looked up all the different ways Jesus healed people in the gospels, searching for some common key, but I could not find one. Sometimes He connected sin with sickness as in Luke 5 and John 5, and sometimes He separated them – John 9. Why did He choose to heal that one man at the pool of Bethesda who did not even ask for His help? He had to step over a multitude of blind, lame and paralysed people to reach him, and He walked away leaving them just as they were, yet He had the power to heal them all.

I began to realise just how much Satan hates the ministry of healing because it brings such glory to God. When he cannot hinder it by doubt and unbelief, he causes us to become *too* obsessed by it. He can then use it to turn our energies away from praying for our friends who need God or taking them to meetings where they might find Him. Instead, Christians flock to healing services to have their sore toes or backaches dealt with because Satan would much rather we used God as a bottle of aspirin than the answer to a lost world.

I think this is what happened at Capernaum. Jesus delivered a demon-possessed man in the synagogue (Mark 1: 23–27) and then healed Peter's mother-in-law. By evening the whole district had heard the news, and they all arrived at his door bringing everyone who was sick, and Jesus healed them. But the townsfolk were very upset when they found He was missing next morning, and Peter and his friends were sent off to find Him.

'I must preach in other towns,' Jesus said, 'that is why I came.' But His mission was thwarted when He healed a man of leprosy. 'Don't tell anyone about this,' Jesus told him sternly (verse 44), but the man 'spread the news about everywhere' (verse 45) so that Jesus could not go into the cities He longed to reach, but had to wait in the desert for people to come to Him.

When He went back to Capernaum, the crowds packed the house so tightly that men ripped open the roof to let down a man for healing, but Jesus knew the man was much more worried by his spiritual problems than his physical ones, and He said, 'Your sins are forgiven you.'

It was probably months later when He was again in Capernaum that a huge crowd ran Him to earth, and He said to them (John 6: 26): 'You are looking for me because you ate the bread and had all you wanted, not because you understood my miracles.' When He went on to say, 'I am the bread of life' (verse 35) the Jews murmured at Him (41). They did not like Him to talk about spiritual things, and verse 66 says, 'Because of this, many of Jesus's followers turned back and would not go with Him any more.'

Of course Jesus used miracles to build faith, but they were a means to an end, and not an end in themselves. It was the preaching of the Good News about the Kingdom of God that was His primary mission (Mark 1: 38).

He told Pilate (John 18: 36) that 'My Kingdom does not belong to this world.' Of course He cares intensely about our health and welfare, but He also knows how short our lives are, and how many wonderful things He is planning for our real lives with Him in eternity.

Satan also revels in confusion. So many people have said to me, 'I just don't know what I think about healing any more. Some people are healed and some are not. Why?' Whole churches waver in doubt when they have prayed earnestly for someone who has died instead of recovering. Satan tells them he has triumphed and they just don't see that person as perfectly whole at last.

Of course God does not want us to be muddled and confused, but He just cannot trust us with all the answers yet. Real faith grows when *we* don't know why, but are sure that *He* does. The Lord once said to Helen Roseveare, 'Can you trust me in this, even if I *never* tell you why?'

On the last hungry day of the week, I had to confess that even though the Lord had done so many wonderful things for me, He had not given me any particular scripture, only the conviction that mere bodily healing is not half so important in the light of eternity as our generation believes it to be.

But I was still left with that command in James 5.

'Lord, You know how uptight Tony is feeling about all this,' I prayed just an hour before he was due home. 'Please Lord, help him to share my conviction that we should call the elders in obedience to these verses. You haven't told me how You want me to pray, but I'll leave that to them, and I promise once those elders have come, I will never nag You again about healing.'

As soon as Tony's car turned into the drive, I longed to blurt out to him all that had happened to me that week, and also to get the rebellion matter off my chest quickly. However with all the children talking at once, and Gom and John joining in loudly, I realised I would have to wait.

'I've got to drive down to Bournemouth tomorrow,' Tony shouted over the din, 'come with me, and I'll take you out to lunch.' There was my chance.

I felt a terrible fool telling Tony how I felt, but I sensed he understood, as he quietly squeezed my hand. Then he began to talk, and I suddenly realised just how very hard these last few years had been for him. I also saw how deep his relationship with God had actually become. While my emotions had been vacillating between euphoria and depression via anger and doubt, he had silently plodded on towards God. How easy it is to misjudge people spiritually. It isn't necessarily those people who are always 'talking big' who are growing the most, but neither I nor some of our local Christian friends had understood this.

'Would you mind if we did a James 5 and asked the elders to come round one day soon?' I asked nervously as we began our journey home. Tony said he did not mind a bit, but first there were a few relationships and hurts he had to restore and mend himself! The wave of relief that enveloped me showed just how much hope I had pinned on those three verses.

The following Saturday morning when the elders were due to come, I woke early with a tremendous feeling of excitement. Nothing after today would ever be the same again. I knew that all over the country our friends were concentrating their prayers upon us, some were even fasting, and when we showed the four men into our lounge I knew all the children were praying upstairs.

As they stood around us both in a ring I felt utterly surrounded by love. I never shall forget Brian's face. I could not help thinking how like the Lord he was – he had seen so clearly all the nasty side of me, and yet he still loved me! We had done everything we possibly could to make ourselves ready for healing, yet we both knew we were still unworthy of seeing a miracle. We offered Him again everything we possessed, but still knew that could not buy automatic blessing.

'Nothing in my hand I bring, simply to Thy cross I cling,' I whispered as they put their hands on our heads. We asked for three things: healing for Tony, and for me, and inwardly we prayed for our marriage. I knew that moment was deeply significant in our lives.

Over the next few weeks all those prayers were answered. Tony went to the Kent and Sussex Hospital for all kinds of tests and they pronounced him to be one hundred per cent fit. We both went to Hildenborough Hall for a Christian Marriage Weekend led by Dave and Joyce Ames, and we were able to talk and pray through all our conflicts and anxieties. The Lord did heal our relationship completely, and gave us a new and deeper than ever love for each other.

Daily I seemed to grow stronger and was able to cope with moving house, unpacking tea chests, painting the kitchen and even planting some seeds in our tiny backyard.

The strangest thing of all was that I discovered, within hours of arriving in Tunbridge Wells, that Tony and the Lord had been right all along. It is just perfect for us all here, and I have never suffered one moment's doubt about leaving Mayfield.

It seems like a very specially loving present from God to have Auntie Gerry living just nearby. She moved down to Tunbridge Wells to be nearer her own family as well as all of us. Now she is here as another much-loved granny to the children and steps into the breach with total efficiency whenever there is a crisis.

But life isn't like a fairy story where people live happily ever after, nor is this a book about people who lived victoriously through difficult experiences and came out on the other side with all their questions answered. It doesn't seem as though there are any neat and tidy endings this side of Heaven.

## Chapter Eighteen

Diseases that grow steadily better, or even steadily worse, are easier to cope with than the endless ups and downs of remission and relapse. Each remission brings fresh hope for the future, which is dashed by the following relapse.

The woods have seemed very dark and bleak indeed during the last twelve months. I have had to be away from the family for long stretches of that time, either in hospital or convalescing. It has been the longest-lasting and worst relapse ever.

The Lord asked me three years ago if I could still praise Him in the wintry woods, and to be honest I don't really think I can – not if praise means a constant loud bubbling exuberance. But I am not sure that it does. Psalm 34: 1 in the Living Bible says, 'I *will* praise the Lord whatever happens.' Perhaps praising the Lord has as little connection with emotions as love has. It is an act of the will, an attitude of mind. Once, during that House Group meeting three years ago, God said to me, 'I do not want automatic praise which costs nothing. I want you to learn to praise Me when you are depressed, tempted or not having your prayers answered. That is when your praise and worship mean something to Me.' Maybe praise is just an acknowledgment that He knows what He is doing even if I don't.

A few months ago I was in hospital in London. It was the day I was officially registered disabled. Not a great boost for the morale, I can assure you! My worst fears were realised and I knew that this time I would not be able to go home and force myself to run my own household. I could not even bathe or dress myself or go anywhere except in a wheelchair. I did not feel like a person any more, just a DHSS number.

'Lord,' I whispered as I gazed hopelessly at the wall. 'You know I am a doing, going, giving person. I will never learn to be just a receiver.'

Then I glanced down at the book on my lap which George had sent me, and three words exploded in my face: 'As You did'. It was Sister Basilea Schlink's *The Blessings of Illness*, and this is the sentence that contained them: 'My Jesus, I will humbly allow others to help me, as You did.'

Surely, I thought, He was the greatest 'doer', 'goer', and 'giver' of all time. He 'came not to be ministered unto but to minister'. Then I realised in a flash that He had been dependent on others nearly all his life. He was born in someone else's stable, buried in someone else's tomb, rode on a borrowed donkey and ate His last supper in another man's house. He and His followers had been supported financially by wealthy women (Luke 8: 3), and He was even gracious enough to receive a little boy's picnic lunch.

'If you want to share the fellowship of My suffering you must learn to receive in grateful humility,' He told me gently. 'And when it hurts, hand it back to Me as an offering, which I will use to bless the people who are giving to you' (1 Chron. 11: 17, 18).

Well, I have to confess it has not hurt as much as I thought it would. Marilyn left Burrswood and looked after us for a time. Now, with the help of Lyn, the Kent County Council home help, not to mention Gom and John, we all get along hilariously, while the occupational therapists are reorganising the house with ramps, rails and a lift to make things easier in the future.

One day I received a letter from someone I had never met. Only the day before I had tearfully realised I could no longer use my typewriter. 'I feel the Lord wants me to send you this cheque so you can buy an electric typewriter,' the letter said. Tony went straight out and bought me a specially adapted

153

model which I can even operate while lying down, and the very next day I began to write this book.

Of course the black patches still come, and one week the pain and weakness were not helped by three different friends visiting me with new theories about why I was not healed. All the old doubt and uncertainty returned, just when I thought I had conquered them once and for all. Every time I looked out of the window, I saw healthy mothers playing games with their children in the park and real, painful jealousy knifed me below the belt. So I deliberately looked out of the windows facing the road and not the park, only to see a neighbour driving off to freedom in her little mini car; the doctor had said I would never drive again. Self-pity sneaked up behind me, and the walls of my own home closed in on me like a dungeon. Lyn's cheery voice in the distance, as she did all the jobs I once thought I hated doing, did not help at all. I would have given anything just to clean the loo again, or scrub the kitchen floor.

That night I went to bed, but soon realised it was going to be one of those nights when the pain gets the upper hand. Usually I find pain brings the Lord Jesus nearer to me, because I know for sure that He understands how I feel and sits beside my bed, hurting with me. I also find prayer is easiest then, because when I am in pain, I seem extra sensitive to the many people who are suffering too in different ways, and I chat to the Lord about them, and even picture us both visiting them together in their homes, hospitals or prisons.

Once, in my active Martha days, I had said, 'To work is to pray,' as I hurtled round doing things for people. Now I can't even do much for myself, and I have turned that motto on its head: 'To pray is to work'. It is not just a form of relaxation to me now, it is an exciting professional job and I am learning as the Lord's apprentice.

But that night He seemed so far away, and I was still plagued by the unresolved emotions of the week. When the pain reached a level I could not handle I groped for my store

of powerful drugs the pain clinic prescribe for occasions like
that one. While I waited for them to act, I opened my Bible
and chanced to read Romans 10: 12–13: 'God . . . richly
blesses all who call to Him . . . everyone who calls out to the
Lord for help will be saved.'

'All right, Lord – I'm calling,' I muttered, 'I just can't
cope with my feelings or this pain.'

Our bedroom is a bit like Spaghetti Junction in the
mornings, and I was still feeling rather vulnerable as I sipped
my first cup of tea next morning. Richard sat in bed beside
me reading his school reading book, Tony and Sarah sat on
the far side of him in deep conversation about her A-level
geography syllabus, Justyn wanted some money (as usual),
and Duncan was playing me his latest Pink Floyd tape while
Jane 'punked' her hair at my dressing table. Naomi had
brought her breakfast up on a tray, 'just in case I was lonely!'
The tears trickled out of the corners of my eyes – what a
failure I was as a mother, I could not even cook them some
porridge.

'Don't be silly, Mummy,' said Sarah briskly. 'We all like
you best this way. Once you were always dashing about, and
so busy we could never talk to you, now you're always home
and ready to listen to us.'

I looked round at them all and suddenly realised they
had each made a definite commitment to God, and were
reading the Bible and praying each day. Surely that is what
I had wanted most of all that night in hospital. Yes, they do
have to do much more to help at home than other children,
but strangely that has built their self-esteem because they
know we rely on them, and could not cope without their
help.

I don't have to strive to *do* things any more in order to be
loved. My family love me for what I *am* and not just for what I
do for them – and the same applies to the Lord! But it has
taken me forty-two years to learn that.

The noise around me increased to a crescendo and then,
quite suddenly, the Lord was speaking to me as well.

'I want you *daily* to take up your cross and follow me,' He said.

'But what do you really mean by that, Lord?' I asked Him, as I turned Richard's page, gave Justyn fifty pence and told Duncan to turn the volume down a little. Inside my head I could see a horrid picture of myself struggling like a martyr, in agony under the exhausting weight of the cross, but the Lord cut sharply across that image.

'It was like that for Me, but not for you. Your cross is a symbol of victory, you must take it up in triumph. I know you cannot handle these feelings of jealousy, doubt, self-pity and despair, but when they come take up your cross and hold it out between them and your mind. "*In* all these things you are more than conquerors"' (Rom. 8: 37 RSV). I tried it and it works!

While it is only honest to say that this last year has not been easy, it is also true to say that all eight of us have received a very real peace. Of course that peace is attacked sometimes – as I have just described. But we are not striving after something all the time and wondering, 'Is God going to heal at this service or through this person? It is *not* that we have given up hope or given in to the disease and stopped fighting, but rather that God has pushed that physical part of life into the background and filled our time with so much that is enjoyable and lovely. Life *is* fun once again; three years ago I would never have believed such a miracle was possible! After all, life really does not consist of what you can do, or what you have. It's how you feel deep inside that counts.

This peace makes talking about the Lord easier than it ever has been before. When I used to chat to people about Him in supermarket queues or at the school gate, I often became conscious of an odd expression creeping into their eyes.

It's all very well for her to talk, I could almost hear them thinking. Happily married – six healthy children – nice home – good health. If she had my problems she wouldn't talk so glibly about God's goodness.

156

I never observe that look in people's eyes now. They can see I am handicapped, and responding to my smile they soon start to chat, and I find they are hungry for God. In a world that seeks happiness in health, wealth and achievements they are fascinated to find it in someone who obviously does not have these things that the world so highly prizes. Underneath their gleaming veneer, people feel very frightened – their jobs are insecure, their marriage unstable or even finished – they fear the bomb, cancer and old age, while depression is an epidemic. To find that God gives joy and peace *in* these things, as well as release from them, fascinates people, and they will listen to me simply because I am disabled. I no longer constitute a threat as I must have done in my bossy Martha days.

Then, I probably wanted to serve God for the wrong motives. But since I have realised how completely He identifies with us in our difficulties I am beginning to see that He also wants us to identify with *Him* in *His* sufferings. Jesus did not stop suffering when He dismissed His spirit that day on Calvary. Because He loves us He will go on being hurt until the last one He loves is free of pain. Jesus wept when He saw the anguish of Mary and Martha (John 11: 33, 35). He still weeps now when tragedies devastate His people. We expect Him to ease our pain, but how can we ease His? If we really love Him we long to do so. He has no hands now to comfort and show practical love, no visible face to smile and reassure – He relies on us to be His physical body. So we serve Him to give Him pleasure – not to earn our salvation, curry His favour or boost our own morale. When he sees people He loves comforted and helped He shares their joy just as surely as He felt their pain.

The other day Gom took me back to Firtoll woods to see the bluebells and the sun playing down through the new green beech leaves. I could not help remembering that gloomy winter day when I had stood here before. Eunja's dream had not come true, yet she had prayed earnestly before she rang me, believing that God wanted her to tell me about the dream. Why had God allowed me to be frightened like that?

When I returned home I looked up all the Bible references to dreams and was astonished by how many there were. It does seem that God uses dreams to communicate with people both in the Old and New Testaments. I don't know why He allowed that dream, but one thing I do know is that it blessed me. I had never considered death before – young, strong and happy people seldom do. But everyone needs to be pulled up short at some time and forced to consider how they feel about dying. I might never have faced the issue without Eunja's dream.

Through that experience I did discover that Christians have no need to fear death, and when they reach the actual point of dying it can be a glorious experience. Over the last three years I have met numerous people who are afraid to die, but in Hebrews 2: 14 we are told that 'Through His death Jesus destroyed the Devil who has the power over death, and in this way set free those who were slaves all their lives because of their fear of death.'

This generation fears death and illness above anything. Many Christians follow this trend and become obsessed with the healing God undoubtedly can give us. I've noticed that the people who are most preoccupied by the healing ministry are often those who in life most fear death and detest illness.

When Christians insist that the death of a much-prayed-for sick person is Satan's triumph, it can imply that the worst that can happen to us is death. I don't believe that any more. For a Christian, death is the beginning of everything that is lovely, and the shorter our lives, the sooner we can taste the glories of eternity. Of course it is tragic when we have to leave behind us people we love, but again we have to trust God to look after them better than we ever could.

F. B. Meyer once wrote, 'It is given to some to teach, others to work and some to suffer as a ministry.' That's a very unpopular idea these days, now that the ministry of healing, having lain largely dormant for centuries, is being revived by God. Only the deliberately blind can deny the miracles that are happening, but why must we claim that it is *always* God's will for his children to be physically well in this life? I believe that Satan has brought this heresy into our thinking today, and he is using it to crush and discourage many who believe without a doubt that God can heal, and who would fifty years ago have been radiant in the joy of discovering that His 'strength is made perfect in weakness'.

F. B. Meyer went on to say, 'The child of God is often called to suffer because nothing will convince onlookers of the reality and power of true religion as suffering will do, when it is borne with Christian resignation and fortitude.' In these days of body worship, are we not forgetting that 'My strength shows up best in weak people'? Could not God sometimes be glorified *more* by helping a person in an illness than by removing it?

Suffering seems to give Christians the opportunity to grow spiritually more than anything else. By trying to oust suffering from the 'victorious Christian life' we risk spiritual immaturity. There are no pain-free short cuts to growth – though Satan would have us think there are.

These days we make God too small. We think that if we rub Him in the right way, like Aladdin's lamp, He will lavish on us anything we ask for, and remove all problems from our lives. We live in an age of stereotypes but God, who made each blade of grass different, is the God of the individual. We read a book or hear a talk by someone to whom God has given a special blessing, gift or healing, and we feel like second-class citizens when He does not do exactly the same for us. But He could not treat us all the same when He made us different.

Every time I have a remission, I am convinced that the Lord has healed me for good, and every time I have a relapse the same old depression washes in. But I wanted to write this book while I still don't know all the answers, because I think that all too often we pretend to other people that we're in a constant state of victory partly to convince ourselves. To me, it's better to admit that we are often bewildered and muddled up inside even when we *know* that God is in control. That tension is always there, and I think that it's intrinsic to our faith.

Psalm 73 says, 'What else have I in Heaven but you? Since I have you, what else could I want on earth? My mind and my body may grow weak, but God is my strength. He is all I ever need . . . But as for me, how wonderful to be near God . . . and to proclaim all that he has done!'

# Turning Point

## Is there hope for broken lives?

Jennifer Rees Larcombe

**Hodder & Stoughton**
LONDON SYDNEY AUCKLAND

Acknowledgments for the Bible versions used
in this book can be found on p.vi.

ISBN 0 340 60163 9

Typeset by Hewer Text Composition Services, Edinburgh.

Hodder and Stoughton Ltd
A Division of Hodder Headline PLC
338 Euston Road
London NW1 3BH

To P. and J., with grateful thanks
for teaching me how to forgive.
Without your help, I could not have
written this book.

# CONTENTS

# FOREWORD

We are delighted to commend Jen's latest book, which answers so many of life's questions in such a humorous, compassionate and sensible way.

We all face bereavement in more ways than we probably realise – not only through the death of a loved one. We can go through the same emotions when we lose our car keys or wave goodbye to our daughter on her first day at school! We often feel riddled with guilt because we are not meeting other people's expectations of our behaviour at any given time. This book sets the record straight by enabling us to understand and face the emotions we are experiencing.

Paul wrote to the Corinthians: 'What a wonderful God we have – he is the Father of our Lord Jesus Christ, the source of every mercy, and the one who so wonderfully comforts and strengthens us in our hardships and trials. And why does he do this? So that when others are troubled, needing our sympathy and encouragement, we can pass on to them this same help and comfort God has given us' (2 Cor. 1:3–4, LB).

Jen has learnt these lessons in the school of life, sometimes through almost intolerable circumstances. We are grateful to her for passing on these lessons and we are confident they will be a blessing to every reader.

*Roy and Fiona Castle*

# PREFACE

This is a book for those who boil with anger behind smiles that say, 'I'm all right, everything's fine.' It is for people who are full of those questions that Christians aren't supposed to ask, and doubts that would shock their friends at church – if only they knew about them, it's for those who wake at five in the morning and start on a 'What if . . . ?' cycle – 'What if I can't cope . . . ? What if the money runs out . . . ? What if I never get better?' It's a book for the person who is convinced that he or she must be the only Christian who feels depressed, or for extroverts who can sit smiling broadly in the middle of a room full of people – and yet feel so lonely that they wish they were dead. Feeling broken like this inside is horrible. I know, because I once felt like that myself.

Lives can be shattered and dreams destroyed for all kinds of reasons. Sometimes it happens through large, dramatic events, but just as often people experience a gradual and secret realisation that they are not now the people they used to be or hoped they might become. We can be 'broken' by someone else, or our lives can be smashed by our own mistakes, but often there seems to be no one specific to blame – except God himself. Whatever or whoever caused it all, the sense of inner brokenness is devastating, and we begin to fear that our lives will be like this for ever.

I believe we *can* be mended – I certainly was, and I have seen too many other lives remade to doubt that it can happen. The mending process takes time; it cannot be rushed. But for me there was a definite turning point, a moment when my lost hope began to be restored and the tide turned. I have come to believe that this turning point is the key to rebuilding broken lives, and so I decided to write this book. It comes to you with my love and prayers, and I hope it will feel personal – the hand of a friend reaching out in the darkness.

Most of the chapters in this book offer tips and strategies which I have found personally helpful when coping with all the odd feelings of anger, fear, confusion and despair which seem to hit most of us after some kind of major loss. The chapters finish with a meditation or a story from the Bible which has helped me, and a prayer

I would like to thank the people I mention in the book for kindly allowing me to do so. They are all real people, but to spare them any embarrassment I have changed their names and some of the minor details of their stories. Most of all, I should like to thank a remarkable bunch of people, all of whom have discovered this mysterious 'turning point' in their own lives. They gave me their promise to pray every day as I worked on the manuscript, and I have constantly felt the power of their prayers over the last few months. This book comes to you with their love, too, and they have prayed for you already, many times over. They are some of the most amazing people I know, yet many never leave their homes because of disability or chronic illness – and all have gone through deep personal suffering. Perhaps the rest of the world might not think they were powerful, but they most certainly are! Their power comes from their unshakeable belief in God and his ability to mend broken people.

---

*There is hope for a tree that has been cut down; it can come back to life and sprout. Even though its roots grow old, and its stump dies in the ground, with water it will sprout like a young plant.* (Job 14:7–9, GNB)

# ACKNOWLEDGMENTS

Many thanks to Dr Jenny Brown for all her help concerning medical details; to Dr Sarah Williams for her advice; to Cath Isaaks and the Burrswood Counselling Team; to George and Yvonne Adams; and to Murray Gabriel – who had the worst job of all: correcting my spelling mistakes. Most of all, thanks to Tony and our children, who put up with burnt dinners for many months while my mind was on other things.

# 1

# THE DAY THE TEAPOT WAS BROKEN

My granny had a teapot. It was no ordinary teapot. In fact, it was far too precious to be used at all – except on Christmas Day. For the rest of the year it stood in isolated splendour behind the glass doors of her display cabinet. 'A thing of beauty is a joy for ever,' she would tell me as I squashed my nose up against the diamond panes and gazed at it in awe. 'That teapot belonged to your great-great-grandmother,' she would add, using the reverent whisper she generally reserved for church. 'It's very valuable. It's my little nest egg – so I won't be a burden to anyone when I'm old. If anything goes wrong I can always sell the teapot.' To me, she was old already, and we all knew she would never sell the teapot – whatever happened. If the house caught fire, I am sure she would have rescued her precious antique before she even considered saving herself.

Then one Christmas a dreadful thing happened. At first it was just like any other Christmas. All the members of the family were gathered at Granny's house by midday, and the Christmas dinner tasted just as wonderful as usual. The only slight hitch came after the pudding had been carried in, blazing with blue brandy flames. Everyone was enjoying their share when an anguished cry from my small brother managed to turn sixteen startled faces in his direction. He had swallowed the shilling piece, which was always hidden somewhere among the currants and raisins. He was convinced he would die at any moment, but it seemed to be the loss of a whole shilling that *really* worried him!

By three o'clock, however, he had forgotten all about it as we squashed into the front room to hear the King on the BBC Home Service. In those days people still stood up for the national anthem – even after a large Christmas dinner. Then came the ceremonial opening of the presents while Grandpa puffed his way through one of the fat Havana cigars we always gave him in a sandalwood box. By this time, the crackling fire had raised the temperature in the crowded little room to sauna proportions.

'I'm getting very dry, my dears,' said Granny. 'Let's have some tea.' It was probably the last beverage anyone fancied just then, but we knew she needed an excuse for the teapot's annual ceremonial appearance.

It was while we were all milling about in the kitchen after tea that the fatal accident happened. I can't remember which of my uncles dropped the teapot, but the crash cut a horrified silence right across all the happy noises in the house. 'If only you could turn the hands of a clock backwards,' was my instinctive thought. 'Then it wouldn't have to happen.'

My granny had hard, red, quarry tiles on her back kitchen floor. I remember standing looking down at the pieces of teapot, scattered in all directions over the shiny surface – sharp, jagged, painful pieces surrounding a pathetic heap of soggy tea leaves. Then I looked up at Granny's face, and I will never forget her expression. Something precious, beautiful and irreplaceable had gone for ever. The future was no longer safely insured, and a lifeline to the past had been severed.

Somehow that moment stuck in my memory. All the characters in the scene were left suspended in time, like a video put on hold. Years later, it all came back to me as I lay in a hospital bed in London. Once again I felt the same sickening devastation as I realised that my life had been smashed, just like the teapot, and the pieces lay in fragments around me. I had been seriously ill, and the doctors were not at all sure that I would ever make a full recovery.*

'You are very lucky to survive,' the nurses told me. 'Lots of people die from what you had.' I was not so sure I was lucky when I realised that the illness had left me handicapped in many ways. 'How will I ever cope when I get home?' I thought miserably, when I found I couldn't even stand up without the floor jumping up to hit me, and I slurped tea all over the bed because my hands refused to grip the cup. 'I can't even look after myself properly, so how on earth will I manage the children?' When I tried to tell people how I felt, my words often jumbled themselves up into a hopeless mess that no one could understand. Worst of all, a catheter bag stood waiting to trip up my visitors every time they approached the bed. Would life, trapped in a body like this, be worth living?

---

* I have described this more fully in *Beyond Healing* and *Unexpected Healing*.

It had all seemed so perfect – before. We had six children, the youngest was only four years old and all of them were healthy and happy. We had just finished doing up our dream house in the country, and the garden was well stocked and neatly planted with vegetables and fruit. We had been living out the ideal existence we had always longed to achieve, but when I began to realise that the self-sufficient 'good life' in the country would be impossible now I was disabled, I felt as if our happiness had been smashed for ever – just like Granny's beautiful teapot. All our dreams and hopes seemed to lie around me in sharp, scattered pieces – how would I ever get them all back together again?

I know now that this sense of personal devastation is far more common than I realised then. I frequently meet people these days who say, for all kinds of reasons, 'My life just seems to have fallen apart.' The statement sounds like a cliché, but I cannot think of a better way of describing how it actually feels.


### Some 'Teapots' Break Suddenly

Sometimes the crash comes suddenly and dramatically. Perhaps you open the front door to two policemen who tell you that your husband has died on his way home from work. Or, the hospital consultant may say, 'I'm afraid it's cancer.' Or: 'Sorry, but you're redundant,' your employer announces. Or perhaps you find a note from your wife telling you she has gone to live with someone else – and she's taken the children with her.


### Some 'Teapots' Break Gradually

Sometimes the pieces fall apart more slowly. You find it hard to remember the exact moment when you realised that the relationship you thought was going to be permanent was beginning to crack and split; when the friends at church you loved and trusted began to turn against you; when you first noticed the 'clay feet' of the person you admired, relied on and trusted completely. Or you can't pinpoint exactly when the healthy body that had always obeyed you began to let you down. Perhaps the 'teapot' took so long to fall to the floor that all you can really be sure about is the fact that it is certainly broken now.

## Some 'Teapots' Are Only Made of Dreams

Some 'teapots' never actually existed outside of your own dreams and hopes – but that does not make the moment you recognised their loss any less agonising. It is possible to wake up one morning to the fact that you will never now be the person you always intended to be: the goals you set for your life were unattainable after all.

When Marion left Bible college, she would have gone anywhere for God. She was willing to evangelise the world like Billy Graham, or care for the poor like Mother Teresa. Ten years later, her life had narrowed to the confines of a suburban flat and the needs of three small children. She was overweight, unhappily married, and spiritually smothered by a boring church.

Shelley had always hoped that 'when she grew up' she would throw off her shy, retiring nature and develop the kind of sparkling personality that would draw other people to her like a magnet. At forty-five, it suddenly dawned on her that she was still on the outside of any group, marginalised, and usually ignored. The career she had hoped for had never quite happened, and now her life consisted of caring for her elderly mother, struggling with a dull office job, and babysitting for her sister's children.

Gill was about the same age when she finally realised her marriage was never going to be as romantic and tender as she had been convinced it would be on her wedding day. In fact, it had turned sour – and she was living with a husband who had even stopped trying to pretend that he loved her. The children she had hoped would take Cambridge by storm had turned into monsters who refused to work at school, and who made life unbearable for her at home.

Shattered dreams can be every bit as painful as shattered reality.

## Some 'Teapots' Broke Long Ago

Other 'teapots' have been broken right back in childhood. Often I meet people who go through life feeling 'broken inside – not quite a complete human being'.

'I've always felt like that,' said Mary. 'I don't know why. I can't seem to remember great chunks of my childhood – they're lost in a kind of grey misery. I'm afraid it has something to do with things my father used to do to me, but I can't bring myself to remember them. I don't *want* to remember them. But if I'm honest, I know that whatever was done to me during those grey patches has left me unable to be a normal woman, to marry, to relate to men – even to have the confidence to get the kind of job I know I am capable of doing. Yes, I suppose I've always felt worthless, no good to anyone, broken on the inside.'

Sometimes it is not abuse in childhood that breaks the 'teapot', but some kind of severe loss. As these children grow up, they often try to bury their distress and deny the painful effects of it; but until their grief is acknowledged and dealt with, they are left with a broken 'teapot' inside, lying unmended in painful pieces.

Most of us can fool the outside world quite successfully. We wear a bright smile that says, 'I'm coping, I'm fine,' but inside we feel as if our lives, our dreams, our personalities and our relationships are all lying in little jagged pieces on a red-tiled kitchen floor. As we stand surrounded by the ruins, we probably wish that the hands of the clock could be turned backwards.

### 'You'll Just Have to Come to Terms with It'

I remember a chirpy little student nurse saying that to me as I lay there in the hospital bed. I could have hit her. She was only trying to be helpful, but I thought, 'What does she know about it anyway?' People who have never had their 'teapots' broken trot out that irritating little phrase so glibly. 'You'll just have to accept the new situation and learn to live with it.' It sounds so easy – until you try it! How can we come to terms with something utterly horrible? After all, who wants to be trapped for life in a body that no longer functions properly? Who wants to live alone grieving for the one and only person who made life bearable? Who wants to sit at home all day, pushed out, forgotten and useless? Accepting that life is now irrevocably different is perhaps one of the hardest things that a human being ever has to do. We do not *want* to come to terms with this new kind of life – all we want is the old one back!

'You can do anything if you try hard enough.' That was something Granny often used to say. Probably the first thing she thought after her teapot was broken that Christmas afternoon was, 'I can soon mend it.' After the gasp of horror and the pungent silence in the kitchen, I remember the culprit uncle scrabbling round the floor on hands and knees scooping up all the pieces he could find: his neck purple with embarrassment as it bulged over the collar of his best white shirt.

Outside the back door in the icy darkness stood the dustbin, its lid frosted just like the Christmas cake. It was full of turkey legs, bits of cracker, tight balls of wrapping paper, and cold Brussels sprouts. My uncle began to hurl the bits of teapot in on top, until my grandmother's indignant voice halted him from the open doorway.

'Whatever are you doing?' she demanded. 'You can't throw it away!'

'Mother, that teapot will never hold tea again,' he said firmly, as half the spout went into the bin.

She simply refused to accept such a terrible thought. 'Anything can be mended,' she declared and, pushing past him, began snatching the pieces from among the greasy debris, collecting them carefully in her apron. I can't remember what happened after that, so I guess my parents must have deemed it tactful for us to leave rather hastily.

'This *can't* happen to me!' is how most of us initially feel when something dreadful happens, and it is usually only much later that we begin to realise that the damage is irreversible. We then either accept the situation or are destroyed by it.

Perhaps I should say right now that I did not cope very well with this business of 'coming to terms with it'. In fact, looking back on those first two years of my illness, I can see just what a mess I made of it. It was not living with constant pain and fatigue that got me down, nor was it my disabilities and the restrictions of my life. What really floored me was the way I reacted to it all. A whole range of bewildering emotions that were quite out of character kept taking me by surprise, and caused me to say and do things I heartily regretted.

## Why All the Secrecy?

If only someone had told me that *everyone* feels like that when their 'teapots' are broken. No one warned me that I would feel so angry. No one said that depression is normal after severe loss, so when despair almost drove me to take my own life I thought I must be going mad. No one explained that I might feel like shrivelling up with guilt at the suspicion that it could all be my fault, or that it is common for people to argue and bargain with God – and ask 'Why?' a thousand times a day. When I floated through life, cut off from other people in my own separate bubble of space, I had no idea that this sense of isolation and loneliness is par for the course. These reactions take nearly all of us entirely by surprise, but somehow they have to be lived through *before* we can reach that moment when we can honestly say, 'I have accepted my life the way it is now.'

People try to hurry us to that point of acceptance because we are so hard to live with before we reach it – well, I certainly was! Many of my Christian friends looked askance at my angry outbursts or were shocked by my depression.

'Where's your faith?' they said. 'You ought to be praising the Lord instead of being so negative all the time.' I knew I was behaving badly – lashing out at everyone in sight – but I felt as if my life, as I had known it, was being hurled into the dustbin, just like Granny's teapot, 'never to hold tea again'. I simply did not know how to cope with all the unexpected feelings and reactions that kept on building up inside me. Now, looking back at myself struggling along that lonely road towards adjustment, I can see how much it would have helped to know someone else who had 'been there', and to discover from them some of the things that helped speed their journey. I hope this book will be a 'personal contact' for others who are travelling along behind me.

There is another reason why I wanted to write this book. Two years after I was first rushed into hospital, we reached a terrible time where everything seemed to be going wrong. Not only was I still constantly ill and in pain, but our marriage seemed to be falling apart. I couldn't cope with the children because insecurity made them all so difficult to manage, and we were just about to move from our home in the country. I just did not know where I fitted into the world any longer, or what was going to happen next. At this lowest point of all, something very remarkable happened that transformed the whole scenario for all of us. It was not a great dramatic miracle of instant healing; instead, it was something that can happen to anyone and everyone who wants it. But before I tell you about it, I must finish the story of Granny's teapot.

## The Mended Teapot

After our hasty departure on that fateful Christmas afternoon, I did not see Granny for a number of months. I often thought about her, and wondered if she would manage to glue all the bits of her teapot back together again with her tube of thick brown glue. It was the following July before I went back to see her again, and the first thing

I did was to dash straight into the dining-room. Pressing my nose flat against the doors of the glass cabinet, I looked for the teapot. It wasn't there. Only a dark circle where the velvet had not faded showed where it had once stood so proudly. Poor Granny, I thought. She had failed.

Sadly, I turned round, and there on the window ledge in the sunshine I saw it – what was left of it, anyway. Obviously, she had not managed to find all the pieces: most of the spout was missing, as was the lid, and the handle looked very odd. Like an excavated Egyptian vase in a museum, the teapot was full of little jagged holes and cracks. But Granny had 'green fingers'. She could make anything grow – anywhere. She had filled the carcass of the teapot with rich compost, and out of those holes grew all kinds of beautiful little plants and flowers. Miniature ferns and variegated ivy poked their way out of the gaps, and a begonia with tiny orange flowers cascaded from the hole where the lid should have been, reminding me of soap bubbles escaping from an over-filled washing-machine. The teapot looked so lovely that it took my breath away.

'It's not the same; it never will be,' said Granny, coming up behind me. 'But everyone who comes to see me these days tells me how lovely it looks. I always used to say, "A thing of beauty is a joy for ever",' she added thoughtfully, 'and I suppose it *is* still beautiful, but in a different sort of way.'

---

*God can do wonders with a broken heart so long as you give him all the pieces.* (Victor Alfsen)

# 2

# INSIDE THE BROKEN TEAPOT

My granny's broken teapot had a happy ending, but not all the stories of broken lives finish quite so well. Some 'teapots' take years to mend, and others stay in fragments for ever.

How is it that some people seem able to adapt to massive trauma and upheaval and, like Granny's teapot, allow their lives to be reshaped and given a new purpose? Other people experience similar tragedy, but they leave the broken pieces in the dustbin and give up on life completely, while their friends say gloomily, 'How sad, he never got over it.'

Why do some people gather up the pieces and hold them tightly, as if the jagged shards were some kind of comfort? These little fragments of the past are all they have to cling to now. In fact, they become so absorbed in them that they never consider that the future is also there, waiting to be lived.

Others collect the broken pieces and arrange them carefully in the display cabinet as a perpetual reproach to the person they blame for the disaster. Being 'a broken person' becomes a way of life. They show the fragments off to everyone who comes near them, endlessly requiring pity, and gaining comfort (and even importance) from the attention.

There are probably hundreds of reasons for staying in pieces, but I believe there is a way that broken lives can be mended. It happened like this for me. It was two years after I first became ill that I reached that 'all time low' that I mentioned in the last chapter. It was one

---

*The Lord is near to those who are discouraged; he saves those who have lost all hope.* (Ps. 34:18, GNB)

Saturday morning just before we were due to move from our home in the country. The children were all being diabolical, my pain level was uncomfortably high, and the house seemed full of packing cases that tripped us up or ripped our clothes with their sharp metal corners. Tony made some bright but irritating comment that triggered off a major row, and suddenly all I wanted to do was go away by myself and scream very loudly indeed. 'Everything had got on top of me' may be yet another cliché, but it describes exactly that feeling of being weighed down and crushed by problems that no one seems able to solve.

Struggling out of the house on my elbow crutches, I fell over, face down, in a lake of manure at the bottom of our garden.* I struggled in the dung, vainly trying to get myself back on to the grass, but my arms and legs were not strong enough. I felt as if the manure was sucking me down, and in the end I simply had to give up and sit still until someone came along to pull me out.

I was crying with rage, not only at the indignity of being stuck in that ghastly mess, but at the frustration of being trapped in a similar way by my problems. I wanted to vent all my fury on the person who had disintegrated my nice, well-organised life, and turned it into a mass of stinking muck – but who was really to blame? I had been so angry with Tony that morning that I had thrown the steam iron at him, but it was not his fault that I was ill. Nor were the doctors at fault because they could not cure me. My friends irritated me with their tactless advice, and the children drove me up the wall with their bad behaviour. I was angry with all these people, but suddenly I realised who I was really holding responsible . . .

### It Was God Himself

Lying in the muck, I told God what I thought of him for allowing me to become ill in the first place, and then refusing to hear all those prayers for healing. I was so abusive that I deserved to be struck

* See *Unexpected Healing*, p. 93.

> *God has blocked the way, and I can't get through; he has hidden my path in darkness.* (Job 19:8, GNB)

down by lightning, but instead I really believe he answered me. These words formed themselves inside my head: 'I know about the mess, but I want to be in the centre of all those problems with you, and I would be, if only you would let me.' As I lay there in all that filth, I felt utterly overwhelmed by his love – it really was the most amazing experience of my life! Gradually I began to realise that for months I had been blaming God for everything that had been going wrong. By holding all these grudges against him, I had pushed him out of the centre of my life and allowed the problems and worries to take his place.

It was a long time before anyone came to find me. Somehow, as I sat there, I kept on thinking of Granny pulling the pieces of broken teapot out from among the rubbish and carefully collecting them in her apron. I found myself giving God the fragments of my life one by one – the broken body, the broken dreams and hopes, the broken marriage and family security, and – most of all – the broken faith in his goodness and care. I asked him to come into the middle of the mess my life had become, to take control of it, and to mend it for me.

I believe he did that. I did not feel any different at the time, but a few weeks later I was aware that something had definitely happened. It was not that the circumstances of my life suddenly became easier; it was the way I felt about those circumstances that had changed.

It was 'letting go' of the past and of my hidden resentment against God that made room for him to come back into the central place and begin to mend me from the inside. He did not put me back together in the way I would have expected, but he did allow new things to 'grow' out of the broken places. In the past, my happiness had come from outward things such as good health, a perfect home, and an identity in the village community; so that when they were lost, my happiness went too. Having God in the centre gave me a new kind of inner happiness that has nothing to do with the outside circumstances of life. It is a supernatural peace and joy that goes on bubbling away internally – however difficult the outside circumstances may be.

Soon the rest of the family caught this 'peacejoy' too, and the children settled happily into our new home and our marriage became stronger than ever before. I had the time to write books and speak

---

*He heals the broken-hearted and bandages their wounds.*
(Ps. 147:3, GNB)

from my wheelchair in churches and Christian meetings, and the very fact that I was always at home made it possible for other hurting people to stop by for a chat. I was no better physically, and in fact my health deteriorated drastically over the next six years, but I think God mended my 'teapot' all the same. Being ill had not finished my life – it had simply changed its shape.

I always seem to see things in pictures, and this is the way I visualise what happened to me after falling in the cow dung. The following diagrams show what I was like during those first two years of my illness. God was there, but pushed right out on the edges of my life. The problems filled the centre and dominated my thinking.

When I asked God to come into the centre of my life, his love began to push the problems out to the edges, making them seem so much less important. They were still there, but they no longer obsessed my thinking and defeated me. The more I allowed God to pour his love into me, the more he could do to help and mend me.

## That Vital Moment of Letting Go

I have often tried to picture my granny sitting at her kitchen table, carefully trying to glue all those bits of china back together again. How did she feel when she first realised that she had not managed to find all the pieces in the dustbin? Did she wonder if it was worth continuing with the intricate repairing job if her precious teapot could never be perfect again? Did there come a moment when she let go her memory of the teapot as it had been, and began to picture it in a new shape?

How did she feel about the person who dropped it? I know she was furious with him at first, because her ears always turned red when she was angry. Did she ever consider making him feel guilty by displaying the wreckage in her cabinet? Perhaps she did, but later she must have decided to set aside her resentment, or she could never have lavished so much loving care on reshaping her treasure.

The more I think about it, the more convinced I am that this 'letting go' of what is past, and also of the person responsible for the 'breakage', is the key to rebuilding broken lives.

## Who Is Responsible?

'Teapots' do not break all by themselves – we can always find someone to blame.

---

*God says, 'The mountains and hills may crumble, but my love for you will never end; I will keep for ever my promise of peace.'* (Isa. 54:10, GNB)

- Sometimes the culprit is obvious – the husband who walked out, the boss who gave us the sack, the father who abused us – or perhaps a whole chain of people contributed to our misery.
- Sometimes we only have ourselves to blame for the mess we are in, yet oddly it can be harder to forgive ourselves than anyone else!
- When the answer is not so obvious we often blame God – just as I did. 'If he really loved me and had the power the Bible says he has, then he would have healed me,' was my unvoiced accusation.

To forgive means to give up a grudge and to stop blaming someone. Being willing to do that for the person who 'broke our teapot' seems, in some mysterious way, to set us free to live again.

### 'But Forgiving a Man Like Him Is Quite Impossible'

'Everyone I meet keeps on telling me I must forgive him!' Those were the words of a friend of mine, Fiona, and they were said to me some years ago. 'They make me mad! It's easy to spout on about forgiving and letting go of the past when you've never been hurt badly yourself! If they were married to someone like him, they'd find forgiving impossible too!'

Since then, I have met many other people who feel the same as Fiona, and I believe she was right: forgiving is impossible when someone has devastated your life and damaged the people you love. Yet her life stayed in ruins until she had forgiven her husband. So how did she manage to do the impossible?

#### *She had to get help from outside*

Back in the days when I was surrounded by umpteen screaming babies and toddlers in temper tantrums, I was asked to a coffee morning talk entitled 'Anger in the Family'. I thought it might do me good! It was there I met Fiona.

> *Everyone says forgiveness is a lovely idea until they have something to forgive.* (C.S. Lewis)

Before the official proceedings began, we chatted as we munched homemade biscuits, and she told me she had been a Christian for ten years and went to a church on the other side of town. Our children were all about the same age, and we were getting on so well that I felt mildly irritated when the speaker began her talk. My irritation did not fade either as she told us about her two perfect daughters, both away at boarding school, and her husband – who seemed to have a highly paid job and a positively saint-like disposition. As I listened, I felt that even *I* could keep my temper in such idyllic circumstances. Towards the end of the talk the speaker began to talk about forgiveness, and suddenly I felt a volcanic eruption in the seat beside me. With a snort of disgust, Fiona leapt to her feet and sent her chair crashing into the lap of an astonished-looking lady in a pink velvet hat. Everyone in the room looked on aghast as Fiona stormed out of the room, banging the door behind her. I slid out in her wake because I had noticed the distress in her face, and was just in time to see her disappearing upstairs to the crèche in one of the bedrooms. I caught up with her on the landing, and she turned on me like a cornered animal.

'Leave me alone!' She almost spat the words at me. 'You lot make me sick! All happily married, well off, smug little Christians. And yet you tell me to forgive!'

'I'm sorry,' I said nervously, 'But p'raps if you explained . . . ?'

'He doesn't even *want* to be forgiven – he's telling everyone it's my fault we broke up. He's spreading the most amazing lies just to put himself in a better light. I must have been blind – or thick! It had all been going on for months before I twigged – she even went to our church! We were in the same housegroup; she was my *friend*! I just don't know how they could . . .'

'What's happening now?' I ventured.

'He wants a divorce, but my kids cry for their daddy every night. Their security's shot to bits because we've got to move – he wants to sell the house so he can use his share to set up home with her! They'll have to change schools and, worst of all, I'll be out at work full time unless he gives us more money. How could he do all that to his own

---

*He pulled me out of a dangerous pit, out of the deadly quicksand. He set me safely on a rock and made me secure.* (Ps. 40:2, GNB)

kids? And yet everyone seems to imply I'm the wicked one because I
can't forgive.'

By that time, the meeting below must have finished because up the
stairs behind us surged the speaker and the lady of the house. They
obviously knew Fiona and her circumstances well. I could hardly
believe my ears when the speaker said sweetly, 'My dear, you really
must forgive and forget. Why don't we have a little prayer together?'

Fiona's response is best forgotten, but sadly she is typical of so
many who are urged into making some kind of mental assent or
verbal statement far too soon. Just to keep everyone happy they
comply, but real forgiveness does not happen in the head; it comes
from the heart, and when nothing inside seems to change they feel
they have failed.

Fiona, like everyone else, needed to feel the pain first, express the
anger, grieve the loss, and experience the sorrow before she was
ready to face the issue of forgiveness. She was afraid to come too
close to God because she thought he too would force her to forgive.
First she simply needed to talk. Then, gradually, over many months,
she began to turn back to God again and open herself up to his love,
rather as I did in the cow dung. One morning she was finally ready to
be made willing to forgive. The following week, when I popped in to
see her, I found this little prayer pinned on her kitchen wall: 'Lord, I
can't forgive them, but please put your love in my heart and forgive
them for me. And please forgive me for not being able to forgive.'

Now, years later, her children have left home and she is in charge
of a small private nursing home. She loves her job, and in her spare
time is heavily involved in her church's activities. Her 'teapot' is
certainly mended, and I asked her, 'Did you find it easy to forgive in
the end?'

'No way!' she replied vehemently. 'It's taken me years – and even
now I can't be quite *sure* I have forgiven entirely. I think it's
something you have to keep on working at – for ever. But life
changed for me the moment I decided to spit out the hate, and breathe

---

*Forgiveness is not a sweet, platonic ideal to be dispensed
to the world like perfume sprayed from a fragrance bottle. It
is an unnatural act which is blatantly unfair and achingly
difficult. Long after you have forgiven, the wound lives on in
the memory.* (Philip Yancey)

in the love of Jesus. I've had to do the same thing millions of times since, because the resentments and angry feelings keep coming back in waves, but every time I "spit out and breathe in", I feel better. I still think it would have been impossible for me to forgive on my own. I needed Jesus to forgive through me, and then of course he was able to heal all the damage those two did to me and the children. In fact, despite everything, I'm really pleased with how well the children have turned out!'

'Would you mind if I wrote about what happened to you?' I asked her.

'Not now, I wouldn't,' she replied, 'now I'm mended. But do tell people they *must* be willing to allow God to "do it *his* way". He must be the boss. He has to be in complete control of everything if we want him to mend us. Otherwise, he's limited like a back-seat driver who can't help much in an emergency. He has to sit in the driver's seat and take the wheel before he can control a skid or avoid a crash. And,' she added finally, 'tell them that forgiving takes time, even with God's help!'

Perhaps, like Fiona, you feel you are being pressurised by others into making a hasty decision to forgive before you are really ready. If so, it might be better to put the whole subject on the 'back burner' while you read the rest of this book. Towards the end of the book there are some practical tips on letting go which you may find helpful.

## God's Presence

'There's no one I can really blame for what's happened to me, and how can God mend me when I don't feel he's there any more?' If you are feeling like that, it may be a help to know that many other people feel the same. Experts agree that one of the results of shock and intolerable stress is a complete loss of the feeling of God's presence. So whether you feel his presence or not, it does not alter the fact that he *is* there and he *can* help you. You simply have to make the decision to ask God to mend your life. The rest is up to him.

> *He who cannot forgive others breaks the bridge over which he must pass himself. For every man has need to be forgiven.* (George Herbert)

## But It Can't Be That Easy!

You're dead right. It isn't that easy – even with God's help – and when I fell in the cow dung, I would have lashed out at anyone who suggested that it was.

When my granny pulled the bits of teapot out of the dustbin, she was only just *beginning* her repairing job – not finishing it. The process of mending and adjustment usually takes a lot longer than most of us think that it should! Human beings cannot adapt suddenly to massive changes without all kinds of unexpected and disconcerting side effects, even with God in the driver's seat of their lives. As I said in the last chapter, some of these reactions can be most embarrassing, particularly for people who want to live the Christian life.

Everyone in the village loved Martin. He had been their vicar for twenty-seven years. 'He's got a big round red smile, and he laughs so much that he bounces when he walks.' That was the way one six-year-old member of his congregation described him in the parish magazine, and most people felt it was an apt description. Yet when Martin's wife died after a long and agonising illness, he lost his 'round red smile' completely for a while and shut himself away in the vicarage study.

'I've helped so many people through bereavement over the years,' he told his brother-in-law, who was also a clergyman, 'but I never thought it actually felt like this. Surely a man who has served the Lord for as many years as I have shouldn't feel depressed like this. And the anger!' His parishioners were surprised too.

'Fancy the vicar behaving like that!' said the postmistress. 'He snapped my head off the other day, and he couldn't be bothered to visit my auntie in hospital. You'd have thought his faith would have meant more to him than that, wouldn't you?'

Martin was not suffering from some deep spiritual problem: he was actually behaving like a normal human being going through what the experts call 'the grieving process'. Such experts devise diagrams to show us what to expect, and they make it look as if it is all a well-charted journey through clearly defined stages:

---

*What wound did heal but by degrees?* (William Shakespeare)

- shock
  - denial
    - recognition
      - anger
        - fear – anxiety
          - guilt
            - despair – depression
              - isolation – loneliness
                - questioning – bargaining
                  - and finally, acceptance

However, people are all different. We don't all move through the process from one nice neat stage to another in an orderly sequence. Some people start in the middle and finish near the beginning, while others do the whole thing backwards. In fact, it can feel more like a crazy game of snakes and ladders when our emotions send us zooming up and down and back and forth with quite remarkable rapidity. Some people even say they feel as if they are experiencing several of the emotions all at once! We just have to keep on reminding ourselves that the process is different for each of us, and we all travel through it at our own individual pace.

### *Warning!*

There is nothing tidy and systematic about this process that I have christened the 'Broken Teapot Syndrome'! So don't feel you have to wade through this book chronologically. If you are full of questions and plagued by endless 'whys?', turn straight to Chapter 8. If you are so angry you feel like a walking volcano ready to flare up at anyone who comes too close, take a look at Chapter 9. Just let the book scratch you where you itch most!

---

*Jesus said, 'He has sent me to . . . deliver those who are oppressed . . . downtrodden, bruised, crushed and broken down by calamity.'* (Luke 4:18, AMP)

## The Puzzled Spectators

The rest of the world sits around and watches us playing this weird game of snakes and ladders, but few of them understand what we are going through.

'If someone in my family had died, I think people would find it easier to understand why I keep crying,' said Rhianan, who had just had her leg amputated. She was right; everyone would have rallied round to support her through a bereavement, but few understand that other losses can feel almost as bad. It is possible to grieve for a job, health, ministry, reputation, marriage, friend, money or a home.

## A Secret Kind of Grief

Amanda lost both her parents in a car accident when she was only five, yet she appeared to grow up quite unaffected by the loss. Then, when she was thirty-five, she lost her job. It was only a minor tragedy in comparison with her childhood experience, but somehow it triggered off the memories she had buried and they all came surging to the surface. She went through the whole grieving process just as if her trauma had happened yesterday. It seemed ridiculous to admit she was crying for a mother she lost thirty years before, so instead of having the support and sympathy that people receive when they are 'publicly' bereaved, she had to suffer in secret.

Grieving for the loss of broken dreams and shattered hopes is just as embarrassing and quite as painful. Because this kind of pain is harder to acknowledge or express, people going through these secret crises can become so agitated internally that they may go into a depression and even suffer a complete breakdown.

## Why Is It Harder for Christians?

Secular 'experts' tell us that all our muddled emotions are perfectly normal, but we find it difficult to cope with them because we think:

> *Forgiveness is the key which unlocks the door of resentment and the handcuffs of hatred. It breaks the chains of bitterness and the shackles of selfishness.* (Corrie ten Boom)

- Christians should be tranquil and accepting, not angry.
- Christians should trust God, not keep on asking 'why?'
- Christians should be full of joy and triumph, not depression.
- Christians should be outgoing, not isolated and lonely.
- Christians shouldn't worry: they should praise God – and sing hymns loudly!
- Christians shouldn't always feel guilty, because Jesus died for them.

So we push these awkward feelings down behind a 'bright Christian smile' and deny their existence – even to ourselves. Christians, though, are human beings, not robots or angels, and human beings happen to feel all this and far more when their 'teapots' are broken. Later in the book it might be good to look at some of these emotions and discover ways of coping with them, and even how they can be turned around and used creatively to our advantage.

Although Christians can feel as devastated as anyone else by personal disaster, we have one huge advantage: we do not have to face the misery of it all on our own. Yet there have been times when I've felt so badly hurt that it was hard to accept that truth, so it has always been a great relief to me to know that one of the greatest 'saints' in history also found it difficult.

---

## A Meditation

'There's nothing to worry about,' she told everyone who came to the house to ask how Lazarus was that day. 'He'll be well soon, because we've sent for Jesus. He'll be here any time now.'

'Mary, your brother is dying,' said the physician from Jerusalem. 'He can't possibly last through the night.'

She smiled confidently up into his grave face as she replied, 'But Jesus of Nazareth is a friend of ours. He loves Lazarus and me, and

---

*Listen! I stand at the door and knock; if anyone hears my voice and opens the door, I will come into his house and eat with him, and he will eat with me. (Rev. 3:20, GNB)*

our sister, Martha. If he heals strangers he's never even met before, and any old beggar who asks him, then he's absolutely sure to heal Lazarus – because he loves him. He'll be here in a minute, you'll see.'

However, by the next morning Lazarus was dead.

'No! You mustn't do that,' said Mary, as Martha began to pull the sheet up over the face they both loved so much. 'Don't you remember that story Peter is always telling us, about the young girl in Capernaum? She was dead at least an hour, but Jesus suddenly arrived, just in time, and brought her back to life. I'm going to the gate to look up the road for him. He'll be here soon.'

For hours she sat there, watching. 'Come on in, for goodness' sake!' snapped Martha. 'Can't you see how much you're leaving for me to do? We'll have half Jerusalem over here for the funeral. I've got hours of baking to do; come and give me a hand. Our brother will rise again at the resurrection on the last day. Mooning about out here won't bring him back any sooner.'

They buried Lazarus at sunset; and as they rolled the stone over the mouth of the grave, Mary's last hope was buried in the darkness with her brother.

Four days later, the funeral party was still going on, and Martha was far too busy to notice Mary. She sat motionless in the house, surrounded by crowds of friends and relations, but totally alone all the same. It was a comfort to know they were there, but she could not talk to them.

'She loved him so much,' they all said sadly, but how could she tell them the greatest agony was not the loss of Lazarus? Jesus hadn't come. He hadn't even sent a message to tell them why. She was exhausted from trying to understand him.

There was a commotion going on in the road outside, and children were shouting, 'He's coming down the road!'

'Quick, Mary,' said Martha, gripping her arm, 'Jesus is here – we must run to meet him before he reaches the village.'

Mary shook her head. Why should she go to him now? He hadn't come to her when she needed him. How could she possibly look him in the face, knowing he could so easily have prevented all this?

With a shrug of annoyance, Martha ran on without her and was met by this challenging question: 'I am the resurrection and the life, he that believes in me will live, even if he dies. Do you believe that?'

Her answer still echoes triumphantly down through the years. 'Yes, Lord, I believe you are the Christ . . .'

But Mary still sat motionless in the house. 'Come on, do!' protested Martha, shaking her crossly. 'He's asking for you!'

So she had no choice, she had to go. When she finally reached the place where he was waiting, all the emotions she had been holding down for so long finally burst out. 'If only you'd come, my brother wouldn't have died!' she exclaimed. She wanted to make him feel guilty – to pay him back for letting her down – yet she wanted so desperately to hold on to her dwindling faith in his love.

As Jesus watched, he could see the pain in her face as so many confusing emotions struggled beneath the surface. He did not ask her why she had not come out to meet him with Martha, why she had hidden away from him, looking for comfort from others instead of running to him. He did not compare her with Martha, whose faith was so strong. He did not reproach her for doubting him. He did not explain or answer her questions – he loved Mary too much to bother about any of those things. The only thing that mattered to him at that moment was the way she was feeling. As he stood there silently, he minded so much for her that he wept.

He loves you just as much as he loved Mary of Bethany. He is weeping for you too. Mary finally ran and flung herself at his feet. All he says to you at this moment is, 'Come to me.'

## A Prayer

*'Come to me, all of you who are tired from carrying heavy loads . . .'*
(Matt. 11:28, GNB)

Yes, Lord Jesus, I am tired: tired from carrying this load of grief and disappointment; tired of being reduced to a heap of bits and pieces; tired of struggling with all these conflicting feelings, and tired of making endless plans that I'm too tired to carry out. I can't possibly think about being built into anything new just yet – all I need is someone to comfort me because I'm hurting so badly. People I loved and things that I valued have been wrenched away, leaving my heart lacerated and bleeding. I feel as if I have been emotionally punched and beaten, and inside I'm nothing but bruises and festering wounds.

*'Come to me . . .'* (Matt. 11:28, GNB)

I think I can dare to come to you because you understand; you were beaten too. You were left wounded and humiliated to bear the pain of it all, alone.

*'Come to me . . . and I will give you rest.'* (Matt. 11:28, GNB)

Rest. Yes, I need rest so badly; but I'm restless with pain. Maybe rest means healing? If I exposed all these wounds to you, asked you to come into the pain with me, right to that hard core where it hurts most, would your love pour in to bathe the wounds, soothe the bruises and eventually bring perfect healing to my soul?

*'Come to me . . . "for I am the Lord, the one who heals you".'* (Exod. 15:26, GNB)

Lord Jesus, I do come to you and give you my bruises and sores, my conflict and confusion, and in exchange I receive your healing, comfort and rest for my weary soul.

---

*He jests at scars who never knew a wound.* (William Shakespeare)

## STOP FOR A MOMENT

'People say it was Jesus Christ who mended their broken lives, but how can a character from history help me now?'

*Jesus is not simply a character from history, though – he is actually God himself. He stepped down into our world and became a man, so he could show us what God is really like and how much he loves us.*

*He was constantly mending broken people. He healed bodies physically, but he cared about how people felt on the inside too.*

'What can a dead man do for me?'

*Jesus died a terrible death, but because he was God, death could not hold him. He rose after three days, and he still lives in this world today – still doing the same job of comforting, mending and restoring.*

'How is that possible?'

*The Bible tells us how the Spirit of Jesus returned forty days after his body had ascended to heaven. He no longer has a physical body, but he lives by his Spirit in the bodies of people who ask him to do so. When Jesus lives in a person by his Spirit, gradually he helps that person to think as he thinks, to see other people as he sees them, to feel about them as he feels about them, and to act towards them in the way he would act. The more room inside himself – or herself – that someone makes for Jesus, the more he is able to fill that person up with his personality and his power. That is what the word 'Christian' really means – someone who has Christ in their lives. Take out the letter 'a' in the word Christian and it spells 'Christ in'.*

---

*I will lead my blind people by roads they have never travelled. I will turn their darkness into light . . . These are my promises and I will keep them.* (Isa. 42:16, GNB)

# SHOCK AND DENIAL

Before we begin to examine in more detail the confusing kaleido-
scope of reactions and emotions which usually follow any loss,
perhaps we should look at the period when most of us feel nothing
at all. Experts call this vacuum the stage of 'shock and denial'. This is
how one of my friends described it:

'I was like a zombie, going through the motions of life quite
automatically – without thinking about the past or the future. I just
kept on doing silly little jobs to fill the time. People used to say, "Why
don't you have a good cry, dear?" but I couldn't. I felt too discon-
nected.'

Another friend said:

'I kept thinking, "This is only a bad dream, tomorrow I'll wake up
and find everything's back to normal".'

### Shock

Perhaps this numbness is actually necessary. Our minds seem to
need space to work through the implications of what has happened,
so they switch off the emotions and render us incapable of feeling
anything. In fact, shock seems to work for the mind rather like an
anaesthetic works for a critically injured body, helping it over the
worst part of the trauma.

Yet this anaesthetic effect can have its problems. We may lose the

---

*But for you who revere my name, the sun of righteousness
will rise with healing in its wings.* (Mal. 4:2, NIV)

bad feelings, but we can also lose the good feelings too, and, as I said in the last chapter, some people become very distressed because they feel they have 'gone dead' spiritually. When they find they have lost all the joy that prayer or worship once used to bring them, they fear they have lost God himself. This numb feeling can persist for months, so they think they are in the 'dark night of the soul', instead of in a normal stage of the grieving process.

On the other hand, shock can induce a feeling of euphoria. I remember lying in hospital in 1982 and being so relieved *not* to be dead that I felt marvellous – just as if I were floating in God's presence. All day, and most of the night, I listened to praise tapes on my personal stereo and was convinced life would always be like this. When I came home from hospital, I came down to earth with a nasty bump!

That bump seems to happen to a lot of other people, too. As the shock wears off, the full realisation of what has happened can be so painful that they retreat into the second part of the process: denial.

## Denial

When Granny went fishing about in that dustbin declaring indignantly, 'Anything can be mended,' she was denying the horrible possibility that her beautiful teapot might be permanently broken. The following people are all doing the same thing:

'He isn't going to be allowed to spoil my life; I'll find such a good solicitor that he'll be *made* to come back to me.'

'There *has* to be a doctor somewhere in the world who can make me well again.'

'My wife hasn't really got multiple sclerosis. The doctors must be wrong. It's all in her mind – she could walk if she tried.'

'Somewhere there must be someone who'll lend us enough money to get our business back on the road again.'

'Of course I'm not going deaf! The trouble is, young people nowadays can't be bothered to speak clearly.'

'God will heal me [or my child]. So many people are praying for us that he's bound to perform a miracle.'

*God is light; in him there is no darkness at all.* (1 John 1:5, NIV)

## Christians and denial

I often used to think it would have been easier for me to 'adjust' to life
as a disabled person if I did *not* believe in a God who answers prayer.
I knew he had the power to put everything right for us, yet in spite of
all the prayer that went up from our friends at church, he did not
seem to be doing so!

Of course, humans must have hope or life is pointless; and when
adversity strikes, it is right to fight back – and people with a
tenacious will to survive recover much better than the pessimists
who give up. However, there does come a time when it is right to face
reality in order to adjust to things as they actually are. God wants to
give us a new life, but he can't while we are still determined to
reconstruct the old life. Jesus said, 'Happy are those who mourn; God
will comfort them' (Matt. 5:4, GNB), but he cannot begin to comfort
us until we admit we are broken and badly hurt.

## Beware of the 'Hold Up' Factor

The 'hold up' factor is what I consider the greatest danger we face
during the whole mending process. All the stages we go through
during this bizarre game of snakes and ladders are normal reactions,
but it is vital to keep on moving through them. We must plod on
continuously, taking each stage at a time and never allowing
ourselves to stand still and become stuck in one particular attitude
or thought pattern. For instance, it is normal to be angry when we are
badly hurt, but if someone holds on to his or her anger for too long it
becomes a way of life; such people then develop such huge chips on
their shoulders that they seem to stay permanently trapped in the
ruins of their 'broken teapot'.

There is a 'hold up' factor connected with each of the various
stages that we will be considering in the next few chapters, and I will
describe them all as we go along. People seem to get held up in this
denial stage because they refuse to accept the event that has changed
their lives. They do this in three ways:

> *The light that shines through the darkness – and the
> darkness can never extinguish it.* (John 1:5, LB)

1. They deny what has happened by insisting everything will be back to normal soon. The people I have just described, who refused to believe they would remain ill, alone or deaf, are examples of this.
2. They deny the pain of what has happened by not letting themselves feel their reactions.
3. They deny the event ever happened by 'forgetting' it completely – the 'buried video' approach (see p. 47).

## Everything Will Be Back to Normal

Perhaps the most extreme example of the first method mentioned that I have ever come across was when we were moving house. The estate agents sent us particulars of a very nice-sounding property in just the right area. We made an appointment and went round to see it. A woman of about forty-five opened the front door, and seemed quite happy to show us around her home. One of the bedrooms was obviously a child's room. School clothes were left out ready to wear on the bed, a cricket bat lay beside them, homework was spread out on the desk, and a model aeroplane was half finished on a table.

'How old's your son?' I asked, in order to make conversation.

'Eleven,' she replied proudly. 'He's a lovely boy.'

We liked the house very much, so we went to the agent and made an offer. Later that day, it was accepted. A week after that, our doorbell rang and the lady's husband stood on the step. He looked embarrassed, angry and distressed, in sequence, as he explained that the sale was off.

'It's happened so many times before. I nearly get her to the point of moving, but in the end she can never face it. You see, our only son was killed eight years ago. She just can't bring herself to believe he has really gone. She feels she has to wait there for him with everything ready in case he comes home one day. But life has to go on, doesn't it?' he finished, and there was a note of desperation in his voice.

---

*Once the little child in us is healed, then the adult can get on with their life.* (Russ Parker)

## Denying the Pain

This is the second way that people get held up in the denial stage, and I met someone like that when I was asked to speak at a Ladies' Day held in a church in the North of England. The 'hub' of the proceedings was a lady called Rose, who won my complete admiration by her ability to dispense tea for a hundred thirsty women at frequent intervals, cracking a continuous string of jokes while she did so.

'Isn't she wonderful?' whispered someone in my left ear. 'Her son committed suicide a few months back. He got very depressed after he failed his exams, but she never talks about it.'

As I was speaking that day, I kept on seeing Rose's face as she listened through the kitchen hatch. Her expression was frozen and quite without emotion. At the end of the day, when most people had left, I was just putting on my coat when she hurried up to me. 'Thought you might like a quick cuppa before you go,' she said, holding out yet another paper mug.

'You look tired,' I said, 'after all that tea pouring.'

'I'm all right,' she replied firmly, 'but I think I may have something wrong with my throat. It feels so tight and painful these days, I can't seem to swallow.'

'Could I pray about that?' I asked her gently. She nodded, and we closed our eyes as we stood there side by side in the empty hall. As soon as I began to pray I had a vivid picture. The whole of Rose's throat and chest was filled with a huge block of ice. I described it to her and then I said, 'Rose, I think it's made of all the tears you can't seem to shed. They're frozen solid, and they'll do a lot of damage if you don't allow Jesus to melt them with the warmth of his love.'

'I can't cry,' she replied firmly. 'It wouldn't be a good witness if I gave in to it. And there's no point in getting all emotional, you've just got to put on a brave face and get on with it, haven't you?'

---

*Something in us prevents us from remembering, when remembering proves to be too difficult or painful . . . We are not entirely successful however, because the memory is buried within us, and influences every moment of our growth. Sometimes it breaks through the prison and strikes at us directly and painfully.* (Paul Tillich)

'Rose,' I said, 'just because you are a Christian does not mean you are exempt from pain.' I got her to sit down, and even managed to make her drink my tea while I talked. 'When Jesus was a baby, Mary and Joseph met an old man one day called Simeon. He knew exactly who this tiny baby really was, and he was so delighted that he took him in his arms and thanked God. Then suddenly he looked up into Mary's face and the smile died away from his eyes. She must have looked so happy that day, but Simeon was "seeing" her thirty-three years later, bent with grief as she stood by the cross where her son was dying in agony. "A sword will pierce your own soul too" (Luke 2:35, NIV), he murmured quietly. Rose, a terrible thing has happened to you. It must feel exactly as if a "sword has pierced your soul". You are wounded just as severely as if you had been stabbed physically. If you ignored a stab wound, you'd bleed seriously and probably go into shock. Or the wound might become infected and cause all kinds of severe problems. I think you badly need to ask Jesus to treat this wound of yours.'

'No!' she said, as her clenched fist squashed the empty paper cup to pulp. 'If I start to cry, I'll never stop.' And with that, she hurried away towards the kitchen.

'Isn't she wonderful!' The same woman was talking again into my left ear. Like so many other Christians, Rose simply did not realise how dangerous it can be to freeze her feelings.

## *Why do we get stuck like this?*

I am beginning to wonder if sometimes we get stuck because we are unwilling to face the issue of who we really blame for what happened. For instance, there is Beth, who was disabled after her car skidded on a patch of ice. Beth admitted she had not been concentrating too well that morning, but the accident seemed to be 'just one of those things'. Five years later, Beth finally managed to admit that deep down she had always felt her lack of concentration was due to sleepless nights spent worrying over her rebellious teenage daughter. Secretly, she had felt so bitter that their relationship had broken down completely.

---

*Freedom is what we have – Christ has set us free!* (Gal. 5:1, GNB)

---

'But surely it's not very nice to go looking for scapegoats to blame for all our troubles?' people say. 'And it doesn't matter, anyway.' But it *does* matter, because our subconscious minds know exactly who we are blaming for all our misfortunes. While our 'culprits' lurk down there like nameless shadows, shaped like a question mark, they can hold us back from the new life ahead because no one can 'let go' of a shadow.

Discovering that I had been blaming God for allowing me to be ill, and being able to leave behind those grudges in the cow dung, was the moment my 'teapot' began to mend. Rose, denying the pain she felt after her son's death, did become quite ill soon after we met. It was nothing serious, just infections that would not clear up and exhaustion that her doctor put down to depression. In the end, she had to give up her job and church work for a while.

Looking back now, she realises she dared not allow all that grief to be released because there was so much anger tangled up amongst it. She could not bring herself to admit it, but subconsciously she was furious with her son for committing suicide. She was also angry that he had allowed himself to drift into the unsavoury relationships and destructive activities that she felt had led to his depression and death.

One day, when she was visiting her doctor, she exploded – and finally managed to put into words all the resentment she had been hiding for over a year. 'How could he do such a thing to us?' she asked the doctor, and then felt terrible as soon as the words were out.

'The doctor was so kind,' she told me later. 'He said a lot of people feel angry like that after someone dies, even as a result of an accident, but he said I would have to let my son go before I could move on through my journey of grieving. He was right, too. That was the day I managed to cry – in fact, my husband thought I was never going to stop. Somehow everything came to the surface, and finally I did manage to get rid of it all. It was a turning point for me, and things have been much better since then.'

---

*You will know the truth, and the truth shall set you free.*
(John 8:32, GNB)

### The 'Buried Video'

Some people not only deny their feelings, but they wipe the event
that caused those feelings right out of their memories. The usual way
for our minds to cope with traumatic events is by 'reliving' them
endlessly for a while. The memories of all we have seen and felt go
round and round in our heads like an endless video replay. Although
it can be most distressing, this internal video is part of the mind's
natural healing mechanism, and after a while the repetitive memory
fades or the replays become less frequent. Sometimes, however, the
experience is too painful to handle, so we simply 'bury the video'. In
other words, we exclude all the bad memories from our minds. For a
short period of time this might work quite well as a coping strategy,
so long as we are willing to recall the incident and work through our
reactions to it as soon as we feel strong enough. The problems begin
when we continuously refuse to dig that video up again. The human
mind never forgets anything, so the original incident remains in the
subconscious like a festering wound, causing irrational fears, behaviour problems or difficult relationships.

I know all this is true because long ago when I was a child I 'buried
a video' that has caused me trouble for the last forty years. It is only
recently that I finally managed to dig it up and dared to watch it
again. Perhaps if I explain how I was helped to do this, it might
encourage other people whose 'teapots' broke when they were
children.

### The 'Teapot' that Broke Long Ago

In June 1991 Tony and I went together to a Communion Service in a
church that we do not usually attend. That morning, the Gospel
reading was from Matthew 6:14–15, and for some reason these words
seemed to stick in my mind: 'For if you forgive men when they sin
against you, your heavenly Father will also forgive you. But if you do
not forgive men their sins, your Father will not forgive your sins.'

'Goodness!' I thought, 'those are strong words.' I have a terrible

> *If the Son sets you free, then you will be really free.* (John
> 8:36, GNB)

habit of daydreaming in church, and suddenly I 'saw' myself arriving eagerly at the gates of heaven, only to be told by St Peter, 'Sorry, luvvy, there was that person you said you couldn't forgive, but really you meant you *wouldn't* forgive. So you can't come in here because your own sins aren't forgiven.'

The idea was so nasty that I shuddered and returned to earth rather rapidly. 'But do I have anyone I need to forgive?' I asked myself. I couldn't think of anyone at all, so I tried to concentrate on the sermon that had just begun.

This was on forgiveness, too, and the preacher talked about the man Jesus described in Matthew 5 who came to worship God at the altar carrying his offering. Jesus pointed out that it was useless for him to try to worship God because he was holding a grudge against his brother. He had to put down his offering and go at once to try to put right that broken relationship.

'The matter was so urgent, he even had to do it before the closing hymn!' declared the preacher, glaring at us severely from the pulpit. Perhaps he had the same naughty imagination as I have, but he made his point so well that several people wriggled uncomfortably. 'So don't come up to take communion this morning until you are *sure* you are willing to lay down anything you hold against someone else,' he concluded, and I felt relieved I had no grudges on my conscience. All the same, I felt I had better make quite sure, so I said the quick prayer that was to have a monumental effect on my life.

'Lord, please show me if there *is* someone I need to forgive.' It was when we reached the Lord's Prayer that the familiar words I must have said a thousand times suddenly stuck in my throat. 'Forgive us our sins as we forgive those who sin against us . . .'

In my head I heard a harsh voice shouting, 'Jennifer Rees, you are the stupidest child I have ever had the misfortune to teach!' I smiled – almost fondly. 'That was Miss Mitchell,' I thought. 'Surely God can't be serious, I'm not upset about that poor old thing – I can hardly remember her, and anyway she was quite right to call me stupid!'

At seven I had been sent to a private school for girls, and I soon discovered I was the only one in the class who couldn't read. (I was fourteen before I finally mastered the art.) When I tried to write down

---

*I feel I'm on a journey and I don't know where I'm headed, but I trust the driver.* (Roy Castle)

all the stories that teamed in my brain, no one could read the jumble of back-to-front words and bizarre spelling. Maths was no better because I could never work out whether five was more or less than seven, and I caused chaos in gym lessons because I did not know my left from my right, and always marched in a different direction to everyone else! Nowadays, all those problems would have been given some fancy name, but words such as 'dyslexia' were not invented when I was at school, so they labelled me 'backward' instead. Poor Miss Mitchell was lumbered with me in her class for four years – everyone else moved up in September, but not me.

By the time I was eleven I was so totally humiliated that I ran away and refused to go back to any school – ever again. They call that by another name these days, 'school phobia', but it felt to me like cowardice – and I have been deeply ashamed of it ever since.

In church that day I couldn't really think of anything I needed to forgive Miss Mitchell *for*, but just to make sure I said a hasty 'I forgive her Lord', before going up to the communion rail. Yet I had no idea as I knelt there just how many memories and feelings I was pushing down behind my tranquil expression. I had become so used to smothering them, I did not even realise I was doing so.

### *The recurring nightmare*

The first thing I noticed after that service was that my recurring nightmare happened more frequently than usual. Ever since I ran away from school I constantly dreamed I was being dragged back to face a sea of jeering faces and swirling navy gym slips. I had never taken much notice because frequent dreaming is an occupational hazard for most writers, and anyway it was so lovely waking up to find I was an adult safely in bed beside my husband.

Then two months later I had a letter. It was from the only girl who had been my friend in those four years at school. We had never met, or even been in touch, since the day I ran away.

'Let's make a date and get together,' said her letter. I looked

> *For the Sprit that God has given us does not make us timid; instead, his Spirit fills us with power, love, and self-control.*
> (2 Tim. 1:7, GNB)

forward to seeing her again, but was rather disappointed to find she no longer had pigtails and a brace on her teeth!

'At least you're a bit slimmer than you used to be,' she said.

'Yes, I was as fat as a barrel, wasn't I!' I laughed. At least I could remember that, but reminiscing about old times was surprisingly difficult for me, because I seemed to have 'lost' those years almost entirely.

'Miss Mitchell was a marvellous games teacher,' said my friend nostalgically, 'but I don't think she liked you very much!'

'I can't really remember her,' I said vaguely as I tried not to hear that voice shouting across the netball pitch: 'You're supposed to *catch* the ball, not stand there until it hits you! You're too revoltingly fat to walk, let alone run!'

'I've got a photo of her,' my friend said, as she rummaged in her bag. 'I took it last year at the school's centenary.' I went ice cold all over as I looked down at the face I had 'forgotten', and found that in reality I remembered it in minute detail. It seemed quite extraordinary that a woman of fifty could be so terrified of a mere photograph, but I was so afraid that I felt sick. I was oddly angry too. 'How dare she say I was stupid!' I thought, 'And how could she make the whole class laugh and jeer at me?' Hastily, I pushed these awkward emotions back in the dark cellar where I had been hiding them for forty years, and I managed to pin the smile firmly back on my face as I handed back the photo. 'Good job I've forgiven Miss Mitchell,' I thought, as I locked the cellar door once again.

But I had not really forgiven her at all, because I would not allow myself to acknowledge how much she had hurt me. It is foolish to say, 'Forgive and forget,' because we can't forgive until we are willing to *remember*, and that was something I was far too afraid to do just then. Until we identify the person who damaged us, we will never be free of the damage that person caused.

---

*For God . . . made his light shine in our hearts to give us the light of the knowledge of the glory of God in the face of Christ.* (2 Cor. 4:6, NIV)

### *Getting to the root*

About eighteen months later, something happened that at the time I did not realise was connected with Miss Mitchell. I went to see my great friend Marilyn Baker, the blind singer, and her companion, Tracy, who is deaf. I respect their ministry of inner healing greatly. Marilyn can 'see' things and Tracy can 'hear' things that most people with ordinary sight and hearing never perceive at all.

I went to them because of a very long-standing problem of my own. Perhaps we all have a besetting sin, something that seems to grow up in our lives like a tangling weed, getting in the way of the good things and spoiling them. We keep cutting it down, but it shoots up again to defeat us. I had been grappling with my very embarrassing 'weed' for years, and was totally sick of it. 'I need to get at the root of this thing,' I kept thinking, 'then perhaps it could be pulled out once and for all.' So just after Christmas I went all the way round the M25 to Watford, hoping that Marilyn and Tracy might 'hear' and 'see' what the Lord wanted to say to me.

My 'weed' was an eating problem. I was a fat child, I became an even fatter teenager, and then in my early twenties I developed anorexia to the point where I resembled a skeleton. Ever since then I have struggled with the humiliating misery of compulsive eating followed by endless starvation diets. I told Marilyn and Tracy all about it, and added, 'I've put on so much weight recently I don't have anything in my wardrobe I can wear!'

They listened to the Lord silently for a time, then Tracy said, 'I feel the root of all this has something to do with words that were spoken to you once. Perhaps by a teacher?' I felt startled because I certainly had never mentioned Miss Mitchell. Then Tracy added, 'Her words have also caused you to drive yourself because of a vow you made.'

I could see that being told so often I was stupid could have accounted for the crushing sense of inadequacy and failure that has dogged me for forty years. I have always driven myself to ridiculous limits to prove I am not as inadequate as I fear I am. So I guessed I must once have vowed to prove Miss Mitchell wrong, but how could she possibly be responsible for making me fat?

---

*In him was life and that life was the light of men.* (John 1:4, NIV)

So Marilyn and Tracy prayed a prayer to cut me off from the vow I could not remember making, and I drove home – eating several bars of chocolate on the way and feeling that I had failed yet again! Now, though, I believe that their prayers made possible what happened a month later.

It was late in January when I went to the North of England to give a talk entitled 'The Power of Words'. I explained how the things people say to us can bind us almost like a curse, changing the very way we think and feel about ourselves. By way of illustration, I mentioned Miss Mitchell and how her words had made me feel I was always a worthless failure. I also said I had 'forgiven' her, and that I believed the way to be freed from the effects of harmful words was to forgive the person who originally spoke them to us.

It all sounded quite good and everyone seemed to be nodding in agreement, but I was in for a nasty shock! In the meeting that night was a missionary teacher called Ann. She and I had been pen friends for years, so we arranged to meet for coffee before I returned home the following day.

'There is something I feel I must say,' she began awkwardly. 'You haven't forgiven Miss Mitchell at all, have you?' I was stunned.

'Yes I have,' I protested.

'Something tells me you have only forgiven her in your mind,' said Ann, 'but not from the heart – because in your heart you hate her.'

'I've never hated anyone in my life,' I protested. 'I think I was terribly frightened of her, but . . .'

'Have you seen her lately?'

'Oh no,' I said hastily, 'I never want to see her again.'

'That's the problem then,' replied Ann. 'You're only in the first stage of forgiving – the part that happens inside us – but the second part is all about moving towards the other person to offer forgiveness in a tangible way. When we have been hurt we shrink away from the person who inflicted the pain by "keeping out of their way", but while we are still doing that we are only at the half-way mark. I think you should go to that teacher of yours.'

'I really can't see the point,' I said, 'and anyway I used to think she was *ancient* forty years ago. If she's still alive, she must be about a

---

*True grieving uncovers the wounds and mourns them with painful energy until healing is achieved.* (Mary Pytches)

hundred and fifty by now.' But I knew Ann was looking at me with her kind, but penetrating, brown eyes. 'All right,' I said at last, 'when I get home I'll see if I can trace her.'

The secretary of my old school was most helpful when I rang. Miss Mitchell was alive and well, she told me, and even gave me a phone number. I was shaking all over as I tried to make my thanks sound sincere. Even after a strong cup of tea, I still could not muster up enough courage to ring the number on my notepad, so I took my dog Brodie for a walk in the park and tried to think what I could say when I finally managed to dial it.

In the park, my speech sounded very mature, confident and business-like, but once I heard that familiar voice say, 'Yes? Speak up, can't you?' I was reduced to a quivering child who was almost too afraid to remember her own name. I realised she had always been able to make me feel like that, and the louder she had shouted at me, the more stupid I became.

'I was in your form,' I managed at last, 'for four years. I wondered if I could just pop in s-some t-time, there's s-something I want to give you.' Well, there was! I wanted to give her my forgiveness, even if I intended to express it through a bunch of flowers rather than in words.

'How about next Tuesday at eleven – sharp?' suggested Miss Mitchell. I thanked her profusely and collapsed in a sweaty heap in my armchair. I was not at all sure I could go through with this, and my feelings towards Ann at that moment were far from affectionate.

An awful lot seemed to happen inside me during that week. Tony was away on a conference in the Ukraine, so I had plenty of time to watch the 'videos' I had buried for so long. I began to realise just how many of my lifelong problems could be traced back to those four years in my childhood. The more I thought about the things that had crushed and broken something inside me, the less I wanted to go near the person I felt was responsible. And what was I going to say to her? That question worried me considerably. 'All is forgiven' sounded perfectly ridiculous! And had I really forgiven her anyway?

The whole situation seemed too much for me to handle, until one

---

*The deaf and dumb sign language for forgiveness is signed by wiping the palm of one hand firmly across the other as if removing any stain or mess that clings to it.* (Russ Parker)

morning when I was reading Luke 6 in an amplified version of the New Testament, and I realised Jesus told us to 'Pray for the happiness of those who curse you, implore God's favour upon those who abuse you – who revile, reproach, disparage and high-handedly misuse you' (6:28, AMP). I was beginning to blame Miss Mitchell for doing all those things to me, but Jesus knew what he was about when he told us to pray for our own particular enemy because, as I soon discovered, prayer has the most remarkable effect.

First of all, it kills hate. As I prayed for Miss Mitchell, I pictured myself bringing her into the presence of God, and the two of us standing side by side before him. Somehow it is impossible to stand there like that with ice-cold anger in your heart. God's love seems to melt it away like snow in the morning sun.

Prayer also began to help me see her from God's angle instead of my own. As I prayed, I began to wonder if some hurt that Miss Mitchell had once received could have caused her to be so aggressive. Then about three days later, I discovered the answer to that question. Someone who had known Miss Mitchell for many years was able to tell me about the terrible things that had happened to her as a child. There is an old French proverb that says, 'To understand all is to forgive all.' I was not sure I was quite ready to 'forgive all', but it certainly helped me to understand.

Then one morning, as I was asking the Lord yet again how to handle my Tuesday visit, I suddenly realised I was not going to Miss Mitchell to offer some grand gesture of forgiveness: the main purpose of my visit was to ask *her* to forgive *me*! It is a terrible thing to hate someone for so many years and to blame them for all your personal weaknesses and failures. As I looked up everything Jesus said about forgiving, and searched the commentaries in order to understand what he meant, I began to realise that forgiving means 'setting free'. The Greek word is *aphesis*, the same word Jesus uses at the grave of Lazarus when he emerged all bound up like an Egyptian mummy. By not forgiving Miss Mitchell, perhaps I could have bound her spiritually by the grudges I held against her. Some commentators think that this is what Jesus meant when he said, 'Whatever you bind on earth will be bound in heaven, and whatever you loose on earth will be loosed in heaven' (Matt. 18:18, NIV).

There was another verse I discovered that week: 'If you forgive anyone's sins, they are forgiven. If you refuse to forgive them, they are unforgiven' (John 20:23, LB). Did that mean that as I prayed for Miss Mitchell I was saying to God, 'Please let her off the eternal punishment I feel she deserves for hurting me'? Could this be what Jesus meant when he told us to show mercy (Luke 6:36)? It was all getting a bit too deep for someone like me. However, I was not so stupid that I could not understand that I had sinned by hating her for so long and blaming her for so much. I felt I had to confess that to God as quickly as possible.

Then the horrendous thought struck me. Would I have to *ask* for her forgiveness too? The idea sent me into a panic. It was bad enough to imagine facing someone who completely terrified me and saying, 'I forgive you,' without having to tell her about the resentment I had felt towards her as well. Of course, I knew that would not be what God wanted me to do in a literal sense. It would feel more like a spiteful revenge than an act of penitence to let her know she had been hated for so long. No, it would be the attitude of heart in which I went that mattered, and I prayed that if it was possible to express the sentiment in some way that did not cause her pain, that God would show me how to do it. In the event, that is exactly what he did.

## The willingness to forgive

By the Monday, so many thoughts were churning and tumbling about inside me that I must have been very hard to live with, and the three 'overgrown' children who are still at home had a very rough time.

'You must be going senile, Mum!' said Duncan, and even Brodie looked offended. During the evening, I decided to look out a photo of myself as a child to take with me the following day – so at least Miss Mitchell might have some chance of remembering me. I went rummaging through the box from the attic until I found one that must have been taken very soon after my first day at the school. I sat holding it for a long time, looking at the small, thin face that stared apprehensively up at me. 'That child looks haunted,' I thought, and when I went to bed I put the photo on the table beside me.

I never sleep well when Tony is away, and the thought of that

---

General James Oglethorpe said to John Wesley, 'I'll never forgive!' John Wesley replied, 'Then I hope, Sir, that you will never sin.' (John Wesley, quoted by David Augsburger)

appointment the next morning certainly did not help matters. At about two o'clock I finally gave up trying to sleep and put the light on. Often when I wake like that it seems to be because the Lord wants me to pray in a specific way, so I asked him if that was the case now.

Suddenly I thought, 'but the child in the photo is *thin!*' My mental impression of myself as a child was that I was always grotesquely fat, rather like a Miss Piggy puppet, but the child in the photo could have been accurately described as 'skinny'. Therefore I must have got fat after my first day at school.

### Reliving the event

As I sat up in bed looking at the photo, something began to happen that I think was one of the most extraordinary experiences of my life. If I had not described it on paper the next day, I would not believe it really happened. The memories that I had buried became so vivid that I felt I really was back at school again. I could smell the distinctive 'cloakroom' aroma, which was a blend of stale sweat, disinfectant and old plimsoles – with a dash of cooked cabbage from the kitchens close by. I felt that sick feeling of desolation that always came when my mother dropped me off at the door, and then drove home without me. Quite abandoned, I was left to face probable annihilation all alone. I could see the child in the photo as if she was nothing to do with me, although I seemed to know how she was feeling.

In my hand I was clutching a grimy arithmetic book full of the sums I had got wrong the day before – all eighty of them. I had been told to take them home and get them right overnight – or else. I had worked at them until I was too tired to think straight, refusing all offers of help, because I felt Miss Mitchell would know, and that would make it even worse – for she loathed cheats.

Why don't children tell their parents when they are being bullied or abused? It took me four years until I dared to explain what school was really like. Whyever did I wait so long? Perhaps because I felt too ashamed, and this is probably true for others as well. I believed Miss Mitchell when she said I was the stupidest child she knew, and I remember the way my mother had looked when she was told I was backward. Both my parents were brilliantly gifted and extremely attractive people, and I always felt that I was a great embarrassment to them – particularly when I grew so enormously fat. So I never 'told' because I felt it was all my fault they had a dud for a daughter.

So there I stood, cringing with fright, clutching a book full of sums that were bound to be wrong and facing yet another day of insults, derision and humiliation – perhaps even physical pain. I could feel the rumble of hundreds of feet pounding the boarded corridor and suddenly I was right in my own nightmare, as girls in gym slips swarmed around me shouting contemptuously, 'You're a fat moron – a thick idiot!' Then I could hear her shouting. She was coming towards me through the crowd – nearer and nearer – and I felt sick with an old familiar dread.

'Lord!' I muttered, 'Help me!'

### Warning!

It is never right, or safe, to relive painful memories alone. We must go back to the place where we were hurt with Jesus himself beside us, and preferably some other friend as well.

None of mine were handy at two o'clock in the morning, but my urgent cry for help was answered instantly. I sensed Jesus really was there. I seemed to see him standing beside that small, thin, frightened child, with one big, kind hand on her shoulder. As the face of the monster loomed closer, distorted with rage, the hand on the child's shoulders tightened reassuringly, then just as the monster was ready to strike he stepped between her and me, taking the abuse, the pain and the misery himself – because he cared so much. In my head I heard these words ringing like church bells on Christmas morning: 'Surely he has borne our griefs and carried our sorrows, (Isa. 53:4, AV). 'The insults which are hurled at you have fallen on me' (Rom. 15:3, GNB).

Suddenly, it was all over. The child was free for ever from the memory, because *he* had borne everything in my place. I sensed there was something very important that I needed to do after that, and I realised the child in the photo was saying, 'Miss Mitchell, I forgive you freely for everything you did or said to me. I let go of all blame and set you free from the grudges I have carried against you ever since. And please forgive me for hating you and binding you so long.'

It had been no use forgiving Miss Mitchell as an adult on behalf of the child I had once been. One adult can easily forgive another, because as adults we also have power, and we forget just how small and helpless a child can feel. We need to relive by memory the painful events to make real forgiving possible. Exactly the same applies to forgiving any hurt, even if it happened last week. We must not deny the pain we felt, and we need to go back mentally to the moment our 'enemy' hurt us so that we can release forgiveness to them at the point in our memory when the damage was done.

## *Healing the wounds*

Suddenly Miss Mitchell was gone, as was the school – and the cloakroom smell – but I was aware that the child was still hurt and in need of healing. She had been emotionally wounded so many times in those four years. 'Watching our buried videos' helps us understand these wounds, but only Jesus himself can heal them and set us free from their destructive effects. So I asked him to do that, and later during that long night something very strange happened. I 'saw' another picture. Jesus himself was sitting at the foot of a huge wooden cross holding the child that had once been me. At first I was pleased, until I realised she was wriggling about, restless and fretful. 'Lord, whyever isn't that child more contented?' I asked indignantly.

His reply was perfectly clear and plain, 'She will not allow me to comfort her and she grows into an adult who will not always turn to me for comfort, either.' He looked so sad that I really felt mortified, and I sat there for a long time trying to think what he could mean. Then another memory came back into my mind. I saw myself walking into the sweetshop on my way home from school. My mother, who was generous to a fault, always heaped me with pocket money and I would go in and buy quantities of chocolate and toffees each day.

Somehow the sweets eased the pain of the day and made life seem bearable again. I would still eat a huge tea when I arrived home, and go on nicking and picking all evening. No one ever seemed to notice. It was no wonder I was soon too fat to play netball! Obviously it was not a sin at the time, for the child in me had been crying out for love and acceptance. It was then, though, that I discovered a method of easing pain that I have used countless times ever since, instead of going direct to the Lord for comfort. I had deliberately turned away from him and craved the counterfeit comfort of food.

So here was the root of my lifelong 'weed', and I asked the Lord to pull it out, once and for all. I believe that he did. I had asked him thousands of times before, but perhaps I could not be forgiven and delivered until that night when I finally forgave the person I subconsciously blamed for causing it all. Surely it is as we forgive that we can be forgiven.

Then the word 'fear' kept coming into my mind, and I realised that fear had also become one of my 'weeds', causing everything from chronic worry to a total inability to face certain situations. If I ever encounter someone aggressive and angry, I simply go to pieces – and all those endless feelings of inadequacy stem from the same root. Of course, fear itself is not a sin, but running away from it can be. And some of the more subtle techniques I have devised to avoid the things I fear have been very wrong indeed.

It is also not a sin to feel inadequate, but it *is* wrong to drive yourself unmercifully to prove that you are not. Misplaced energy like that can destroy relationships, and it must be a terrible strain living with someone who constantly has to prove she is 'Super-woman' – in case the world realises just how stupid she actually is!

Suddenly I remembered the day I made the vow Tracy had mentioned. I had been standing in the middle of a field full of stubble one autumn, when I was about ten. I remembered the flocks of migrating birds swirling in the sky above my head as I said, 'In spite of what I am, somehow I'll make my parents proud of me one day.' As well as removing the seed of fear that night, I believe the Lord delivered me from the bondage of achievement hunting and the slavery to other people's desires and expectations.

It was about five-thirty in the morning when I finally knew it was all done. I felt as if I'd had a major operation – as indeed I had – but I also felt gloriously free. Just as I was falling asleep I saw the figure of Jesus walking away into the distance with a little girl holding his hand. She hopped and danced away with him in the kind of carefree abandonment she would never have known forty years before.

### We are not stuck for ever with the damage

Sometimes when people 'watch their childhood videos', they can think, 'I'm stuck with all these problems because of what was done to me!' But after all that happened to me that night, I really do believe that inner healing and deliverance from the tangling weeds of sin come through being willing to allow Jesus to help us forgive the people who hurt us. It dawned on me that night just how ridiculous I was to hold someone from my childhood responsible for causing all my weaknesses and failures.

It is not what people do to us that cripples us, but how we react to what they do. I chose to allow the roots of those weeds of sin to remain and grow in me through the years. I was not responsible for what people did to me, or did not do, but I *was* responsible for how I coped with it – for the food, the desire to prove them all wrong, and the fear that makes me run away.

## *The second part of forgiving*

As I drove up the hill towards Miss Mitchell's cottage the following morning I have to admit I was so terrified that I had to grip the steering wheel very tightly indeed. I knew that the 'child me' had been set free the night before, but the 'adult me' felt a perfect fool! I still didn't know what I was going to say and the flowers on the back seat had cost far more than I could afford. In fact, as the car turned into her drive I couldn't help thinking that the first half of forgiving, the bit that happens in our own hearts, is an awful lot easier than the second part – when we have to do something that demonstrates it!

By one minute past eleven, I was sitting nervously on the very edge of my chair in Miss Mitchell's front room. I was very much the little girl and I could hear myself prattling and giggling like an eight-year-old. 'For goodness' sake, get a grip on yourself!' I told myself furiously. 'Remember you've published sixteen books, so you can't be completely inadequate!'

She must have realised I had something on my mind, and she came to my rescue by cutting abruptly across the chatter.

'Why did you come?'

'To lay some ghosts,' I said nervously. 'I wasn't very happy at school, you see.' She looked surprised. 'I couldn't read, if you remember, or write, either.' Then I took a deep breath and added something I had wanted to say to her so many times during the years in between. 'Nowadays, they would say I was dyslexic.'

She looked at me so strangely I wasn't quite sure what she was thinking. Then at last she said, 'Yes, we didn't know much about that kind of thing in my day. We used to tell parents of difficult children that their offspring were either lazy or thick.' I cringed, but then she added, 'I think perhaps we might have been rather cruel.' I am not sure if she meant it as a kind of indirect apology, but I certainly took it as such.

After that, conversation became much easier and we both relaxed. When she finally showed me out, something very significant happened. She said, 'I'm sorry you were unhappy at school.' I reached out and took the hand I had been so afraid of as a child, and held it for a moment. 'Well I'm sure that wasn't your fault,' I replied. 'You couldn't have known how I felt, could you?' And we kissed each other warmly.

The transaction was done, we had both offered and received forgiveness, and we parted with promises to meet again. As I drove home, I felt a great sense of peace.

I was fortunate to have such a gracious 'enemy', but reconciliations are not always made so easily. You will find some practical tips from other people in the chapter on forgiveness (Chapter 11). There are also some ideas for expressing forgiveness to someone who has died.

------

## A Meditation

It was one of those awkward step-families, where everyone has the same father, but different mothers – so no one knows quite where they belong. He was almost the youngest of twelve, and that did not help him either, but the fact that his father adored him caused his greatest problem. His older brothers hated him for it. Of course, he never imagined their jealousy would drive them to such terrible lengths, so he was taken totally by surprise when one day on a lonely hillside they grabbed him and threw him down the shaft of an old, dry well. He had seen murder glinting in their eyes, so as he huddled in the darkness waiting for them to come back, he was convinced they would pull him out and slit his throat. In the end it was greed that saved his life. His brothers found a way of making some money, as well as ridding themselves of him for ever.

Perhaps in the hard, lonely years of slavery that lay ahead, or during his imprisonment in the dungeons of Egypt, Joseph may often have wished he had died quickly at their hands instead of having to face all the suffering his brothers caused him. Did he block out the memories of his childhood? Perhaps he did, because when life improved for him and he even became Prime Minister, he did not go straight back to find the father who had loved him so much, nor did he even send him a reassuring message.

Then one day, there they were, standing before him in the state reception room of his grand home: the ten brothers who had mocked him as a child, robbed him of the best years of his life, and hated him so much they had tried to destroy him. So many memories must have come flooding back into his mind, but he could not tell them who he was because he couldn't forgive – not then – because it all still hurt too much.

For months or even years he struggled with his emotions. One moment he was weeping like a child at the joy of seeing them again, the next he was harshly throwing them into gaol. He lavished good things on them and then played cruel tricks, hiding money in their grain sacks, seizing one as a hostage, and accusing another of stealing his silver cup. Then when he had finally proved to himself that their hearts were no longer as black as he had always feared they were, he called them in and forgave them. It felt as if the wall of a dam had finally given way as all the pent-up pain and grief finally gushed out, and he cried so loudly that everyone in the palace could hear him.

However, many years later, the writer of Genesis tells us that Joseph's brothers were still not quite sure they were truly forgiven:

> When Joseph's brothers saw that their father was dead, they said, 'What if Joseph holds a grudge against us and pays us back for all the wrongs we did to him?' . . . His brothers then came and threw themselves down before him. 'We are your slaves,' they said. But Joseph said to them, 'Don't be afraid. Am I in the place of God? You intended to harm me, but God intended it for good to accomplish what is now being done, the saving of many lives. So then, don't be afraid. I will provide for you and your children.' And he reassured them and spoke kindly to them. (Gen. 50:15–21, NIV)

## A Prayer

### *For those who find it hard to face life as it is*

'*Come to me all you who are tired from fighting reality . . . "for the Spirit that God has given us does not make us timid; instead, his Spirit fills us with power, love, and self-control".*' (2 Tim. 1:7, GNB)

Lord Jesus, I am afraid – I don't want it all to be like this. I can't bear to live through one more day feeling like this. Yet I know you understand how I feel. You did not want your life to go the way it did either. You wanted people to listen to what you had come to tell them, not turn against you and reject the love you offered them. You did not want to go up to Jerusalem and face the final horror. Yet you set your face like flint – and went. You looked hard at reality, and had the courage to move towards it. Help me not to shrink away. Help me to set my face towards reality as you set yours. I give you this feeling of dread and foreboding, and in its place I receive your courage.

### *For those who find it hard to face life as it was*

*'Come to me all you who are tired of fighting the dark shadows of the past . . . "for I am the light of the world. Whoever follows me will . . . have the light of life".'* (John 8:12, NIV)

Lord Jesus, come with me into the darkness of the cellar where I have hidden so many frightening things. I've shoved feelings down there because there wasn't time to process them – memories I couldn't face, emotions I thought were wrong and must be suppressed, fears, doubts, resentment, and yes, furious anger! Shine your light on these things I never wanted to see again, and help me remember things I would much rather forget. Handle my reactions with me, and show me how to bear the pain of it all. I am so afraid of the dark; please come with me, and one by one we can bring these things to the surface and out into your sunlight. Lord, I am ashamed that I felt as I did, and as I still do. Forgive me, heal me, help me to let it go. I give you my darkness, and in exchange I receive your light.

## Perhaps the Lord Would Respond Like This

'The people walking in darkness have seen a great light; on those living in the land of the shadow of death a light has dawned.' (Isa. 9:2, NIV)
'Arise, shine, for your light has come, and the glory of the Lord rises upon you.' (Isa. 60:1, NIV)

## STOP FOR A MOMENT

*Refusing to forgive and harbouring anger damages our bodies, our minds and our spirits.*

### Physical Damage

*Modern research is leading many doctors to believe there is a definite link between negative emotion and some types of physical illness. Work done by doctors such as Friedman and Simonton conclude that unresolved anger and guilt can trigger and maintain some forms of heart disease and certain types of cancer. Other researchers feel that the same link exists in some rheumatic conditions, and in problems with the digestive system. A number of doctors also feel that difficult relationships can upset the natural immune system, making some patients more prone to attack by viruses, infectious diseases and conditions such as MS and ME. Dr W. Munro says, in his book Beat Stress, 'The psyche will often "dump" unresolved emotions and pain into the body when it is overloaded.'*

### Mental Damage

*Some psychiatrists believe the same factors can play a part in causing various types of depression, phobias, panic attacks, eating disorders and many other neuroses.*

### Spiritual Damage

*Jesus says that when we flatly refuse to forgive, we are cut off from God because he cannot:*

- *hear us when we pray (Mark 11:25)*
- *accept our worship (Matt. 5:23)*
- *forgive our sins (Matt. 6:14–15)*

*Not only can our spiritual growth and personal relationship with God be impeded in this life, but we could even be eternally damaged. Some theologians say that if we won't forgive we don't go to heaven, because we can't be forgiven ourselves. I don't know if they are right – I am not a theologian – but I wouldn't like to take the risk!*

Forgiving is impossible for most of us, but Jesus would not have told us to do it unless he meant to help us! He said, 'With man this is impossible, but with God all things are possible' (Matt. 19:26, NIV). Jesus also said, 'Apart from me you can do nothing' (John 15:5, NIV). And St Paul declares, 'I can do everything through him who gives me strength' (Phil. 4:13, NIV).

# 4

# LONELINESS AND ISOLATION

When people begin to emerge from the numb sensation of shock, one of the first feelings that can hit them is isolation – and it seems to recur relentlessly throughout the entire process of mending.

'I went back to work for the first time the other day . . . everyone was very friendly and I got through the day pretty well, but the thing I found so hard was the loneliness. Crazy! I was surrounded by so many people I knew well, yet I felt this overwhelming sense of being cut off and not part of them any more . . . trapped in my own little bubble of space.' That was part of a letter from a man whose wife had recently died.

It is easy to understand this lonely feeling when the person or people we want and need most are suddenly missing. A huge empty space is left where they ought to be. 'When I look beside me, I see that there is no one to help me, no one to protect me. No one cares for me,' was how King David described this sensation in Psalm 142 (v. 4, GNB).

One woman commented after her husband's funeral, 'Everyone was there. The whole family came to the funeral, and lots of old friends from way back. It was good to see them all, but I kept on thinking, "If only he was here with me – to share all this – so we could talk about it all tonight over hot drinks – laugh at all the funny little things." But he'll never be there beside me – ever again. I'll always have to face things alone from now on, won't I?'

Often a move can bring about feelings of loneliness and isolation: 'I

---

*When I lie down, I go to sleep in peace; you alone, O Lord, keep me perfectly safe.* (Ps. 4:8, GNB)

always thought, "How lovely to retire to a little cottage in the country." But I wasn't prepared for the abject loneliness. No bustling shops, all my church friends gone, no neighbours shouting at each other – it's so quiet I can't sleep!'

## They Can't Possibly Understand

Sometimes, though, this sense of loneliness does not have quite such an obvious cause. When we are facing personal devastation for whatever reason, we can feel surrounded by a swarm of well-wishers who all seem to say, 'I know just how you feel', but how can they? No one in all the history of the world has ever faced quite the same set of circumstances as you are facing now. You are unique. No one else thinks, acts and reacts just as you do. No one else's body feels pain in the same way as yours does. No one else can possibly get into your mind and see these events from your point of view. You really are alone in all this. Yet everyone you meet seems to have a nephew, a friend or a mother-in-law who has had exactly the same thing happen to them.

People always seem to know what you ought to do, and they make you feel even more isolated by their disapproval when you fail to take their unasked-for advice. They shower you with platitudes and send you cards with trite little messages written all over them. But they *don't understand*! 'My days have passed; my plans have failed; my hope is gone. But my friends say night is daylight; they say that light is near, but I know I remain in darkness' (Job 17:11–12, GNB) was how Job described this, and he certainly had a difficult time with his friends!

---

*Whoever goes to the Lord for safety, whoever remains under the protection of the Almighty, can say to him, 'You are my defender and protector. You are my God; in you I trust.' . . . He will cover you with his wings, you will be safe in his care; his faithfulness will protect and defend you.* (Ps. 91:1–4, GNB)

### Embarrassment and Fear

There are other occasions when we could do with a few of these well-wishers back again, however irritating they may be:

'The first time I went out into the village after Bill died, it was terrible. People looked at me with frozen faces, not liking to smile or say anything. I suppose they must have felt embarrassed – not sure what to say, or frightened of saying the wrong thing. So they crossed over the road rather than meet me head on. Others hurried into shops or just looked the other way. I felt so utterly lonely that I didn't know what to do with myself. If only one of them had just come up and given me a hug.'

Another woman said: 'When our fourth baby was born with a hare-lip and cleft palate, it seemed so odd taking him out in the pram. With all the others it had been such fun pushing the new baby up to the school gate. Everyone came over to have a look, say nice things, and make cooing noises. But with Peter . . . no one came near us, it felt like being invisible.'

One woman who has had a stroke said: 'People are afraid of illness, I suppose. Steven pushes me out in the wheelchair to the shops sometimes, but neighbours often won't look at me or say "good morning" like they used to when I was well. They just talk to Steven. Perhaps they think, "If she can have a stroke at her age, I could have one too." The thought worries them so much they ignore it – and that means ignoring me as well.'

King David must also have felt like this: 'I had hoped for sympathy, but there was none; for comfort, but I found none' (Ps. 69:20, GNB).

### He Ought to Be Over It by Now!

Most 'spectators' do not understand just how long grieving takes. This is yet another cause of loneliness and misunderstanding.

---

*You hold me by the hand . . . What else have I in heaven but you? Since I have you, what else could I want on earth? My mind and my body may grow weak, but God is my strength; he is all I ever need.* (Ps. 73:23–26, GNB)

---

'Everyone was round here like a swarm of bees at first,' one friend of mine told me. 'But I felt so dazed I didn't need them – in fact, I wished they'd go away. Once the numbness wore off I felt awful, and began to need them all badly, but by then they thought I ought to be getting over it and had drifted back to their own lives.'

## I Just Can't Face People

When Beattie was involved in a car crash on the motorway, the whole church seemed to rally around to support the family. After being discharged from hospital, she remembers how people were 'always popping round with flowers, cakes and even whole meals wrapped in tin foil. I felt so loved, but when at last I got the plaster off my legs, they couldn't understand why I didn't come back to church. I didn't know myself really – it sounded so silly to say I was too scared. There were other families in the church by that time who were going through the mill, and everyone's attention moved on to them. That was when I began to feel isolated and forgotten.

'Every Sunday I tried to go back, but the thought of all the smiling faces and the noisy chorus-singing frightened me. I felt I would panic if I was stuck in a crowd and couldn't get out if I wanted to. After a while, I began to feel I didn't dare come out of my house at all; I felt safe inside, but couldn't cope with big shops and lots of people.

'I missed my friends at church so much, but they soon forget you if you don't show up on a Sunday, so I began to feel cross with them all – kind of bitter and hurt inside. I thought they couldn't be bothered and didn't care any more. The gap got wider and wider until I didn't *want* to see them. I turned in on myself, I suppose, and got very depressed and weepy.

'When I went to the hospital for my check-up I mentioned this fear of being with people, and I was so relieved when the doctor said it was entirely normal and a symptom of Post Traumatic Stress.

'"It will pass," he told me, "but it may take you two years to become desensitised." Actually, it didn't take more than a few weeks, because once I knew the feeling had a medical explanation and

---

*And I will be with you always, to the end of the age.* (Matt. 28:20, GNB)

wasn't just me being silly, I was able to ask one of the pastoral team to come round and pray with me about it. His wife helped me so much that first day I dared to go back – she walked in with me and we sat together. After that day, I gradually began to get back into the life of church again. Just knowing that my feelings were normal helped me turn the corner.'

## A New Dimension

When we feel our lives have stopped completely, we often find it hard to realise that the rest of the world is still whizzing on just the same as ever. The following comments illustrate this:

'I heard someone laughing in the hospital corridor outside my room, and I thought, "How can people still laugh?" Then I thought, "But why shouldn't they, it's just another Tuesday morning for them".'

'I looked out of the window and saw people hurrying off to catch the London train or walking their dogs, and I thought, "How can they, when Brian is dead?" '

'At first I felt like a car, broken down on a motorway. Shunted on to the hard shoulder while everyone else went driving along at high speed, bound for exciting places to do important things, leaving me behind and forgotten.'

Traumatic experiences change values, and turn priorities on their heads. In fact, they actually move us as people into a new dimension, so that a lot of the people who used to travel comfortably through life with us are suddenly left behind. Their interests and involvements seem oddly trivial and childish.

On several occasions during the eight years that I was ill, my condition became life threatening, and I had to be hastily admitted to hospital. While this was very hard on my children, I do think it

---

*Jesus said, 'A time is coming . . . when you will be scattered . . . You will leave me all alone. Yet I am not alone, for my Father is with me.' (John 16:32, NIV)*

helped them develop a very sound set of values. One of our daughters was fourteen during one of my acute episodes. One day, when she came home from school, she threw her bag down on the kitchen table with rather more force than was usual for a gentle character like her.

'What's up?' Tony enquired.

'It's spots!' she said crossly. 'All they can talk about is *spots*! But what do little things like that matter when Mum might be dead by tomorrow?'

## Self-imposed Isolation

Recently, I was on my way to speak at a coffee morning in a Baptist church, and I took Brodie, my dog, to keep me company in the car. We arrived early, so I took her into a nearby park for a walk and there I met a young woman who also had a black labrador. Dog-lovers never wait to be introduced, and soon we were chatting away. I explained where I was going and asked if she knew the church. She looked as if she was going to cry as she replied, 'I used to go there – but I can't any more.' She went on to tell me about a terrible day, two years before, when she had lost her temper and battered her small son very badly. 'I knocked his front teeth out by banging his face against the banisters. My husband had just left me and I was at the end of my tether, but I never should have hurt my son like that. He looked terrible, and of course everyone kept asking him what had happened. I was so ashamed that I never went back to church again. I keep away from all my other friends too. I don't feel I deserve to have company after that.'

We sat down on a bench and talked about forgiveness for so long that I was nearly late for the coffee morning! The best bit of this story is that she came along to it with me, and received such a warm welcome that she has been going every week since.

## Invisible Walls of Protection

When I spoke about loneliness at a ladies' conference once, a girl called Barbara was talking to me at the end when she suddenly burst into tears.

---

*Thy presence fills my solitude.* (Longfellow)

'I've been a loner for a long time now,' she told me. 'But really I can't think why – I never used to be like this. I go to a good church and I'm reasonably happy in my job.'

After we had prayed and asked the Lord Jesus to show us the cause of her isolation, she began to tell me about something that had happened to her four years before.

'I don't really want to talk about it,' she admitted. 'In fact, I've never told anyone else.' She had been on holiday in Tenerife when one night she had been attacked and raped by a stranger in the hotel car park. 'I never went to the police. I felt so degraded, so ashamed. I was a virgin, you see, and I felt as if I had lost something precious. Somehow, I got myself back to my room. All I wanted to do was have a bath and get clean again – or try to, anyway. I don't think I've ever really felt clean since. It's stupid, I know, but I can't stop myself from feeling guilty – as if it was my fault. The others on the holiday with me just thought I was ill in bed with a tummy bug for the next few days, and I felt too ashamed to tell them because we were all from the same church.

'As I was flying home, I decided to leave the whole thing behind me and never think of it again. But ever since, I've had an odd feeling of being cut off – even from myself – sort of shut in behind walls. My Christian life's gone dead on me too, and I feel distant in all my relationships. There's a really nice boy at church who wants us to get serious, but I can't seem to make a commitment somehow.'

We prayed together, and then I explained that when we are hurt we often build invisible walls round ourselves for a while as a kind of protection.

'I know I've done that,' she said tearfully, 'but I don't know how to take them down again.'

'You could ask Jesus to do it for you,' I suggested. 'Sometimes he has to demolish these protective walls before he can begin rebuilding our broken lives.'

'But I'm not really sure I want him to demolish them,' she replied uneasily. 'I would feel so exposed, and I've got used to hiding the real me from people now.'

'But Jesus would never do anything suddenly and brutally, like a demolition gang moving in with grappling irons and dynamite,' I

---

*With my God I can scale a wall.* (Ps. 18:29, NIV)

assured her. 'When we put him in control of the mending operations, he actually builds his own wall of protection round us *before* he starts dismantling our own walls. Then he usually works away on us very slowly and gently. In fact, he will melt your walls away gradually by his love. The more you expose yourself to that love, the more he will be able to do for you.'

A look of sheer relief began to spread over Barbara's face. I can't say she went home radiant and instantly healed of her problems – she did not. For months, she regularly visited a Christian counsellor who was able to help her gradually forgive the man who had attacked her, but the moment when her ultimate healing began was when she gave the Lord permission to come inside her lonely sanctuary.

## Beware of the 'Hold Up' Factor

The invisible walls we construct to keep out other people can be a safe retreat while we are vulnerable emotionally, but we can become permanent prisoners in our own fortress unless at some point we deliberately decide to come out and start relating to others normally again.

There are all kinds of colourful examples of this 'hold up' factor in fiction. Silas Marner, in George Eliot's book of that name, felt so hurt by his church community that he went off alone and lived as a recluse in an isolated cottage. Miss Haversham of Great Expectations is Charles Dickens's version of the same phenomenon. She remained alone after being jilted on her wedding day, cut off from the world by echoing corridors and locked doors, while her wedding finery decayed around her.

The danger of this lonely stage is that when the people who once filled our world have suddenly gone, we feel so devastated that we never make new contacts. It either seems too much of an effort to make new friendships, or we fail to get close to new people because we stubbornly refuse to let go of people we have lost.

> *Sometimes He takes away that which is most precious so that into the void of a life that is utterly broken He may pour the glory of his indwelling love.* (Dr Alan Redpath)

## People Need People – Even the Shy Ones

Hiding away in isolation for too long can be dangerous for many reasons, but one of them is that we need a 'dustbin' for our 'rubbish'! Talking to someone who really cares is a wonderful way of getting rid of painful feelings, and can be tremendously healing. However close God may seem when we are distressed, we also badly need human beings to listen to us as well. Perhaps Jesus comes to us most easily wearing the body of an ordinary person. Once, when my oldest son Justyn was only five and not very happy at school, I went to meet him. He trailed across the playground towards me, his little, white, tear-stained face looking up at me pathetically from the hood of his grey duffel coat.

'Whatever went wrong, darling?' I asked him.

'Everything,' was his tragic reply. 'My sums wouldn't come right, the teacher was cross, and no one loved me all day.'

'That's not true,' said his six-year-old sister reproachfully. 'Jesus loves you, and he's with you – even in the toilet.'

'Yes, but Jesus doesn't have arms these days to cuddle sad people,' was Justyn's profound reply.

### Warning!

It is very hard to find the right person on whom to dump our emotions. We begin to remove a brick or two of our protective wall when we think we can trust someone, but then suddenly we realise they are looking at us blankly or even with a hint of contempt, so we hastily build the wall back up again and pin back the smile that says 'I'm fine'. The next time someone comes close enough to talk, we feel too vulnerable to risk it. We need to find someone who will not:

- crush us or make us feel silly
- bombard us with good advice
- listen to all we say, and then relate it to everyone else at church under the guise of 'a prayer topic'
- rush us through the mending process too quickly

---

*In a desert land he found him, in a barren and howling waste. He shielded him and cared for him; he guarded him as the apple of his eye.* (Deut. 32:10, NIV)

---

- stop us from moving forward (there are people who will want to wrap us up in cottonwool sympathy, keeping us prisoners to their own need to be needed)

We need someone who will listen to us, accept us as we are at this moment, and walk beside us without condemnation. People like that are rare, and during the eight years I was ill I made some bad mistakes until I specifically asked God to send me the right person at the right time. I soon discovered he had the remarkable knack of bringing along human 'arms' whenever he saw that I needed a metaphorical cuddle. Perhaps it is far safer to leave the choice of our friend and confidant to God rather than blundering up to the wrong person and being hurt yet again.

## The Challenge

Someone once said, 'Loss is inevitable, but growth is optional.' It sounds very irritating, but it does happen to be true. Each of the stages in the Broken Teapot Syndrome faces us with a challenge: we can use it to help us move on in our growth towards God, or we can refuse the jump like a horse in the show ring. The questions the Lord asks us in our isolation are:

- 'Will you exclude me as well as everyone else?'
- 'Will you allow me to come in and fill your emptiness?'
- 'Can I be the friend and companion you need so badly just now?'

Perhaps the day when I felt most abandoned and lonely was also the day when I allowed him to come to me through my own invisible wall. I have written about this before, in *Unexpected Healing*, but the moment was so special that I make no apologies for telling the story again. It was just over two years after I first became ill, and soon after I had fallen in the cow dung. We were on holiday in Yorkshire, and one day Tony took the children off for a long hike over the moors, leaving me alone in the car park.

> *No-one came to my support, but everyone deserted me. May it not be held against them. But the Lord stood at my side and gave me strength.* (2 Tim. 4:16, 17, NIV)

'You'll be all right, won't you, Mum?' they said, as they settled me in the wheelchair with a little rug over my knees like an old granny. 'I will,' I lied, forcing myself to sound cheerful, but as I watched them walking away up the path to the moors my smile slipped away and the tears took its place. Other families were also eagerly setting out for a day's hiking, and the empty car park felt very bleak indeed. By that time, I was beginning to get used to expressing my feelings to God, so I said to him, 'I could have done so much for you, if only you'd heard all those prayers and healed me.'

I *felt* (rather than heard) his reply: 'Lots of people are willing to *do* things for me, but not many are willing to be my friends, and that is what I want most of all.'

That single fact was probably the most important thing I learnt in all those eight years of illness. We ourselves – our friendship and company – are far more valuable to God than any service we could ever render to him. Yet so often, when our 'Teapots' are smashed, the greatest distress we experience is *not* being able to do all that we once thought was important. We value ourselves by what we can achieve, so when the power to 'produce results' is taken from us, we feel worthless, useless and fit for the scrap heap. God values us not for our achievements, but for ourselves and for our company. We are so valuable to Jesus that he gave up everything he had to win our friendship – his life in heaven, and then his life on earth.

Most friends expect a measure of give-and-take in relationships, and that is why so many of the less faithful ones back away when we do not seem to be 'mending' as quickly as they feel we should. Their motives for being our friends are, to a certain extent, selfish. Morever, the kind of friendship that Jesus offers to us is utterly unselfish. He is willing to hang in there with us, however long this mending process takes, however difficult we are to live with, and however violently we express our reactions. He is always there, night or day; he never gets bored with the same old stuff coming up over and over again, and he always understands us completely.

Out of the terrible feeling of isolation I felt that day in Yorkshire came the discovery that God was my friend. If that love relationship of trust and intimate friendship is actually the most important thing

---

*A man of many companions may come to ruin, but there is a friend who sticks closer than a brother.* (Prov. 18:24, NIV)

any human being can acquire then anything that helps us towards that goal is good. So whenever we feel that lonely, empty, lost feeling creeping up on us, if we form the habit of turning to Jesus and asking him to fill our solitude with himself, then even our most unpleasant experiences can become our greatest blessings.

---

## A Meditation

She stood alone, waiting, as the evening shadows gathered around her. She was always waiting these days; and she was always alone. People were hurrying and bustling all around her, but they did not seem to notice her standing there, separated from the rest of the world, isolated by shame. Women were on their way home from the well to cook their husbands' food, but she had no husband and often these days she had no food either. The men were closing up their market stalls, calling to each other as they finished their day's work, but she had no work, except this, and now she was getting older even the other street women excluded her from their company.

She stepped back further into the shadows. Dim light was her only hope of bread tomorrow – it hid her greying hair and the wrinkles round her eyes. Fortunately, soldiers were not fussy – and this was a garrison town. She shuddered as a wave of utter degradation swept over her. What a way to earn her bread, selling her body to Gentile pigs.

It had been one of them who had started it all, long ago when she was a young girl, happy and carefree in this very marketplace. He had walked by, his helmet flashing in the sunshine, and she had loved him. Yes, that was the beginning of her shame, and now at the end of it all she could never undo her mistake and start again. Righteous people never forgive, and this town was full of righteous people.

A group of men were coming down the road. Suddenly alert, she stepped forward to take a closer look, but their clothes were dusty from the journey and very shabby. Men like that had no money to spare, and she sighed, for she was hungry. Perhaps she should try anyway? You could never tell, and the evening light was kinder now, so she let her shawl slip from her long, unbraided hair and stepped out into their path.

She had done it a thousand times before, but still she hated it. She had been kicked into the gutter too many times by righteous men, and felt the blows from their sticks. Of course, the Pharisees never hit her; they would not defile themselves by touching an outcast like her, but the disdain in their faces as they turned away hurt far more than any blow. Were these men righteous, she wondered.

The leader stopped. Perhaps he was a customer? She looked up into his face, expecting to see the usual greedy glance of appraisal, but instead she encountered an expression she had never seen on anyone's face before. This man neither despised her nor wished to use her. In fact, his smile gave her the strange feeling that she was loved – really loved for the very first time in her life.

They stood there in the busy roadway for a long time, and somehow she felt his eyes were looking right into her soul, reading all the degradation and disgrace, but without condemnation. Then at last he put out his hand and gently touched her shoulder. It was only a simple gesture, but it made her feel that, in spite of knowing everything she had ever done wrong, she was still deemed valuable – and that it might, even now, be possible to begin again.

'You are forgiven,' he said softly. 'Your shame is covered, your past is wiped clean.'

Then he was gone. Bemused and dizzy, she stood gazing after him. 'Who was that man?' she asked, grabbing the coat sleeve of one of his followers.

'That was Jesus,' he replied simply. 'The Messiah himself.' She gasped.

'Then he really can forgive sins,' she whispered. 'Am I really free at last?'

All through the evening she searched for him, up and down the little streets and alleyways, but no one would tell her where the strangers had gone, and they laughed at her scornfully.

'That Jesus is a righteous man,' they said. 'What would he want with a woman like you?'

She was almost desperate – what if he had left the town before she could give her gift to him? The tears were running down her painted cheeks as she stumbled along clutching her precious bundle. She had to find him. Suddenly, a child's footsteps came pattering up the street behind her.

'Hey, you!' he shouted cheekily. 'I know where he is, that man you want.' She turned suddenly, her heart beating wildly. 'He's at supper with Simon the Pharisee,' and he added with a mocking laugh, 'but you won't be welcome there!'

The child was right, of course. She had suffered more from Simon than any other man in town. He would not even allow her shadow to contaminate him, and his righteous indignation had caused him to make her a public example in the marketplace on several painful occasions. Of course, she ought to have realised that the Messiah would want to spend his time with people like Simon, men who had never sinned. Yet the man who had smiled at her today was not like Simon at all. There was acceptance and warmth in that smile, not contempt. And the memory of his smile gave her the courage to go to him.

It was not difficult to slip unnoticed into the house and across the courtyard; the servants were too busy with the meal to notice her. The drone of conversation came from a room where the lamplight flickered warm and inviting, and through the arches she could see men reclining on couches around the table. He was there all right, but she sensed at once that he was uncomfortable. His feet were still caked with the grime of his journey, and dust powdered his hair and beard. What were those servants thinking about, to insult a guest by not offering him water for washing, or oil for his head?

She crept closer; she must make him look in her direction before she was discovered, and the shouts and blows began. Respectable people like Simon would not tolerate an outcast defiling their home. The Pharisees, though, were so busy arguing about theology that they did not notice her as she slid to her knees at the foot of their visitor's couch.

From under her cloak, she took out the present. It was not much to give the Son of God himself, just a jar of scent, but it was all she had in the world. She had been saving it as a nest egg to keep her from starvation when she got too old to . . . work. Now she wanted to give him everything she had, holding nothing back for herself.

As she watched him, the tears began again: tears of sadness for a whole life thrown away; tears of repentance for the other lives she had ruined through her trade; tears of relief, too, that at last the terrible weight of guilt had gone for ever. They splashed down on to his dusty feet, and in her embarrassment she quickly wiped them away with her hair, hoping he would not notice.

But of course he did notice – and looking round, smiled at her again. He did not need to speak; she knew that to him she was not an outcast, excluded and alone. She could walk away from her past and live again, because at last she had found someone who could remove her shame. Such a surge of relief swept through her, followed by such an overwhelming sense of love, in that moment she determined in her heart to serve this man-shaped God for the rest of her life. What, though, could she possibly do for him?

Then she remembered his feet. She could at least take away the insult Simon had dealt him by washing them for him. As she broke the seal from her jar and let the valuable perfume trickle away, the pungent scent filled the house with its sweetness. The Pharisees looked around startled. There was a stunned silence as they saw her kneeling there, followed by a rumble of disapproval. 'Fancy letting a woman like that actually *touch* him!' said one in disgust.

Jesus looked round at them, and sadly shook his head. 'You think you are righteous,' he said, 'But you are caught by the most deadly sin, pride, which tells you that you have never sinned at all. Yes, this woman has sinned greatly, but she is forgiven. Do you see how she loves me? Her love is so great that it has transformed her life. She loves much because she has been forgiven much. Those who feel they have no need of forgiveness can never love like that.'

## A Prayer

*'Come to me, all you who are tired from carrying a heavy burden of loneliness . . . "for I will never leave you; I will never abandon you".'* (Heb. 13:5, GNB)

Yes, Lord Jesus, I do feel lonely. Most of what I valued is gone. Loss seems to surround me like a great wide ocean, leaving me cut off on an island, quite alone. Loss on all sides, loss in every direction, loss, loss, loss as far as the eye can see. All I can hear are the echoes of familiar voices and laughter from the past, and all my hopes and desires lie shipwrecked on the rocks around my island. The memories of all the things I wanted to do, places I wanted to visit, people I wanted to meet, merely mock me now that I am stranded here in this desolate place.

No one else knows I'm lonely. People can't see it by looking at me

---

*I will not leave you as orphans; I will come to you.* (John 14:18, NIV)

from the outside. How could they ever understand unless they had been there themselves? But you have. You must have been lonely so often, because the people you loved best always seemed to misunderstand what you said and did. That night in the garden when you faced the worst ordeal of your life, you desperately needed your three best friends to be there for you, but they let you down and went to sleep. They couldn't come with you into your private anguish, and when the soldiers came to torture and kill you, they ran for their lives.

So, because you understand, will you come into my loneliness and share it with me? Then, because I know I am not alone after all, please give me the courage to stop excluding other people. They could be the very ones you might be sending to me, friends who are willing to be your arms to comfort me, your mind to understand me, your hands to hold mine and steady me, your smile to reassure me, your voice of compassion. Please breathe on these separating walls and begin to melt them away. Yet, Lord, I am so afraid of being exposed to the world out there; please help me.

## Perhaps the Lord Would Respond Like This

'Do not fear, for I am with you; do not be dismayed, for I am your God. I will strengthen you and help you; I will uphold you with my righteous right hand' (Isa. 41:10, NIV).

## STOP FOR A MOMENT

*During the mending process it can be dangerous to make major moves or changes that you might regret when you finally emerge with a new, reshaped 'teapot'. Right now, you cannot trust your feelings, and one day you may wish that:*

Fear *had not made you leave your job now that you feel more confident and able to cope again.*

Isolation *had not made you choose to move to that cottage in the wilds, now that you want to be near people again and are sick of being a hermit.*

Anger *had not made you leave your church and resign from that committee, or get out of teaching for good.*

Loneliness *had not rushed you into making a relationship that you now find is a disaster.*

Denial *had not made you suppress your righteous anger so that you accepted a compromise and left someone who depends on you to suffer the consequences.*

Depression, *causing a temporary loss of faith, had not caused you to resign from your ministry.*

Painful feelings *had not made you walk out on your marriage before giving God a chance to help you work through your feelings.*

Guilt *(the false kind) had not made you feel so worthless that you gave up being a housegroup leader or Sunday School teacher.*

*You need to let the mending process happen gradually, until you find the 'new you' at the far end, then make any life-changing decisions. Of course, some decisions have to be made quickly, but God really can be trusted to help you make the right ones. We just tend to sit and wait for a voice to boom at us from the skies above. Yet God does not seem to do that. He seems to guide us while we are on the move, but we can always trust him to stop us from doing the wrong thing. We take a step in one direction, and if he does not block our progress we continue walking along that road. If, however, we do hit a barrier, then we should change direction until we find a clear path to follow.*

*'If you wander off the road to the right or the left, you will hear his voice behind you saying, "Here is the road. Follow it"' (Isa. 30:21, GNB).*

# 5

# FEAR

Fear, anxiety and worry are all very predictable reactions when our 'teapots' are smashed, and their causes are easy to find:

'I hate the dark. Now I'm alone in the house at night, I'm too afraid to sleep.' Being alone is a very common cause of fear, and so is the feeling of not being able to cope.

'John did everything for me, sorted out the mortgage, income tax, the bills. He made all the decisions, and he could mend anything from a hole in the roof to a dripping tap. Now that he's gone, I just don't know how to cope with it all, and I feel worried all the time.'

Some people say they feel all right during the day, but wake up at about three in the morning in a cold sweat, and start on the 'What if . . . ?' cycle:

- What if I can't make it on my own?
- What if I can't get a job?
- What if the children get out of hand without a father's control?
- What if the finances don't work out?
- What if I get too lonely to face life at all?

## Reactions to Fear

### In illness and pain

The following comments are typical of the fear that people experience concerning illness:

'I feel very positive most of the time since finding out I've got cancer, but then I suddenly think, "Suppose the doctors aren't telling me everything." Then I start wondering if the next scan will show it's reached the liver, and how much longer I would have. I usually wind up getting so worried that they won't give me enough pain control that I have to take something for my headache!'

'Mostly I can cope with this disease and the irritating disabilities it causes, but I know it's progressive, and I'm so afraid that one day I'll be trapped inside myself, not able to speak or move at all.'

'I'd willingly go through this myself; it's watching my child suffering that terrifies me so much – and the constant anxiety that we might lose him.'

### *A loss of identity*

'I don't know who I am any more. All the little things that made up my life have gone: the ordinary everyday routines, activities and responsibilities, my role and position in the "pecking order" of life, all the people I met every day and worked beside – they were my props and I've lost them all. I feel as if I'm walking off the edge of a cliff into nothingness. The uncertainty terrifies me.'

### *It can come in 'monster' waves*

'If I go out to the shops I get these terrible panic attacks. My heart begins to pound, and I hear rushing noises in my head. I'm too afraid to move in any direction, I feel like I'm choking, and I get this awful pain in my chest. The first time it happened I thought I was having a heart attack and was going to die on the spot.'

### *It can be milder, but continuous*

'It's always there just under the surface. I don't suppose I look worried; people wouldn't guess if they meet me out in the street, but I'm constantly tense and edgy. And I get butterflies in the tummy nearly all the time.'

---

*He did not promise to take from our paths the events that we fear, but he did promise to take away from us the fear of those events.* (Tom Rees)

### *It can paralyse us*

'Recently I've begun to feel that I can't face people; I can't think what to say, and I'm afraid they'll discover just what a wreck I've become, so when I hear the doorbell ring, I freeze. I just can't open the door, so I sit quiet and hope they think I'm out.'

### *It can make us run*

'I was walking down the High Street when I saw someone from our old church coming towards me – one of the people who'd been so critical and beastly before we left. I turned tail and pelted down a side street. She must have seen me, and I felt such a fool, but I was just too scared to meet her again.'

## The Plight of the Earwig

Most human beings fear change – it threatens us. Change, even change for the better, makes us feel unsettled and insecure. It is not surprising that we often feel afraid during this mending process, because it is really a journey through change. At the beginning, Granny's teapot stood perfect behind the glass doors of her display cabinet; at the other end of the change process, it had become a fascinating plant holder on the window ledge. There would have been a time in between those two points when the half-mended teapot was neither one thing or the other, because it was in the middle of being changed. A person in this state can look back at the life he or she once had and feel separated from it, but the life still to be lived is shrouded in uncertainty because the person has not arrived there yet. So there is a nasty sensation of not belonging anywhere – and that is very frightening. I remember going to our housegroup one evening when I was feeling exactly like that, and someone quoted a saying of Cardinal Newman. It did not help me at all, and it probably won't help you either! But here it is anyway:

> *When we walk in the shadow of his protection nothing can ever harm us again. They may hurt us but they can never crush or destroy us for we are always safe when we walk with him.* (Tom Rees)

'To live is to grow,
to grow is to change.
So to live successfully is to change often.'

The very thought that God might be developing us into a new kind of person is frightening. Most of us were perfectly happy as we were – we felt safe in the old familiar rut of long-held attitudes, thought patterns and routines. Caught in the middle of the process of change, we feel as vulnerable as an earwig when changing its skin. The earwig carries its skeleton on the outside, so its body can only enlarge during the few hours when its hard outer layer has been shed and the new, soft exterior is in the process of hardening. Naturally, the earwig is very vulnerable indeed during these times, a prey to any greedy blackbird. It can't feel safe until its soft white skin has become brown and hardened into a new outer shell. Sudden change often makes we humans feel the same!

## The Challenge

This fear is perfectly normal – but for Christians it poses a problem. The Bible says 'Fear not, at least 365 times, and we are also told, 'Don't give in to worry . . . it only leads to trouble' (Ps. 37:8, GNB). So are we being sinful and letting the Lord down when we feel anxious? Once again, let's remember that just because we are Christian, we do not stop being human. Human beings suffer from stress when their security is threatened, and stress pumps into the bloodstream the 'fight or flight' chemicals that saved our ancestors from sabre-toothed tigers. When we are stuck in a situation we cannot fight, flight is our only option, and therefore fear is both natural and inevitable. It is what we do with the fear that matters. Will we let it destroy us or work for us?

There are possibly two questions that the Lord is asking when fear

*Do not cling to events of the past or dwell on what happened long ago. Watch for the new thing I am going to do. It is happening already – you can see it now! I will make a road through the wilderness and give you streams of water there.* (Isa. 43:18–19, GNB)

shakes and rattles the half-mended pieces of 'teapot', and the first one is:

● 'Do you believe I have the power to keep you safe?'

As I said in Chapter 3, fear has always been an enemy of mine. Once, when so many things were going wrong for us that I felt terrified of what might happen next, I went to have coffee with a friend of mine. On her sitting-room floor stood an old wire birdcage, and prowling all round it were seven kittens. They were so big they were really cats, but I guessed they looked like tigers to the occupant of the cage! They hissed maliciously through the bars with obvious evil intent, and clawed viciously at the door catch. Guessing the poor little bird must be scared to pulp, I stepped in among those savage monsters to take a closer look, but the perch was empty and there was no sign of a bird in the cage. Instead, I saw a cheeky little hamster lying on his back in a bed of cotton wool, contentedly nibbling a peanut. Now and again he looked up at those claws and teeth as if to say, 'I know my owner cares enough about me to make sure those bars are strong enough for my protection – so I'm going to enjoy this nut and say nuts to you!' I prayed that the Lord would give me as much faith as the hamster, and went home feeling considerably better.

The second question is:

● 'Do you believe I am speaking the truth when I say, "Do not be afraid – I will save you. I have called you by name – you are mine"?' (Isa. 43:1, GNB.)

Most of us would reply promptly, 'Yes, of course I believe all that,' but at the very back of our minds there is often a tiny seed of doubt. Many of us have rather an abstract, academic or secondhand kind of faith. When we are fit, earning a good salary, and surrounded by people who love us, we can go to church and sing loudly about Jesus meeting all our needs, but how can we know for sure that he really will – until the crunch comes and our faith is put to the test?

At the start of any airline flight the airhostess always stands at the

---

*How I plead with God, how I implore his mercy, pouring out my troubles before him. For I am overwhelmed and desperate, and you alone know which way I ought to turn.* (Ps. 142:1–3, LB)

front of the cabin and tells everyone what to do if the plane should crash. No one ever seems to listen as she points out the emergency exits and models the lifejacket. People sit nonchalantly reading their newspapers, but do those passengers ever think, 'I wonder if that little bit of orange plastic she's waving about would *really* hold me up if this plane came down in the sea? Would it *really* inflate on impact as she says it would?' Well, of course they can't be sure until that 'unlikely event' actually occurs. Yet surely it is when our lives are crashing and our faith is put under pressure, that we are forced to ask, 'Is it *really* going to work?'

Because Jesus loves us so completely, he longs for us to trust him to look after us in every way. In fact, we are insulting him when we say we love him without also trusting him. Peter tells us that our faith is more precious to God than gold (1 Pet. 1:7), and without it we cannot please him (Heb. 11:6). It is that implicit, hamster-like trust that he wants to develop in us during this stage of the Broken Teapot Syndrome.

When my friend Trisha discovered she had multiple sclerosis, her husband walked out and left her prey to all kinds of anxieties. 'It seemed so unfair,' she told me. 'I could just about understand that he couldn't cope with illness and didn't want to see me gradually deteriorating, but you would think the least he could do was to see I was all right financially.' He was late with her maintenance cheques every time, leaving her sick with worry over the unpaid bills. In the end, he stopped sending anything at all and she had to take him to court.

'The whole thing was a constant nightmare,' said Trisha. 'I was forced to put the house on the market because the MS was making it impossible to live with so many stairs. Yet my husband demanded his share of the sale, so I knew I wouldn't be able to afford a bungalow – they always seem more expensive. I just didn't know what I was going to do, and I felt absolutely beside myself with worry.

> *I alone know the plans I have for you, plans to bring you prosperity and not disaster, plans to bring about the future you hope for. Then you will call to me. You will come and pray to me, and I will answer you. You will seek me, and you will find me because you will seek me with all your heart.* (Jer. 29:11–13, GNB)

'Then one day I felt "confronted" by the Lord. He seemed to say to me, "Are you looking to *me* to sort your finances out, or to Terry?" I had to admit that I felt it was my husband's obligation to look after me – after all, I was his responsibility, the courts had said so. He jolly well owed it to me after walking out just because I became ill. But then I realised that the Lord wanted to be "my provider", to take the responsibility of my care and maintenance, just as if he had become my husband. I did have to struggle with that, but in the end it was a very important part of my being able to forgive Terry for rejecting me. (That was something I was working through at that time.) Letting him off the debt I felt he owed me helped me to let go of all the bitterness and resentment I had been feeling towards him. I made a definite decision to rely on the Lord in the future. If he wanted to meet my needs through Terry, well, that was fine, but if he wanted to use some other way, that was fine too. I stopped nagging his solicitor when cheques failed to arrive, or writing abusing letters to Terry or screaming at him down the phone. Whenever some emergency arose, I just said, "Lord, what are you going to do now?" And somehow the needs were always met.

'Mind you, they weren't always met instantly! I sweated a bit when I finally sold the house and had about six weeks to get out and nowhere to go. The council wouldn't give me a flat because Terry was supposed to provide me with a home, but of course he wouldn't give me enough to buy something suitable for my disability. I was desperate, and wondered what on earth the Lord would do about it. Then, most unexpectedly, I heard that an aunt of mine who had recently died had left me her bungalow. It was on the other side of town, but my mobility allowance came through just then, so I could get an adapted car that made it still possible to get back to see my beloved friends at church. A lot needed doing to the bungalow, but I lived there in the meantime, and the money Terry finally gave me was enough to pay for everything to be made easy for me as a disabled person. Now my favourite verse is Philippians 4:19 (NIV): "My God will meet all your needs according to his glorious riches in Christ Jesus." '

---

*The Lord himself will lead you and be with you. He will not fail you or abandon you, so do not lose courage or be afraid.* (Deut.31:8, GNB)

When, like Trisha, everything and everyone who represents safety and security in our lives is removed, and we have no way of meeting our own necessities any more, our need for God is paramount, and that is when we really discover for sure that we can trust him.

## Doesn't God Want Me to Be Mature and Self-reliant?

One day Jesus startled a group of confident, well-qualified men by telling them he wanted them to become like small children again. They had been arguing for hours about which of them had the most to offer the new Kingdom they thought Jesus was about to set up in Jerusalem: which of them would make the best Prime Minister, and who should manage the finances. They all thought they had abilities and personal qualities that Jesus could use to meet the needs of his Kingdom, but before he could use any of them they had to learn to trust him.

Some commentators say Peter's own little son was the child Jesus called, and, lifting him up on to his knee, he said to those big, proud, self-confident men something like this: 'Until you recognise you are as helpless and dependent as this child you can never be important in my kingdom' (Matt. 18:3–4, paraphrased).

## God Brings His Children up Backwards

When I was expecting our first child, Sarah, I used to love feeling her kicking round inside me. She was totally dependent on me to meet her every need, and she belonged to me completely. The moment she took her first gasp of breath and the midwife cut the cord, I had to begin letting her go. Our assignment as earthly parents was to turn this totally dependent scrap of humanity into a self-sufficient adult who could function without any help from us whatsoever.

The first steps towards this goal were a delight to us. One day, as we pushed cereal into her mouth, she grabbed the spoon and shoved it into her ear – or was it up her nose?

> *When anxiety was great within me, your consolation brought joy to my soul.* (Ps. 94:19, NIV)

'Oh look!' we cried in wonder, 'she's feeding herself!'

When she took her first tottering step we rang all our friends and exclaimed proudly, 'She's walking – already!'

Then the really big day came: she used her potty. I was so thrilled with her sheer cleverness that I felt like showing the contents to the milkman!

It hurt like mad to hand her over to the teacher on her first day at school, but I knew I had to let go if we were ever to achieve the goal of her independence. From that time on, the steps she took away from us gradually lengthened, and we watched with pride as we taught her to meet her own needs instead of always looking to us to meet them for her.

'If you want money, you earn it,' we said, as we sent her off in a heatwave or a thunderstorm to pick fruit on the local farm.

And finally, we accompanied her to her chosen university, and had to watch her walk away into the huge building while we travelled home in desolation without her. She soon came back again, of course – along with her dirty washing! It was not until she had her own home and career that we knew we had finally launched her into the world as an independent adult, able to earn her own living and solve her own problems.

God works backwards. Usually by the time he becomes our Father, we have already become self-sufficient adults. God knows that in this universe our only hope of true and lasting happiness is to depend on him entirely. Trusting in ourselves and our own abilities may sound very 'manly' and adult, but it is actually a recipe for disaster on this dark planet. We are not the giants we think we are, and God never designed us to live without him.

So he has to work on us – backwards – gently dismantling each of our little self-sufficiencies and allowing our earthly props to be removed. His ultimate aim is for us to depend on him for everything, just as Sarah depended on me during those nine months in the womb. St Paul describes this by saying, 'In him we live and move and have our being . . . We are his offspring' (Acts 17:28, NIV). Only when we reach this state of utter dependency, and are fully under his control, can we safely function in this world. The Broken Teapot

---

*His never-failing love protects me like the walls of a fort!*
(Ps. 31:21, LB)

Syndrome may feel to us like a catastrophe, but it could have huge potential in God's eyes, because, as Sören Kierkegaard said, 'God created everything out of nothing and everything which God is to use he first reduces to nothing.'

King David was one of the greatest soldiers and statesmen who ever lived, and the stories of his achievements still ring triumphantly down through the years. Yet his secret was this utter dependence on God; and, except for two unfortunate occasions, he never made a decision without first turning to God for his guidance. Towards the end of his life he wrote, 'My heart is not proud, O Lord . . . I do not concern myself with great matters or things too wonderful for me. But I have stilled and quietened my soul; like a weaned child with its mother, like a weaned child is my soul within me' (Ps. 131:1–2, NIV).

## Lost in the Forest

Like many babies born in the war, I did not see much of my father during the first few years of my life. And when he did come home, he didn't have very much to do with me.

'Babies are noisy, smelly creatures that ruin everything,' was the way he described me in his diary. My noises and smells were left to my nanny to cope with, and he and I hardly coincided at all until the day he offered to buy me an icecream. I must have been about three, and my mother and I were staying in my grandparents' house in Scotland. My father arrived to spend a few days with us, and he obviously felt it was time I had some paternal contact.

My reactions to his overture of friendship were mixed. Icecreams were a rare treat in those days of rationing, but they could only be bought in a shop in the next village – a long walk away. (Petrol was rationed, too.) Could I really dare to go off alone with this big, remote stranger with the loud, deep voice? However, greed overcame fear and I opted for the icecream. We set off, walking stiffly and silently down the path by the sea.

It was about three o'clock on an October afternoon and the light already seemed to be failing. 'You can't walk very fast, can you?' my

> *Cast all your anxiety on him because he cares for you.* (1 Pet. 5:7, NIV)

father commented, as my short legs tried to keep pace with his long strides. 'I think we'll take the short cut through the forest or we'll never get there before dark.'

The forest! Terror seized me. All my bedtime stories seemed to contain wolves and trolls who lived in forests. I had never been in one, but I was sure they must be frightful places. All desire for icecream was lost in a wave of nausea, but I was far too overawed by this big man to express my anxiety – even when he lifted me over the granite wall and the eerie darkness of the trees engulfed us. Not even the birds were singing.

Forest paths all look much the same, and we had walked until my strength had almost gone before he admitted we were lost.

'Never mind,' he said, 'I'm sure we just need to keep going downhill and we'll hit the sea eventually.' So we left the comparative safety of the track, and plunged in among the trees themselves – where, of course, the wolves and trolls were sure to live!

Branches scratched my face and pulled my hair, slippery roots tripped me up, and huge wood ants' nests impeded my progress. Yet the pain from my grazed knees and scratches was nothing in comparison to my terror of those wolves. I did not actually see one, but I was sure their yellow eyes were looking at me from the black holes between the rocks and moss-covered boulders.

It was like the worst nightmare I ever had, but suddenly everything changed. A huge hand came down from high above me and took mine. It was warm and reassuring, and so big that it engulfed my wrist and forearm as well as my hand.

'Come on, you're doing well, I'm proud of you,' said my father. 'We'll remember this adventure all our lives.' Somehow, it was easy after that. His hand held me up; when I slipped, it stopped me from falling – lifting me right over those painful boulders and piles of sharp pine needles. We began to talk, even laugh, as we struggled along together, brought close by shared adversity.

When we finally discovered a stile leading into a field, we both whooped with joy because we saw the village below us with the sea beyond. 'Come on,' he said, 'let's run so we can get there before they

---

*You can sleep without fear; you need not be afraid of disaster . . . for the Lord is with you; he protects you.* (Prov. 3:24–26, LB)

close the shop.' Icecream never tasted so good, and we drove back triumphantly in a taxi.

That walk through the forest holding hands established a relationship of love and trust with my father that lasted for the rest of his life. 'My soul clings to you; your right hand upholds me,' says Psalm 63:8 (NIV). Since then, I have often thought that the art of clinging to God's hand is easiest to learn during the times of greatest fear. As Psalm 37:23 (NIV) adds, 'If the Lord delights in a man's way, he makes his steps firm; though he stumble, he will not fall, for the Lord upholds him with his hand.'

## The 'Hold Up' Factor

Five years ago, Joyce had a breast lump removed. It was benign and no further treatment was necessary, yet she has never recovered. She looks ill, always seems to be in pain, and suffers from all kinds of unpleasant symptoms. She has had to give up her job as a nursing sister and spends most of her time in bed. Yet endless visits to many different hospitals and all kinds of tests and investigations have never shown anything wrong physically. She is not unique in her suffering. Recent studies carried out by Manchester University's Department of Psychiatry and the Institute of Psychiatry in London have confirmed that nearly a third of all patients who go to their GPs with a physical symptom have no detectable physical illness.

Just a few days after Joyce had her operation to remove the lump, her husband died, and three months later their only son went off to university. Was it the fear of life on her own and the demands of a stressful job that trapped Joyce permanently in her 'broken teapot'? Could illness have become her way out of situations she felt too afraid to face?

---

*Don't worry about anything; instead, pray about everything; tell God your needs and don't forget to thank him for his answers. If you do this you will experience God's peace, which is far more wonderful than the human mind can understand. His peace will keep your thoughts and your hearts quiet and at rest as you trust in Christ Jesus.* (Phil. 4:6–7, LB)

No one can answer that question, but many doctors have always maintained that how we think and feel influences our physical health enormously. We are not only bodies; we are minds and spirits as well. One man can have a serious heart attack, but be back playing golf again a few months later, while another man suffering an attack of similar severity is so afraid of further trouble that he wraps himself in cottonwool and stays an invalid for the rest of his life.

The doctor in charge of the largest Intensive Care Unit in the USA was recently interviewed on television. He said his research showed that fear plays an important part in a patient's rate of recovery. When patients who are fearful and apprehensive are admitted for major surgery, they are likely to take longer to recover, require higher doses of analgesics and face a greater chance of post-operative complications than patients who are not afraid.

I bumped into Joyce the other day, hobbling painfully into the post office with the help of a stick. 'It's my hip,' she complained, 'but the doctor says there's nothing he can do. I reckon he thinks I'm making it up,' she added with a sigh. The bleak expression on her face has haunted me ever since.

Dr David Goldberg, Professor of Psychiatry at Withington Hospital in Manchester, maintains that although many doctors dismiss psychosomatic pain as imaginary and incurable, the pain experienced can be greater than that suffered by patients with organic disease. Yet they receive little sympathy from the rest of the world. People like Joyce are written off as hypochondriacs and malingerers, but they *are* ill – ill with fear. They are the truly 'incurable', because no modern drugs or miracle surgery can give them back their health.*

There is hope, however, even for these 'no-hopers'. Jesus can mend the unmendable. I believe that he is saying to all those who cannot face getting back into 'real' life again and feel they may be retreating into illness: 'Will you trust me – even in the grip of such a huge fear? I am not asking you to travel alone along the road that lies ahead; I will

* Obviously not all psychosomatic illness is caused by fear.

*There is something supernatural in all disease which man cannot explain.* (Hippocrates, the pioneer of the science of medicine)

walk it with you. Let me flood your mind, soul and body with my
own health and vitality. I came to give you life in all its abundance –
will you say "yes" to that life and walk into it with me?'

See! The winter is past;
the rains are over and gone.
Flowers appear on the earth;
the season of singing has come,
the cooing of doves is heard in our land.

The fig-tree forms its early fruit;
the blossoming vines spread their fragrance.
Arise, come, my darling; my beautiful one,
come with me.
(Song of Songs 2:11–13, NIV)

## Practical Tips for Coping with Fear

### *Talk about it*

Talking out our fears usually helps a great deal. The smaller worries
are easy: most of us discuss those so easily that the rest of the world
runs for cover when they see us coming! It is the really enormous
fears that we find hard to put into words, yet by doing so we can
diminish them in size quite dramatically.

Dick had been in hospital for three weeks, undergoing extensive
surgery. He never asked the medical staff about their diagnosis, and
he avoided the subject when his family and friends visited him. He
was pretty sure he knew what was wrong, but somehow he simply
could not put his worst fears into words. At night, when the ward
was quiet at last, he would lie longing for sleep, but it was then that
these nameless, unexpressed fears loomed very large, and his whole
body felt so rigid and stiff that sleep was quite impossible.

---

*Save me from sinking in the mud; keep me safe from my
enemies, safe from the deep water. Don't let the flood
come over me; don't let me drown in the depths or sink into
the grave.* (Ps. 69:14–15, GNB)

One morning, another patient stopped by his bed for a chat. 'You've got cancer too, haven't you?' he said casually. 'I know because I've just had the same op., and I heard the doctors talking about you.'

One hour later they were still talking, and later that afternoon, when Dick's wife came to see him she said, 'What's happened to you? You look ever so much better. Have they changed your drugs or something?' Dick smiled. He knew it was talking that had helped him, not pills, and that night he slept wonderfully.

A week later, when he left hospital, he soon discovered that it is one thing to talk to another patient, but quite another to discuss your fears with a wife and family. As the weeks went by, a prickly silence settled over the household. 'How much have they been told?' Dick wondered, while his family thought, 'He doesn't seem to have a clue what's wrong.' In the end, the atmosphere became so tense and relationships so strained that a wise Macmillan nurse gently but firmly helped Dick and his wife to share their feelings with one another. The relief was enormous.

'I was waiting for you to say something,' said Dick.

'And I was waiting for *you* to say something,' said his wife. The shadow that had begun to divide them melted away, and they were close to each other again.

### *A more energetic method*

Martin Luther was often full of fear, and this was his coping strategy: 'When I am assailed with heavy tribulation, I rush out among my pigs, rather than remain alone.' On another occasion he said, 'I exorcise the devil when I harness the horse and spread manure upon my fields.'

My friend Ruth devised a rather less smelly way of coping. She found the first few months after her husband died very difficult indeed.

> *Do not be afraid – I will save you. I have called you by name – you are mine. When you pass through deep waters, I will be with you; your troubles will not overwhelm you. When you pass through fire you will not be burnt; the hard trials that come will not hurt you.* (Isa. 43:1–2, GNB)

'I've always been an early bird,' she told me. 'I go downstairs, make a pot of tea, and just sit with the Lord for an hour before breakfast. For years that's been my best time of the day, but after Brian died I found all the worries came crowding in on me as I sat there in the mornings. I struggled with them, told myself off, and generally felt wretched. Then I decided to try a change of routine. I still got up early, but, instead of my "quiet time", I got the hoover out and tackled the cleaning. Did my bits of cooking for the day, scrubbed the kitchen floor, scoured the bath – anything I could think of that was downright physical. Then at eight o'clock I was good and tired. I seemed to have used up all that nervous energy, and I was ready to sit down with the Lord quietly.'

### The irritating method

There is nothing so maddening as being told to 'count your blessings', but that was exactly what helped George, a businessman with a very stressful workload. 'Probably most people get things completely out of proportion if they wake in the night,' he said, 'and their worries seem to spin round and round like a whirlpool. That's just how I felt all day long as well, when I got into that anxiety state a few years back. I just couldn't seem to control my thoughts at all – until I decided to be positive, and made myself concentrate on what was going right, rather than always thinking about the things that were going wrong.'

### Walking away

People who are born with naturally placid temperaments can often look down on us born worriers and condemn us as unspiritual. Yet if we can use worry as a trigger for prayer, then surely the more we worry the better! At least, that was always my theory until one day I realised that expressing my worries to God in prayer was not at all the same thing as *relinquishing* them to him in faith.

When our oldest daughter Sarah left home and went to university, she was the first of our six 'chicks' to leave the nest. I knew that her faith had been very wobbly during her 'A' level years, and she made no secret of the fact that she wanted to 'experience Oxford' in the fullest sense of the word and not be tied down by some 'stuffy old Christian Union'. She had every intention of leaving God behind at home. I can't ever remember being more worried than I was the first few days after she had gone. I knew the people she met during her freshers' week and the societies she joined could influence the rest of her life. For eighteen years I had always been able to take care of her in thousands of ways; now she was right out of my control and influence. 'Turn your worries into prayer,' I reminded myself firmly. So I sent a constant barrage of muttered prayers aloft day and night.

'Oh Lord, help her. Oh Lord, be with her. Oh Lord, help her . . .' On and on it went like a chant, but I was so preoccupied that I burnt the toast, blackened the sausages, forgot messages, and generally rendered myself useless with worry.

'This can't go on,' I told myself after a few days. 'I'm not really praying because there's no trust involved.'

So I went up to Sarah's unnaturally tidy bedroom and on a shelf I found my mother's old Bible, worn and shabby with many years of use. I opened it and laid it down on Sarah's bed. Then I wrote her name on a scrap of paper and laid it on the Bible.

'Lord,' I said, 'here she is. She is *yours*.'

Then I closed the Bible, enclosing the piece of paper – 'Just like the hands of God,' I thought, as I turned and deliberately went away, leaving her in his care. Each morning I went back, opened the Bible, and prayed again for Sarah in detail, but finally I would close the Bible and relinquish my concern by the simple act of walking away. For me, prayer can be a bit abstract and intangible sometimes, so doing something active like that helps me a lot.

A few days after I had started to pray like that, we had a phone call from the John Radcliffe Hospital in Oxford. A voice said, 'Sarah has been involved in an accident, and she has back injuries.'

'Fine way you have of looking after her,' was my unworthy prayer as we drove down the motorway. Sarah spent the rest of that term on her back, isolated from all her new friends and involvements.

'When I came up to Oxford,' she told me later, 'I thought I didn't need God any more, but as I lay in hospital I knew that I did.' She gave herself to him in a new, adult way, and was able to lead many other people to him during her university years. God really did know what he was doing.

## A Meditation

It was the last time they would all be together like this. None of them realised that, of course, except perhaps Judas. The shadow of a terrible sin already darkened his face as he sat there, fiddling nervously with a piece of bread. Poor Judas, there was still time to change his mind, but when he finally got up and sidled away into the darkness, the sorrow he left behind in the heart of Jesus must have been terrible.

However, there were still the other eleven, and Jesus needed to turn his attention to them, because time was running out and he had so many important things to say. They had been with him constantly, working, travelling, eating, laughing and facing all kinds of adventures together. And here they all were at the end of those three special years, enjoying a meal that they had no idea would seem so significant in the years ahead. He loved them so much as he looked round at their happy faces, laughing in the candlelight.

'My children, I shall not be with you very much longer,' he said gently. Like anyone else who saw death approaching, he wanted to give these people he loved the precious assets he had valued most in life – just as silver spoons, four-poster beds and stately homes have been handed safely on through the years. He had no money to leave them, not even a little carpenter's business, and his clothes were shabby from the dusty roads, but he had something far more valuable than anything else. What good are silver spoons, fine furniture or grand houses if their owner is tormented by fear? Or money, work and clothes to someone who is too miserable to enjoy them? So looking round he said to them:

'Peace is what I leave with you; it is my own peace that I give you . . . Do not be worried and upset; do not be afraid' (John 14:27, GNB); 'I have told you this so that my joy may be in you and that your joy may be complete' (John 15:11, GNB). Peace and joy are the perfect antidotes to fear and misery.

His heart must have been heavy as he thought how much they would need their inheritance in the years to come. He knew they must face the terror of persecution, the fear of travelling to dangerous places, storms at sea, shipwrecks, aching homesickness, hunger, cruel beatings, stonings, insults and lying accusations, then the lonely dungeons and, for most of them, a violent, painful death.

Yes, he knew they would often be afraid, and how he must have longed to save them from it all. He had the power to do so; he could have changed them all into angelic beings who were above human cruelty, but he needed them to be men for a little while longer. The job of telling the rest of us about his love could only be done by human beings. So he gave them his peace to keep their hearts and minds through the tensions and anxieties, and his own personal brand of joy to give them strength to face everything that mankind, and even Satan himself, would throw at them. Those eleven men have handed that inheritance on down through the generations, so that this 'peacejoy' can be ours too – just for the asking.

## A Prayer

*'Come to me all you who are tired of being afraid . . . "For I, the Lord your God, hold your right hand; I, Who say to you, Fear not, I will help you".'* (Isa. 41:13, AMP)

Lord, I have that one great dread – you know the one I mean – my worst fear. To me it feels like my own Calvary, and the path towards it resembles a crucifixion. I know that thinking about it is probably worse than the actual reality will be when it comes, but you too were afraid in your Gethsemane. You cried out to your father God, pleading with him to change his mind and take the horrible cup away from you. You were a man, and you were afraid like the rest of us. Yet you took your fears and walked with them right to the bitter end. You faced that worst fear of all, the cross itself, and you walked right through it to the far side, and beyond to resurrection and renewal.

Lord, help me to do the same. I want to avoid my Calvary just as you did, but I know there is only one way – and that is to go forward towards it and then through it to the far side. But I am still afraid, I am not as brave as you. But I give you my fear, and I ask for your help as you walk beside me towards the thing I dread. 'Even if I go through the deepest darkness, I will not be afraid, Lord, for you are with me . . . I know that your goodness and love will be with me all my life' (Ps. 23:4, 6, GNB).

## STOP FOR A MOMENT

*It was in Ireland that I discovered something that has helped me profoundly in coping with just about every single emotion connected with the Broken Teapot Syndrome. One glorious sunny afternoon a friend took us for a drive along a rocky Irish coast road. The sea was actually turquoise as it lapped round the little coves and sandy bays, and tall stone towers stood at intervals along the cliffs.*

*'Why don't the lighthouses have any doors?' we asked.*

*'Because they're Irish,' our friend replied with a twinkle in his eyes. 'Hundreds of years ago, all along these shores, were little sleepy fishing villages full of happy people minding their own business, when along came the Vikings in their long boats. Up the beach they came and terror reigned. Every man killed, the women raped, and the children taken as slaves. Crops and huts burnt to the ground, and nothing left to show for it but corpses.' He was warming to his story even if it was growing a little in the telling. 'Well, we Irish didn't like that, so we decided to build these high towers. A wee man would be sitting at the top, looking out to sea. When the raiders were sighted, he rang a bell so everyone could run for safety into the tower.'*

*'But how did they get in without a door?' I protested.*

*'The door was high up on the side of the tower, and the wee man would let down a rope ladder. When the last man was inside, he'd pull it back up again. Then there'd be nothing at all the old Vikings could do but go home again.'*

*'Didn't they wait until the people were hungry enough to come out?' I suggested.*

*'Sure, but the tower would be filled with all the provisions they could ever need. So, because those towers were there, the people could live happily, knowing there was always somewhere safe where they could run.'*

*Later I had to speak in a church and the first song they sang was based on Proverbs 18:10 (NIV): 'The name of the Lord is a strong tower; the righteous run to it and are safe.' The verse meant everything to me after seeing those strong towers of refuge earlier in the day. I realised that words like 'fortress', 'stronghold' and 'refuge' are often used to describe the Lord in the Old Testament, and of course Paul loves telling us about all the benefits we receive when we are 'in Christ'.*

*The concept of the Lord being like a huge, safe, protective fortress to which I can run and be safe whenever the need arises has been such a help ever since. One day, for instance, I was furiously angry. Someone close to me was making my life extremely difficult without any apparent concern or regret. For months I had struggled with my feelings until irritation had become outrage, and on this particular day I felt my anger getting quite out of control. So I took my dog Brodie to a lonely place in the countryside and stamped round the fields muttering, growling and even shouting when I was quite sure no one was within earshot.*

*'Lord, take this anger away!' I kept demanding as I shook my fist heavenwards. But he did nothing to help me at all, and if anything my rage became even more intense. Then suddenly I remembered those Irish towers, but how did you get into a tower if it was not made of solid stone? Suddenly, it dawned on me: it was the name of the Lord that was the strong tower. Out loud I began to say the name of Jesus, and round and round the muddy field I stamped, repeating it all the while. At first, nothing happened, and I felt such a fool; but there is an enormous, earth-shaking, life-changing power in the actual name of Jesus Christ. Before long, I began to feel the anger recede, and a tangible calm like strong walls began to rise up around me. I was safely 'inside the strong tower' by the time Brodie and I finally reached home, wet and mud splattered, and my anger over that particular situation has never troubled me since.*

*The following week I told someone else about this coping strategy when she told me about her fear of crowded places. She looked most doubtful when I explained the idea to her, but later that day she phoned to say, 'It worked! As soon as I began to say the name of Jesus I felt as if safe walls were rising up all around me, my heart beat slowed down, and my breathing returned to normal.'*

*You probably won't believe that this works – until you try it. So why not decide now that the next time you are overrun by your particular 'Viking', you will run into Jesus himself by repeating his name. Like the Irish towers that contained all the necessary provisions, when we are 'in Christ' we really can find the antidote to whatever negative emotion is attacking us at the time. 'In Christ' you have 'every spiritual blessing' (Eph. 1:3, NIV) and 'everything we need for life and godliness' (2 Pet. 1:3, NIV).*

# DESPAIR AND DEPRESSION

Sadness and sorrow are understandable after the loss of something or someone very precious, but many Christians seem to feel that despair and depression are right out of bounds! Yet experts say that practically all human beings go through some degree of depression within the first five years after a major loss. Doctors describe it as reactive depression. For some it is no more than feeling 'a bit low' for a few weeks, while others may spend a year or more feeling that life is grey and pointless and not worth the effort. In its most acute form, it can cause a total failure to function normally, 'a complete breakdown', and rest, medication and even hospitalisation are necessary. In all its forms, reactive depression is normal – even for Christians; yet so many look on with disapproval when one of the others slithers down the 'black snake' and lands on the darkest square on the game board.

Depression *is* the very roughest part of the entire Broken Teapot Syndrome. I remember feeling utterly desolate. A misty, grey cloud shrouded me constantly, affecting my every action, thought and feeling. Worst of all, God seemed to have abandoned me, just when I needed him most.

These days I am quite often asked to be part of seminars for Christians going through depression – or living with someone who is – and I asked one group recently to write down in a few words how they felt. Here are some of their responses:

*Surely there is no greater attachment in life than the attachment to your self-image?* (Michael Hanson)

'I can't feel that God's there any more.'
'God seems to be hiding his face from me.'
'God is out of sight and between us is a blank, black wall.'
'I've lost touch with God and my Christian life's gone dead.'
'Darkness with no light at the end of the tunnel.'
'No point in going on, there's nothing to live for.'
'Like being in a deep dark well.'
'Everything's grey. The world's lost all colour.'
'As I wake up I feel as if a load of heavy, wet sand is pouring over me, pushing me down into the bed. Can't face the day. Can't make decisions – not even what to wear.'
'A black cloud hiding the sun and covering the horizon.'

King David wrote: 'Lord, I call to you for help; every morning I pray to you. Why do you reject me, Lord? Why do you turn away from me?' (Ps. 88:13–14, GNB.) And in Proverbs it says: 'A man's spirit sustains him in sickness, but a crushed spirit who can bear?' (Prov. 18:14, NIV.)

## Doubts

Doubts about God's love, and even his existence, also seem to come with the 'depression package' and many people in the seminars confessed they were plagued by them:

'I can't believe God loves me – because I'm so totally worthless myself, I assume he thinks the same.'
'I sometimes think he must be a sadist to let me go through something like this.'
In Lamentations it says: 'I am one who knows what it is to be punished by God. He drove me deeper and deeper into darkness and beat me again and again with merciless blows' (Lam. 3:1–3, GNB).
It is possible to be depressed without feeling gloomy and doleful at

---

*Answer me now, Lord! I have lost all hope. Don't hide yourself from me . . . Remind me each morning of your constant love, for I put my trust in you.* (Ps. 143:7–8, GNB)

all, and these doubts may be the only symptom that shows. So instead of seeing these doubts as part of the depression and accepting that they will pass in time, we begin to feel we are losing our faith and failing completely.

## Hopelessness

It is useless to talk brightly about the 'process of change' to people who are depressed, or to remind them that God is moving them on into a new kind of life. Depression takes away all hope for the future and makes life today feel pointless and futile. Verses like 'Surely goodness and mercy shall follow me all the days of my life' (Ps. 23:6, AV) are hard to believe when you are convinced that this state of despair is going to be permanent. 'I'm never going to get out of this,' commented one member of the seminar group.

King Solomon described his feelings like this: 'It is useless, useless, said the Philosopher. Life is useless, all useless. You spend your life working, labouring, and what do you have to show for it?' (Eccles. 1:2–3, GNB.)

## Tiredness and Lethargy

Depression is not only a feeling of despair, but an illness that affects the emotions, the body and the mind. Many physical symptoms seem to be part of it, and these often take people by surprise:

'I feel tired and lethargic all the time.'
'All motivation has gone.'
'The day stretches ahead endlessly. I'm bored, but there's no energy to do anything interesting.'
'My house is a tip, but I can't be bothered.'

Comments from 'the spectators', such as 'Why don't you just pull yourself together and snap out of it?', can hurt terribly, because you

---

*The Lord is close to the broken-hearted and saves those who are crushed in spirit.* (Ps. 34:18, NIV)

*would* – if only you *could*! Such people force you to look on the bright side when, from where you stand, there is no bright side to see.

### Christians and Depression

Perhaps it is the fear of that kind of misunderstanding that makes many of us keep quiet about how we are really feeling. To me, depression felt like utter failure. 'As a Christian, I shouldn't feel like this' is something people often say in the seminars. Perhaps many of us have a mental image of the 'Christian' we feel we ought to be, someone who is constantly full of joy, and who dashes round helping people who are miserable.

I now realise that our friend George thought he should be like that. He was part of a whole gang of friends that Tony and I used to go around with before we were married. None of us ever realised that George was depressed after his particular 'teapot' broke, so we were badly shaken when we heard that he had hanged himself. He left a note telling us he was sorry, but he could no longer live with the hypocrisy of knowing he ought to be able to praise God when he no longer felt that he could.

George died more than twenty-five years ago, but his memory still haunts me. If only we had realised he was feeling so bad, and if only he had gone to his doctor for help. It is because of George that I always urge people who admit they are depressed to swallow their pride and go and see their GP. Dr Marion Ashton, a psychiatrist, once told me that, in her opinion, Christians were the most difficult group of patients to treat.* 'They find it so hard to admit they are depressed, so they may function below their potential for years, feeling tired and lacking enthusiasm. Medical science could do so much to help them, if only they could be brave enough to go to their doctor and receive his treatment as a gift from God.'

Perhaps another reason for the stigma attached to being depressed

* See *Where Have You Gone God?*

> *O my soul, why be so gloomy and discouraged? Trust in God! . . . he will make me smile again, for he is my God!*
> (Ps. 43:5, LB)

is that it can be caused by some deepseated spiritual problems. I remember once, when I was depressed, listening to a tape on the subject by a leading Christian conference speaker. While I lay in my bed cringing, he reeled off a long list of things that can cause depression:

- unresolved conflicts
- blocked goals
- swallowed anger
- unconfessed sin
- bitterness
- lack of forgiveness
- self-pity
- delayed or long-denied grief
- unacknowledged guilt

There were probably more things that I have forgotten, but I do remember trying to work out which ones were behind all my misery. In the end I became so upset that I felt they probably *all* were, and I wanted to sink through the bed in shame. What if my friends at church discovered what a disgrace I was as a Christian? I was sure they would all be running down the checklist with me in mind if they ever guessed I was depressed. I never actually told anyone, not even my husband or my two best friends. Perhaps it was easier for me to deceive everyone because I was physically ill at the time, and that created a perfect smokescreen – as it does for many people.

Of course, all those things listed above can cause depression, but during the Broken Teapot Syndrome the most usual cause is a reaction to the trauma we have recently gone through. Therefore it is probably wiser, while we are depressed, not to go digging down looking for reasons when all our energy is needed just to survive through the next hour.

---

*Praise be to . . . the God of all comfort, who comforts us in all our troubles, so that we can comfort those in any trouble with the comfort we ourselves have received from God.* (2 Cor. 1:3,4, NIV)

## Does Anything Help?

Looking back at my own depression and by talking to many other sufferers, I have managed to glean just a few suggestions that do seem to help some people, some of the time.

### *It will pass*

Repeating the three words 'it will pass' has been a real help to several people – simply because they are true. This depression *will* go away eventually, even though we may find that hard to believe at the time.

### *Go with the flow*

That is another good little phrase to remember. Fighting depression and allowing yourself to become agitated or angry about it only seems to make things worse. Looking for instant escape routes or sudden healing can lead to disappointment and further despair. Although there are people who have been healed instantly through prayer, depression seems to lift very gradually for most of us – so usually it is best just to keep plodding on through to the other side.

### *Look out for surprises*

I have a battered old notebook that I call my prayer journal, and in it I found these words that I wrote because I felt they were from God:

'Look carefully as you walk through today. I made so many beautiful things, which others say are useless. Savour them with me. Relish these small surprises.

'The sun shafting through a chink in the curtains and making all that dust which irritates you dance and swirl in a world of exquisite colour.

'Or the intricate pattern on the wings of the fly that buzzes against the glass at your window – and nearly drives you mad. The tiny

---

*Don't you think that some of us must know the trials of misty weather if we are to be enabled to understand when others are in the mists?* (Amy Carmichael)

bubbles reflecting the light in yesterday's glass of stale water standing forgotten on the table.

'Out of these tiny glimmers of hope your joy will be reborn. I have placed these surprises ready for you to discover along the path today, so watch out for them carefully because they could easily be missed.'

I can remember deliberately looking out each day for one of these unusual 'treasures of darkness' (Isa. 45:3, NIV), and then noting it down in my diary at night.

> Open our eyes, thou sun of life and gladness,
> That we may see that glorious world of thine!
> It shines for us in vain,
> While drooping sadness enfolds us here like mist. (Keble)

## Act as if

Blaise Pascal, the seventeenth-century mathematician and theologian, once said that if our faith has gone, we need to act as if we still possessed it until it returns. Those three words, 'act as if', have not only been a help to me over the doubts, but in all kinds of other situations as well.

A friend of mine who is part of an amateur dramatic society had to play the part of a very depressed woman in a play that they performed seven nights in a row. She was excellent in the part, but by the Friday she admitted she had let herself get into it a bit too well! 'I began to feel depressed myself. I couldn't switch it off somehow. I found myself shuffling about with my shoulders drooping or flopping wearily into a chair with a heavy sigh. When I heard myself talking in a minor key with all my sentences going downhill at the end, I thought, "I'll be glad when Saturday night's over!"'

If 'acting depressed' can make you feel depressed, then might it not work the other way round? It has been medically proved that a smile on the outside can actually make you feel better on the inside – but if

---

*I am weak and poor, O Lord, but you have not forgotten me. You are my Saviour and my God – hurry to my aid!* (Ps. 40:17, GNB.) *I am poor and needy, but the Lord takes thought and plans for me.* (Ps. 40:17)

anyone had suggested that I try that when I was depressed, I might well have hit them!

## God still believes in you

When I felt my faith in God's love was slipping away, I used to panic because I thought that if I lost it completely he would not be able to help me any more. Thinking like that is just about as stupid as the small child who feels invisible when he closes his eyes! Francis James put it like this: 'It is not my grasp of God that matters most, but His grasp of me. The thing that matters most is not even my conscious-ness that He holds me fast, but just the blessed fact of it.'

## 'It is not your faith that counts, but God's faithfulness'

Once, after weeks of trying to work up faith for healing, our vicar said something that helped me profoundly. 'It's not our faith that counts, but God's faithfulness.' The relief was enormous, particularly when he added, 'We do not need to have a great faith, we just have to trust a great Saviour.'

## Find a prayer partner

I would not tell anyone I was depressed, so no one was specifically praying for my protection in the wilderness. When I finally dared tell the hospital chaplain,* he began to pray for me every day; it was then that my depression began to lift.

We should never underestimate prayer. It connects us to the limitless power of God, just as an electrical plug pushed into the socket puts all the gigantic power of electricity at our disposal. I don't understand *why* prayer works, any more than I understand elec-tricity. I just know they both do work! Find someone who will pray for you regularly – although not necessarily *with* you, because that

* See *Unexpected Healing*, p. 75.

---

*The Lord's unfailing love and mercy still continue, fresh as the morning, as sure as the sunrise. The Lord is all I have, and so I put my hope in him.* (Lam. 3:22–24, GNB)

might become the kind of strain you cannot take when you are depressed.

## *Tell God how you feel*

I found it very hard to tell God how I felt, because prayer was impossible at first. The only way I could communicate with God was by writing him short notes in my journal. Looking back at them now, I am horrified at how rude some of them were, but at the time it really helped me to be brutally honest. Later, when I finally confided in the chaplain, he reassured me greatly by pointing out that Jesus had also been honest like that when he expressed his anguish without any reserve whatsoever. As he hung alone in the darkness on the cross, he felt (as I was also feeling) that his Father had abandoned him completely. So he summoned up his last scrap of strength and cried out into the lonely darkness, 'My God, My God, why have you abandoned me?' Just knowing he understood from experience how I was feeling was a vast comfort at the time.

## *An alternative way of communicating*

Even writing notes to God was quite beyond my friend Ruth after she had spent eighteen months nursing her husband through cancer:

'When he was gone, praying or going to church were "out" for at least six months. I felt brain dead, and the hymns unhinged me completely. So I used to creep into church during the week sometimes when no one was there, and sit quietly in a pew. Just being with God. Not saying anything, just reminding myself that he could see just how I felt. I always felt comforted as I walked back home.'

## Beware of the Blankets and Sheets

May, who lives alone, was signed off work for three months last year

---

*All your waves and billows have gone over me, and floods of sorrow pour upon me like a thundering cataract. Yet day by day the Lord also pours out his steadfast love upon me.* (Ps 42:7–8, LB)

with depression. 'I would wake up in the morning feeling so terrible that I couldn't face the day, so I often used to pull the bedclothes over my head and just stay there. Yet when I did make the effort to get up, even if dressing, washing and doing my hair exhausted me completely, I felt so much better for doing it. I only sat in the chair all day, but at least I felt more like a human being. Perhaps when you don't feel good, you can try and look good!'

Jenny found it helped if she made herself go out of her house, even if it was only to the shop on the corner. By the time she had chatted to someone about the weather and the price of butter, she felt more in touch with ordinary, everyday life.

## Beware of Amateur Psychiatrists

As we have seen in other stages of the Broken Teapot Syndrome, talking about how we feel is vital – but never more so than during depression. However, talking to the wrong people can be disastrous. There are far too many well-meaning people these days who see themselves as amateur psychiatrists. If we begin to open ourselves up to them they can go crashing around our subconscious minds in hobnail boots, or compound our sense of worthlessness by their condemnation. One nineteen-year-old girl who was being 'counselled' by someone like that was told to throw away all the drugs the doctor had prescribed because she was 'now healed'. However, she did not *feel* healed, and a week later she jumped in front of a train.

There are certain people who are experienced and recognised counsellors and, although they have received a training, they work under the control and guidance of the Holy Spirit. Secular counsellors and psychologists can help us to understand our hurts, but Jesus can actually heal them; and he seems to do this most often through the prayers of his servants. You are not alone: there is a whole network of people who want to allow the compassion of Jesus to flow through their personalities to help you. It is better to talk to an experienced counsellor than a hundred of the other kind.

---

*Let he who judges me, first walk two weeks in my moccasins.* (Red Indian proverb)

### Beware of the 'Hold Up' Factor

When we are severely depressed we carry such a vast burden of misery that we cannot add to it by considering the problems or needs of anyone else. *We* become the centre of our own universe, and see others only as they relate to us – what they do for us and give to us. Their problems, feelings or needs cease to exist, and we cannot reach out to them in order to give them any help or emotional support. We resemble the following diagram: looking to others to meet our needs, but unable to do anything in return.

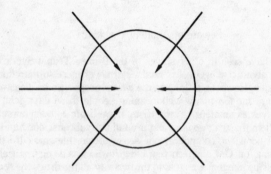

The opposite diagram represents a person before depression: receiving help and support, but able to give to others in return.

During the worst of the depression we cannot help but resemble the first diagram. As the depression lifts, however, the self-absorption can remain and become a way of life. Negative attitudes and self-centred thought patterns can be acquired during depression, and self-pity makes us feel everyone else must be better off than we are. Some people stay trapped like this permanently, so absorbed by their own needs and problems that they lose the habit of noticing that other people have pressures too. People trapped like this talk about themselves all the time, and demand so much from others that they drain them dry.

---

*This land that was desolate is become like the garden of Eden.* (Ezek. 36:35, AV)

---

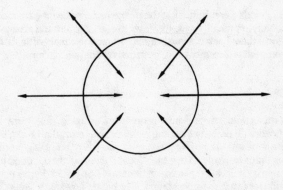

*Turning the arrows back outwards again*

My depression was definitely on the way out when it dawned on me that I was in danger of being trapped by this particular 'hold up' factor. I wrote one of my notes to God in my diary that day: 'This book is full of endless prayers for me, but I never seem to pray for other people any more, do I?' The realisation came because I had looked at Tony. It sounds odd, living with someone and *not* looking at them, but that day I had noticed how worn and tired his face looked, and I remember thinking, 'This depression has been horrible for me, but I bet it's been even worse for Tony.'

Sometime during the following week, my friend Grace rang to say she was coming to see me. She is the most sympathetic and sensitive friend I have ever had, and it is always easy (and safe) to pour out all my worries to her; but that day I made a conscious decision that I would also ask her how *she* was feeling, and then really listen when she told me.

The next step was to ring someone who I knew was feeling low as

*Some wandered in the trackless desert and could not find their way to a city to live in. They were hungry and thirsty and had given up all hope. Then in their trouble they called to the Lord, and he saved them from their distress. He led them by a straight road to a city where they could live. (Ps. 107:4–7, GNB)*

well. Sounds easy! But using the phone had terrified me for months. Gradually, in small ways, we have to start turning the arrows and pointing them back outwards again. I found it a real battle, but it is the only way to combat this destructive 'hold up' factor.

## The Challenge

All this could make some people say, 'But I've lost my self-confidence. I can't help being self-centred, now that I can't face meeting people.' Depression certainly robs us of our self-confidence, but is that loss really so terrible? Could it even be turned round to our advantage if it were placed in the hands of Jesus? Perhaps 'self'-confidence is not so important as most people nowadays think that it is. Maybe 'God'-confidence is what we need even more.

Surely in this stage God is asking:

- 'Will you allow me to come into the centre of your self-absorption? Will you let me fill the "self" part of you – the self-occupied, self-fulfilled, self-assertive, self-conscious place at the core of your being?'
- 'Will you let me be your confidence, in place of the self-confidence you have lost? Then together we can go out to other people – and you will be able to see them as I see them, and I will be able to meet their needs through you.'

'Blessed is the man who trusts in the Lord whose confidence is in him' (Jer. 17: 7, NIV).

One summer afternoon in 1989 I was sitting in my wheelchair overlooking the beach on which my children were playing. For some months I had been slightly depressed, and I had so hoped this holiday in Devon would see the end of it. By that time I had been ill for seven years, and the strain of coping with the pain and weakness on top of trying to be a good mum, write books and speak at

---

*He changed deserts into pools of water and dry land into flowing springs. He let hungry people settle there, and they built a city to live in. They sowed the fields and planted grapevines and reaped an abundant harvest.* (Ps. 107:35–37, GNB)

meetings was all proving a bit too much. (Those were the days when I was still trying to prove that I was not inadequate.)

As I sat there, I hated the thought of going home the next day and having to get back into 'life' again. The depression had certainly broken the small amount of self-confidence I had regained since I first became ill. I couldn't face the half-finished book that lurked in my computer and the speaking engagements that glared at me from my diary. I didn't pray; I just sat there gazing bleakly at the tide slapping and sucking round a red Devon rock just beyond the beach. Suddenly, I knew that Jesus himself was standing on that rock. I did not actually see him, but I knew he was there, and the sense of his presence was overwhelming. I am embarrassed to say that I did not dissolve into a flood of praise – instead, I told him all about my inadequacy and apprehension.

'Why do I always get so scared of doing things and why didn't you make me like all these powerful people who have so many wonderful gifts?' (In other words, 'Why couldn't I have taken after my parents?') Five words instantly popped into my head, and I knew without doubt they were his answer.

'All you need is me.' That puzzled me at first, then gradually I realised he wanted to be everything to me – not only to meet all my needs, but the needs of others through me. I wonder if Paul was describing this when he said, 'I am most happy, then, to be proud of my weaknesses, in order to feel the protection of Christ's power over me . . . For when I am weak, then I am strong' (2 Cor. 12:9–10, GNB).

Ten months later, Jesus healed me physically,* but I have never regained my self-confidence. I am still terrified before I have to stand up to speak or when I begin a writing project, but I am no longer trying desperately to cover up this sense of inadequacy. I see it as an asset, because it makes me turn to the Lord so he can make up for my deficiency.

* See *Unexpected Healing*, Chapter 15.

---

*Who is this coming up from the desert, leaning on her beloved?* (Song of Songs 8:5, LB)

## A Meditation

She stood shaking with fear in the middle of a huge, surging crowd of people. They were pushing and pulling each other – all eager for the best view – but no one ever touched her; they backed away when they recognised who she was. It had been like that ever since the bleeding began twelve years ago, and she had been living with despair ever since. Was it a baby she had lost? A foetus torn prematurely away from the wall of her uterus, leaving a wound that simply refused to heal? The constant bleeding, coupled with her tears of regret, had slowly sapped away her strength, leaving her listless, weary and ill. In her culture, bleeding like that meant she was unclean, and so was anyone that she touched. There could be no more intimacy with her husband – she was not even allowed to cook his food or wash his clothes.

At first they had hoped one of the big city doctors from Jerusalem might be able to help. She had gone from one to the other, using up all her dowry, but their treatments had been humiliating, exhausting and painful. Worst of all, none of them had been successful. Her husband had given up on her – he was within his rights to do so – and now she was alone, her money all gone, and repeated disappointment had gradually killed her hope. She was excluded from her community, the market, the synagogue, and even the temple itself. There was no role for her in life, she was useless, discarded like rubbish, and left to the rot of despair.

Sometimes the emotionally injured feel like that too; their wounds never seem to heal, and over the years they go on bleeding until all their joy has drained away and the perpetual twilight of chronic depression closes around them. Like that woman, they too can go from this person to that in a fruitless search for healing. They expose their souls to painful internal examinations and conflicting diagnoses, until their inner resources of dignity and self-respect have all been absorbed. So often these people are also outcasts in our Christian communities, labelled 'the church problem', and hastily avoided whenever possible.

Jesus was closer now. The clamouring crowd closed in around him, demanding his attention with shrill, excited cries. She had come here to ask for his help as well, yet he was really the last person she wanted to face. This man who said he was the Son of God must surely shrink away from her uncleanness. And all those years of hope deferred had made her wary. Suppose he could not help her either? But there was no one else to turn to now; she was at the end of her endurance and had nothing left to lose.

Standing always made the pain worse, and she was doubled over with it by the time she reached him, almost crawling in the dirt and dust. He had walked on past by the time she managed to reach out towards him and clutch at the hem of his coat.

He stopped. He always stops. If only we would go to him directly instead of putting our hope in all those 'big names' and 'spiritual superstars'. He cannot resist faith that goes to him directly and reaches out a hand in desperation. People who are at the end of themselves can always touch him instantly – as she did. All his undivided attention was hers at that very moment. It can also be ours when we reach out. He may not always help us in the way we expect or as quickly as we would wish, but in his way and in his time he always helps.

He did not draw back disgusted by her as other men would have done. He spoke to her gently, using the most tender and personal name he could have chosen. He called her 'daughter'. Then he sent her away with his own peace resting on her, like a fresh set of clothes or a new identity. No longer just the 'community problem', she was clean. He had taken away her despair, and in exchange he gave her back hope and dignity.

## A Prayer

### *For a grey day*

*'Come to me all you who are weary from carrying heavy burdens of worthlessness, regret and chronic misery, and I will give you "a crown of beauty instead of ashes, the oil of gladness instead of mourning, and a garment of praise instead of a spirit of despair".'* (Isa. 61:3, NIV)

Lord Jesus, it's an awful place, this wilderness: bleak, empty, desolate. The wind blows dust into my eyes so I can't see where I'm going, and I walk round and round in endless circles, getting nowhere. I'm so tired I just want to stop and crawl away under some rock, but I'm afraid I might be lost for ever if I stop walking. I keep on tripping over jagged little stones on the pathway, and feeling compelled to stoop down and pick them up. These endless stones are my 'if onlys':

- 'If only I . . .'
- 'If only I hadn't . . .'
- 'If only I could still . . .'
- 'If only he was here . . .'
- 'If only I had more . . .'

Collecting these 'if onlys' has become compulsive, and I can't seem to stop. I stuff them into my pockets as I walk, but they are heavy now, there are so many of them. They weigh me down and I'm too tired to carry them any longer.

Can I give all these 'if onlys' to you, Lord? Could I place them into your hands like the little pebbles and shells a child collects and presents to its father for safe keeping? I know that whenever I manage to give you my worthless things, you always give me something far better in exchange. So in the place of all these 'if onlys' and 'might have beens', I will receive from you the new life you said you would give me. The way I feel right now, I find it hard to believe a new life is possible, but I receive it from you by faith – and I thank you.

### For a black day

*'Come to me all you who are torn by anguish and terrible mental distress because I know how it feels . . .'*

*'Then Jesus went to a place called Gethsemane . . . He began to show grief and distress of mind and was deeply depressed. Then he said to them, "My soul is very sad and deeply grieved, so that I am almost dying of sorrow".'* (Matt. 26:36–38, AMP)

> *'And being in an agony of mind . . .'* (Luke 22:44, AMP)

> *'And he took with Him Peter and James and John, and began to be struck with terror and amazement and deeply troubled and depressed. And He said to them, "My soul is exceedingly sad – overwhelmed with grief so that it almost kills me".'* (Mark 14:33–34, AMP)

Lord, nothing seems to help when I am bound here like this at the very bottom of the deepest pit in the darkest part of the valley I am being forced to struggle through. I can see the faces of my friends peering down at me from high above my head – they are right up there in the sunlight, anxiously watching as I squirm in agony down here below them. *But they can't understand.*

I am glad you are not a God who looks down on me like that, without knowing how it feels. Just remembering that you have been here in this same pit before me is my only shred of comfort at this moment. Yes, that helps so much.

## Perhaps the Lord Might Respond Like This

'You are not alone in that bleak place. I am with you to shield and guard you, even when you cannot feel me near. You think of yourself as useless rubbish, flung away in that wasteland, but to me, who made the entire universe, you are the very apple of my eye; the focus of my attention. I know you find it hard just now to believe that I love you, but I long for you to accept that I do, by faith. I want you to know that I love you now, just as you are this moment. I am not waiting to love you one day when I have rebuilt you and made your life productive and beautiful again. You are the apple of my eye, and there is nothing that you could ever do that would make me love you any more than I do at this moment, because my love for you is complete.'

*Even when we are too weak to have any faith left, he remains faithful to us and will help us for he cannot disown us who are part of himself, and he will always carry out his promises to us.* (2 Tim. 2:13 LB)

## STOP FOR A MOMENT

*One of the nastiest things about the Broken Teapot Syndrome is the
feeling of being worth nothing in the world and forgotten by other
people. 'God can't be interested in me,' we think, 'because I'll never be
able to do anything big or important for him.' However, Jesus tells us
that this is absolutely not true.*

*That summer when we were in Devon, I felt just like that. It was
most frustrating to be in a paradise of cliffs, beaches and lazy blue sea
and to have no energy to do more than sit gazing blankly out of the
window. Right in front of me was a very high hedge, and among its
shiny green leaves lived several billion sparrows – well, it seemed that
many to me. I even tried to count them one day, but they acted like
sheep and sent me to sleep instantly.*

*As the days slid by, I became increasingly fascinated by those
sparrows and the way they repeated the same sequence of activities
over and over again throughout each hour of the day. Their routine
was always the same:*

*Hop down from the hedge, peck, flutter back up again.*
*Hop down, peck, flutter back up.*
*Hop down, peck, flutter back up.*
*Hop down, peck, . . . flutter back up.*

*And so on, probably thousands of times a day. The sparrows only
seemed to take a break when it was time to roost in the hedge for the
night.*

*A friend had lent me some sermon tapes for the holiday, and most
of them were by a cousin of mine, the Rev. David Pawson. One drowsy,
hot afternoon I was listening to one as I watched the inevitable activity
in the hedge, then suddenly I heard him mention sparrows: 'Are not
two little sparrows sold for a penny? Yet not one of them will fall to the
ground without your Father's leave and notice. Even the very hairs of
your head are all numbered. Fear not then; you are of more value than
many sparrows' (Matt. 10:29–31, AMP).*

*David went on to explain that in biblical times the normal use of
the phrase 'fall to the ground' did not mean 'die and fall to the
ground', but should really have been translated 'hop to the ground'.
He then went on to say, 'It is just conceivable that a loving God might
be touched by the tragic death of a poor little sparrow as it keels over
and falls off its perch, but that is not what Jesus was saying. He
meant that every time each individual sparrow hops to the ground,*

*God knows about it, and is watching with complete attention.'*

*I stopped my cassette player, too amazed to take in anything further. God Almighty knew each one of those sparrows in the hedge individually, and watched its 'hop down, peck, flutter back up' routine every time it ran through it – each and every day of its life. Multiply that by all the sparrows that 'hop down, peck, flutter back up' in every corner of the earth and you really begin to see what a staggering thing Jesus was saying. It occurred to me that Jesus must have enjoyed watching birds as much as I do, because on another occasion he said, 'Look at the birds of the air . . . your heavenly Father feeds them. Are you not much more valuable than they?' (Matt. 6:25–26, NIV.) The value of an object is measured by the price someone is prepared to pay for it. Two sparrows were only worth one penny, but Jesus thought you and I so valuable that he was prepared to give up all the riches of heaven for us.*

# GUILT

Feelings of guilt, remorse and endless regret play a very large part in the Broken Teapot Syndrome. There are two distinct types of guilt: genuine guilt, when we know for sure that we are to blame for breaking the 'teapot', and false guilt, which is simply a reaction to grief. This counterfeit version traps people on an endless treadmill of self-reproach:

'It's all my fault, if only I'd noticed he wasn't well, and *made* him go to the doctor.'

'I wish I'd gone on that holiday he was always talking about; now it's too late.'

'Perhaps he wouldn't have left me if I'd lost a bit of weight or kept the house a bit tidier.'

'I'm always a failure. Nothing I do ever seems to succeed.'

'Why, oh why, did I lend him the money to buy that motorbike?'

'It must be my fault.'

The last quote is often how parents of handicapped children feel, or patients who receive a grim diagnosis. They seem to feel it is a punishment for some real or imagined failure in the past. People who have been raped or abused may also feel that they were secretly to blame for what happened:

'For three years my eighteen-year-old step-brother used to abuse me sexually,' Penny told me. 'He had a knife, and he said he'd kill me if I didn't go with him to the shed on the allotments and do as he said.

---

*Mere sorrow which sits and weeps out its regrets is not repentance. Repentance is sorrow converted into action.*
(David Augsburger)

I was only eight when it started. Ever since, I've always felt this awful feeling of guilt, like a big black cloud hanging over my head and shoulders. I never dared tell my mum or teacher what was happening because I thought they would say it was my fault, and I suppose that I thought so too, really.

'At church when the word "sinner" was used, I always thought, "that's me". Anything that went wrong in my life, like breaking my leg on holiday or losing my job, I always thought it was only what I deserved. It was years before I dared tell my doctor about the abuse, and when I also told him about my feelings of guilt he just shrugged and said it was perfectly normal – and that people often feel like that after they've been raped or abused.'

The doctor was right: false guilt is normal after trauma, but when we have put God in control of our mending process there must come a time when we climb off this irritating treadmill and ask him to set us free from our misery. He can certainly do this, so long as we are willing to be honest with him. Penny went on struggling with her black cloud of condemnation until, during counselling, she was encouraged to ask God if there was a more valid reason for her feelings of guilt. Almost at once, the word 'hatred' came into her mind.

We are not responsible for what happens to us, but we *are* responsible for our feelings and reactions, i.e. the resentment, self-pity and anger that we feel as a result of the incident. Penny had hated her step-brother, both at the time of the abuse and ever since. She had also implacably refused to forgive him for what he had done to her. Before she could finally be free from the effects of his abuse, she had to repent and let go of her hate. Someone we refuse to forgive is always there, handcuffed to us perpetually, and the only way the chains can be broken is by forgiveness. The difference that this 'liberation' made to Penny's life was enormous, and she found that her false guilt totally disappeared when the genuine guilt that had been hidden beneath it was dealt with at last.

---

*If we say that we have not sinned, we make God out to be a liar, and his word is not in us.* (1 John 1:10, GNB)

## The Red Light on My Washing-machine

During the last thirty years, our permissive society has decided to abolish guilt, declaring it to be old-fashioned and harmful. Yet genuine guilt is a much maligned emotion. On my washing-machine is a red light that flashes when something is going wrong. When I see it, I know I must stop the machine and call in the expert quickly before irrevocable damage is done, and the whole machine has to be thrown on the scrap heap. God built guilt into our systems to act like that red light. Untreated sin is fatally dangerous to us, because it cuts us off from him. On the other hand, guilt can be instantly removed by 'calling in the expert', God himself. He really can set us free from guilt, and it seems such a tragedy that so many people struggle with it unnecessarily.

Pat was told her guilt was 'all part of grieving', so for four years it spoilt her happiness completely. Her first marriage had been a disaster, and it was only for the children's sake that she and Reg had remained under the same roof. When he died suddenly in his early forties, Pat was able to marry a man she had secretly loved for ten years. 'On paper' this new marriage looked perfect, but something seemed to be making Pat edgy and depressed.

'I keep thinking I've got no right to be happy,' she told a friend who was a social worker.

'Guilt is such a self-indulgent emotion,' replied her friend. The comment did not help Pat at all – it left her feeling guilty for feeling guilty! In desperation she began to attend a nearby church, and the minister was finally able to help her. Under all that false guilt lay a genuine need to be forgiven for her part in the unhappy relationship. Pat had always seen herself as the 'injured party' in her first marriage, blaming everything that went wrong on to Reg. She had not allowed herself to feel a single qualm about deceiving him with her secret affair. She was greatly helped by writing a list of all the ways in which she felt she had failed Reg – the sheer length of the list astonished her – and once she was able to ask for forgiveness, all her long-denied guilt was gone. 'I suddenly feel like

---

*But if we confess our sins to God . . . he will forgive us our sins and purify us from all our wrongdoing.* (1 John 1:9, GNB)

it's spring,' she said, when she gave her testimony in church the morning she was baptised.

## When We Break the 'Teapot' Ourselves

What about the guilt someone feels when he or she *is* responsible for a terrible tragedy?

'I met my friend on the way back from the shops and we got talking. I was feeling fed up that day, what with the baby crying all night and Tim grizzling all day. Tim was just three, and he hated me talking to my friends. He started pulling at my skirt – pestering to go home – and I got cross. He started mucking round on the pavement with her two kids, who were a lot older than Tim. The next thing I remember was that awful screech of brakes behind me. I should have kept watching him; I knew that road was dangerous. I'll never forgive myself.'

For five years after Tim's funeral Janet hardly left her house. All the things she had once enjoyed, she felt she should no longer do, but of course she gave herself other reasons for giving them up. Watching television made her eyes hurt, gardening strained her back, knitting was too tiring, and she never felt well enough to make love. In fact, she never felt well at all. The doctor could find no physical reason for that, but subconsciously she felt she had no right to be happy or healthy ever again – since it was her inattention that cost Tim his life.

So how did Janet walk out of the ruins of her 'teapot'? Only one person was willing to go on being Janet's friend, in spite of constant rebuffs, and that was Sue, who was a Christian. Gradually she helped Janet to see that Jesus stepped down into our world so that we need not be destroyed by guilt. Janet had always thought of Jesus as 'a good man' who showed us what God was like, so she was startled when Sue explained who he really was.

---

*Sometimes we remain unhealed because we nurture the picture of ourselves as victim and the other as monster, we are disturbed when we see that we too may need to be forgiven for nursing our bitterness and in some cases building a whole life-style around it.* (Russ Parker)

---

'People began to be angry with him for claiming to be God by saying he could forgive sins,' Sue told her. 'So they killed him, but he did not need to die. It was not some terrible accident: he planned it all in advance. At any moment while they were beating him, punching him and hammering great iron nails through his hands and feet, he could have summoned billions of angels to his rescue, but he chose to remain suspended up there in agony on the cross until the torture ended in his death. He did all that because he wanted to lift all our guilt away by taking the punishment that really ought to have been ours for all the things we regret. He took the rap so we could be free.'

It took Janet months to absorb it all, but Sue 'fed truth to her with a teaspoon' and slowly Janet realised that Jesus did not want her to go on carrying that terrible load of shame and reproach. He wanted her to:

- bring it to him
- tell him about it, holding nothing back
- tell him how sorry she was
- give him the whole lot – and then let it go
- receive his forgiveness
- walk away free, leaving it all with him

Janet was sitting in Sue's garden one hot summer's afternoon when she finally made her once-and-for-all transaction. She gave to Jesus all her guilt, and then received in return his forgiveness – and it was done, for ever.

'It's over,' she said with a deep sigh of relief, and she lay back in her deckchair and allowed the sun to bathe her in warmth. 'It feels like God's love pouring all over me,' she said happily. 'I never need to feel bad like that again.'

---

*At last he came to his senses and said, '. . . I will get up and go to my father and say, Father, I have sinned against God and against you. I am no longer fit to be called your son . . .' He was still a long way from home when his father saw him; his heart was filled with pity, and he ran, threw his arms round his son, and kissed him.* (Luke 15:17–20, GNB)

## How Do We Know We Did It Right?

Repentance and receiving forgiveness are internal and happen secretly in our hearts, and therefore some of us need to do something external and tangible to prove to ourselves that it has happened. Once I was feeling very bad about something particularly nasty that I had done, and somehow a muttered 'Sorry Lord, please forgive me' just did not seem enough. So I wrote a long letter to the Lord, describing it all in detail and how I felt about it. Then I got in the car and drove 10 miles to Mayfield, the beautiful Sussex village where we used to live before I was ill.

In the churchyard stands a huge wooden cross that has always been one of my 'special places'. Carrying my letter, I walked very slowly up to the cross and knelt down in its shadow. Then I read my letter out loud to the Lord, and after I had received his forgiveness I added, 'I'm going to leave all this guilt here with you now, Lord, and when I walk away I won't take it with me.' So I screwed up the piece of paper tightly and buried it in the loose earth at the foot of the cross. When I finally drove home I felt wonderful, and every time I was tempted to feel guilty about that same old sin, I remembered I had left it behind, buried for ever.

### *Beware of the fire alarm!*

Some people set light to their letters and lists, or even flush them down the loo. One friend of mine tied hers round a rock and hurled it into the sea. Others have used a stone to represent all the things they are ashamed of, and when they have confessed them, they drop the stone over a cliff or throw it away in the dustbin.

All these 'visual aids' are helpful, but a friend of ours once had a very embarrassing moment after using one of them. George teaches RE in a boarding school for girls, and one day he was trying to explain what happens to our sins at the cross. The class compiled a list of all the things they wanted to 'dump', and George stuck the paper on a metal cross that stood on his desk, and then set light to it. He hardly had time to blow out the match before the smoke alarms

---

*Our love for him comes as a result of his loving us first.* (1 John 4:19, LB)

went off, and within minutes the entire school, several hundred strong, was lined up neatly in the courtyard while four fire engines hurtled up the school drive. Poor George had a terrible time explaining things to the Fire Chief!

### Finding someone to witness the transaction

Finding another person to act as a witness often helps to make this invisible give-and-take feel more real. James 5:16 tells us, 'Confess your sins to one another and pray for one another, so that you will be healed' (GNB). Even though we know it is Jesus who forgives our sins, we cannot see or hear him, so it can help to have someone there to represent him. This person listens to our confession on his behalf, then tells us in words we can hear that we really are forgiven. Finally, he or she prays for healing for us and for others from the wounds our sins have caused. Knowing that our witness believes we are really forgiven helps us should the flames of our own faith flicker in a draught of doubt.

## Fighting Feelings with Faith

Our faith does flicker. Our minds tell us we are forgiven instantly when we repent, but we don't find it so easy to *feel* forgiven. A man who has had his leg amputated often goes on feeling pain in that leg long after it has been removed. He knows that his knee or his foot isn't there any more, but it can take quite a long time for his mind to realise that. The same applies to guilt. It is this clash of faith and feelings that most of us find so difficult, so here are a few methods that people have found helpful in retraining their minds and emotions:

> *The Lord is merciful and loving, slow to become angry and full of constant love. He does not keep on rebuking; he is not angry for ever . . . As far as the east is from the west, so far does he remove our sins from us. As a father is kind to his children, so the Lord is kind to those who honour him.* (Ps. 103:8–13, GNB)

1. Talking to yourself is not always a sign of madness; it can actually help to 'reprogramme' the mind. If we are told something often enough and firmly enough, we soon begin to believe it. Telling ourselves is just as effective! So try talking under your breath to these feelings of guilt. Whenever they bother you, say, 'I am *not* guilty any more. Jesus took all that blame when he died for me. I am free of whatever I did, or fear that I did.'

2. Another excellent way of combating the guilt waves is to turn them instantly into a prayer of gratitude by saying, 'Thank you, Jesus, for dying to rescue me from these horrible feelings.'

3. A friend of mine who was having a terrible job kicking his guilt habit wrote this on a large piece of paper: 'If we confess our sins to God, he will keep his promise and do what is right: he will forgive us our sins and purify us from all our wrongdoing' (1 John 1:9, GNB). Every morning when he got out of bed, he claimed the promise by standing on the piece of paper and repeating the verse out loud, then he added, 'I am forgiven, regardless of how I feel, because God said I am and he's never broken a single promise yet.' Doing something physical like that helped him to realise his freedom was real.

4. Living with someone who constantly abuses us verbally can be devastating, but some people endure it *from themselves*. An internal abusive voice keeps up a continuous tirade of accusations. 'Look at the mess you've made of your life. You're useless! You've blown it so often you can't expect God to forgive you yet again.' We simply do not have to put up with abuse like that. We should tell that invisible bully that Jesus does not think we are worthless. He told us to forgive our brother seventy times seven, so it stands to reason he's going to do even better himself!

### Beware of the 'Hold Up' Factor

Once I rescued a little field mouse just as he was about to be mauled by our ginger cat. I scooped him up, physically unharmed, and

> God cannot work His greatest good in a heart that harbours a grudge. Grace may flow like a river, but a grudge in your heart may well dam the stream. (Selwyn Hughes)

carried him back to his cornfield in an empty Marmite jar. Even when he was safely on the ground in familiar territory, he still stayed inside the darkness of the jar, shivering with fright because he could not believe he was really free to live again. It is tragic that so many Christian people seem to remain permanently trapped by guilt because they are never quite sure they are forgiven.

One evening I was asked to speak on the subject of 'Peace in a Troubled World' to a ladies' coffee club. I arrived at the hall, nervous as usual, and sat down in the front row beside a red and grey wheelchair, very like the one I used to have myself. I was soon talking to its occupant, Monika, who was one of those chirpy people, always ready with bright smile or a joke. Yet I sensed that her cheerfulness was only a mask, and it was a real effort to keep it fixed in place.

The time came at last to climb on to the rickety platform and give the talk, and after it was over quantities of homemade cakes and clotted cream were served by way of a reward to the long-suffering audience! I did a lightning calorie count, and decided to flee temptation by going back to find Monika – and it was then that I discovered her mask had slipped. It was rather unnerving to look suddenly right inside the real person. She seemed to want to talk, even though I guessed she had not found talking about *real* things easy for a very long time.

She told me she had been a 'manse kid', for her father was a Baptist minister. 'People put me on a pedestal; they used to say to their children, "Why can't you be good like Monika, the minister's daughter?" I hated it because I knew I wasn't good at all. I did all the right things, sang in the choir, and taught in the Sunday School, but when I was nineteen I discovered I was pregnant. I felt terrible. I really loved my dad – he was such a kind man. I knew what this would do to him. It was a country community, everyone would know. He would feel shamed in front of the whole district. I felt I couldn't do that to him so . . . so, I got rid of it.'

Her voice trailed away in a mist of unshed tears and she sat looking at me helplessly. 'I regretted it as soon as it was done,' she continued at last. 'I felt such a terrible feeling of loss. I've never had another baby. A few months later I found out about the MS. That

---

*The more we see our sinfulness, the more we see God's abounding grace forgiving us.* (Rom. 5:20, LB)

was my punishment, wasn't it, being stuck in this wheelchair? A life sentence, but it's what I deserve.'

As Monika was talking I had been going cold all over. Suddenly, I could not keep silent any longer.

'Monika,' I said gently. 'You couldn't possibly think that God would send a horrible thing like multiple sclerosis as a punishment, could you?'

'Why not?' she said dully. 'I killed my baby just because I was ashamed to own it.'

'But Monika, you told me you were a "manse kid" – your father was a minister. Surely you must have heard him explain that Jesus took the punishment for *everything* and *anything* we could ever do wrong? Haven't you ever asked him to forgive you?'

'Of course I have!' she retorted furiously. 'Every time I've been in a church since. But he still hasn't forgiven me.'

'But he forgave you the very first time you asked him,' I told her. 'In fact, you've been forgiven for years. God punished *Jesus* for that abortion, so he would not punish you as well by sending the MS. You are forgiven regardless of whether you feel forgiven or not.' Then I found myself saying, 'Perhaps you just couldn't forgive yourself!'

Slowly, a tinge of colour began to seep into Monika's white cheeks. Her smile followed – and this time it was a real smile that came from deep inside her, not a mask that was just stuck on the outside. I wish I had a photograph of how she looked at that moment.

'So the MS just happened,' she said. 'It wasn't God's judgement after all.' At that point, the caretaker came over to us and jangled his keys menacingly. Nearly everyone else had gone home long ago.

As I was helping her into her specially adapted car, she looked up at me and said, 'Yes, you're right. I couldn't forgive myself – in fact, I almost *wanted* to be punished. Perhaps I wouldn't let Jesus take the punishment because I felt I ought to suffer myself. What a fool I've been!' I have not met Monika again since then, but I did speak to her minister's wife about a year later.

'She's like a different person since that long talk you two had in the village hall,' she told me. 'She never seemed to be able to accept the

---

*All who will take God's gift of forgiveness and acquittal are kings of life because of this one man, Jesus Christ.* (Rom. 5:17, LB)

MS before; it always made her a bit bitter under all that cheerfulness. But she's thrown herself into life since then. She goes to the local MS group, and is really using it as a means to reach out to others.

People say 'I'll never forgive myself for this' after some tragedy – and the world also expects us to have that kind of attitude. They feel, as we often do, that we have no right to be happy after damaging someone else's happiness. God knows we don't deserve to be happy either, but because he longs for us to be happy, he has taken the blame and the shame that we deserve and put them on to Jesus instead. When we insist on punishing ourselves, we are really insulting him by refusing the precious gift of happiness that cost Jesus so much. The trouble for many people is possibly because they are not quite sure that God really loves them personally.

## The Challenge

Perhaps God could be asking us these questions:

- 'Do you really believe that I love you?'
- 'Do you believe that you do not have to earn my love, and that I do not withhold my love until I have made you more worthy of it?'
- 'Do you believe you are safe in my love, so there is nothing you could ever do that would stop me loving you?'
- 'Do you believe that my love for you is personal, and not simply part of a vague benevolence for all human beings? That it is you, yourself, that I love, and that I have even numbered all the hairs on your head?'

If you have any hesitation over answering 'yes' to any of these questions, turn to page 142 and you might discover why.

## What About the Person We Hurt?

Does our forgiveness from God depend on our saying 'sorry' to the person we hurt? Definitely not, because in certain cases it would be

---

*Right actions in the future are the only true apology for wrong actions in the past.* (David Augsburger)

impossible, or even unwise, to do so. I think, however, that God wants to see on our part a *willingness* to apologise, to restore the relationship and, where possible, to make restitution.

There is no doubt that when we can manage to say we are sorry, we so often take a huge leap forward in our relationship with God – and experience a tremendous release of joy. Maureen, a friend of mine, saw that happen in a rather special way.

She was in her home one afternoon with only her cleaning lady. She had always had a terrible fear of being burgled, so it felt like a nightmare come true when two men pretending to be window cleaners forced their way into the house. They dragged both women into the kitchen, gagged them, then threw them roughly to the floor and tied them to the leg of the table. The beautiful house was ransacked, and everything that was valuable was loaded into the 'window cleaners' van and driven away. When Maureen's husband discovered the two women, they had been left for five hours struggling to breathe through their tight gags, and were stiff, cold and in pain from their many bruises.

The police caught the two men and they were eventually found guilty and sentenced, but Maureen had been so badly shaken by the whole incident that she was ill for a long time afterwards. She was a Christian, but the very thought of trying to forgive her attackers was difficult. Her vicar suggested that it might help her struggle if she began to pray for them, and this she did every morning for the next two years. Then one day she received this remarkable letter:

> Dear Mrs Parkside,
> I am one of the men who did that break-in at your house. Since I've been in here, I have received a lot of help from the chaplain. I now feel I want to become a committed born-again Christian. He feels it might be a good idea if I wrote and told you that I am very sorry for frightening you that day. I hope you will forgive me.

Maureen was thrilled, and she was able to visit the prison and meet her attacker, whose Christian faith has been flourishing ever since. Incidentally, Maureen's health steadily improved from the time she began praying for her burglars.

---

*There is now no condemnation for those who are in Christ Jesus.* (Rom. 8:1, NIV)

That was a story with a happy ending, but on certain occasions it can be sheer self-indulgence to dump our guilt and pain on someone we have seriously sinned against when they knew nothing of it beforehand. There are no absolute rules, because people are all different, so it is vital to seek the advice of someone wise before doing anything hastily.

### It can be risky

There is a particular risk involved when the victim is not yet willing to forgive us. A friend of ours had been having a long-standing disagreement with an older member of his church, who he had always accused of being a 'stick in the mud' and holding the whole church back from blessing. The argument had been rumbling on for a long time, but our friend began to feel sure that the Lord was showing him that he had hurt the other man a great deal over the years. He even began to see that what he had thought was his zeal for God could have been youthful arrogance, and his tactlessness had started the whole row in the first place. So very nervously he went round to his 'enemy's' house and gingerly rang the doorbell.

'I've just popped round to say I'm sorry for all the distress I must have caused you,' he said, when the door opened.

The old man glared down at him from the step and replied, 'Well, it's about time too! And while you're here there's a few things I'd like to get off my chest.' Half-an-hour later he was still talking.

Our friend managed to react in a very Christ-like way by shutting his mouth tight and refusing to defend himself (see Matt. 27:14), but when the old man finally drew breath, he looked at him directly and said, 'Look, I'm really sorry, but all I can say is, please will you forgive me?'

A second later the door was slammed in his face, and he crawled home wishing he had never gone round there in the first place. Did he do the right thing by 'going to his brother'? At the time, he may not have thought so, but looking back a year later, he could see that his spiritual life, which had been drab and dull for a long time, suddenly sprang back into life after that painful interview.

### Danger! High risk of infection!

That incident taught me that there are few things calculated to make anyone feel more of a fool than asking forgiveness and having the request ignored or refused. At best it leaves us with a sense of loss and incompleteness, and at worst we can become so hurt and bitter we 'catch' our victim's unforgiving attitude. Perhaps when we have done everything on our part to put matters right and the person still won't forgive, then we just have to remember that it then becomes his or her problem, not ours. We are free of it for ever.

---

## A Meditation

He never intended to be dishonest, but the expenses of keeping up such a high position were enormous. They had to have a house close to the palace, and a large one at that, because of all the parties and official receptions they needed to give. Then there was the estate up in the Judean hills – they had to have that to escape when pressures at work were high, and of course the children needed seaside holidays, so the house by Lake Galilee was vital. His wife needed expensive clothes and jewellery to maintain their status, and the cost of keeping thousands of slaves and servants was astronomical. None of it could be avoided, but paying for it all was a nightmare.

At first he only 'borrowed' occasionally from the King's accounts. Juggling figures from one ledger to another was easy for him – he was in charge of all the royal finance – and naturally he meant to pay everything back. However, as the children grew larger, so did the bills, and he was dipping deeper and deeper into the King's exchequer. He was far too important for anyone to check up on him, and the King himself was away abroad most of the time.

Then came the day when he realised that his debt was so enormous that he could not repay it even if he sold everything he had, and it would no longer be possible to conceal the deficit when the King next returned home.

He sat in his marble office shaking with fear. He was ruined. He would lose everything and he faced nothing now but public disgrace and death in the debtors' prison. The awful thought of that dark, airless dungeon under the royal barracks kept him awake all that night. He had only been there once, but the memory haunted him still: hundreds of people herded together on straw like animals, trampling their own filth; naked in the darkness and the suffocating stench; dying of disease and starvation.

No! The prospect was appalling. His wife would be dragged there with him while the children would be sold as slaves. When he thought of what that would mean for his beautiful daughters, he gave up the pretence of sleep and paced up and down trying to make a plan. He must do something quickly – pay it back somehow. However, that morning the King returned unexpectedly and sent for the accounts. It was too late! The chancellor's time had run out. As he stood beside the King, watching as he worked slowly through the ledgers, he felt sick with apprehension.

'Guards!' The inevitable had happened: the debt was discovered. The soldiers had almost reached him, but just before he felt their hands seize him he flung himself down before the white marble throne.

'Please, Sire, show mercy!' he cried desperately. 'Give me time to pay!'

At first, as he huddled there, cringing on the floor, he thought the stress must have affected his mind. What he was hearing could not possibly be true. The footsteps of the guards died away into the distance, and he thought he heard the King's voice say,

'I forgive, let's forget all about it.' He was sure he was imagining it until he felt a hand gently pulling him to his feet. 'Come on, my friend,' smiled the King. 'We've got work to do, let's get back to these accounts.'

'Sire,' stammered the chancellor, 'I owe you millions.'

'I know,' said the King, 'but I said, let's forget it.'

'But surely you can't still want me to work for you?'

The King looked straight into his eyes and replied, 'I have forgiven you so much that I am sure you will serve me loyally for ever more.' The chancellor knelt once again, but this time it was to kiss the King's hand.

'I will always obey you, Sire,' he muttered.

'Will you?' replied the King softly. 'Then remember I want you to treat other people as I have treated you.'

'I will!' promised the chancellor, and backed out of the state apartments on a pair of very unsteady legs.

Home through the palace gardens he ran, bathed in sunshine and euphoria. It was springtime, and the world was full of flowers and new green hope for the future. He could live in peace again, free of the threat of slavery and that ghastly debtors' dungeon.

'It's all right!' he shouted, as he burst into his wife's bedroom, 'We're saved!'

She looked up at him crossly from the couch where she was

reclining, 'What on earth do you mean?' He had forgotten that she knew nothing about his debts, and as he told her the whole story he could see she did not believe him.

'You've been drinking again,' she said scornfully. 'The King would never write off a debt as big as that.'

'But he said he would!'

'He said he would,' she mimicked. 'And you believed him?'

'Well . . . yes,' he faltered uncertainly.

'You stupid man! You'll see, he'll go off again on his travels, and when he comes back he'll have changed his mind completely. Once he's had time to think, he'll realise what a fool he would be to trust a man like you. Why, you're nothing but a nasty little thief – why should he ever trust you again?'

'What shall I do?' he mumbled as he flopped down into a chair beside her.

'Raise the money to pay it all back, of course!' she snapped. 'And do it *quick*! You're supposed to be a financial genius, so start making some clever investments. We'll live simply for a while, and then when the King next comes home you can present him with his money.'

'If he hasn't changed his mind, he could be very insulted,' said the chancellor, as he remembered the way the King had smiled at him that morning. Then he added rather wistfully, 'He did *say* he'd forgiven me.'

'You've only got his word for that,' said his wife sharply.

As he walked back again through the palace gardens, he did not notice the flowers or the spring sunshine. His head was bent in thought as a thousand schemes chased themselves round his brain. Only the day before he had been asked to finance an expedition to discover new diamond mines in Ethiopia. There was a double fortune to be made, but he would have to raise the capital quickly before anyone else heard about it. 'I'll close on everyone who owes me a single groat,' he thought grimly. Just then, he looked up to see one of his young scribes hurrying towards him. 'And here's the first bird for plucking. He doesn't owe me much, but he'll serve as an example to the others, and frighten them into paying up quickly.'

'You have a debt to pay, young man,' he said sternly. The scribe had asked him for the loan a couple of years before. He was getting married and wanted to buy a small house. He should have had time enough to pay it back by now; but the young man's face turned white.

'Sir,' he said, 'please give me a little more time, my wife has just had our first baby and there were so many expenses. I'll pay you very soon, I promise.' But the chancellor lunged at him and grabbed him by the throat.

'I want that money by tomorrow morning!' he roared. 'Tomorrow – or else . . .'

'Sir, please, not the debtors' prison . . . my wife . . . the child?' He had fallen to his knees in the pathway and the chancellor had to step on to the grass to avoid him as he swept towards the palace. It was all most distasteful, but it had to be done – it was just part of the business world.

However, the young scribe was well liked in court circles and his wife was very beautiful. People felt outraged at the sight of them being hauled away by the guards as the bailiffs invaded their home. The plaintive cries of the baby added a final touch of pathos to the story that was soon buzzing about the palace. When the chancellor began demanding money from all and sundry, his already waning popularity plummeted and the indignation of the entire palace staff rose against him.

'Fancy treating his own scribe like that! Someone ought to make a complaint to the King!' And someone did.

'How could you do such a thing?' It was a very different royal face that confronted the chancellor now.

You can read how the story ended in Matthew 18:32–35 (GNB): '"You worthless slave!" he said. "I forgave you the whole amount you owed me, just because you asked me to. You should have had mercy on your fellow-servant, just as I had mercy on you." The King was very angry, and he sent the servant to jail to be punished . . . And Jesus concluded, "That is how my Father in heaven will treat every one of you unless you forgive your brother from your heart."'

If only the chancellor could have believed he had really been let off his debt, he would have been able to let others off their debts to him. In this story, was Jesus saying that when we believe God has forgiven us for so much, then the comparatively small wrongs that others do to us will be easy to forgive?

## A Prayer

*'Come to me all you who are tired of carrying a heavy load of shame and humiliation for "I am He who blots out and cancels your transgressions, and I will remember your sins no more".'* (Isa. 43:25, AMP)

Lord Jesus, I can't look up into your face. I feel too dirty, shameful, disgusting. My soul feels violated. I have been shamed, exposed and humiliated. I've got nowhere left to hide now everyone knows. I feel they blame me for what happened, and I'm always conscious of them whispering and looking at me oddly.

*'Come to me, for they said of me, "He had no dignity or beauty . . . We despised him and rejected him . . . we ignored him as if he were nothing. But he endured the suffering that should have been ours . . . Because of our sins he was wounded, beaten because of the evil we did. We are healed by the punishment he suffered, made whole by the blows he received".'* (Isa. 53:2–5, GNB)

Help me to look up at you. I know your body was abused and ill-treated by people who did not care what they were doing to you. You were left to hang up there, naked and exposed, while people stared curiously at you. People blame me for things that weren't my fault, but that is what they were doing to you too. Scornful faces and reproachful eyes surrounded you as well.

Help me to remember that although you were shamed up there on the cross, you were never shameful. Help me to remember that although I may be shamed, I am not shameful either, because you have made me pure and clean by what you did for me on that cross. I give you my wretchedness, so you can hold it with your own, and in exchange I receive your purity and innocence. I do not deserve it, but I receive it with grateful joy.

### Perhaps the Lord Might Respond Like This

'You are precious in my sight, and honoured, and I love you' (Isa. 43:4, AMP).

## STOP FOR A MOMENT

*I constantly meet active and enthusiastic Christians who secretly admit
that they have never felt sure that God really loves them. That was my
problem once, and I always ask them this question: 'How did you get
on with your parents?'*

*As we grow up, we seem to paint ourselves a portrait of God that
looks a lot like the adults who were important to us as children. We
think he will treat us as they always did. These personalised pictures
are always inaccurate, because none of us was brought up by perfect
people, yet we seem to base our concept of God's character on them
rather than on the Bible, and end up with a distorted view of what he is
like.*

*Try going through the following checklist and see if you can spot
yourself:*

- *Were your parents angry and abusive? Did you sometimes even
  suspect that they enjoyed hurting you? If so, you may find it difficult
  to be sure that God is not waiting round the corner ready to 'get you'
  or watching your pain from a distance with his arms folded.*
- *Did your parents love you, but feel it right to punish you often? If so,
  you may find it terribly hard to believe God really has forgiven your
  sin without* punishing you first.
- *Did they have impossibly high standards for you? Were they only
  pleased with you when you achieved high marks at school and won
  every possible race on sports day? Did you only feel worthy of their
  love when you were clean, quiet and being extremely good? If so, you
  may struggle constantly to please God, but never quite feel that you
  have. Perhaps you are the kind of person who can't say 'no' to any
  request for help and goes dashing around trying to do good, kind
  things in the hope that the more you achieve for God, the more he
  will love you.*
- *Were your parents very busy people who were always hurrying off to
  do important things somewhere else? Were you never allowed to
  'bother' your father with your little concerns? If so, you may think of
  God as cold, distant and remote, far too high above you to care how
  you feel.*
- *Were your parents moody, changeable and inconsistent? Perhaps
  one day they seemed to love you, and the next you were just in the
  way. If so, you may have a problem believing that God's love is
  changeless.*

- *Were your parents very loving people who were always looking after the needs of others in the caring professions, the church or at home with numerous brothers and sisters? If so, you may always feel that God must care far more about people who have big problems, so that you should not take up his time with your smaller worries.*
- *Did your parents split up? Perhaps the one you loved the most left and you felt abandoned? If so, you may find it hard to feel sure that God will not suddenly drop you.*
- *Did your parents adore you, sacrifice everything and everyone else for your needs, and fall over themselves running around to gratify your smallest whim? Did their whole existence revolve around you and you alone? If so, you may find it hard to accept that God loves you enough to say 'no' to your demands sometimes. To you, being loved always meant being given exactly what you wanted, so when things go wrong now you automatically think you have lost God's love.*

*We do not have to be bound by the erroneous thought patterns we inherited from childhood. It is vital that we chuck away these counterfeit portraits of God, and begin looking at the genuine picture that the Bible paints. If you are still struggling over all this, try repeating one of the following verses three times a day – it's a bit like taking medicine!*

*I have loved you with an everlasting love; I have drawn you with loving-kindness.* (Jer. 31:3, NIV)

*I will never leave you; I will never abandon you.* (Heb. 13:5, GNB)

*Can a mother forget the baby at her breast and have no compassion on the child she has borne? Though she may forget, I will not forget you!* (Isa. 49:15, NIV)

# 8

# QUESTIONING AND BARGAINING

When Babs lost her nineteen-year-old son in a motorbike crash, it was yet another chapter in a whole series of disasters that had been hitting her family for the last three years.

'Why should it all happen to such nice people?' Everyone in the district seemed to be saying something like that, and when Babs went to see her vicar she was certainly right in the middle of the stage of questioning and bargaining.

'Life's just one gigantic "Why?"' she said miserably. 'Sometimes I think the Lord must be testing us – trying to teach us something. And that makes me furious. Why should my son lose his life just so I'll learn something I didn't want to learn anyway? But then I tell myself that God doesn't do horrid things like that, so it must be Satan attacking us. That makes me scared stiff, because if he's running amok, then what's he going to do to us next? Someone suggested a curse might have been put on the family, and yet another friend was convinced that it was all because of some sin in a previous generation. I'm so confused. I keep saying to the Lord, "I'll do anything you want, go anywhere you like, but just don't let anything else go wrong for our family."'

---

*Thousands follow Christ when he gives them what they want, few follow him when he confronts them with what he wants.* (Selwyn Hughes)

## The Law of Cause and Effect

Poor Babs, she was hurting so badly, and groping around desperately for an explanation. Most of us human beings feel safer and more in control of our lives if we can provide neat answers for everything that happens. Right from our earliest childhood, 'why' and 'because' go hand in hand:

'Don't touch the fire.'

'Why?'

'Because it will burn you.'

As adults, we feel that if we could only discover the cause of our problems, we might be able to put things right – or at least avoid it happening again.

So naturally anyone going through the Broken Teapot Syndrome is full of questions, but so often there are no easy answers to life's greatest tragedies. When insurance companies can't find a culprit to blame for a disaster they call it an 'act of God', but for people who believe in a God of tenderness and compassion that answer creates a thousand new questions.

'Surely he couldn't be behind all this?' we think, as we frantically clutch at our disappearing faith. 'I wouldn't put my worst enemy through such misery – and God is supposed to love me.'

Perhaps people with a strong faith find this stage of the grieving process even more difficult than it would be, say, for an atheist. We believe that God is in control of the universe and also the tiniest details of our lives, so why, when he has the power to protect us, has he allowed all this to happen? The stage of questioning can feel like a terrible onslaught to our faith, just at a time when we are most vulnerable.

## We May Ask Questions

We must give ourselves permission to ask 'Why?' because God does not want mechanical robots or mindless 'yes men'. We also need to let ourselves feel the confusion and the frustration, and not bottle it all up with a label saying 'Poison, do not touch'. God gave us minds,

---

*Seek his face and not his hand.* (R.T. Kendall)

and we should use them – instead of passively accepting the party line of our particular church circle.

It can be destructive to go round asking numerous different people, 'Why is this happening to me?' They will all be happy to tell you (in fact, many won't even wait for you to ask), and they will all give you advice on how to put things right. The only problem will be that all their opinions may be different, and if you try to follow all their suggestions you will soon feel demented! (I know, I fell into this trap myself!)

As I have said before, a Christian counsellor or your own minister is probably the best person to help, because there may well be things you need to discover. God never sends these calamities to punish us, but he can use them to open our eyes to sins that we may have buried away, unconfessed. Sometimes there is another cause that his power can deal with, such as a curse, occult interference or some binding from past generations. These things are worth investigating because they can so easily be removed by God's power.

## When Questions Become Dangerous

Yet there is a point when we have to realise that while we stand on this earth, bound by the limits of time, we shall never be able to see human suffering from God's perspective. Many people have tried to do so and written books on their conclusions, but all they can really offer us are tiny fragments of truth. The questioning stage begins to become dangerous when a person begins to spend too much time and energy dashing here and there after these fragments, because if their search goes on too long they could lose sight of God in a dry, intellectual maze of theological theories.

## The Challenge

In this stage, perhaps the Lord is asking us: 'Will you trust me without any explanations?'

*You may yourself ebb and flow, rise and fall, wax and wane, but your Lord is this day as he was yesterday.* (Samuel Rutherford)

Dr Helen Roseveare had spent many years establishing a hospital in the remote rainforests of what was then the Belgian Congo. The health of thousands of people was improved by her work and many lives saved. Then in 1964, during the vicious civil war, her hospital was attacked and she herself was brutally beaten and raped. She was forced to return to Britain, and her work at the mission station was left in ruins for a long time.

She was a Cambridge graduate, a scientist with a brilliant mind, and had been trained to look for answers. So naturally she asked God why he had allowed all that to happen, and she felt that she received this response from him: 'Will you trust me if I never tell you why?' Dr Roseveare's acceptance of that tantalising challenge was a profound help in the development of her personal relationship of trust in God, and through sharing it in her books and talks it has blessed many others.

Although questions are normal, therefore, there has to come a time when we let them go and realise that we will never understand God – he would not be God if we could. Our human intellects are too small to reach him, but we can reach him by faith. Of course, our faith is also too small to reach him, but once he sees the tiniest spark, he adds to it until we have all we need.

Through all our questioning he says, 'I do not expect you to understand me, but I do expect you to trust me.' If we can manage to make that quantum leap of faith, all our questions can be turned round to produce a huge growth spurt of faith that will benefit us eternally.

## Beware of the 'Hold Up' Factor

If at the end of all the questions we conclude that it was all God's fault, we might decide to blame him for all that has happened, and angrily exclude him from our lives for ever more.

The 'hold up' factor in this stage is a permanent resolve never to forgive God, which results in a total breakdown in the relationship.

> *Change and decay in all around I see, oh thou who changes not abide with me.* (Henry Francis Lyte)

### Letting It All Out

It is vitally important to remember that this permanent anger is not the same as feeling angry with God *sometimes*, and telling him so. Many of the greatest saints in church history have been angry with God – and survived. My favourite, St Teresa of Avila, was on a mission of mercy when, late on a stormy night, her coach was stuck in rising flood water, miles from civilisation. She was elderly and frail, but all night she and her nuns had to tramp through deep mud and driving rain. They were wet, cold and extremely hungry. As usual, St Teresa prayed out loud as she went, but her sisters were amazed (and perhaps relieved) to hear her say to the Lord, 'Well, if this is how you treat your friends, I'm not surprised you have so few!'

Many Bible characters were also honest with God about their feelings. Moses, who spoke to the Lord 'face to face, as a man speaks with his friend' (Exod. 33:11, NIV), obviously felt confident enough in their relationship to say bluntly, 'If you are going to treat me like this, take pity on me and kill me, so that I won't have to endure your cruelty any longer' (Num. 11:15, GNB).

Jeremiah felt utterly let down by God on several occasions, and in Jeremiah 15 he admits that he is angry – and then adds, 'Why do I keep on suffering? Why are my wounds incurable? Why won't they heal? Do you intend to disappoint me like a stream that goes dry in the summer?' (Jer. 15:18, GNB.)

Job, of course, was more outspoken than anyone: 'Listen to my bitter complaint. Don't condemn me, God . . . Is it right for you to be so cruel?' (Job 10:1–3, GNB.) 'Can't you see it is God who has done this? . . . I protest against his violence, but no one is listening . . . God has blocked the way . . . he has hidden my path in darkness. He has taken away all my wealth and destroyed my reputation. He batters me from every side. He uproots my hope and leaves me to wither and die . . . The hand of God has struck me down' (Job 19:6–21, GNB).

Job said a great many other things too, but (as we shall see in the next chapter) anger must be released – it cannot be allowed to become a long-term, deliberate attitude of blame. Job 1:22 tells us

---

*Jesus Christ is the same yesterday, today, and for ever.*
(Heb. 13:8, GNB)

that, 'In spite of everything that had happened, Job did not sin by blaming God' (GNB).

## Is It Wrong to Be Angry with God?

Perhaps we could dare to try to see our anger from God's point of view. In order to do that I have constructed an imaginary situation where one of my children might be extremely angry with me because I have prevented him doing something, or denied him something he wanted very badly. As a loving parent, I could see that what he wanted would be utterly destructive, but that he was too young to appreciate the sensible reason for my refusal. I love him so much I would be very sad that he did not trust me, but I would accept that his angry reaction was normal – so long as he expressed it correctly – and soon.

(a) If, however, the anger remained for many months, and he expressed it by locking himself away in his room in a world of brooding, resentful silence, and refused to speak to me or anyone else in the family, I should be most concerned.

(b) He could do me a lot of damage if he stormed off to express his anger to other people, telling our friends at church all kinds of things they never knew about me before!

(c) I would be terribly upset if he diverted the anger he felt towards me on to other members of the family and started punching the smaller ones, kicking the cat, or even smashing the china.

(d) The expression of anger that would hurt me most of all would be if he slammed out of the house in a rage, vowing never to return.

(e) As a parent, I would far prefer him to come to me with his anger direct and tell me how he feels. When my children manage to do that in real life, the whole thing usually blows over quite quickly and finishes with a muttered 'Sorry, Mum' from them and a hug of forgiveness from me.

God is a far better parent than any of us could ever be, so he understands our immaturity and our furious reactions. As Susan

---

*Now, Job, make peace with God and stop treating him like an enemy . . .* (Job 22:21, GNB)

Jenkins puts it, 'For we beat upon his breast from within the circle of his arms.'

The following chapter on anger contains some guidelines for expressing our feelings to God, but sometimes we are afraid to do that, so we hold it all in, as in example (a), locking ourselves away from God and others at church while we seethe and simmer internally, and our fellowship with God is suspended. That would hurt him very much because he values that friendship with us so highly.

God's relationship with other people could be damaged by our anger if we expressed it as in example (b), by spreading our doubts and dissatisfactions all round the church and denting other people's faith.

So often we transfer our anger on to others, as in (c), by venting it on them unfairly because we are too afraid to go to God direct. We quarrel with the vicar because he fails to call, or with our friends because they 'don't understand', or we roar at the children and slap the baby. Because God also loves the people we are hurting, it causes him added pain to watch their suffering.

Example (d) is, of course, the 'hold up' factor, and it is the expression of anger God dreads the most, because he longs to turn round in our favour all the suffering we encounter in this life, to transform it for our benefit and for the good of those we love. When we refuse to forgive him, he cannot 'work all things together for good' (Rom. 8:28) and the whole situation becomes destructive.

---

## A Meditation

People described Jo as a self-made man, but he never agreed with them. 'If you give your life to God, he'll always take care of you' was one of Jo's many little 'sayings', and his teenage children always groaned when he trotted it out yet again. But Jo had done exactly that soon after leaving school with no official bits of paper to help him get

---

*Perhaps the issue for Christians is simply this: is God there for me, or am I there for God? Does He exist to do my will or do I exist to do His?* (Justyn Rees)

established. He had taken a job labouring in a building firm, and less than twenty years later he owned the firm – and several others.

'People can always be sure of quality in one of my houses' was another of Jo's sayings, and his success lay in the fact that it was true.

He adored his children, even when they were going through the worst of their teenage rebellion, and he was always up at six in the morning, praying for them each by name – 'Just in case they forget to pray for themselves'. The family home was large and beautiful, but somehow Jo still managed to give thousands away to charity, saying as he wrote the cheques,'The more you give to God, the more God gives to you.'

The rugged world of the building trade respected Jo, but at church he was genuinely loved. 'Jo's a good man, he deserves to be happy,' was a sentiment shared by the whole district.

Then one day, Satan went to see God.

'Where have you been, then?' asked God.

'Oh, just walking about, looking at things,' replied Satan nonchalantly. 'Keeping an eye on the people you call your friends.'

'So you'll have noticed Jo,' said God, with a little smile of pride. 'Now there's a man who really loves me.'

'Well, "loving you" pays him well enough!' replied Satan tartly. 'He knows which side his bread's buttered. Just look what he gets out of it! You can't resist pouring blessings on him, can you? Look at his bank account! And doesn't he love that reputation you've built for him? Everyone asking his advice, and thanking him with tears in their eyes. I'm not surprised he loves you!'

God sighed. He knew what Satan had in mind.

'I'll prove to you that your fine friend Jo only loves you for what he gets out of you,' continued Satan with a sneer. 'Let me take it away – everything he values in life. We'll soon see if he loves you then.'

God's heart was heavy. For a long time he had been wanting Jo to have certain special things – precious assets he had not yet been able to give him. However, these treasures could only be discovered in the

---

*When we agree to the disagreeable things in life the life of Christ presses to the fore and the Lord is manifested and glorified through us, and it is then that we become broken bread and poured out wine to feed and nourish others.*
(Oswald Chambers)

darkness of adversity (Isa. 45:3). If he let Satan attack Jo, these valuable things could be his. Yet God shrank away from the very thought of it. He loved Jo, he was the very apple of his eye, and even though he could see clearly how much blessing he could bring to Jo's soul through Satan's plans, he still loathed the idea of the pain he must suffer in order to gain the prize.

There was also the very real possibility that he could lose Jo altogether. It was a terrible risk, and not one that God was prepared to take lightly.

'Come on,' said Satan impatiently. 'Why are you holding back? If you know Jo loves you, then you must know he'll trust you.'

With another sigh, God gave Satan the permission he needed.

'But you must not touch him personally,' he warned. Satan nodded, and went away whistling confidently.

'It's only the recession,' Jo told his workforce the day he had to lay off another twenty men. 'Things will soon improve. "The good Lord looks after his own" – that's what I always say.' Yet the work contracts seemed to be drying up completely, while the bills grew bigger by the day.

The offer from the London Consortium looked like the break he had been praying for, but he still spent two days fasting for guidance before he threw in his lot with their venture. He was so sure that he could trust them that he put up his house, and everything he owned, to raise the money he needed to buy himself in on the deal.

The crash came with devastating suddenness. It seemed as if in just one day he had lost his business, his home, his cars and his money, while the humiliation of bankruptcy was staring him in the face. None of that seemed to matter at all when they broke the news to him about the accident. The children had been at one of their wild parties. The building had caught fire, and they were not among the survivors.

At first the shock caused a kind of euphoria. Jo felt he was positively being carried along by the power of God. At the funeral he coined another of his sayings: 'The Lord gave it all to me, he has a perfect right to take it away again.' People quoted that all over

---

*He plied him with many questions, but Jesus gave him no answer.* (Luke 23:9, NIV)

Britain, and even used it in sermons as an example of patience under trial.

'What a good witness Jo is to his faith,' said everyone who knew him.

'There!' said God, next time he saw Satan. 'I told you Jo would never stop loving me.' Satan was still feeling rather sore; his good ideas so often seemed to backfire on him. Perhaps he should make a last attempt?

'Well,' he said with a shrug. 'Jo's a big strong man. He knows he can build his business back with his marvellous reputation. You let me get at him through his health – *then* he'll soon stop trusting you.'

God loathed the very thought of it, but he also knew Jo had not received quite all those good things yet.

'You have my permission,' he said sadly, 'but remember, you may not kill him.'

'It's one of these viruses,' the doctor told Jo's wife Helen. 'He'll get over it.' But Jo did not get over it.

'These things take time,' said the doctor a month later.

One day in August, when five months had elapsed, Helen said, 'Why don't you snap out of this? Get up and find a job! Why should I have to slave away supporting us both while you lie there in bed all day?'

Jo rolled over towards the wall; he could not bear the sight of her vicious face. They were living in a small, two-roomed flat by then, on the shabby side of town, crowded on top of each other until irritation soured their marriage.

'Call yourself a Christian! Fat lot of good all that stuff did you in the end!' He could still hear her voice, even with the pillow over his head. She had never been as committed to church as he had been; now he secretly wondered if she had not been right all along.

When the door slammed behind her at last, he sighed with relief. At least he had eight hours peace from her nagging while she emptied bed pans at the geriatric hospital. What had he done to

---

*Do you know the mind and purposes of God? Will long searching make them known to you? Are you qualified to judge the Almighty? He is as faultless as heaven is high – but who are you? His mind is fathomless – what can you know in comparison?* (Job 11:7–8, LB)

her? he thought, as remorse stabbed him painfully. She hated it there, and earned a smaller pittance than he would once have given his building apprentices. Her hands were as rough as her tongue these days, and she kept saying she wouldn't stick it – or him – much longer. He couldn't blame her!

It was hot at the top of this tower block. The man who built it had been a rival once, and as Jo looked round the shoddy room he reckoned the fool needed shooting. Once he and Helen would have been lying on a beach somewhere, during August heatwaves like this, but now they were forced to sweat the summer out in a jerry-built oven. A fly buzzed against the windowpane and made his headache even worse. Everything ached these days, every joint in his body hurt as he eased his position on the lumpy mattress. He was thirsty, but the physical effort involved in dragging himself to the kitchen next door was too great to consider.

'Why are you doing this to me, God?' he snarled. 'You've taken everything now, haven't you? I hope you're satisfied.' Not even his reputation remained to console him. Some of the people who had lost their jobs or their investments when his business crashed were turning nasty now, calling him a liar and a dishonest hypocrite all round town. They would have sued him if he had anything left to make it worth their while. Worst of all, his Christian friends seemed to believe their accusations, and he even had letters saying this sickness must be God's way of calling him to repentance. His friends had stopped coming round with flowers and cakes, and the phone never rang these days.

'You know for sure that I've never lied or cheated anyone, God,' he raged, 'so why don't you stand up for me?'

Last week the worst had happened: his doctor seemed to lose patience with him. 'I think these symptoms are all in your mind,' he had said. 'The hospital tests are negative. Where's your courage, man? Can't you face up to life? You should get up and take yourself out for some good long walks in the country and stop all this self-pity.'

Jo had been furious. 'Walks in the country? Can't you see I can't

---

*When my thoughts were bitter and my feelings were hurt, I was as stupid as an animal; I did not understand you.* (Ps. 73:21–22, GNB)

even stagger to the toilet without sweating with weakness?'

He'd said a great many other things as well, but of course the doctor had won with his parting remark to Helen as she showed him to the door: 'I'll make an appointment for him with a psychiatrist; it's time we got him back to work.'

Helen had loved it. She'd been on the phone in the next room all that evening and now everyone would know. 'Fancy a man with all that faith sinking as low as that,' they'd all be saying. 'Lying in bed malingering until they had to get a shrink to convince him he was a fraud!'

'You know I'm not making it up!' he muttered towards the cracked plaster of the ceiling. 'Aren't you listening to me any longer?'

At midday the phone rang. Jo was both surprised and pleased, but the struggle into the next room took him so long that it had stopped before he reached it.

As he stood clutching the table and fighting the waves of dizziness, the phone rang once again. It was Bruce, the senior elder at church, but his voice sounded so condescending that he could have been addressing a naughty member of the Sunday School.

'Since we heard how your doc is feeling about you, we've been praying quite a bit,' he began. 'More likely, gossiping,' thought Jo bitterly. 'The other elders and I feel we should come round and see you this evening,' continued Bruce. 'We feel we have various words from the Lord for you. Would eight o'clock be all right?'

'What do they want?' protested Helen when she arrived home. 'I've had a long day, I'm too tired after work to start making tea for that lot.'

'Don't bother then,' snapped Jo, adding crossly, 'I've had a long day too, and I'm tired just from doing nothing.'

'Whose fault's that?' she replied acidly. 'It's time you told all that church lot to get lost, if you ask me.'

'I didn't ask you!' growled Jo, who knew perfectly well he agreed with her.

The four men were looking ominous as they filed into the bedroom. They stood round the bed, gazing down at him without

---

*I will give you the treasures of darkness, riches stored in secret places, so that you may know that I am the Lord.* (Isa. 45:3, NIV)

saying anything at all for so long that Jo felt quite unnerved. Who did they think they were, anyway? They had all sat under his preaching for years, and he had picked them out to be elders himself. One of them had worked as his employee, two of the others he had helped out of serious financial difficulties, and he'd led young Graham to the Lord in his own sitting-room.

When he was beginning to think they would never break the silence, they started on him – one after the other.

'We all feel we have different aspects of the truth to share with you, Jo,' began Bruce. 'As a church we have prayed and fasted for you regularly over these months; and, as you know, we have held a special service of healing for you, but we have always been praying for a physical illness. We didn't realise, until we heard that your doctor says . . .'

'I'm making it all up,' put in Jo bitterly.

'Well . . . quite . . . but I feel that all this must be due to some sin you won't face up to. Some dishonest business deal you haven't confessed yet, perhaps?' At the start of his illness Jo had confessed so many things to these four elders that he felt naked every time he thought about it, but it had made no difference to his health. 'Search your heart, Jo,' continued Bruce, 'be honest with us for once.'

'For once!' said Jo. 'God knows I've never been anything else.'

'If God knew that, Jo,' said Bruce, shaking his head sadly, 'surely he would have told us four elders, don't you think?'

'Jo, I feel it's all a matter of faith,' said the man who had been the best chippy Jo had ever employed. 'A man like you ought to have enough faith to tell this sickness to go – instantly.'

'I'm afraid it has something to do with your wife's attitude,' added the third elder, and Jo heard an indignant snort from the far side of the bedroom door. Helen wouldn't like that, he thought grimly.

'Surely you must realise, Jo, that God never wills sickness like this for his children,' said the last man piously. 'He wants us all fit and well and out there serving him. You just don't want to get well, do you? You're not even trying.'

'Yes, but God could be teaching him something,' interrupted Bruce.

---

*Have you ever noticed how the same trouble that turns one Christian sour is used by another to refine and sweeten his life?* (Selwyn Hughes)

'I disagree,' said the fourth man, 'but even if you were right, why doesn't Jo just learn it quick, then he could be better instantly!'

Something inside Jo snapped. He sat up in bed and shouted, 'If it was as easy as that, do you think I'd still be stuck here like this? And if Christianity is all about kicking a man when he's down, you can keep it! You're always coming here with "words from the Lord" for me, but they keep changing! Why can't he make up his mind? Get out of here – and you can tell God from me that if he can't look after me and mine better than this, I'm through with him!'

'Jo!' said Bruce reproachfully, 'perhaps if you stopped treating God like an enemy he might bless you with your health again.'

'Get out!' yelled Jo. 'It's him who's treating me like an enemy, and I've had enough of it!'

Helen had her say as well – once they'd gone – and it developed into the biggest row they'd ever had. The whole 'delightful' evening finished when she packed her bags and left to stay with her best friend Susan.

'You can jolly well look after yourself in the future!' she shouted, as the door slammed with awesome finality.

The night was hot, oppressive with the heavy threat of thunder. Even the irritating fly had abandoned him, and as he lay there in the darkness he had never felt so utterly alone. 'That's it then,' he thought, as somewhere in the distance a church clock struck two. 'There's no one left who cares a rap about me now.'

But that was where Jo was wrong. He was not alone in that hot airless room. If only Jo could have seen the face of God at that moment. It was so close to him, he could have touched it by faith had he tried. The look of anguish would have astonished him. God's compassion longed to reassure Jo and comfort him. His heart was breaking as he watched him lying there.

'Trust me, Jo, please trust me just a little bit longer.' God said it several times, but Jo had lost the knack of listening to his voice.

Satan was watching Jo too, during that fateful August night. He

---

*In a human sense, it is understandable how most of us shrink from disappointment, bereavement and other trials, but in a divine sense, these are the very things that God uses to deepen His work of Grace in our lives.* (Selwyn Hughes)

was sitting in the corner of the hot little bedroom smiling in triumph.

'How are the mighty fallen,' he remarked nonchalantly.

'He hasn't reached the crisis yet,' said God. 'You wait.'

'Yes,' said Satan with a cunning smile, 'I can afford to wait.'

'If I could have just five minutes with God,' said Jo out loud. 'By golly, I'd ask him a few questions!'

'Trust me,' urged God silently while Satan smirked.

A sudden feeling of desolation came over Jo.

'If I haven't got God any more, then I've got nowhere left to run,' he muttered.

'Come to me, Jo,' breathed God. 'Trust me just a little bit longer.'

'I keep thinking I hear someone saying, "trust me",' said Jo, poking at his ear crossly. 'P'raps I am going mad after all, and I've started hearing voices.'

'Trust me, Jo.' There it was again.

Jo had the uncanny feeling that God was challenging him. 'Suppose all this happened because he wanted me to trust him – whatever.' Jo pulled himself up the bed a little – he felt he was having some kind of revelation. 'Trust him without any of my props – trust him just because I love him – for himself, and not what he gives me. Suppose that's what he's been after all along?'

'Well Jo?' said God. Heaven waited in breathless suspense and Satan fidgeted restlessly.

'Well, I suppose I might as well trust him,' whispered Jo at last. 'Because I'm darned sure I've got nothing else left but him now.' Then he added slowly, 'But then, maybe if I've got him I don't really need anything else anyway.' He paused, searching his mind for one of his sayings, but for once he failed completely. Then back into his mind came the words of someone else – he was sure he had heard them somewhere before – and he repeated them softly to himself. 'Though he slay me, yet will I trust him,' and 'when he has tried me I shall come forth as gold.'

Jo sat very still; he did not dare to move. God had not answered any of his questions, but suddenly he felt quite overwhelmed by his love. It seemed to pour down on him directly from heaven itself like

---

*Let Almighty God be your gold, and let him be silver, piled high for you. Then you will always trust in God and find that he is the source of your joy.* (Job 22:25–26, GNB)

thick, golden liquid. Gradually it filled the room, and swept away everything but its own tremendous reality. Tears seeped from the corners of Jo's eyes and dampened his rugged cheeks.

'Lord,' he whispered, 'I'm so sorry I doubted you. I said some stupid things, didn't I? Honestly, I didn't mean most of it. Forgive me. And I'm sorry I was so angry with them all at church. They didn't mean to be heartless.' He had the oddest feeling that God might be angry with them too, so he hastily added, 'Please forgive them too for not seeing what you were really up to. Don't go punishing them for that – they were only trying to help.'

Then, lying back, Jo closed his eyes and slept like a contented child. He never saw Satan slink away, defeated and shamed. Nor did he see the angels dancing with delight on the scruffy covers of his bed. But all heaven rejoiced that night as he slept, and there was a smile on the face of God.

I am not quite sure how this modern version of the age-old story of Job should end. Jo has to get better, of course, and, if the original story of Job is anything to go by, he becomes a multi-millionaire! I am not sure if even my imagination will allow Helen to have lots more children at her age, but perhaps they could adopt?

However we decide the story should finish, there is one vital fact we must not overlook. Job's fortunes were restored after he had:

- repented of his anger against God (Job 40:3–4; 42:3, 6)
- forgiven God through an experience of renewal (Job 42:5–6)
- forgiven his infuriating friends by praying for them (Job 42:10)

Then, and only then, could his story reach its happy-ever-after ending. God does not always restore everything to us in a physical sense during this life, but we must reach the same point as Jo before we can emerge whole from our Broken Teapot experiences.

---

*In all the changes, confusion and uncertainty there is only one cast iron fact that we can cling to with perfect confidence. Whatever is happening to us, God can make it all work for our good and the benefit of those we love – if we allow him to do so.* (Jean Rees)

## A Prayer

*'Come to me all you who are tired out from carrying heavy loads full of questions and confusion, for "I alone know the plans I have for you, plans to bring you prosperity and not disaster, plans to bring about the future you hope for".'* (Jer. 29:11, GNB)

'My God, my God, why . . . ?' 'If it is possible, take this cup of suffering away from me . . .' Lord, these are your own words and I echo them, but I also want to reach the point of adding, 'Nevertheless, not my will but thine be done.' I want to stop trying to buy your favour with promises of money, service or good behaviour, to stop trying to manipulate you by prayer, fasting and sacrifice. From now on I want to allow you to have your way in this situation, and use it to bring good things to everyone involved. My Father, I do not understand you, but I trust you.

## Perhaps the Lord Might Respond Like This

'I cannot give you all the answers, because – as a human – your view of the universe is as limited as that of the ant who wriggles between the stalks of grass in a field. From where I am, I can view the whole earth in one glance. I can see the jagged mountain peaks, the quiet rivers and the icebergs floating in dark blue water. I can also see each blade of grass in your field. You feel you are struggling round in circles, but I can see clearly where you are going and each obstacle you will face among the matted roots and muddy soil. How do I explain to you how beautiful the world looks from up here? You could never understand with your limited experience. But one day, when I lift you up here to see it all with me, from my perspective, then you will look back down at your field where you struggle now and laugh at the tiny things you thought were insurmountable. Trust me just a little longer – one day you will see it all, *and* understand.'

---

*And He doesn't explain, He trusts us not to be offended, that's all.* (Amy Carmichael)

## STOP FOR A MOMENT

*Had the real Job been able to see that a spiritual battle was taking place above his suffering, he would no doubt have found the whole thing considerably easier to bear. For us, struggling through our own misery and confusion, we do at least have the benefit of his story. It does not give a complete answer – like all other explanations it is just a fragment of the truth – but it does show us that we are not actually alone.*

*Knowing that, like Job, we are watched by the two Superpowers could make us feel like little pawns in a game they are playing above our heads – until we remember that we decide which of them wins: Satan, when we allow our problems to destroy us; or God, when we allow him to work them all for our good.*

## Warning!

*If you have not yet had time to release your anger fully to the Lord, you may find the following exercise too difficult at present.*

## Take Two Sheets of Paper

*At the top of the first sheet, write 'The Facts', then underneath make a list of everything that happened when your 'teapot' broke – the actual events and the losses they caused. Here is an imaginary example:*

## The Facts

*My marriage broke up*
*I lost my financial security*
*I lost my teenage children; they left home, disgusted by both of us*
*I lost the security of having a husband*
*I lost the companionship*
*I lost the house I loved*
*I lost my friends through having to move away*
*I lost my Christian status as the wife of a housegroup leader*
*I lost my church, and the new one is horrid*
*I lost my ministry (Sunday School); they don't need me here*

*Both God and Satan want to use this set of circumstances to implement their plans. God wants to use them to bring you good, whereas Satan wants to use them to harm you. So divide the second piece of paper down the middle with a vertical line. At the top of the left side write, 'Satan's Objectives' and on the right side, 'God's Objectives'.*

## Satan's Objectives

*On Satan's side, write down what harm you guess he might hope to achieve. For example:*

> *He wants to make me bitter and angry with my husband for leaving*
> *He wants me to think God is angry with me or doesn't care any longer*
> *He wants to destroy my children's faith and cut them off from us*
> *He wanted to destroy my ministry with the children and house-group*
> *To send me to a church where I am not asked to help in any way*
> *He wants to see me lonely, miserable and bored*

*Your own list will probably be much longer, so do give yourself time to think carefully.*

## God's Objectives

*Look back at your sheet headed 'The Facts' and try to see them from God's angle, then write down on his side of the paper what good he might be wanting to achieve for you. For example:*

> *He wants to help me trust him to meet all my needs*
> *He wants to develop my friendship with him by filling my loneliness with his companionship*
> *He wants to give me a new, warm, forgiving heart*
> *He wants to build my children's faith by my example*
> *He wants me to meet my new neighbours so that I can tell them about him*
> *He wants to use me to bring his reality into this new church*

*Again, don't hurry. You may be amazed at just how long this list can get.*

*When these two battle plans are laid out side by side, it is easier to see just how important we are in the centre of it all. As I said, it is up to us to decide which side wins by how we choose to react. During the whole Broken Teapot Syndrome we may not feel that we control the confusing circumstances, but we do control whether they bring good to us and those we love, or whether we let the circumstances destroy us completely.*

# ANGER

'I've always thought of myself as a reasonably well controlled man; I was punished if I lost my temper as a child. But for two years after I had my stroke, I seemed to boil with anger most of the time. The smallest thing would set me off, and I'd go into these terrible moods when I wanted to lash out at everyone in sight for no apparent reason. Poor old Alice took the brunt of it, and I remember one day, when she was getting ready to go out with one of her irritating girlfriends, she said that she'd left lunch in the microwave. I saw red, and we had the worst row of our married life – she even threatened to leave me.

'Then one evening she asked a colleague from my old firm for dinner. She thought it would cheer me up, but all he did was go on about all the office gossip, and I was so rude in the end that poor Alice didn't know where to put herself. The worst explosion of all happened at church. I'd been feeling upset because things had got so sloppy without me there to keep them on their toes (I'd been administrator for years), but it was the sight of the noticeboard in the church porch that finally did it. I lost my cool, and snapped off the heads of everyone that morning. I felt so ashamed of myself later – getting angry like that was no way for a Christian to behave.'

Tom is not the only Christian to be plagued by anger. It is probably the most dominant emotion in the entire Broken Teapot Syndrome. I am giving it the last place on the list not because it is the least important, but because – for most of us – it seems to be the hardest emotion to handle. Perhaps this is because anger makes us

---

*A fool gives full vent to his anger.* (Prov. 29:11, NIV)

want to hurt someone, and if we cannot get back at the person who caused it all, then we get frightened by the feeling that anyone else will do! Anger makes us react in different ways:

1. *We fight back.* We defend ourselves from further attack by attacking in return, using either our voices to shout, swear and argue, or our bodies to punch, hit, kick or throw crockery. Or we fight back the dignified way, and call in a solicitor to stand up for our rights.

2. *We save it.* We say nothing at the time, but think, 'I'll make him pay for this one day.' While we wait for our chance to get even, we tell everyone we meet how badly he behaved so that they will be angry with him too. We find ourselves hoping that she is unhappy with her admirer, or wonder what would happen if he had a breakdown and lost his job. We might even think how much easier everything would be if he or she were dead.

3. *We divert it* – by venting it on someone else, i.e. shouting at the milkman or kicking the cat when it's really the boss who crossed us.

4. *We turn it inwards.* We hurt ourselves because we dare not hurt others, by inwardly 'shouting' abuse at ourselves, punishing our bodies through excessive physical exertion, reckless driving, nail biting, self-starvation or wild eating binges.

5. *We freeze it* – by turning it into hate: the 'never ever again' kind of ice-cold anger. 'I'll never speak to them again . . . go near him . . . trust her . . . I will never forgive.'

6. *We deny it.* We swallow it down behind a smile that says, 'It doesn't matter, it didn't hurt, of course I'm not angry,' while we lock the anger carefully away in a sealed compartment and pretend it isn't there.

Christians face a dilemma over anger. 'You've got every right to be angry, you can't be a doormat when someone treats you badly,' we are told by the world. 'It's a healthy reaction, and you must let it all come out,' say the experts. But somehow we feel it is 'not done' to bawl and scream abuse at a church meeting, and it isn't scriptural to

---

*Everyone must be quick to listen, but slow to speak and slow to become angry. Man's anger does not achieve God's righteous purpose.* (Jas. 1:19–20, GNB)

give the vicar a black eye. So the 'fight back' method is out, and we opt for methods 2–6 instead – often with disastrous consequences.

Anna had been a minister's wife for twenty years, and keeping the peace between her husband and his flock had taught her to keep her anger under tight control. She was a slim, attractive woman in her early fifties, but she came to see me because she wanted prayer for all kinds of physical symptoms that medical tests could not explain. 'Life's a bit of a mess,' she said wearily. 'Ours was one of the largest Baptist churches in the country. We used to get three hundred regularly on a Sunday morning, but last week there were fifteen people there! It's been such a bad witness, all the gossip and infighting.'

'How did it happen?' I asked.

'Leslie took on an assistant pastor, Trevor – he seemed a super young man, full of spiritual dynamite, and determined to go places in the Christian world. However, it wasn't long before we realised that all he was after was power, and he started stirring people up against Leslie, saying the church was being held back because he was so traditional. When Leslie tried to tell the elders about his misgivings over Trevor, he was accused of being jealous.

'In no time at all, the church was divided down the middle, and it all came to a head when Trevor went off with two-thirds of our membership to start a new fellowship in a school, less than two miles away. Lots of people were so disillusioned that they just stopped going anywhere at all.'

She had told me the story quite calmly, her face expressionless, but something was worrying me.

'You must have felt very angry?' I ventured.

'Angry? Oh no, just sad,' she replied quickly.

'But they hurt you?' She hesitated, apparently struggling with herself as a tinge of red coloured her pale face.

'Well, before the church split up it was a little difficult because Trevor started a rumour that our marriage was breaking up, and that I wanted to control Leslie and dominate the whole church. Then he even spread the word around that my pressurising was making

---

*You are never more vulnerable to sin than when your anger is out of control. Will you use your anger, or let it use you?*
(David Augsburger)

Leslie ill. Because it was only silly gossip, I took no notice. Of course, in the end it was Trevor who made Leslie ill – the whole thing took its toll and he had a terrible breakdown. He nearly died after taking an overdose, and was in the psychiatric hospital for months. That was really the end, because even the people who still came to church began to say it was a sign that God was judging him; and, with no minister, the place soon emptied.'

'How is Leslie now?' I asked.

'He's at home, he potters in the garden – sometimes – but mostly he sits and stares into space. The doctor says he'll probably get better, but his whole personality's changed. He never speaks to me unless he has to, and if he can't snap out of it soon we'll have to leave the manse to make way for a new minister. Goodness only knows where we'll end up then.'

'But how does all this make you react?' I persisted.

'Well, I feel it's my duty to expose Trevor for what he is,' she said grimly. 'A "wolf in sheep's clothing". I've written letters to the powers that be and done my best to open as many eyes as possible. Of course, I can't do much since I became ill myself – that's why I feel I need some prayer.'

'Anna,' I said, when we had asked the Lord how we should pray, 'I feel that anger is causing a lot of your problems.' She looked quite astonished.

'I haven't been angry once throughout all this,' she protested. 'I've learnt to control it.' In reality, she had only learnt to *deny* it. We may think we are behaving like Christians by not losing our tempers, i.e. not letting our anger show, but invisible anger is just as wrong. *We* are supposed to follow the teachings of Christ, and Jesus tells us plainly that *all* anger is bad (when it is sparked by a wrong done to us) (Matt. 5:22).

Obviously Jesus would not approve of the 'fight back' method. He says that when someone hits or insults us we are not to retaliate (Matt. 5:39). The 'save it' method is out, too, because when he talks about anger in Matthew 5:21–24 he does not use the Greek word, *thumos* (a sudden flame that quickly springs up, but just as quickly

---

*Be gentle and ready to forgive; never hold grudges. Remember, the Lord forgave you, so you must forgive others.* (Col. 3:13, LB)

dies down), but uses the word *orge* (long-lived anger that we nurse and brood over). He warns us that 'hell fire' is the consequence of this kind of anger, because it makes us devalue others and he forbids us to plan revenge (v. 39), or to stand up for our rights (v. 40). He also says that what we *think* in our minds is the same as *doing* it. We should hope for good things for our enemy, because wanting nasty things to happen to him or her is as bad as arranging that they will. To imagine killing the person is actually murder!

Jesus would also not approve of the 'divert it' method because he would not want other people to be hurt by our rage. The same applies to the 'turn it inwards' strategy. He loves us, and so does not want us hurt either.

The 'freeze it' reaction in his eyes would be the worst of all, because it denies the possibility of ever forgiving. We have already discussed what that could do to us (see p.44).

So that only leaves us with the 'deny it' option, which most Christians take without realising that this is also condemned in the Bible. 'Get rid of all bitterness, passion, and anger' (Eph. 4:31), and to do so as quickly as possible (Eph. 4:26–27). 'See that no . . . root of resentment, rancour, bitterness or hatred shoot forth and cause trouble and bitter torment and many become contaminated and defiled by it' (Heb. 12:15, AMP).

Jesus does not condemn *all* kinds of anger. He was obviously angry himself on a number of occasions, but always on behalf of others and never because of wrongs done to himself. The Bible tells us, 'in your anger do not sin' (Eph. 4:26, NIV), so there must be times when it is right to *use* anger to lend us the courage to confront bad situations. This is what Jesus did when he demolished an entire livestock market singlehanded, with only a few bits of old rope and lots of righteous indignation. Abraham Lincoln was angry when he saw the slave market in New Orleans, but he used it to give thousands of slaves their freedom. Tolstoy's anger blazed out against war, Gandhi was angry about oppression, and Shaftesbury, Elizabeth Fry and Wilberforce used their anger to confront injustice. Anger comes as a reaction to pain, but for most of us the pain is caused by injuries

---

*And when you stand and pray, forgive anything you may have against anyone, so that your Father in heaven will forgive the wrongs you have done.* (Mark 11:25, GNB)

others inflict on us, and that kind of anger is not the 'Jesus kind'.

## Handling Anger

This wrong kind of anger must be dealt with promptly and efficiently, and here is a formula that I have personally found very helpful. I hope to explain it as this chapter unfolds.

1. Name it
2. Understand it
3. Express it
4. Confess it
5. Explain it
6. Let go of it
7. Use it

Most of us find no. 1 so difficult that we never get any further, and I have learnt from experience just how easy it is to ignore buried anger to the point where it becomes dangerous.

When my mother had a stroke she was already physically frail from serious heart disease. The mental confusion that the stroke caused seemed like a final insult. Our six children were all still tiny, the youngest little more than a baby, but we felt it was right for her to come and live with us. She had to sleep downstairs in our living-room, which did not leave much space in our ordinary 'semi' for the rest of us. In fact, we soon began to feel like rats confined in an overcrowded cage.

Mother used to wake up at three in the morning and demand her breakfast, and if I dashed out to the shops during the day I would discover on my return that she had wandered up the road looking for me, probably in no more than her petticoat; or she'd had an unfortunate accident trying to reach her commode.

Yes, I was angry an awful lot of the time, but I did not realise I was angry because there was no way I could admit it – even to myself. Her constant, unreasonable demands made me feel angry, but it

---

*Be kind to each other, tender-hearted, forgiving one another, just as God has forgiven you because you belong to Christ.* (Eph. 4:32, LB)

would have been unthinkable to let her see it because she couldn't help being confused, and it was distressing her enough as it was. Most of my anger came because I loved her and didn't see why God should let her suffer like that, and because my ceaseless efforts to make her happy always ended in failure and frustration. I could not have told Tony how I felt because it would only have made things even worse for him. Everyone else in the world would have said, 'Get her into a home,' but I loved her too much for that. So I felt guilty for being irritable and firmly swallowed my anger.

One morning, when Mother had upset her cup of tea all over her newly changed bed, I suddenly knew I was going to explode – and I had to run out of the room to prevent myself from screaming abuse or even hitting her. I stood in the kitchen, trembling all over with the effort of controlling myself, while trying not to hear her plaintive voice demanding yet another wash and a clean nightie.

I suddenly recognised my anger for what it was and I remembered a foster child called Debbie that we once had. She had a terrible fear of vomiting. When all the other children caught a tummy bug they got rid of it in the usual way and soon felt better. Debbie could not let herself be sick, so the poison remained in her body until she became quite ill. As I stood there in the kitchen I suddenly thought, 'That's what I'm doing to my anger. Holding it all in like this must be bad for me.' Perhaps because I have always found it helpful to think in pictures, I suddenly 'saw' all this swallowed anger going down inside me and being stored in a huge internal tank, like a cesspit situated deep inside me. The thought was so unpleasant that I have never forgotten it.

When someone, for whatever reason, continuously forces down anger over a prolonged period, the anger has to go somewhere. Perhaps we all have one of these underground reservoirs where our unexpressed anger bubbles away undetected and the same old bitter thoughts revolve endlessly in our minds. As more and more fury is pushed down, this underground chamber has to be constantly enlarged to hold the ever-increasing volume.

---

*The test of forgiveness lies with healing the lingering pains of the past and not with forgetting that the past ever happened.* (Lewis Smedes)

## Naming the Anger

Rumpelstiltskin, that nasty little tyrant in the fairy story, had great power over a princess in distress until the moment he was named. Then he disappeared in a puff of smoke. I think anger is like that. It has such destructive power while we deny its existence, but once we name it for what it is and stop calling it 'hurt feelings' or 'my irritable nature', and once we face the fact that we *are* angry and we have a very valid reason for being angry, there is a chance that Jesus can help us to deal with both the anger and the reason. After all, it would hardly be fair for God to make people with the capacity to be angry, and then condemn most forms of anger, unless he intended to help us manage it correctly – or even learn to use it creatively.

## Understanding the Anger

People who are hurting seem to boil with anger a good deal of the time, as I did while I cared for my mother. We know this huge tank of anger is there, smouldering away under the surface, and silly little things like tea spilt on bedclothes or an untidy church noticeboard spark a flame of irritation that we try hard to smother. We say, 'The spilt tea made me angry', but if we are honest we know these little things are not the real cause. A far bigger lake of frustration lies beneath these trivial pinpricks.

### *When our sources of satisfaction are under threat*

This is what James, the brother of Jesus, says about anger: 'Where do all the fights and quarrels among you come from? . . . You want things, but you cannot have them . . . you strongly desire things, but you cannot get them, so you quarrel and fight' (Jas. 4:1–2, GNB).

> *If a brother sins against you, go to him and show him his fault . . . If he listens to you, you have won your brother back . . . 'Lord, if my brother keeps on sinning against me, how many times do I have to forgive him? Seven times?' 'No, not seven times,' answered Jesus, 'but seventy times seven.'* (Matt 18:15, 21, 22, GNB)

What is it we want so much that we become violently frustrated when we cannot have it? Surely the greatest 'wants' in our lives are to be loved, accepted and needed. The pain when these three crucial needs are not met is so unbearable that we will do anything to find the people or situations that supply them:

1. Being loved makes us feel secure. We find this love first in our parents, then our friends, romantic attachments, spouses and children.
2. Being accepted builds our feeling of worth. This comes through being valued by the people who matter most to us, our family, friends, identity group and workmates. It matters vitally to us to be the kind of person they find attractive, and to live up to their ideals, desires and patterns of behaviour.
3. Being needed makes us feel significant and important as a person. This comes from our work, career, charity activities, clubs, home and possessions, power, positions of leadership, and Christian work or ministry.

When the 'teapot' crashes we may lose the people on whom we depended to give us the love we need, we may no longer be able to do the things that made us feel worth something in our family and community, or we may no longer fill the role or position that made us feel important and significant in our corner of the world.

### Tom's anger

All this causes a feeling of devastation, because we have lost the ways in which we had always met our vital needs. A lot of the fear and depression comes through their loss. The anger comes because the goals we set ourselves in order to achieve this feeling of being loved, accepted and significant are blocked off. All the things we set out to do have been thwarted, and the frustration that results is enormous, but so often we do not know why.

Tom, the man I mentioned at the beginning of this chapter, said, 'I wanted to lash out at everyone in sight for no apparent reason,' but

---

*Our wounds tie us to the past and if we try and forget them, then we keep the past as a jailer over our present. To relive is a commitment to remember and to forgive.* (Russ Parker)

once he realised what the reason was, he reached a turning point. After two years of constant bad temper he went to a Christian counsellor, who helped him to see that all three of his crucial 'life needs' were under attack as a result of his stroke. In spite of the way he treated poor Alice, his greatest fear was that his disability might turn her away from him, because their love had always been the source of all his security. His anger was triggered every time she left him to look after himself, so she could go out with 'her irritating girlfriends'. In his position as a partner in a large firm of London solicitors, people looked up to him – and that made him feel 'he mattered' and had something to contribute to the world. Hearing all the office gossip reminded him that life was going on perfectly normally without him and made him feel as if he no longer counted. His self-worth came through his role as administrator at church. Now he could no longer be the hub of church life he felt devalued and rejected.

Tom emerged from his 'broken teapot' when he found new goals and a different way of meeting his needs – but more about that in the following chapter.

### Anna's anger

It was so easy for me, standing outside the situation, to see that Anna's secret anger was there because Trevor's 'takeover bid' had blocked so many of her life goals. She needed to feel loved by her husband, her security depended on it, but his illness had changed him and he was cold and distant. She needed to feel accepted in order to maintain her self-worth, and being loved and appreciated by a large congregation who had valued her ministry had always provided that. Now she felt most of her friends had rejected her because they believed the lies about her, or left the church just when she needed them most. Her significance in her corner of the world was also under fire, now no one knocked on her door for advice or practical help, and her status in the town as a minister's wife looked

---

*Paul said, 'I want to know Christ'* (Phil. 3:10, NIV). *To love someone is to long to know him or her even better. And he also said, 'More than anything else . . . we want to please him.'* (2 Cor. 5:9, GNB)

as if it was coming to an end completely. The thought of swapping the status symbol of a lovely big manse for a retirement flat in some strange town where no one knew her felt to her like being 'chucked on the scrap heap'.

Of course, there was also a lot of the right kind of anger too. She was right to be furious when she saw how her husband was suffering so unnecessarily. While Anna insisted she was not angry, though, all these conflicts went on battling inside, completely undetected by her.

It often helps people when they suddenly feel anger surging up inside, and while they are counting up to ten, to ask themselves, 'Which of my needs is being threatened here and what goals are being blocked?'

### Danger! Beware of One of the Greatest Hazards!

To function efficiently, all human beings need to feel loved, accepted and needed, as we have seen, and we look to certain people, activities or roles to satisfy these needs. When our 'teapot' breaks, we often lose these vital sources of satisfaction and we have to search for new ways of meeting our needs. Until we find them, these needs are screaming out to be met – and most of us will do anything to smother the resulting pain. We turn to various things that seem to soothe this pain for a while, but sometimes these very things become 'hold up' factors that prevent us from finding new ways to meet our needs. For instance, certain things such as alcohol, sleeping pills and tranquillisers can be a help at first, but if taken too much for too long they become addictive. Other less obvious things can also be just as habit-forming and destructive: food, nasty videos and magazines, doubtful books and films, casual sex, gambling, or extravagant spending that leads to debt.

Make sure you run for comfort to the 'strong tower' (see p.102), because the Lord says this about people who run in the opposite direction: 'My people have committed two sins: they have turned

---

*One thing I ask of the Lord . . . that I may dwell in the house of the Lord [in his presence, his company] all the days of my life.* (Ps. 27:4, NIV)

away from me, the spring of fresh water, and they have dug cisterns, cracked cisterns that can hold no water at all' (Jer. 2:13, GNB).

## Expressing the Anger

Understanding why we are angry does not help completely, of course: we need to find a safe way of expressing our anger without hurting anyone else. On the day that my mother tipped tea over the bed, I made a firm resolve to have my 'inner tank' drained as soon as possible. I knew I needed to express the anger in some way, but how?

As the mother of a large family, I have always felt it best to allow anger to be legitimate, so long as expressing it does not hurt anyone. Experts may well disagree, but then perhaps they don't have six children! When our second baby was born, Sarah was not yet two. We thought at first that she was delighted with 'her baby', then I began to find her sharp little teeth marks in Justyn's foot or mysterious bumps on his head. Rather than teach her to store her anger or deny it, we went to a jumble sale and bought a large, motheaten cuddly toy which became known as Debbie Teddy. It lived in the corner of the playroom, and we explained to Sarah that we understood that she wanted to hurt Justyn, but we couldn't let her because it made him sad; instead she could punch, kick and bite Debbie Teddy, because Teddies never get sad about anything. It worked marvellously for a week or so, and then backfired on us badly because Sarah and Debbie Teddy became so devoted that punching and kicking were out of the question! Yet I cannot remember Sarah ever hurting Justyn again.

As I changed my mother's nightie I considered finding a plump cushion, or knocking up a batch of dough and kneading it violently. I even thought of fetching a hammer and nails from Tony's tool shed and banging out my anger that way. However, I rejected those options: my anger was bigger than that. However, people do find a physical expression helpful such as going for a jog, digging the garden, scrubbing the floor. All those things work well, except for people like Tom in his wheelchair, but he found a substitute in his computer games.

I've always been a 'words person' and therefore I find that expressing anger in that way helps me most. Of course, words can hurt people far more than sticks and stones, so that leaves us with the problem of who to say the words to. It is possibly best not to say them to the person who caused the anger, because the situation may be so volatile that the result could be murder!

There was no one else I could talk out my anger with at that time, and anyway I am sure the very best person to go to is God. In the last chapter we looked at expressing anger towards God himself, but this is something quite different: it is not directing anger *at* God, but pouring it out *before* him.

I had been denying my anger for so long that I felt I wanted to make the expression of it a special occasion, so when a friend said she would take my mother out for the day it gave me an excellent opportunity. Another playgroup Mum said she would keep my two youngest boys for the afternoon and 'give me a real break', so for the first time in years I was quite alone in the house. This was definitely 'clean out day' for those anger tanks. It seemed sensible to get myself into the right mood, so I spent the morning doing all the jobs that make me most bad tempered – and I fasted, too, that day. Eating has not only been one of the ways I have coped with my fears, it has also acted as a lovely, cosy blanket to cover my anger, and I always want to stuff myself with chocolate biscuits when I'm cross. Fasting allows anger to come to the surface, and that's just where I wanted it to be.

By the time my stomach told me it ought to be lunchtime I was almost ready, so I had a bath, washed my hair and put on a clean set of clothes. This was not only because I had cleaned out the chickens and tidied the garage, but because I felt the occasion was so important that I wanted to purify myself as they did in Old Testament times.

Finally, I took the phone off the hook so nothing would disturb me, and locked the back door. Coming into the presence of God is always an awesome thing. In our church we do not go in for visual prompts to worship, such as icons or crucifixes, but that day I felt I needed something to make the whole thing real. So I found a poster that showed two big hands held out as if to a child, and I stuck it on the kitchen wall. The picture helped me to think of God the Father. Then I lit one of the leftover Christmas candles to represent the refining fire of the Holy Spirit. I set the candle on a little table under the picture, and added the cross I had made that morning from two bits of fencing wood. Father, Son and Holy Spirit were all represented, and I was ready at last.

First, I sat down at the table and wrote a long and detailed list of everything that made me angry about life as it was. It took a long time, because it covered several pages, but when it was done I stood in front of the little table and reminded myself just how very great God is. He was there with me, even though I could not see him or feel his presence. Remembering the time when Moses stood before him, I slipped off my shoes. The place where I stood was 'holy ground' (Exod. 3:5). God really would hear what I told him, and I was not just going to express all my anger into empty space. He loved me infinitely, and he cared intensely about how I was feeling.

Then I held the list out to him, and began reading it out loud. I felt such a fool at first, but fortunately, as we lived right out in the country, no one could hear me – if someone had, I might have been certified!

Should you decide to try this way of communicating your anger to God, I am sure that you too will also find it hard to let go of all the filthy, revolting bitterness of your innermost being and to lie there exposed to his sight. It could even be one of the hardest things you have ever had to do. So many of us were brought up in families that denied feelings, and were taught that expressing anger is wrong, so this exercise will be a real psychological hurdle.

Do let yourself feel the strength of your anger as you express it. If you dare, go back to times in the past and stand in your imagination where you stood then, and feel as you felt then. Experience the ferocity of your rage, because unless you are aware of its full power you will never realise its potential danger to yourself and others. Feel it fully as you express it to God. Don't panic halfway through; don't stop to consider just how great and powerful and holy God is. Don't let yourself think how easily he could squash you like an insignificant ant if he chose. He *is* holy, he *is* powerful, he *could* squash you right now, but he also loves you. God has been eagerly waiting for you to throw all this anger at his feet so that he can pick it up and absorb it all for you.

## Confessing the Anger

When my anger was finally expressed and poured out before God, I felt I wanted to kneel and ask him to forgive me for allowing that anger and bitterness to collect down there inside me for so long. All anger (except the Jesus kind) is sin, because it comes when our 'I wants' are not met, so basically it results from selfishness. As I knelt there, I sensed that God was cleaning me out inside, just as I had swept out the garage that morning. All that filthy, rotting anger was gone. It was as if his power was washing out any remaining slime left clinging to the walls of my 'cesspit', scouring them clean, white-washing them, and making everything inside me fresh and new again. The experience was completed when I asked the Holy Spirit of Jesus to come and fill that empty space where all the anger had been, and I felt the warmth of his love flowing into my soul.

Finally, I found the roasting tin we use for turkeys at Christmas and, placing it on the table beside the cross and the candle, I set light to all the sheets of paper and watched my anger writhing and twisting grotesquely as the words disappeared for ever in the refining fire of God's Holy Spirit. The blackened remains went down the kitchen sink, and I just had time to scour the roasting tin thoroughly before my mother was back demanding her tea.

It would be nice to say here that I was never angry again, that I nursed my mother like a perfect saint from that time on. Sadly, that wouldn't be true – perhaps keeping that internal Bitterness Tank free of collected anger has to become a daily job after that initial spring clean. It helped me to understand this when a friend of mine was taken ill in the night while staying with us. She was rushed into hospital for an emergency operation to remove an abscess in her pelvic cavity, and for some time after the surgery a tube was constantly draining away the remaining infection and pus.

During the difficult patches in our lives, when our stress levels are so high that a lot of anger is produced, we do need to keep on expressing and confessing it continuously to the Lord throughout each day, rather like the drip, drip, drip of that drainage tube. If we leave it to collect again for a long period, we will be back in hospital for a further major operation!

## Explaining the Anger

By 'explaining' I mean waiting until we have calmed down, and then telling the person who made us angry how we felt, and, because anger always causes barriers, trying to mend the relationship. We will be looking at practical ways of doing this in Chapter 11, and there is also a section there on how we handle this 'explaining' when the person concerned is dead.

Here, I simply mean, for example, going to the boss and saying,

'Look, I really did find it a bit too much when you gave me all those extra letters to do on a Friday afternoon. Couldn't we sort out a better system next time?' Or saying to the family, 'I'm sorry you're sick of sausages, and I will try and be a bit more creative in future, but it really dents my self-esteem when you criticise my cooking.' That sounds a bit ridiculous, and it certainly wouldn't work in our house, but there is a serious principle behind it.

When Jesus was talking about anger and relationships in Matthew 5:23–24, he tells us to settle our accounts with others very quickly so that they do not escalate and become impossible to pay. In other words, we need to deal correctly with the very first spark of anger, so that it does not become a raging forest fire.

Suppose an imaginary husband remarks mildly that he wishes his wife would grill the sausages rather than always frying them. Her self-esteem is threatened, and a niggle of irritation makes her prod his weak spot: significance. 'If you had a job we could afford steak!' shouts the wife. This produces a small flame of anger, because being unemployed whacks at his need for significance. In turn, he uses the flame to attack just where he knows it will hurt her most, and so it goes on all day, tit for tat, back and forth, and each time a larger amount of anger is generated until a major argument erupts before nightfall.

'I can't think why I ever married you!' is a major attack on security, and soon such huge amounts of anger have been generated that, if left unchecked over a long period, can lead to the kind of raging inferno that divides relationships. Or it could be frozen into the 'I will never ever again' kind of ice-cold hate. There are couples who do not split up, but who stay together for years without ever speaking again.

The Bible says, 'A gentle answer quietens anger' (Prov. 15:1, GNB), and if that first spark of anger over the sausages had been dealt with by a frank explanation or a quick apology it might have changed everything. 'Do not let the sun go down while you are still angry,' says St Paul (Eph. 4:26, NIV): in other words, only carry one day's burden of anger at a time and keep short accounts. 'Let no debt remain outstanding, except the continuing debt to love one another' (Rom. 13:8, NIV).

## Letting the Anger Go

It took Anna a long time to admit she was angry, perhaps because her 'righteous indignation' became confused with the wrong kind of anger.

'Bad situations must be confronted if there is ever to be justice in the world,' she said one evening, as we sat by the fire. 'If Trevor is left unchecked he may do untold damage by his strange ideas. I feel I must take further steps to make people see him for what he really is.'

'Isn't that a bit like taking revenge?' I said it softly, but she heard all right – and for one moment I almost thought she was angry! Instead, she managed to smile as she calmly replied, 'Surely if something is wrong we have a duty to put it right?'

'That is true, but perhaps you are not the right person to do that, seeing that you are emotionally involved?' I suggested.

'If I don't, who else will?' she demanded.

'Couldn't you leave it to God to choose the right person? Surely it is a father's responsibility to deal with a wayward child, and not the responsibility of a sibling, particularly the sibling who has been wronged.'

'God doesn't expect us to be mindless doormats!' Anna said snappily and, looking at her watch, decided it was time she left.

As we met each other regularly, she gradually began to understand just how many of her sources of satisfaction had been threatened by Trevor's actions, and with that understanding came the ability to acknowledge that her anger was there. However, after that point she stuck, excusing herself by saying, 'I can't face up to all this heavy stuff while I'm feeling so ill all the time – and now I'm getting depressed on top of everything else, I just feel I must have space.'

So we talked about other things when she came, until I began to suspect that she was afraid to express and confess her anger in case she would then have to forgive, and her hatred of Trevor was still far too real to allow that.

'Of course I'm willing to forgive Trevor,' she would say suspiciously often, 'but I'm not quite ready to do it yet.' It is hard enough for most of us to admit to anger, but very few will ever acknowledge hate. There was nothing I could do but go on praying for her as the weeks went by.

Then one March weekend, when Anna was staying with her mother who lived close to us, she came round to see me on a Saturday evening. I realised at once that something was different about her, so I asked her directly what it was.

'Well, it only happened this week,' she admitted. 'I've been going to an ecumenical prayer group during Lent, and there's this little old nun who comes along to it. She's such a sweetie. She asked me if I'd like to see the convent where she lives, and I went on Monday afternoon. I had been feeling that something was happening to me inside for a few days,' she added awkwardly. Years of being 'the minister's wife' made it very hard for her to admit any spiritual need of her own. 'I think it's this business about life goals and crucial needs; I think the Lord has been challenging me to trust him to meet *all* my needs, instead of always trying to find ways of meeting my own. Anyway, I told Sister Elizabeth about all that, and she took me into a little oratory off the Convent Chapel, and prayed such a beautiful prayer – asking the Lord to show us what he wanted to do for me.'

Suddenly I noticed that tears were trickling down Anna's thin cheeks. It was the very first time I had ever seen her cry. She went on to explain how the little nun had helped her to express her anger in very much the same way as I had done once. They even burned a long list of all the things that Anna felt that Trevor had taken from her.

'I think it was realising that I could trust God to meet all my needs that finally helped me to get it all out into the open. After we had burnt the papers, that dear old lady even sprinkled me with holy water as a sign that I was cleansed. I dare not think what people would say about me if that got round our Baptist church!' And then I heard her laugh for the first time too! So often, buried anger holds good feelings down as well.

'What about . . . forgiveness?' I asked cautiously, and her smile died away.

'Soon,' she replied, 'but not quite yet.'

Anna and I went to church together the following evening and it was such a special service that Anna spent most of it in tears at the far end of the pew, and I must say I was a bit weepy myself. When it finished, I knew I needed to get to Anna before we were caught up in all the usual chit-chat, so as soon as the other occupants of the pew had left I slid along to sit beside her. She put her head down on my shoulder and wept again.

'I think I've got there at last,' she said.

'Got there?' I asked.

'You know, you nagged me about it often enough. I've reached that place now, but I don't really know what to do now and it scares me a bit.'

So we asked the Lord to show us what he wanted to do for her at that minute, and as we sat there in silence I began to see a picture in my head of a little alpine path, winding up through the fir trees. Anna was trudging up this, struggling under the weight of a very heavy backpack. The path was steep and stony and she often stumbled as she struggled upwards.

Then I saw the path had emerged from the trees on to a stark and rugged mountainside and suddenly I realised it had ended abruptly, leaving the Anna in my picture to stare down into a dark chasm, so deep there seemed to be no bottom to it at all. On the far side, just a few feet away, the path continued, and across the abyss on the far side stood Jesus, his arms held out in welcome.

'Yes, that's exactly how it is!' she said, after I had described the picture to her. 'I've known for months that I would have to decide to trust Jesus completely one day. While I've been fighting for our rights, and trying to sort out our future and prevent Trevor damaging anyone else, I haven't been trusting the Lord to sort it all out. I suppose it's been pride, really, but this evening I kept feeling he was waiting for my decision. It was urgent that I made up my mind one way or the other.'

'How do you feel about that?' I asked, remembering all her questions and prevarications.

'Scared,' she replied, 'because I feel there is something I have to do first, before I leap over that chasm.'

We prayed again, and the picture came back to me very clearly. I saw that if Anna was going to manage that leap across the chasm, she would have to take off her backpack and leave it behind.

'What do you think is inside it?' I asked her.

She frowned in her effort to get into the picture with me.

'Perhaps it's my props,' she suggested, 'the things I always used to think were so important in my old life.'

'Is there anything deeper down in the bag?' I asked her, and she flushed.

'Yes, but I don't want to look at them.' The struggle took Anna a long time, and she was silent for what seemed to me like hours. Finally she looked at me and said, 'Jen, they're all the grudges I've been carrying against Trevor and the other people who left the church and said such terrible things about Leslie and me. I think,' she added with a sob, 'there's a lot of hatred in that bag too.'

'Are you going to be able to leave the bag behind you when you leap that chasm?' I asked. Again she was silent for a very long time.

'I want to,' she said slowly, 'but I just don't see how it's possible to forgive someone who did such a lot of damage.'

'I think Jesus is saying, "try it",' I said gently.

'I can't!' she said, suddenly drawing away from me. 'It's too hard, why should God expect me to forgive them on top of everything else he's asking of me these days?'

'Try it, Anna,' I said again.

'He'll have to lift me across the chasm then,' she said morosely.

'He can't,' I said. 'You've got to take that backpack off and make the decision yourself to jump. No one can help you with that. Once you are over on the far side, *then* he'll help you with the "how to" part of forgiving.'

Anna finally made that leap of faith with many tears shed on my shoulder. I can never wear that orange blouse without remembering the great sodden patch she left behind on it as she made her quantum leap. At last she looked up at me, with red, swollen eyes, but a radiant smile.

'I've never seen one of your "pictures" before,' she said, 'but I just saw myself in his arms. Saw them tight round me and I realised the utter safety of my position in life now. I am truly *in* Christ. He is my sufficiency. I've just told him, "I shall love you whatever you do, or don't do. I shall love you whether you make things easy for me or not. I shall love you because you are all that matters to me in the world now." Why, oh why, has it taken me so long to reach this lovely place?' Then she added, 'It's not enough to be willing to forgive – one day you have to make that leap and decide to do it.'

## The 'Hold Up' Factor

Anna was profoundly right. That is what the 'hold up' factor is all about in the anger stage: refusing to forgive the person who broke the teapot.

Many people walk all the way through the stages we have described and right up the mountain path, but when they reach the chasm, they stop, look inside their backpacks, and decide they cannot leave those grudges behind. So they put them back inside again, and struggle off down the mountain with the heavy bag still on their shoulders. These people never come out of the Broken Teapot Syndrome.


## The Challenge: Using the Anger

God's kind of anger rages furiously on behalf of someone he loves. When we use the wrong kind of anger to defend ourselves and to right our own wrongs, God leaves us to it, but when we turn to him and leave him to put matters right in his own way and at his own time, he is committed to helping us. 'Do not take revenge, my friends, but leave room for God's wrath, for it is written: "It is mine to avenge; I will repay," says the Lord' (Rom. 12:19, NIV).

Our wrong kind of anger gets in the way of God's right kind of anger because, 'The Lord will fight for you, and there is no need for you to do anything' (Exod. 14:14, GNB).

Perhaps these are the questions that the Lord wants to ask in this challenge:

- 'Will you let me sort all this out for you?'
- 'Will you let me use your righteous anger to help me defend the other people I love?'

Once Anna had shifted all her hatred out of the way, she was able to see who her real enemy was – Satan, not Trevor. Satan had organised the whole thing, and Anna could be justly angry at what he had done to Leslie and the faith of many younger Christians. So she used that anger to 'do something about it' by going into spiritual warfare through prayer. She felt so much better physically that she found that she could get up early in the mornings for a real time of intercession before her husband woke. She prayed for his health and the broken body of the church, and she prayed for Trevor too. She realised that when Jesus said, 'Behold, I stand at the door, and knock: if any man hear my voice, and open the door, I will come in to him' (Rev. 3:20, AV), he was speaking to a whole church, not simply to an individual. It only takes one person to open the door of a church, a family or any other situation, and to allow the mending power of Jesus to come into the centre of all the pain and hurt.

Anna then gathered some of the women who were still left in the congregation, and with newfound enthusiasm and energy she encouraged them to begin praying with her for the healing of the church. They fasted each Monday and met together in twos and threes at other times of the week.

As Leslie began to improve in health and the life of the church started to move on again, many of the 'scattered sheep' returned to the fold and once more numbers began to grow. In the end, it was Anna who helped both churches to patch up their differences - and today both fellowships are flourishing side by side, one catering more for the needs of younger people, and the original church for older Christians and those with more traditional tastes. A messy situation has been turned into an opportunity for growth, because one apparently defeated woman used the anger she had always denied to give her courage to fight a battle with spiritual weapons.

---

## A Meditation

King David was one of the fiercest fighters of all time, but he was also known as 'a man after God's own heart'. The anger that sent him out to fight Philistines was God's kind of anger; it burned on behalf of his people who were being attacked without mercy.

One afternoon, when he was a very old man, David sat in a shady corner of his palace courtyard, drowsily remembering. His fighting days were over now, but he was living his greatest battles all over again. Then suddenly a dark memory came back to him and he stirred restlessly on his couch. The wind was moaning among the lonely caves of the desert, where he was hiding like a fugitive in danger of his life.

He had been banished from his position at court with his reputation in tatters, stripped unjustly of all he had in the world, and divided from his best friend for ever. It was all because of the jealousy and hatred of King Saul, who was out there in the darkness, hunting him relentlessly like some animal. But he could so easily have killed his enemy during that dark night that he was remembering now. He had discovered him lying alone and defenceless at the mouth of a cave. A sharp spear was in David's hand – should he plunge it into Saul's black heart and end his own problems for ever? After all, God had said that he should be king some day, so perhaps this was the way it was 'meant'. However, David had turned away, and left Saul to God's anger and vengeance.

He woke with a start, almost expecting to find himself still in the desert, but the beauty of his palace surrounded him. God's anger had burned on his behalf, and Saul had long since gone. But the shadow of another enemy had darkened his life since then, and sadly the old man bowed his head as he remembered another terrible day. This memory was more recent, and he saw himself already frail and bent with age. This time it was not jealousy and hatred that was driving him away from all he valued, but the greed of a young man who wanted his crown – his own son Absalom, the son he loved so much he would willingly have died for him.

David, who had always been admired for his bravery, looked like a coward the day he ran away from his city fortress and left it waiting for Absalom. As he trudged away he was cursed and publicly insulted by one of his son's supporters.

'Your majesty, let me go and cut off his head!' said one of David's men as the old king was pelted with stones. But David shook his head and said simply, 'It may be that the Lord will see my distress and repay me with good for the cursing I am receiving today.'

That is how it had happened in the end, and once again it was God's anger and not David's that came to his defence. As David sat there in the evening of his life, he wrote his final Psalm as a tribute to the powerful but terrible anger of God Almighty.

'My God is my protection, and with him I am safe . . . In my trouble I called to the Lord . . . In his temple he heard my voice . . . Then the earth trembled and shook . . . because God was angry. Smoke poured out of his nostrils . . . He tore the sky apart and came down . . . flashes of fire came from the lightning . . . when you rebuked your enemies, Lord, and roared at them in anger. The Lord reached down from above and took hold of me . . . he rescued me from my powerful enemies and from all those who hate me . . . When I was in trouble . . . the Lord protected me.' (Selected verses from Psalm 18, GNB.)

## A Prayer

*'Come to me all you who are tired of being hurt over and over again, for "I offered my back to those who beat me, my cheeks to those who pulled out my beard; I did not hide my face from mocking and spitting".'* (Isa. 50:6, NIV)

Lord, it's all very well to say I must forgive – it would be easy if everything was all over and done with and safely in the past. But my enemy keeps on hurting me, rejecting me, heaping pain on top of pain, and so many insults that I do not know how to endure it sometimes. I decide to forgive and then bang! He hits me again. I struggle up to my feet and bang! Down I go. Bang! Another humiliation. Bang! Something else is taken away. Bang! Bang! Bang! Over and over again. This repeated pain is driving me mad; how can I possibly forgive something like this that goes on and on? Bang! Bang! Bang! Yet you did.

I suppose it wasn't *afterwards* that you forgave; you did not wait until you could look back on your enemies and see them in retrospect; it was while they were hammering in those nails . . . Bang! bang! Bang! . . . that you said, 'Father, forgive them, they don't know what they are doing.' Each of those nail blows into your hands was rejecting all the loving things those hands had done for mankind. They were the very hands that had formed and created those soldiers; they had hidden the iron in the earth out of which the nails were forged. Bang! Bang! Bang! They rejected you, insulted and humiliated you as well, as they hit you over and over again. Yet you still forgave. Oh Jesus, forgive me for not forgiving too.

Lord Jesus, help me to see what it really means to have you living in me. You feel through my emotions, hurt in my body; these things that they do to me, they do to you too. You say, 'The insults that are hurled at you have fallen on me.' Lord, when they smash my life, they smash your life too. When they insult me, they insult you in me. When they steal my reputation and good name, they steal your honour too. I know you feel angry for me and will fight on my behalf. Help me to rest in that fact.

I am glad I can leave you to be angry with them for me, for your anger is so much more terrible than mine could ever be. I *want* your wrath to burn with vengeance until they are punished in full. Yet as you prayed, 'Father, forgive them', you were asking that they should be let off that punishment, pleading that the terrible wrath of God should *not* wreak vengeance on them. Those men will stand next to me in your presence for all eternity as free and as loved as I am. Lord, please give me the same supernatural forgiving grace – help me love my enemy as you loved yours.

## STOP FOR A MOMENT

### Why Is Forgiving So Hard?

#### 1. It Is Unnatural

*No one expects a rabbit to forgive the fox who has just half eaten it. The natural world says 'an eye for an eye' and 'every man for himself', but as followers of Christ we are told not to conform to the standards of this world; instead, 'let God transform you inwardly by a complete change of your mind' (Rom. 12:2, GNB).*

#### 2. It Is Unpopular

*After a two-year-old called Jamie was brutally beaten to death by two older boys, a clergyman suggested in his pulpit that the only way for anyone to cope with such an atrocity is by forgiveness. Immediately, five members of the congregation stormed out of the church. After some outrageous tragedy, some people regard forgiving as weak, soft or downright wrong. A friend of ours, a clergyman in Dover, spent weeks helping grieving relatives after the Zeebrugge ferry disaster. In his address at the memorial service, which was conducted at sea over the place where the ferry went down, he said that only forgiveness could mend broken lives. His words stirred up a hornets' nest of rage from the media.*

*When I went to speak at Enniskillen in Northern Ireland, I met friends and family members of those killed or hurt in the bomb blast there on Remembrance Day 1987. I told them how much it had helped the rest of us to hear how they stated their willingness to forgive so publicly, but was told that the harsh criticism they had received from people who felt they had no right to forgive such evil had caused them almost as much suffering as the tragedy itself.*

#### 3. It Takes So Long

*Forgiveness is not a once-won battle, but a lifelong war. Just before he died, C. S. Lewis wrote to his American friend Mary: 'Do you know, only a few weeks ago I realised suddenly that I had at last forgiven the cruel school master who so darkened my childhood. I'd been trying to do it for years; each time I thought I'd done it, I found after a week or so it all had to be attempted over again.'* Many people give up and feel they have failed simply because they think forgiveness should be as instant as coffee or packet mashed potato. Forgiving is a lengthy process, and it can be the hardest thing Jesus ever asks us to do for him; yet nothing gives him more pleasure than when we make the attempt to forgive. Surely this must be because forgiving was the reason he came to our world in the first place. It cost him everything he had to make forgiveness possible, so perhaps it is no wonder that we find it so costly.

# 10

# ACCEPTANCE

So what is the 'last square' on the game board of adjustment and change – this mysterious 'state' the experts call acceptance? Could it be the moment when we turn away from the empty display cabinet where the old teapot used to stand and catch our first glance of the new teapot on the windowsill? The time when we realise that we are no longer in tragic pieces scattered all over the kitchen floor, but beautiful in a new kind of way as fresh green shoots push their way out of all the cracks, gaps and broken places.

And how do we know when we reach this 'mysterious moment'? On the day I was thinking out this chapter, a curious thing happened. It was one of those beautiful November days, when a rather elderly sun was painting the remaining autumn leaves in quite impossible colours. So I went for a long walk up my favourite valley near Alfriston in Sussex.

The Cuckmere River winds in elegant ox-bow curves between the flinty chalk hills that eventually become the Seven Sisters – this particular river has always fascinated me because it alters its character completely with the changing tides. Sometimes it is nothing more than a little stream bubbling over the stones at the bottom of deep muddy banks. When the tide is in, however, the level

*I will sprinkle clean water on you and make you clean from all your idols and everything else that has defiled you. I will give you a new heart and a new mind . . . I will put my spirit in you and I will see to it that you follow my laws . . . I will save you from everything that defiles you.* (Ezek. 36:25–29, GNB)

of the water rises right to the top of the banks, creating a wide smooth surface on which the swans glide gracefully.

That day, as I walked up the valley, the tide came in after me, and by the time I reached the little bridge at Littlington it was fuller than I had ever seen it before. I noticed it as I paused on the bridge. It was easy to see that the tide was still racing in at high speed because a great sheet of scum, froth and bubbles came racing towards me from the direction of the sea, carrying with it all kinds of straw, twigs and driftwood.

The water was so high that it was not far below the level of the bridge, and as I stood there looking down I thought anxiously, 'If the tide doesn't turn soon, the river is going to burst its banks and flood the cottages in the village.' Then just as the blanket of scum was right under the bridge beneath me, it suddenly slowed down and stopped – and I mean suddenly. It was as if someone had put on the brakes; there was nothing gradual about it. For a moment the water in the river was motionless; it neither flowed in nor out, then a few foamy bubbles from one corner of the slick detached themselves and began to move back slowly downstream. Within seconds, the whole mass followed, and was soon hurrying back towards the sea, from whence it had come. The tide had turned.

I have never seen it actually happen before; usually you only know the tide must have turned because rocks or posts begin to appear that were submerged half-an-hour before. Yet there must always be a moment in time when the tide does turn, whether we happen to perceive it or not. For some people, the Broken Teapot Syndrome seems to get worse and worse as it builds up to a crescendo of misery – just like a floodtide that threatens to burst the banks of their endurance and plunge them into total disaster. Then an event such as a new job, or moving house, or a sudden revelation like Anna's 'alpine leap' or my 'baptism' in cow dung, changes everything so suddenly that they can pinpoint the exact moment when the tide of their affairs actually turned. For others, things improve slowly and imperceptibly so that acceptance feels more like a gentle receding of pain, and a gradual awakening to a new life. Yet even for them, there must have been 'a moment' when the tide turned, even though they were not aware of it at the time.

---

*We will reap a harvest of blessing if we don't get discouraged and give up.* (Gal. 6:9, LB)

This is the stage the textbooks call 'acceptance', but I am not sure I like that word. It conjures up in so many people's minds a sigh of resignation, a surrender to defeat, or a bowing down to an inevitable fate. Real acceptance is not like that at all. In *Beyond Ourselves* (Hodder & Stoughton), Catherine Marshall writes, 'Resignation is barren of faith in the love of God ... Resignation lies down quietly in the dust of a universe from which God seems to have fled, and the door of Hope swings shut.' Acceptance is a deliberate decision to let go of the past, to step away from the person we were and to move into the future. Boldly embracing it rather than shrinking away. Acceptance is a strong word, a life giving experience.

But surely many people successfully reach this place of acceptance without any Christian faith – if it is only a matter of letting go of the past and deciding to step into a new future. Yet acceptance, for Christians, is also something more, because God is involved in the process.

The issue for a Christian is:

1. Now that the past lies behind me, do I still trust God in spite of all that has happened?
2. Now that the future lies ahead of me, do I trust God to be there in it with me and take care of all my needs?

Nowadays, I am beginning to prefer the word 'abandonment'. Acceptance is something you do through your mind, but abandonment has to be done through the heart.

## What Does It Mean to Abandon Ourselves to God?

Strange as it may sound, it was in Marks & Spencer's that I first realised what the word 'abandonment' really means!

Just before Christmas last year, I was in the store looking for a chunky jumper as a present for Sarah's husband, Paul. Among the

---

*God who began the good work within you will keep right on helping you grow in his grace until his task within you is finally finished on that day when Jesus Christ returns.* (Phil. 1:6, LB)

crowds I noticed a little boy of about three, tightly holding on to his father's hand. His eyes were big and round with the wonder of the occasion, which his father was making particularly special for him. They were obviously there to buy a Christmas present for an older sister.

'You see, I wanted her to have slippers with cats' heads on them and *real* whiskers,' he explained earnestly to the startled girl at the check-out desk, as he handed her the pair he had chosen.

'Come on, David,' said his father, and I watched him walk away proudly carrying his green carrier bag.

A while later, when I was queueing up to pay for Paul's jumper, I saw a very different David indeed. He was running frantically through the shop, diving this way and that, round the high counters and displays. He had obviously lost his father, and my instinct was to run up to him and take his hand.

Sadly, children these days have to be warned not to trust strangers, and I decided that he might have become even more frightened if I had approached him. So instead I prayed for him as I wrote out my cheque. Then, with my own green carrier bag in my hand, I went to see if he was all right. In the far distance I caught sight of him standing rigid in the centre of an aisle, his face puce with anger. His precious shopping bag lay on the ground where he had flung it in his baffled fury. He had obviously searched the shop frantically, and had now decided that he had been abandoned for ever and would never be found again. Fear, anger, doubt and utter despair flitted across his face as he stood there, immobilised by his emotions.

This time, I really felt I must take action, but someone else reached him first. She was an elderly lady with thick glasses and bristly warts all over her chin. 'Come along, sonny,' she said, as she grabbed his arm. She meant well, but David shrank away in sheer terror.

Sometimes, when you have run in all directions looking for your security, there comes a moment when there is nowhere left to run; David seemed to have reached that point, so he simply pulled the plug out on the world and collapsed into a heap on the floor. He did not cry, because there is also a place beyond tears and it seemed that

---

*Man's chief end is to glorify God and enjoy him for ever.*
(Westminster Catechism)

he had reached that place. He curled himself into a ball – a defenceless little hedgehog without any prickles. It was then, much to my relief, that I saw David's father appear around the end of the counter.

'David!' he called. What a transformation! The little boy sprang to his feet and ran with quite remarkable speed towards his father. I held my breath, for sometimes when parents find a lost child they lambast them – hard – for being so naughty. I felt as if I couldn't bear that to happen to David, but this father was different. He squatted down to David's level and held out his arms – wide, and David ran straight into them to be lifted high off the ground; his little legs swinging free, in utter abandonment to his father's love.*

## 1. Abandonment Means Trusting God for Everything that Lies Behind Us

Look before you leap! Take a positive look at the past!

One of the most painful results of loss is that so many of the goals we used to aim for in life suddenly become impossible to achieve. Perhaps, for example:

- You always wanted to have a happy Christian family. So when your teenagers get mixed up with drugs and bad company, or your spouse wants a divorce, you feel devastated.
- You always wanted to provide for the people you love, but your bankruptcy and endless unsuccessful job applications make you feel a failure.
- You always wanted to be a vet (or a dancer or whatever), so that

---

* Does that story make you cringe because you think that if that is what abandonment to God is all about, you don't feel it's for you? Do you sometimes find it a bit difficult to trust God completely and feel really comfortable with him? Perhaps you should look back again to page 143 and check that you have not developed a wrong picture of what God is like through contact with people in the past. If you ask God to correct any wrong concepts you have, he most certainly will.

> *And when we obey him, every path he guides us on is fragrant with his loving-kindness and his truth.* (Ps. 25:10, LB)

you felt your life was shattered when the accident resulted in you being in a wheelchair.

- You always wanted to serve the Lord by helping other people, building up your church fellowship, developing a powerful ministry, leading others into the faith, running the youth work housegroup or Sunday School. So when others no longer wanted you or your health broke down, you felt that your life had no purpose.

One of the positive things about the Broken Teapot Syndrome is the opportunity it gives us to consider if such life goals were the right ones in the first place:

- Perhaps the goals we used to think were so important were all good things, but had become *too* important to us. Had they begun to rule our hearts to the point where our lives mean nothing now we cannot achieve them?
- If the things we so badly wanted could be lost as easily as this, were they wise goals to be aiming for anyway? Surely we would be more fulfilled if we aimed at goals that we could be sure of achieving, whatever happens to us in the future.
- Had we managed to achieve those old goals, would they actually have brought us the fulfilment we hope they would have brought us?
- Our previous goals may have been good ones, but were they the goals God wanted for us?

### 2. Abandonment Means Being Willing to Change Our Goals for the Future

What does God think is the most important thing in life? Jesus was once asked that question by a crafty lawyer, but the question was couched in the theological language of his day.

'Teacher, what is the first and greatest commandment?' he asked.

---

*Oh Lord, I know it is not within the power of man to map his life and plan his course . . . Show me the path where I should go, O Lord; point out the right road for me to walk.* (Jer. 10:23 and Ps. 25:4, LB)

Jesus replied promptly in the following vein, 'Loving God with everything you have. All your affections and willpower, with all your physical strength and mental capacity, through your emotions and entire personality. It is our relationship with God that is the most important thing in life, and after that our relationship with other people.'

In other words, there is nothing more important in life than to please God, know him, love him, spend time with him, and make him our treasure and heart's desire. Our goal in life needs to be *him* – not just serving him, or pointing others to him, or doing good, or turning the world upside down. It is not wanting to receive power or spiritual gifts from him, but just wanting *him* for his own sake.

When we want to please God and make him happy every minute of the day, that may mean serving him in all the ways listed above – or perhaps none of them ever again – but when we really want to please him we are willing to leave it to him to decide what he does with us.

This passionate single-minded pursuit of God himself is a goal that is not thwarted by being in a wheelchair or by being kicked out of your church, left to live alone, or robbed of a ministry by the lies and insults of others. It is not affected by any earthly loss, and nothing from heaven will ever thwart it because this is God's goal for us too.

Jesus said, 'Do not store up riches for yourselves here on earth, where moths and rust destroy, and robbers break in and steal. Instead, store up riches for yourselves in heaven . . . For your heart will always be where your riches are' (Matt. 6:19–21, GNB). 'Let Almighty God be your gold, and let him be silver, piled high for you. Then you will always trust in God and find that he is the source of your joy' (Job 22:25–26, GNB).

One of the greatest achievers in history was St Paul. He travelled all over the Roman world making converts and founding churches. When his 'teapot' broke and he was confined to a prison cell, he obviously had time to review his goals and consider what he most wanted out of life.

---

*Happy is the person who remains faithful under trials, because when he succeeds in passing such a test, he will receive as his reward the life which God has promised to those who love him.* (Jas. 1:12, GNB)

'All I want is to know Christ . . . and become like him' (Phil. 3:10, GNB), he said from his prison. That was a goal that was not blocked when he lost his freedom, but had his desire been to change the world he would probably have died of frustration. Was he able to say he had found the secret of contentment (Phil. 4:12) because his goal was the highest one of all, and the only goal that can be achieved by anyone, at any time, in any circumstances?

But how can we 'know Christ'? The idea that suffering brings us closer to Christ is not a popular one these days, but I have seen it happen for so many people that I cannot possibly doubt the truth of it. Many of us can say with Job as he looked back on his terrible experience of suffering, in the past 'I knew only what others had told me, but now I have seen you with my own eyes' (Job 42:5, GNB).

When Paul told us his goal was to 'know Christ', he also explains how that goal can be achieved. The full version of what he said from his dismal prison cell and under sentence of death was this, 'I want to know Christ and the power of his resurrection and the fellowship of sharing in his sufferings, becoming like him in his death' (Phil. 3:10, NIV). Paul had known that 'resurrecting power' once before when he had been in prison; it had been strong enough to burst the Roman fortress apart by an earthquake, setting him free instantly (Acts 16). However, he is telling us that we do not only get to know someone by sharing with them the highest and happiest moments of their lives, but also by sharing with them their deepest and most painful feelings, thoughts and experiences. Through the little prayers at the end of each chapter we have tried to identify with Jesus in his difficult moments as we gave him our own painful feelings and thoughts. It is a habit well worth acquiring.

### 3. Abandonment Means Feeling Safe
### Right Now in the Present

When little David ran into his father's arms, he felt safe. He knew that his father would, and could, meet all his needs. When Jesus said, 'Happy are those who long to be just and good, for they shall be completely satisfied' (Matt. 5:6, LB), surely when he said 'completely satisfied' he meant that God will meet in full our crucial need for love, acceptance and significance. 'Come, everyone who is thirsty – . . . Come . . . buy corn . . . Come! Buy wine and milk – it will cost you nothing! Why spend money on what does not satisfy? Why spend your wages and still be hungry? . . . Come to me, and you will have life!' (Isa. 55:1–3, GNB).

## *The challenge*

### Can God give us all the security we need?

- Can he love us with unearned, unending, uncondemning, unchanging love, which is so enormous it couldn't possibly get any bigger?

### Can God give us back our self esteem?

- Can he accept us individually for what we are here and now, this very minute, regardless of what we do or fail to do, and accept us so completely that our sense of worth and personal value is complete?

### Can God make life worth living?

- Can God's enjoyment of our company and desire to work in partnership with us provide us with all the significance and importance that we need? That is what we have to decide before we make that leap of abandonment.

### Perhaps God might ask us:

- Why have you always looked to people to meet your crucial needs?
- Why are you always hunting for love and security from human beings? They will always fail you in the end, perhaps not deliberately, but death or illness may prevent them from being there when you need them most. But I love you – I will never leave you or forsake you.
- Why have you always wanted people to like you in order to feel accepted and worth something? Why are you always trying to please, to do and say the things that will make the 'right people' approve of you? Why do you always strive to be the person they want you to be? Why worry about the opinions of people, when

humans only affect you in this life? Why don't you care what I think of you when I have your eternal destiny in my power? (Matt. 10:28.) You will never please people consistently enough to give you the affirmation you need. But to me, you will always be precious.

- Why do you look to your church activities, your job or role in the home to make you feel needed and significant as a person? People are so changeable that one moment you are their superstar and the next a mere nothing. Why look to them to make you feel that your life counts for something? When you are dead and gone, what will earthly importance matter anyway? It is your relationship with me that will last for ever. 'What good will it be for a man if he gains the whole world, yet forfeits his soul?' (Matt. 16:26, NIV.) Remember, I honour you, to me you are important. 'I will condemn the person who turns away from me and puts his trust in man . . . but I will bless the person who puts his trust in me. He is like a tree growing near a stream . . . not afraid when hot weather comes, because its leaves stay green; it has no worries when there is no rain; it keeps on bearing fruit' (Jer. 17:5–8, GNB).

God says to us: 'You are precious and honoured in my sight, and . . . I love you' (Isa. 43:4, NIV). In this verse God promises in just one sentence to be the three things we need!

- He says we are loved – that is our security
- He says we are precious – that is our self-worth
- He says we are honoured – that gives us significance

During a lifetime we will probably love quite a number of people, but very few will be really precious to us, but how many people can we honestly say we *honour*? That means esteeming them very highly, taking careful note of their opinions, and attaching great importance to all they say and do. God not only loves us, but he *honours* us too! And that has to be true – because he would have to honour someone extremely highly before being willing to die for them.

So we are absolutely loved, invaluably precious and highly honoured, both now and in the next life – what more could we want?


### 4. Abandonment Means Being Willing for a New Identity

The fear of changing into something new has been the 'hold up' factor for many people, but this last stage of abandonment entails a willingness to accept life as the new 'teapot' God has been designing all this time. Three little things might still be bothering people about the thought of that:

● 'If I depend on God for everything, does that mean I'll have to live alone for ever, with just him for company?'

There may be all kinds of things we want in the new life ahead – a husband, children, new friends, good relationships at work. When we begin to look to God to be the source of all our needs, it does not mean that he will force us to live like a hermit in the wilderness so that he himself can meet all our needs without human assistance. When God wanted to meet the needs of his first friend, Adam, he met them by sending another human being, Eve, to do it for him: 'It is not good for the man to be alone' (Gen. 2:18, NIV). As I have already said earlier in this book, we can always trust God to send along human arms to 'cuddle sad people' when he knows it is arms and a cuddle that we need. However, we do have to remember that God can see our *needs*, but we can only see our *wants*. Only he knows the difference!

● 'Surely it can't be right for God to want us all to spend our lives worshipping him and "sitting at his feet" in contemplation, like Mary of Bethany. He *must* want a few Marthas around to get things done.'

St Teresa of Avila once said, 'Our Lord is best served by a blend of both Mary and Martha', and of course making our personal relationship of love with the Lord our top priority does not mean that he will never ask us to serve him in more practical ways.

Jesus met a man once who was at the height of one of the most terrible Broken Teapot Syndromes of all time. His name was Legion. He had once been an ordinary family man, with a job and a little house in Decapolis. We don't know what went wrong for him, but gradually he began to open himself up to evil until finally he committed himself to Satan entirely, and many demons were sent to invade his life and possess him completely. Terrible anger burned in him, and would burst out at people uncontrollably until he became so dangerous that they threw him out of the community and chained him among the rocks and graves of the dead. His anger had no outlet then, so he turned it on himself as he mutilated his body, cutting and slashing at it with anything sharp he could find. The evil spirits tormented him until he was too afraid to sleep at night; sometimes, panic lent him such enormous strength that he burst the chains that fettered him and he wandered through the hills in the darkness, alone in his terrible isolation and despair. Then one morning at dawn, Jesus walked up the beach towards him.

It only took a moment to set Legion free from the evil spirits and all the anger, fear and despair they had caused, and his broken life was changed into something astonishingly different. When the local farmers came to complain to Jesus about the loss of their pigs, they were stunned when they saw Legion. Here was the man they had feared and despised, sitting beside Jesus, laughing and talking quite normally. It had been years since they had seen him washed, shaved and wearing clothes. 'When anyone is joined to Christ, he is a new being; the old is gone, the new has come' (2 Cor. 5:17, GNB).

The farmers found the whole thing so unnerving that they ordered Jesus to leave at once, without giving him a chance to tell the people of the ten little towns in that district that he had also come to set *them* free – not just Legion. 'Clear off!' they shouted menacingly.

Legion wanted to go with Jesus, to spend the rest of his life with him, 'sitting at his feet and hearing his words', but Jesus knew Legion was his only hope of reaching those towns. Mark 5:18–20 (GNB) says: 'As Jesus was getting into the boat, the man . . . begged him, "Let me go with you!" But Jesus would not let him. Instead, he told him, "Go back home to your family and tell them how much the Lord has done for you and how kind he has been to you." So the man left and went all through the Ten Towns, telling what Jesus had done for him. And all who heard it were amazed.' Mark also tells us how well Legion did his job of spreading the message (Mark 6:53–56). When Jesus went back some time later, the people were all waiting for him, and they 'ran throughout the whole region' gathering together all the other 'broken teapots' for him to mend.

It is a 'changed life' that convinces people more than anything else that Jesus can also help them. One day when they ask you, 'However did you manage to get through that awful experience?', you will be able to tell them 'how much the Lord has done for you and how kind he has been to you'; and it might be your personal testimony that will introduce *them* to him too.

● 'But how do I know what God really wants to do with me in the future?'

It infuriates most of us to have so few of our questions answered, but we are left in no doubt over this one. Like most other fathers, who want their children to 'take after them', God's goal for our lives is to make us like himself. He has always wanted that, since the beginning of time when he said, 'let us make man . . . in our likeness' (Gen. 1:26, NIV). Yet we never knew quite what God was really like until he sent Jesus down to earth to show us. God wants us to take a good look at Jesus and then to become like him.

### *But what does that mean?*

It simply means living in the ordinary circumstances of our lives as Jesus would. Trying to treat the people in our world as he would treat them, looking at them through his eyes, thinking about them as he does, reacting to them as he would and relating to them in the way he might have done when he had a physical body and lived on earth.

Paul says, 'those whom God had already chosen he also set apart to become like his Son' (Rom. 8:29, GNB), and we 'are being transformed into his likeness with ever-increasing glory' (2 Cor. 3:18, NIV).

### *But I could never do it!*

Well, God certainly does not stand at a distance and shout, 'You've got to change and become like my Son, so start working at it right now!' That would burden us with a crushing load of 'oughts' and 'shoulds' just when we feel too weak to carry anything extra at all. And however hard we tried, there is no way in a billion years we could possibly change ourselves to become like him. Instead, God uses exactly the same method as I explained on p. 27. The diagram there shows that when we ask him to come into the centre of our lives, he fills us up completely with himself. Jesus comes into our lives by his Spirit (John 20:22), and as we make more and more room for him, so he is able to change us from the inside until the difference also begins to show on the outside. He gives us a totally new heart to be the seat of our will and affections (Ezek. 36:26); he gives us his mind to think with (Rom. 12:2), and he helps us to develop his personality and attributes (Gal. 5:22). That is the secret of how we become Jesus 'look-a-likes'.

### 5. Abandonment Means Contentment –
### 'In Acceptance Lieth Peace'*

Being a mended 'teapot' may mean a wonderful, exciting new life, far better than the old one ever was, but it could just as easily mean we still have to live alone, remain trapped inside a painful or disabled body; or we may have to go on sharing our lives with difficult, unkind people who misunderstand us and reject our love. We may never get another job or develop a new ministry; we might have very little money and very few friends. Yet we know that all these things are not the sources of our real satisfaction, and we can say with the Psalmist, 'What else have I in heaven but you? since I have you, what else could I want on earth? My mind and my body may grow weak, but God is my strength; he is all I ever need' (Ps. 73:25–26, GNB). That was the verse that came to me that day by the sea in Devon when I 'felt' Jesus was saying, 'All you need is me.'

It was identifying with Jesus at a deep level that made it possible for Paul to say he was completely happy, even though he was confined in that prison cell under sentence of death: 'For to me, to live is Christ and to die is gain' (Phil. 1.21, NIV) and 'I have learnt to be satisfied with what I have . . . I have learnt this secret, so that anywhere, at any time, I am content . . . I have the strength to face all conditions by the power that Christ gives me' (Phil. 4:11–13, GNB).

Little David, when he was lost in Marks & Spencer's, had run frantically all over the store trying to find his source of security. He had worn himself out with his fear, anger and despair, just as we all did when our 'teapots' broke. As David searched the shop, he must have asked himself why his father would let a thing like this happen to him – just as we too have asked questions – but everything would have seemed irrelevant when he finally felt those strong arms holding him tightly and he had completely abandoned himself to his father's love.

So this is the last square on the board. For me, abandonment is finally realising that God himself is the answer to all my basic needs, and trusting myself to him entirely, just as little David relaxed in his father's arms and rested in his love. It is also acceptance, because when we know how God feels about us we can happily accept ourselves, accept other people, and accept life in whatever package it

* Amy Carmichael

may come. 'Oh, how kind our Lord was, for he showed me how to trust him and become full of the love of Christ Jesus' (1 Tim 1.14, LB).

## A Prayer

*'Come to me all you who are broken and need to be mended . . . for "you will have life! I will . . . give you the blessings I promised".'* (Isa. 55:2–3, GNB)

Lord Jesus, I think I am beginning to know you a little better through all that I have been suffering, and still must suffer, because in a small way I can appreciate what you went through for me. Yet all that was in the past, and it might feel a bit far removed from my life here in the present if I was not able to share my own suffering with you and allow you to come into the heart of it with me. This has helped me to feel you close to me here and now, at this present moment.

I admit my life has been broken: my dreams, my hopes, the person I used to be, and the relationships I used to value, all lay in pieces around me. Gradually, one by one I have been giving up all those shattered fragments, together with the grudges and the fears, the sorrow and the pain. Please take my life, broken as it is; I give it to you now as a sacrifice as you gave your life, 'your body broken as a sacrifice for me'.

Help me to live in the difficult circumstances of my life, as you would, and I know that each time I react to people and problems in the way that you would react I shall become a little more like you. Please help my faith not to fail until the day I see you face to face, because the ecstasy of that moment will make everything I have endured totally worthwhile.

'Now we live in the hope of eternal life because Christ rose again from the dead . . . So be truly glad! There is wonderful joy ahead, even though the going is rough for a while down here. These trials are only to test your faith, to see whether or not it is strong and pure . . . your faith is far more precious to God than mere gold. So if your faith remains strong after being tried in the test tube of fiery trials, it will bring you much praise and glory and honour on the day of his return.' (1 Pet. 1:3–7, LB)

# 11

## THE PRACTICAL SIDE OF FORGIVING

Jesus said tantalisingly little about many things, but he left us in no doubt as to how we should cope with the relationships we find 'difficult', and how we should treat the people who cause us misery and pain.

He says we must:

- Forgive them (Matt. 6:14)
- Pray for them (Matt. 5:44)
- Love them (Luke 6:27)
- Not fight back (Matt. 5:39), but do good to them instead (Luke 6:28–29)
- Go to them, and attempt to mend the relationship (Matt. 18:15–17)

Before we go any further, there are two things we should know about these rules:

1. They are impossible without Jesus' help.
2. They are not simply 'nice little suggestions'; instead, they are vital for our eternal well-being. Jesus tells us that on the final Day of Judgement we shall each be treated by God as we have treated others during our lifetime (Luke 6:37–38; Matt. 25:31–46). So if we refuse to forgive, he cannot forgive us (Matt. 6:14).

---

*One should never mention the words 'forgive' and 'forget' in the same breath. No, we will remember, but in forgiving we no longer use the memory against others.* (Helmut Thielicke, a German pastor who endured the darkest days of the Nazi Third Reich)

---

## 1. First, Jesus Tells Us We Must Forgive Them

For many people, the lengthy process of forgiving the 'Jesus way' begins the moment we ask him into the centre of our pain to melt away the hard core of anger that has collected there. He then begins to make us both willing and able to forgive. There is often a specific moment when we make the decision to forgive, and to leave behind us at his cross all the resentment and the grudges we have been carrying. This decision is simply an act of the *will*, and it has nothing to do with *feelings*.

This moment of 'releasing forgiveness' becomes more real to some people if they speak out loud, as if they were addressing the person who has hurt them. They say something like this, 'I forgive you for all you have done to hurt me and I cease to blame you for anything and everything.' Many also find it a help to write out a list of all the ways in which they feel they have been hurt, and then to burn the list, or destroy it in some other way.

### *But surely I should wait until the person begins to change?*

Jesus didn't wait until we were sorry. 'It was while we were still sinners that Christ died for us!' (Rom. 5:8, GNB.) He poured out his forgiving grace before we asked for it. Like a beautiful meal laid out before a starving person, all the benefits of Jesus' forgiveness lie there ready – regardless of whether that person refuses the food or sits down and eats it. Our response to the forgiveness that Jesus offers makes no difference to the way he feels about us.

Jesus also told us to love our enemies, not our ex-enemies – in other words, to love them while they are still deliberately hurting us and appearing to have no idea of the pain they are inflicting. Jesus practised this precept as the soldiers hammered the nails into his hands; he did not wait for them to repent first.

### *But surely forgiveness is a two-way transaction?*

To be complete, it is, but at first forgiving is all about what happens in our own hearts; it is between us and God, and the other person

---

*How long must I wrestle with my thoughts and every day have sorrow in my heart?* (Ps. 13:2, NIV)

does not come into it until later. So the method of releasing forgiveness I have just mentioned is equally effective regardless of whether the person who has wronged you is alive or dead.

### *But my 'enemy' keeps on thinking up new ways to harm me*

Jesus forgave unconditionally. It was not a case of, 'I'll forgive you on condition that you never step out of line again.'

### *But I don't feel forgiving – I keep having such angry thoughts*

A lot of people think they have failed to forgive because they do not *feel* any different after they have made the decision. A few days later, we could be washing up, sitting in church, or rushing to work when we suddenly think, 'But how *could* he have done that to me?' All the old pain comes flooding back again, and a little voice says, 'You've failed again. You'll never manage to forgive! You've been hurt too much.' Forgiving, though, is not something we do just once; C. S. Lewis suggests that when Jesus said we had to forgive seventy times seven, he was not putting a limit on how many different things we must forgive, but how many times we need to forgive the same sin. We have to keep on and on forgiving the same thing until the pain of the offence, and the memory of the moment, is diminished in our minds to the point where it no longer hurts.

These recurring thoughts of resentment are the little poisonous darts that Satan aims at our minds, and we need to be prepared for them. Every morning when you wake:

- Ask the Holy Spirit to fill you once again with the love and forgiving grace of Jesus.
- Ask for the protection of the blood of Jesus over you for that day.
- Put on your spiritual armour. 'Your strength must come from the Lord's mighty power within you. Put on all of God's armor so that you will be able to stand safe against all strategies and tricks of Satan' (Eph. 6:10–11, LB). This is the prayer I often use:

---

*We take captive every thought to make it obedient to Christ.* (2 Cor. 10:5, NIV)

---

Lord, I put on my helmet of salvation to protect my mind from attack.

The breast plate of righteousness to protect my heart from bitterness.

The belt of truth so that I do not see situations and people wrongly or get things out of proportion.

The iron-studded shoes of a Roman soldier, so I will not slip and slide back in the thought battles of today.

I pick up my shield of faith as I declare that I trust your ability to help me keep on forgiving today.

May I wield my sword effectively and use words of Scripture to defeat Satan as you did.

Please bring the right verses to my mind as I need them.

### *Remember the 'spit out, breathe in' routine*

Whenever a bitter thought 'hits' you throughout the day, 'spit it out' instantly and 'breathe in' the forgiving love of Jesus. The thought itself is not a sin, but welcoming it and sucking it like a toffee is.

It is not the memory you are spitting out (forgiving does not mean forgetting); it is the anger generated by the memory that must be instantly rejected.

### *Use prayer as a weapon*

One of the reasons for linking fasting with prayer is surely because the unpleasant hunger pangs remind us to pray. If every time Satan throws one of these thought missiles at us we use it as a trigger to pray for something or someone, he will soon stop this form of attack because he loathes us to pray. (It is probably better to pray for someone quite unconnected with the painful situation – because that has the same effect as 'thinking about something else' while the nurse gives you the injection!)

Praying in tongues also helps some people.

---

*'No weapon forged against you will prevail and you will refute every tongue that accuses you. This is the heritage of the servants of the Lord, and this is their vindication from me,' declares the Lord.* (Isa. 54:17, NIV)

---

### Singing as a weapon

Another good way to fight bitter thoughts is to sing a praise song or hymn – Satan hates praise. You can easily do it under your breath if you happen to be out shopping, but playing a praise tape in the car or kitchen is much easier!

### Saying the name of Jesus

That name is the most powerful name in the universe, and Satan hates the sound of it more than anything else. So when these 'thought attacks' are at their height, repeating the name of Jesus is a wonderful protection.

### Keep handing over the griefs and sorrows

When the bad memories threaten to overwhelm you, picture the cross of Christ between you and the person who hurt you. Keep reminding yourself that Jesus *was* there with you when all those things were happening. He felt the pain and the insults. He wants to carry all your 'griefs and sorrows', so make a conscious decision to shift them on to him every time your 'memory video' reruns. This is done by telling him how you feel, and asking for his healing. Holding on to the hurts might feel comforting, but it is a sure way of falling into self-pity – and Satan loves setting that trap for us.

### Keep a journey log book

Because the journey of forgiveness takes a long time, it helps many people to record their thoughts and feelings in a note book. Putting anger into words and then writing them down in private is a good way of getting it all out of our systems without the risk of hurting anyone else. It is also helpful to record the positive things, such as verses or sayings, moments when God seemed very close, dreams, or advice from other people. These special things can so easily be forgotten, and during the bad times it helps a lot to look back at them.

---

*In the shelter of your presence you hide them from the intrigues of men; in your dwelling you keep them safe from the strife of tongues.* (Ps. 31:20, NIV)

---

## 2. Jesus Tells Us to Pray for Our Enemies

Perhaps Jesus is best known for saying 'love your enemies', but we all know that's quite impossible! Fortunately, he also told us to pray for them – and we need to do that first because only prayer makes the love possible.

Praying for the person who has hurt us badly is usually the very last thing we want to do; cursing them would be far more natural, but that is exactly how the servants of Satan deal with their enemies. They curse them, bind them with spells and incantations, and do things to harm them, either directly or by sticking pins in effigies made of wax or clay. By commanding us to 'bless those who curse you, pray for those who ill-treat you. . . and do good to them' (Luke 6:28, 35, NIV), Jesus is telling us to treat our enemies in exactly the opposite way.

Praying for the person who has hurt us simply means bringing that person into God's presence and standing side by side before the cross. Sometimes it is easier not to use words at all. Peggy, a friend of mine, has a little stone she picked up on the seashore, which represents to her the person who hurt her so badly. Every morning she holds it out on the palm of her hand. As she exposes her enemy to the love of the Lord, her own heart is also open to that love, and she is finding that all her hatred and bitterness is gradually melting away.

Most of us, however, find 'wordless prayer' very hard. We want to say, 'Lord, change this person – he is sinning badly. Chasten him – and do it soon and hard!' The satisfying mental picture of him writhing in repentance, sobbing in his sack cloth, is quite pleasing – until we realise it is not quite what Jesus meant! He asks us to 'bless' by our prayers, and that means asking God to do good things for him.

Strangely, our prayers do not always change our enemy, but they always change us! Sister Basilea Schlink, when writing about a difficult relationship she had once, says this: 'One day in my distress I prayed fervently, then all of a sudden it was as if the finger of God was pointing not at the other person who was causing me such

---

*Lord, stand between him and me. Absorb all the anger that is passing between us. Filter all our feelings through the mesh of your love. You are not bound by a human body so you can hold me in your arms at the same time as you hold him.* (Cath Isaaks)

distress, but at me, "You are the one who has to change".' Perhaps as we pray for our 'enemies', we are reminded of two things that Jesus tells us *not* to do for them: 'Do not judge . . . do not condemn' (Luke 6:37, NIV). Gradually, we begin to see our own part in the painful scenario, and we wonder if it was really all the other person's fault after all. Perhaps we also did or said things that hurt the other person, and although his or her attack on us was wrong, perhaps in some ways we did 'bring it on ourselves'. So praying opens our eyes to our own need of repentance and forgiveness.

### Prayer then begins to help us see the enemy in a new way

It helps to dissolve some of our self-absorption, and we begin to understand *why* 'our enemy' might have acted as he did. One day, as Peggy was holding her little stone before God, she 'saw' a vivid picture of a small boy crying beside an empty double bed. She later discovered that her 'enemy' had lost both his parents when he was eight, and this softened her attitude towards him. Prayer does far more than simply make us feel more sympathetic; it takes us right inside our enemy's skin in order to see things through his eyes, think through his mind, and feel through his emotion. Understanding on this level makes 'loving' much easier.

### Praying helps the good memories to surface

Libby felt her childhood had been overshadowed by her father's terrible rages and frequent bouts of depression. 'All my memories of him were bad,' she said, 'until someone suggested that I prayed for him. Then suddenly, I remembered a lovely day we spent in a swimming pool when we had once been on holiday. He had taught me to swim by holding on to me with arms that felt so big and strong. I would have been about eight, and it must have been during one of his good spells, but I was able to thank the Lord for that one good memory – and in time I began to remember other little things too.'

> *Words may only add to the shame and pain, but a gentle act of forgiveness and acceptance can mean so much more . . . a hand clasp can mean, 'I need your love and respect you, you are important to me.'* (David Augsburger)

### Warning!

Understanding your enemy, though, does not mean excusing what he or she has done. Excusing can make forgiveness unnecessary, and is a form of denial. It is wrong to try and make ourselves think, 'He couldn't really help it.' He *could* help it, and trying to 'make allowances for him' is not placing the blame at the cross, so we are in danger of subconsciously holding on to it instead.

### Prayer means showing mercy

The Greek word that we translate into *forgiveness*, which was in everyday use in New Testament times, could equally well have described someone being 'let off' a debt that they owed. So forgiving means stepping away from our natural desire to punish our enemy, and handing him over to God to punish for us. We do not find that too hard to do when we read in the Psalms of the terrible wrath of God that awaits those who hurt the people who belong to him. Then we suddenly realise that the Psalms were written before Jesus showed men what forgiving really means. He said, 'Blessed are the merciful, for they shall obtain mercy,' and the greatest way we can ever show mercy to our enemies is by asking God to stay his wrath and vengeance, and to let them off all that they rightly deserve. This is more than just praying good things for them in this life – it is asking for good things for them in the next life as well! The hottest and deepest part of hell itself would surely be too good for those soldiers who heartlessly nailed the 'hands that flung stars into space' to a cross of wood. Yet Jesus was making room for them in heaven when he asked his Father to forgive them. Stephen had reached the same depth of love when he prayed, 'Lord, lay not this sin to their charge', as his persecutors stoned him to death. We know his prayer was answered, because one of them later became St Paul!

When we first bring 'our enemy' to the foot of the cross, we tend to look down on him from a lofty height as we say grandly, 'Lord, this poor wretch needs your forgiveness, and he certainly needs mine too.' However, as we stand there in the Lord's presence we begin to realise we are not 'looking down at our enemy' any longer, but we are standing right next to him. Still we instinctively say, 'Lord, I'm right, he's wrong. Compared to him, I'm a saint!' Then we look up into the face of Jesus and suddenly we stop comparing ourselves with our enemy, and we begin to see what we really are – worthless, wretched and vile. Our enemy may always have had a low opinion of us, but he has never even begun to see what we are really like! In horror, we realise that the lies he told about us were *kind* in comparison to the truth he could have told – had he known us as Jesus knows us. The cruel things he or she did were only a fraction of all that we deserved.

As we stand there sweating with relief at his ignorance, we suddenly realise that Jesus is not ignorant! He knows the very worst about us, yet he chooses to pour down on us a continuous cascade of love, grace and mercy. As we realise the extraordinary extent of the forgiveness he offers to us, our attitude towards the enemy beside us changes. For once we are united, because in the light of God's holiness we are in the same hopeless state, both totally unworthy of forgiveness, either from God or each other. Yet his unstinting mercy is there for us both. After a real experience of God's love and grace, forgiveness is no longer a grudging 'ought', and it becomes easy. All we do is turn in imagination to our enemy beside us and simply allow the torrent that has flooded into us to flow on and out to him, just as if we were merely an empty pipe – a channel of God's grace, unblocked at both ends. Whether he chooses to receive it is not our problem; it is his. We, though, have been obedient to another command of our master, 'Be merciful, just as your Father is merciful' (Luke 6:36, NIV).

### 3. Jesus Tells Us to Love Them

If we are honest, most of us think that is really asking a bit too much! Why should we be commanded to love someone who causes us nothing but misery? However, we need to remember that God's goal is to make us like himself, and he shows constant benevolence to bad people in the same way that he does to the good. The sun shines just the same on the fields of the churchgoing farmer and his Satanist neighbour.

It does help a little to know that Jesus did not tell us to *feel* loving – just to love. Had he meant the kind of love that is full of passionate feelings, he would have used the Greek word *eros*. If he had wanted us to love our enemy with all the emotional tenderness we reserve for our families, he would have used the word *storge*. He might have used *philia* if he wanted us to feel for our enemies the same kind of deep affection we have for our very dearest friends. However, the word Jesus selected was *agape*, which is not a feeling or an emotion as much as an act of the will. It is a decision to love someone. As William Barclay writes in *The Daily Study Bible*, 'No matter what he does to us, no matter how he treats us, no matter if he insults us or injures us or grieves us, we will never allow any bitterness against him to invade our hearts, but will regard him with that unconquerable benevolence and good will which will seek nothing but his highest good.'

Hate wants to harm and destroy; love desires another's highest good and happiness. If we simply spat out the hate, we should be left with a vacuum – that is why we breathe in the love of Jesus, so that it can flow back out again from us in place of the hate. Love is a move towards a person to do good to them in any possible way.

The idea of acting in a loving way without first *feeling* love is difficult. I was once part of a housegroup for new Christians, one of whom was Shirley. One day she told the group she had never been able to forgive the 'other woman' who had broken up her parents' marriage and destroyed her childhood security. Now, years later, she had still never allowed her father's second wife 'to step over her doorstep'.

'I suppose now I'm a Christian I'm going to have to forgive her and even try and love her too,' she added. A few days later she called on me in a panic. Her father had just rung to say he and his wife were in the district and wanted to drop in for a cup of tea.

'How do I treat her?' she demanded.

'You welcome her into your home and treat her with love,' I replied.

'But I don't *feel* loving yet,' she said.

'*Act as if* you loved her,' I said, and explained Pascal's little phrase that had helped me so much with depression and doubt, and added Selwyn Hughes's maxim, 'You can act yourself into feelings even if you cannot feel your self into actions.' 'Loving actions come before loving feelings and not the other way about,' I added.

'It worked!' she told me a few hours later. 'I hated her as I answered the doorbell, but then made myself switch on the love of Jesus and pretended like mad. I felt a fraud at first, but by the time they left I caught myself thinking, "Dad did all right for himself in the end – she's really rather a nice person after all." We have promised to keep in touch from now on, and I haven't felt so close to my dad for years.'

### 'Love always protects'

The NIV rendering of 1 Corinthians 13:7 is 'love . . . always protects'. One of the most valuable things we possess is our reputation. We would never dream of destroying our enemy's car or house, yet by defending our own reputation we automatically destroy his. When sympathetic friends want to hear 'our side of the story', the only way we can put ourselves in a good light is by putting him in a correspondingly bad light. By pointing out to others all his sins and failings, we alter the way they think of him in the future. If we make his shortcomings the topic of conversation over a cup of coffee or glass of beer or make him the butt of our witty little jokes, we are demolishing him publicly. If we 'produce' him as a prayer topic, and sadly shake our heads over his 'lack of spirituality', we are not protecting him, and so we are not loving him. Everything we say about another Christian behind his back should build him up in the eyes of our hearers. Jesus tells us clearly that we should talk to our enemy about his faults face-to-face in private (Matt. 18:15). Of course, we can safely talk about him to Jesus himself, but we must be careful how we talk to other people.

### 4. Jesus Says, 'Do Not Fight Back – Instead, Do Good to Your Enemies'

Forgiving is hardest of all for those who live with their 'enemy', and have to face daily insults and humiliation. It is also difficult for those who feel that their enemy is continually working against them to harm them or those they love. In such cases, forgiveness becomes an active and daily experience. So what does Jesus tell us to do about that?

Most people the world over know that Jesus said, 'If someone smites you on the right cheek, turn to him the left cheek also.' Now the only way that the average right-handed man could hit a man like that is by using the back of his hand. In the days when Jesus said this, to hit a Jew in that way was twice as insulting as using the palm of the hand. So Jesus is saying, 'Even if someone offers you the worse possible insult, do not retaliate.'

However, Jesus did not mean us to stand by passively while someone hurts us over and over again. To do that would simply be to allow all the pain to flow into a vacuum. So he also tells us to 'do good to those who hate you'. In other words, 'don't just stand there while he hits you, do something active – pay back the evil he does to you by doing something good to him in return'. Jesus himself did this the night a mob came to arrest him. Peter jumped to his defence and slashed off the ear of one of the men, but Jesus healed him instantly. 'If your enemy is hungry, feed him; if he is thirsty, give him something to drink . . . Do not be overcome by evil, but overcome evil with good' (Rom. 12:20–21, NIV). When Abraham Lincoln was criticised for being 'kind' to his enemies instead of destroying them, he said, 'Do I not destroy my enemies when I make them my friends.'

James, the minister of a large church, had a terrible time when his congregation began to split because of a power struggle. He made a promise to the Lord that every time he heard on the 'grapevine' of some new criticism hurled at him, or a fresh lie being circulated, that he would do some definite act of kindness for the person concerned. 'Sometimes it was only giving them a smile or a wave across the street, or simply a prayer for God's blessing in some specific way,' he told us. 'But it kept my heart sweet and helped me through those horrible months. In the end the trouble all died down, and the Lord's name was not dishonoured by the disintegration of our church community.'

### Not Fighting Back Means Giving Up Our Right to Be Vindicated

Suppose your enemy threatened to destroy your Christian ministry or rob you of your role in life, or your job, by telling lies about you behind your back, or even accusing you falsely to your face. What about fighting back then? As a human being your first reaction would probably be to justify yourself in the eyes of other people, by speaking out in your own defence or by taking legal action. After all, telling lies about people is defamation of character and the person surely ought to be sued for that? Yet forgiving the 'Jesus way' means giving up our right to be vindicated. He said in Matthew 5:40 (NIV): 'If someone wants to sue you and take your tunic, let him have your cloak as well.' The average Jew in those days might well have two or three 'tunics', but only one cloak. It was really a thick outer garment that he wore as a robe in the day, but used as a blanket at night. The law said a man's tunic could be taken as a pledge, but never his cloak – legally, that had to be handed back by sunset. Jesus is challenging here our natural instinct to stand up for our rights. St Paul also condemns disputes, battles and lawsuits among Christians in 1 Corinthians 6:1–6, and then he goes on to say that such things are a sign of defeat: 'Why not rather be wronged? Why not rather be cheated? Instead, you yourselves cheat and do wrong, and you do this to your brothers!' (vv. 7–8, NIV.)

'But surely Christians are in the world to be salt and light, so we must right wrongs and fight injustice!' you may think. Yes, we must, so long as we only 'right the wrongs' done to other people. We must be very careful how we fight injustice when we personally are the victim, because that is not following the example of Jesus who: 'remained silent and gave no answer' when lying accusations were being hurled at him (Mark 14:57–61; Isa. 53:7).

A friend of ours was involved recently in an extremely painful power struggle within a Christian organisation. He made a definite attempt to mend the relationship between himself and his main antagonist, but the other man simply would not respond. Here is part of a letter in which our friend described to us his feelings:

> I felt desperately disappointed when the reconciliation failed, until I realised it was the loss of my reputation and status that was mostly upsetting me. I had hoped that the reconciliation would manipulate him into repairing the ruins of my life, but I saw that if I forgave him it meant leaving all the chaos he had caused in God's hands. I would have to stop working to clear my name, and turn my back on the mess and deliberately walk away. I risked never being exonerated, but I decided that personal justice was not as important to me as the peace with God that I knew I would receive when I forgave.

### Burning the evidence

Marie had been all knotted up inside by bitterness ever since she had been dismissed from her position as 'matron' of a local government home for the elderly. She believed it was because she had been unfairly accused by a member of her staff, and she also felt she had been badly treated by the 'powers that be' in the DSS. For some years, she had kept all kinds of letters and documents stored in her attic, 'just in case' she could one day use them to have herself reinstated.

During a week's retreat in a healing centre, she began to long to be free from all the resentment and anger that had long been causing her many physical and emotional problems. Even with the help of skilled counsellors, she simply could not seem to release it all, and in the end it was felt that there was some kind of block preventing her inner healing. On the last day of her stay, she suddenly remembered the trunk full of correspondence in her attic. 'But I can't get rid of all that,' she protested, when her counsellors told her to go home and burn it. 'It's my last hope of ever getting my rights.'

'Which is more important to you, your rights or your health and peace?' was the challenge with which they sent her home. As she walked in through her front door, she still had not decided what she would do, but by the following evening she 'made the biggest bonfire ever' in her back garden and finally gave up her chance of vindication.

When she told me that story a few months ago, I had already begun to write this book, but all the inspiration had petered out after the first two chapters. I had put the book on the 'back burner', thinking perhaps it was not what God wanted me to do after all. Then when Marie told me about her attic trunk, I remembered a file full of letters and documents I had also put away. They concerned some personal criticism that I had felt was untrue, and I had collected all kinds of material – thinking that one day I might be able to use it to clear my name. Within days of making my own bonfire, the ideas for the book were positively pouring into my computer! Fancy expecting God to help me write a book on forgiveness with all that in my own filing cabinet!

## *Warning!*

Not fighting back does not mean denying natural anger. You *will* feel angry – often! So do turn back to Chapter 9 on anger, and deal with it by the method suggested there.

### *Surely Jesus does not expect us to let ourselves be doormats?*

Jesus told us in Matthew 5:41 (NIV): 'If someone forces you to go one mile, go with him two miles.' He said that to people who lived in an occupied land. Romans could compel someone to be their porter or guide by legal right, and this is what happened to Simon of Cyrene when he was ordered to carry the cross for Jesus that first Good Friday. Perhaps what Jesus meant is that when someone makes unreasonable demands on us, we should do twice as much as they ask, and do it cheerfully and without resentment. He also pointed out (Matt.20:28) that he had come to serve others and give his life for them, not to stand on his right to be served himself.

It is *not* loving to allow a person to become a tyrant and walk all over our human dignity, because that is not good for them. Yet how can we prevent them doing this if we are not to insist on our rights? This is a dilemma that has to be decided in each individual situation; however, it is worth remembering that people always tend to value us as much as we privately value ourselves. Someone who 'walks tall', looks people right in the eye, takes care of their appearance, and holds their head high is usually treated with automatic respect without having to insist upon it. We need to keep on reminding ourselves in situations where we are likely to be put down and despised that we are *not* worthless, useless stooges; we are princes or princesses of heaven, valued highly by God himself, who says we are honoured in his sight (Isa. 43:4). Here again, Pascal's words 'act as if' might be helpful.

## 5. Jesus Tells Us to Go to Him

Mending broken relationships is of paramount importance to Jesus, and it was the reason he came to earth in the first place. He wanted to make a reconciliation between men and God, and he was willing to give his life to make this possible. So it is not surprising that he cares so deeply about our broken relationships, and he makes it clear that forgiveness not only happens inside our hearts, but is also about reaching out to restore contact. Three times when talking about people who hurt us, he uses the same four words, 'go to your brother':

- 'If your brother has a grievance against you, go to him' (Matt. 5:23 paraphrased)
- 'If you have something against your brother, go to him' (Matt. 18:15 paraphrased)
- 'If your brother sins, go to him and confront him' (Luke 17:3 paraphrased)

To say, 'I have forgiven him, but I prefer to keep out of his way,' is not real forgiveness, and it also robs us of all the blessings that forgiveness brings. It can be extremely embarrassing, or even terrifying, to 'go to your brother', but of course reconciliation cost Jesus an awful lot too!

I have often heard people say that when they asked the Lord to show them how and when to make a reconciliation, he arranged it all for them at just the right moment.

Peggy, the friend I mentioned earlier who prayed for her 'enemy' by using a stone to represent him, was most perplexed about how she could make some kind of contact with the hospital consultant who had been so harsh and unkind to her, and whose mismanagement of her treatment had left her crippled and in constant pain. 'I did ring and try to make an appointment, but he would not see me. I thought about trying to find out where he lived and ringing on the doorbell one day, but I feel that "an Englishman's home is his castle", and that that would be unfair. So in the end I prayed that if the Lord wanted us to meet, he would arrange it for me.

'About a year later, I was out shopping when I met him in the street. He didn't recognise me, but I went up to him and shook his hand, saying, "You probably don't remember me, but you looked after me in hospital five years ago, and I would like you to know I'm getting better all the time." He smiled and looked genuinely pleased as we said goodbye. That was all that happened, and I don't think it would have been right to say "I forgive you for all your negligence and for being so vile to me," because that would just have been dumping my negative feelings on him. Surely forgiveness can be just a smile and a handshake?' I am sure Peggy is right, and that releasing forgiving through words can sometimes cause serious damage.

Gayle was forty-two before she allowed herself to remember that her father sexually abused her on a number of occasions while her mother was present. She needed months of help from a counsellor, her doctor and vicar before she was able to face up to what had happened. When she felt she had forgiven in her own heart she decided to go and see her parents, something she had not done for some years. Against all advice, she expressed her forgiveness to them in words. Her parents were horrified, and told her that she had made it all up. Obviously they were afraid that she would make it public and that her father's reputation as a church leader would be ruined, so they wrote to the three people who had been helping their daughter and denied the whole thing vehemently. 'She was always a very deceitful and difficult child,' was how they described her. The poor girl was devastated; it was her word against theirs, and their angry reaction almost finished her attempt to forgive. Had she expressed her forgiveness by being good to her parents and offering them her company as they grew older, things might have ended very differently.

*But suppose all the old feelings come back when I see him again?*

This is exactly what happened to Corrie ten Boom. She and her sister Betsie had been prisoners in Ravensbrück concentration camp, and Betsie eventually died there. After the war, Corrie travelled all over the world speaking about the power of forgiveness, but one day when she was in Germany a man came up to her at the end of a church service. She recognised him as one of the worst of the Nazi guards at the camp, and his cruel treatment had caused her sister terrible suffering. All the memories came pouring back as she looked into his face, but he did not recognise her as he came up holding out his hand.

'I have recently become a Christian,' he said, 'and I want to ask your forgiveness for the things prisoners like you had to suffer in the war.' Corrie stood frozen, quite unable to reach out and take the hand that he was offering to her. Then she prayed, 'Lord, let your forgiveness flow through me to this man, and help me to see him as you see him now.' As she forced herself to take his hand, she felt love and forgiveness flowing through her and she was able to greet him with genuine warmth.

### *When we go to our enemy, we are not:*

- Attempting to make him aware of how much he has hurt us so that he will feel guilty and ask for *our* forgiveness.
- Trying to justify ourselves or putting our own point of view.
- Trying to change his heart and stop him from doing any more damage.
- Trying to be spiritually 'one up' on him.
- Overcoming fear, in the same way that someone who is terrified of snakes might force themselves to visit the reptile house at the zoo.
- Expressing anger in a restrained way by telling the 'enemy' how we feel.
- Making a grand gesture of forgiveness; instead, we must humbly offer it and also ask forgiveness for any pain that we may have caused through our words, actions or attitudes of criticism, resentment or lack of love.

'Going to our brother' is simply an outward and visible sign of an inward and spiritual grace. We have let go and forgiven in our hearts – privately. When we 'go to our brother', it means putting the thoughts and feelings into actions. Some people find it easier to use actions rather than words, others feel the need to talk at depth – either on the first occasion or later. It really does not matter exactly what happens; the important thing is the new relationship of friendship and trust that emerges from the meeting.

### *What if they do not respond?*

Forgiveness is difficult enough when it is mutual, but it really gets tough after we have dared to make an attempt at reconciliation only to have our efforts flung back in our faces with a few more insults added to the pile we are already trying to forgive! In Matthew 18:16, Jesus tells us what to do in that event: 'But if he will not listen to you, take one or two other persons with you . . .' (GNB). It is always a help to get another perspective on a difficult situation, and I am sure that Jesus means this 'third party' to be a mutual friend rather than a couple of 'heavies' taken along to frighten 'the enemy' into submission! Perhaps in present-day terms, the equivalent would be counsellors or other wise people who will pray about the situation, as well as giving advice and attempting to keep the peace.

If that step fails, Jesus tells us to take the matter to the group of believers to whom you belong. Of course, not even bishops, moderators or housechurch leaders can *make* someone else forgive, but surely the value of bringing in all this spiritual 'muscle power' is to battle with Satan through prayer. Hudson Taylor tells us that, 'Men can be moved for God by prayer alone,' but sadly, when a relationship between two Christians breaks down, the church can be so busy gossiping and taking sides that a general punch-up is more likely than a prayer meeting!

Finally, Jesus says something that at first sounds rather strange: 'If he refuses to listen even to the church, treat him as you would a pagan or a tax collector' (Matt. 18:17, NIV). Some people take that to mean we are to wash our hands of the person, and exclude him or her for ever from our lives; however, that is *not* how Jesus treated tax collectors. Matthew himself was a tax collector until the uncondemning love of Jesus won his heart.

Surely Jesus is saying, 'When you have done everything you can by active means to restore peace, then simply go on treating the person in the way I treated the unlovable, with the kind of love that is willing to go on waiting and never gives up hope.'

There is always a sense of deep regret and even rejection, but just because your 'enemy' will not forgive does not mean that your own journey of forgiveness is incomplete. It is a comfort to know that Jesus understands this kind of sadness only too well, having his offer of forgiveness turned down is something that happens to him constantly; however, it never makes him stop being willing to forgive. Surely, through this passage in Matthew 18, he makes it clear that we should not go on 'pestering' by further contacts, but there never comes a time when you exclude an unrepentant person from your heart.

## Mending marriages

Sometimes the most difficult 'enemy' to forgive is the one to whom you were once married. Perhaps it's because love and hate are so closely linked, but some people find it hard to forgive fully after a marriage break-up because they feel that the only possible outcome of forgiveness is getting back together again. When both partners are willing to forgive, this is often the 'happy ever after ending', but for many reasons it is not always possible. Obviously it is not within the scope of a book like this to advise on anything so complicated, but the fact remains that forgiving from the heart is vital – whether such reconciliation means a second honeymoon, or simply the ability to communicate again in a peaceful and friendly manner.

## *But what if the person we need to forgive is already dead?*

Some people think that this makes forgiving impossible, but that is definitely not the case. Forgiveness must still be expressed either by words spoken out loud, or by some kind of concrete action. Some people write a letter to the person who hurt them, describing the incident in detail, and this helps them to live the experience again and bring their reactions to the surface for confession and healing. Forgiveness can then be offered on paper as part of the letter, or spoken out loud before a witness. Forgiveness should also be requested for any hatred and grudge-bearing involved. Some people take the letter to a place associated with the dead person and, if possible, bury or burn it there. They can then finally relinquish the person to God in a prayer.

## *The end of the forgiveness journey*

Forgiving is so close to the heart of Jesus and he positively lavishes blessing on anyone who perseveres with it to the end. Surely the climax comes when we begin to see just how much we have gained from all that has happened. In Chapter 3 I described how Joseph's jealous brothers sold him into slavery when he was a child. They meant to harm him, but as he looked back over all those years in Egypt he was finally able to say, 'But God meant it for good.' The people who have helped me write this book have all found forgiving terribly difficult, but they all agree that Jesus was right when he said, 'Happy and to be envied are you when people despise, hate and exclude you on account of the Son of man. Rejoice and be glad at such a time and exult and leap for joy for behold your reward is rich and great and intense and abundant in heaven' (Luke 6:22–23, AMP).

Someone once said to me:

'When we are able to be positively glad about the horridest things Satan hurls at us, they become like boomerangs whizzing back at Satan, who launched them at us in the first place.'

The following words were found scrawled near the body of a dead child in Ravensbrück concentration camp, where 92,000 women and children died:

O Lord, remember those of ill will,
but do not remember all the suffering they inflicted on us,
remember the fruits we have brought, thanks to our suffering,
our comradeships, our loyalty, our generosity,
the greatness of heart which has grown out of all this.

---

## A Final Prayer

Lord, you know how hard I find this process of forgiveness. Sometimes I think I've finally 'let go' and then something triggers off all those old memories and the bitter feelings they generate. Please help me not to give up. Give me your kind of persistence; keep me working at it even if it takes me the rest of my life. Like Paul, make me able to say, 'Forgetting what is behind and straining towards what is ahead, I press on towards the goal to win the prize for which God has called me heavenwards in Christ Jesus' (Phil. 3:13–14, NIV).

Thank you, Lord, for all that you are doing in my life; for all the repairing, reshaping and renewing that is going on inside me. It's painful at times, but I know it will be worth it in the end. Most of all, I thank you that I do not have to go through all this alone. I know you are there beside me all the time and you will never give up on me, whatever happens. Thank you for teaching me that all I need is you, both in this life and the next. Amen.

It says in the Bible: 'Blessed is the man who perseveres under trial, because when he has stood the test, he will receive the crown of life that God has promised to those who love him' (Jas. 1:12, NIV).